Andrew Johnson

SPEECHES

OF

ANDREW JOHNSON,

PRESIDENT OF THE UNITED STATES.

WITH

A BIOGRAPHICAL INTRODUCTION

BY FRANK MOORE.

BOSTON:
LITTLE, BROWN, AND COMPANY.
1866.

Entered according to Act of Congress, in the year 1865, by
Little, Brown and Company,
In the Clerk's Office of the District Court of the District of Massachusetts

University Press: Welch, Bigelow, & Co.,
Cambridge.

CONTENTS.

BIOGRAPHICAL INTRODUCTION.

ANDREW JOHNSON was born on the 29th day of December, 1808, at Raleigh, North Carolina. While yet in his fifth year, his father lost his life through generous and successful efforts to save Col. Thomas Henderson, editor of the "Raleigh Gazette," from drowning, leaving his wife and son dependent upon themselves for future support. The untoward event of his father's death prevented the lad from receiving even an ordinary education, and, at the age of ten years, he was apprenticed to a tailor in his native town. Devoting himself steadily and earnestly to his new occupation, he thus began life by a struggle with its daily duties, brightened by probable visions of the future, but into which dreams the possibility of an attainment to his present position presumed not to enter.

In the society of his fellow-workmen he became conscious of his great ignorance, and was possessed with a desire to learn to read. The visits to the workshop of a gentleman who lightened the hours of toil by reading to the workmen, still further aroused the ambition of the young apprentice. The volume thus read, (a collection of speeches by

British statesmen,) sowed in his mind a germ which in after-years was developed in the legislative halls. He devoted the hours after his day's work was done to mastering the alphabet, and then asked the loan of the volume that he might learn to spell. The gentleman, pleased at his earnestness and appreciating his ambition, presented to him the book, and otherwise assisted him in his studies. Through industry and patience, aided by a strong determination to overcome all obstacles, success crowned his efforts, and books were no longer sealed volumes to his youthful mind.

At the expiration of his apprenticeship in 1824, he went to Laurens Court House, S. C., where he worked as journeyman tailor until May, 1826, when he returned to Raleigh. There he remained until September of the same year, when with his mother he removed to Greenville, a small town in Eastern Tennessee, at which place he succeeded in obtaining work. Soon after his settlement in Greenville, he married a young woman whose attainments and devotion exerted a marked and beneficial influence on his future life. Sharing in the desires of her husband to acquire knowledge, and in his ambition to rise to distinction, she read to him and instructed him by her conversation as he plied the needle on his work-bench, thus lightening his labor by her presence and encouragement. At night the instructions of the day were continued by lessons in writing and arithmetic. Actuated by the highest motives, his efforts seconded by unflagging perseverance and an indomitable will, he proved an attentive student and a good scholar, and his estimable wife realized the first-fruits of her teachings in his growing popularity with the workingmen of the town in which they lived.

Thinking to improve his fortunes he left Greenville and moved further West, but after an absence of about a year, he returned with his wife to his former home, where he permanently settled. Self-reliance and energy were early developed in his character, while the method of his education sharpened and improved his reasoning faculties. The broad and comprehensive views of the more liberal British statesmen, implanted in his mind by the readings in the old workshop, took deep root; and in his further studies, the principle of Republican government — the fact that it is a government of the people, by the people, and for the people — became the centre around which clustered all his thoughts, hopes, and aspirations.

He saw that the aristocracy of the town, who were supported by slave labor, despised the white man who maintained himself and family by his own exertions; that capital, represented by the few, was to rule, and not the intelligence of the many who earned their bread by their daily toil. This was contrary to all his preconceived ideas, and he devoted himself heart and soul to the correction of the fallacy. By his appeals to the laboring classes he aroused them to assert their right to representation in the town councils, and, in 1828, the young tailor was chosen as Alderman, which position he held until 1830. In this latter year he was elected Mayor, and served in that capacity for the three succeeding years. He was also appointed Trustee of Rhea Academy by the County Court. In 1834 he interested himself successfully in the adoption of a new constitution for Tennessee, by which important rights were guaranteed to the mass of the people, the freedom of the press established, and other liberal measures adopted.

Andrew Johnson was now fairly enlisted in public life. Identified with the interests of the working classes, he devoted himself earnestly to improving their condition, to raising them from the position to which the aristocrats had doomed them, to the independence and dignity of freemen. His zeal in their behalf secured for him their universal esteem; they looked to him as their friend and champion, and were ever willing to advance his interests by their hearty support and by their votes. Consequently, in 1835, having proved himself in every way worthy of their suffrage, he was elected a member of the House of Representatives of the State for the counties of Greene and Washington. He became an active member of this body, but was particularly noted for his opposition to a grand scheme of internal improvements, which he boldly denounced as a base fraud tending to impoverish the State treasury and increase State taxation. This course rendered him unpopular at the time, and at the election in 1837 his place was filled by another representative. Time placed him right on the record, however. The scheme he had opposed proved, as he had predicted, a useless burden on the people, and in 1839 he was again returned to the Legislature.

During the Presidential contest of 1840, between Harrison and Van Buren, Mr. Johnson, in the capacity of Presidential Elector, canvassed the State in behalf of the latter candidate. He has been described as "an effective stump-speaker. His voice at first appears to be whining, but as he warms with his subject seems to entwine itself around the hearts of his followers and holds them spellbound."

In 1841 he was elected State Senator from Hawkins and Greene counties, and during the two ensuing years labored efficiently for the improvement of Eastern Tennessee. In the Senate, as in the lower branch of the Legislature, he proved a useful and active member. He was not an ornamental legislator or hackney politician, but an earnest and able advocate of all that he believed to be right; an open, honest, and hearty denouncer of that which he deemed wrong.

The people, recognizing his abilities, respecting his character, and appreciating his services, determined to enlarge his sphere of usefulness, and in 1843 he was nominated for Congress from the First

District of Tennessee, embracing seven counties. He canvassed the district with his opponent, Col. John A. Asken, a popular gentleman of prominence and ability, and handsomely defeated him. He took his seat as member of the House of Representatives at Washington, in December, 1843, retaining that position by successive elections until 1853.

The State having been redistricted previous to the election of the latter year, that portion in which Mr. Johnson resided was so allotted as to place him in a district having a large Whig majority, and thus he lost his seat in Congress. Gustavus A. Henry, at that time the Whig candidate for Governor, was the leading spirit in this movement, and Mr. Johnson determined to defeat the man who had thus "Gerrymandered," or, as he called it, "Henrymandered" him out of Congress. After an exciting canvass, Mr. Johnson was chosen Governor, and again in 1855 he was elected, this time defeating one of the ablest Whigs in the State, Meredith P. Gentry. During his administration of the gubernatorial duties, which he performed in the most impartial manner, he was active in urging upon Congress the Homestead Bill, and exerted his influence for the spread of popular education. Under his successive *régimes*, much was accomplished for the benefit and internal improvement of Tennessee, and the sons of toil still found in him a zealous defender of their rights and advocate of their wants.

In the year 1857 he was elected by the Legislature of Tennessee United States Senator, for the term of six years, and ably discharged the duties of that office until the spring of 1862, when he was appointed Military Governor of Tennessee. Prior to his election to Congress, his public services had been confined to the limits of his State, but from this time he belongs to the country.

Andrew Johnson was emphatically "a representative of *the people.*" Born of the people, and at an early age thrown upon his own resources, he lived and grew up amongst the people, becoming familiar with their every-day lives and deeds, their opinions, their wrongs and their asserted rights, their inmost thoughts and their highest aspirations. Feeling "the smart of the want of a proper education while young," but proud in the consciousness that for the knowledge he possessed he was indebted solely to his own exertions, he stood in the legislative halls, — Andrew Johnson, Tailor and Statesman, the compeer of any member of either house. Modestly assuming, but thoroughly appreciating the dignity of his position, he never permitted any sneer at his calling, or any attempted disparagement of the laboring classes, to pass unrebuked, and we find him breaking lances with the ablest debaters in Congress.

"Sir, I do not forget that I am a mechanic. I am proud to own it. Neither do I forget that Adam was a tailor, and sewed fig-leaves, or that our Saviour was the son of a carpenter."

He cordially hated aristocracy, and had decided objections to gentlemen, reared in affluence and idleness, arrogating to themselves the right to all the knowledge in the world. When Jefferson Davis superciliously asked, "What do you mean by 'the laboring classes'?" Andrew Johnson answered, "Those who earn their bread by the sweat of their face, and not by fatiguing their ingenuity."

A true Democrat, he was a firm believer in the sovereignty of the people, and held that members of the lower house of Congress were next in power to the people. Respecting statesmen and hating politicians, he claimed that upon the floor of the House the people had a right to be heard. He was thoroughly imbued with the idea that legislation was for the many, not for the few; for the good of the whole country, and not for the benefit of any party.

He was always consistently in favor of retrenchment in governmental expenses, and participated in nearly every debate upon appropriation bills, or acts requiring the expenditure of the public funds. He opposed the Smithsonian Institute, on the ground that it would be a burden on the public treasury, without commensurate good results; — voted against all direct appropriations for the District of Columbia, arguing that any city in the United States would cheerfully contribute to have the National Capital removed to its limits; — debated all bills to increase the clerical force of the different departments, declaring that if the clerks — many of whom he believed to be political vampires doing little or nothing for government during six hours per day, and devoting the remainder of their time to drinking, gaming, and abusing honest legislators in the newspapers — were made to do a decent day's work there would be no necessity for such increase; — introduced resolutions to reduce the salaries of members of Congress, and all officers of the Government, civil, military, and naval, amounting to over $1000, twenty per cent.; also a resolution instructing the Committee on Finance to investigate and report how much and wherein the expenses of all the departments might be reduced; — opposed all appropriations for monuments and funeral expenses, and called for a statement of the items in the bill for funeral expenses of a distinguished member of the House; — denied the right of members to vote themselves books, &c., saying they "might just as well vote to increase their salaries"; — and refused his assent to the purchase of Mr. Madison's papers and Washington's Farewell Address, not from any want of respect for the services and memory of either, but from his dislike to "speculations and jobs."

He was the true and honest friend of the poor, and of the laboring classes, and appeared in Congress as their champion. He introduced the subject of Homesteads into the House of Representatives, and carried it to a successful issue in that branch. He also brought up the subject in the Senate, and debated it at great length, but the bill, as passed, was vetoed by Mr. Buchanan.

Believing that the burdens of the Government should be borne by the rich and not by the poor, he proposed an amendment to the tariff bill, taxing capital instead of labor. He also opposed the tariff on tea and sugar.

He had no faith in caucuses, and held that they gave the controlling power to a few politicians, and prevented a true representation of the people. At different times he offered resolutions to amend the Constitution so that the people should vote directly for President. He advocated the bill to refund the fine imposed upon Andrew Jackson by Judge Hall at New Orleans (H. R., January 8, 1844); was in favor of the Annexation of Texas (H. R., January 21, 1845); discussed the Oregon question asserting our right to 54° 40′, but sustained the administration in the final settlement of the question (H. R., January 31, 1846); addressed the House on the Mexican question, in support of the administration, December 15, 1846, January 5, 1847, and August 2, 1848; delivered an able argument on the veto power (H. R., August 2, 1847); opposed the bill establishing the Court of Claims (H. R., January 6, 1849); made an earnest plea for the admission of California and the protection of slavery (H. R., June 5, 1850); debated the Mexican indemnity bill (H. R., January 21, 28, 1852); also the bill for right of way on rail and plank roads (H. R., July 20,

1852); made a speech on frauds in the Treasury Department (H. R., January 13, 1853), and another on coinage (H. R., February 2, 1853).

While in the Senate, in addition to the measures alluded to more at length in this sketch, he opposed the increase of the regular army at the time of the Mormon difficulties (S., February 17, 18, 1857); had an earnest debate with Hon. John Bell, his colleague, on the Tennessee resolutions inviting Bell to resign (S., February 23, 24, 1857); participated in the debate on the admission of Minnesota (S., April 6, 1858); opposed the Pacific Railroad bill, and repudiated the idea that it was imposed upon him as a Democratic measure (S., January 25, 1859); advocated retrenchment (S., January 4, and February 12, 1859); and warmly defended Tennessee (S., March 26, 1860).

Born and reared in a slave State, commencing and continuing his public career in another slave State, and himself the owner of slaves "acquired by the toil of his own hands," he accepted slavery as it existed and where it existed. Firm in the belief that the agitation of the subject would ultimately lead to the abolition of slavery, and the consequent dissolution of the Union, he deprecated its introduction into the debates of Congress, and was amongst those who declared against the right to petition upon the matter, giving his reasons therefor in a speech delivered January 31, 1844.

He was not an advocate of the extension of

slavery, and was willing to leave the inhabitants of the Territories to decide whether it should or should not exist therein.

"My position is, that Congress has no power to interfere with the subject of slavery; that it is an institution local in its character and peculiar to the States where it exists, and no other power has the right to control it."[1]

Acting under these convictions, he zealously opposed any encroachments upon what he regarded as the rights of the slave States. He continued true to this belief, and was consistent in his course to the very last; and in the stormy scenes in the Senate in December, 1860, we find him demanding new guaranties for the perpetuity of slavery.

But it required the fiery ordeal of the crisis of 1860 and 1861 to develop the strong points in his character, and to reveal his sincere love for and unswerving integrity to the Union. In those dark and terrible days, when each man distrusted his neighbor, the country demanded MEN, — men with comprehension to grasp the great question of the day, — men with foresight to discern its bearings upon the future, — men of strength, "bold to take up, firm to sustain" the glorious banner of a Republic of States, "one and indivisible." It is but stating truth to say, that, amongst the many who were tried in the crucible of those terrible hours, Andrew Johnson came forth a sagacious statesman, an honest patriot, a true man.

[1] Speech in House of Representatives, June 5, 1860.

An ardent admirer of Andrew Jackson, the memorable words of that indomitable patriot — "The Union; it must and shall be preserved" — were indelibly engraven on his heart. In a speech delivered in the House of Representatives, December 19, 1846, in support of the policy of Mr. Polk's administration in carrying the war into Mexico, he had said: —

"I am in favor of supporting the administration in this act, because I believe it to be right. But, sir, I care not whether right or wrong, *I am for my country always.*"

Thus fortified, with the Constitution for his shield he entered upon the stormy scenes preceding the rebellion. In December, 1859, he had denounced the John Brown raid on Harper's Ferry, and said he believed it to be the legitimate fruits of abolition teachings. He wished to have its leader punished under the Constitution, for an hostile irruption into a sovereign State. In 1860 he readily acquiesced in the election, under the same Constitution, of Abraham Lincoln to the Presidency, and feared none of the phantoms which so disturbed the imagination of a majority of the Southern Senators and Representatives. He believed in conciliation, and in view of the increasing excitement at the South, thought the North should be willing to give some new constitutional guarantees for the protection of slavery, and introduced resolutions to that effect, December 13, 1860, which were referred to the

Select Committee of Thirteen. Five days later, in a powerful speech, he denounced secession, and denied the right of any State to withdraw from the Union. He appealed to the Southern Senators to remain in the Union and "fight for their constitutional rights on the battlements of the Constitution." He did not mean to be driven out of the Union; and if anybody must go out, it must be those who had violated the Constitution by passing personal liberty bills and opposing the execution of the fugitive slave law.[1] But treason had already begun its foul work, and he soon saw that the South in its madness would not listen to conciliation or compromise.

Rising above sectional prejudice, and freeing himself from old party associations, he looked beyond the present, and meeting the issue boldly, declared for the Union now and forever.

In the speech delivered in the Senate, February 5th, 1861, he alludes to his having been denounced for his speech in December, but says, "I feel proud. I feel that I have struck treason a blow;" and adds, "I am for preserving the Union; and if it is to be done on constitutional terms, I am ready to stand by any and every man without asking his antecedents, or fearing what may take place hereafter."

Thenceforward Andrew Johnson was to be found in the van, boldly fighting for the Union, and ready, if need be, to lay down his life for its preservation.

At the first session of the Thirty-seventh Con-

[1] See page 77, Speeches.

gress, in July and August, 1861, he presented the credentials of the Senators from West Virginia, with appropriate remarks; on the 26th of July, 1861, he introduced a resolution defining the objects of the war, as follows: —

Resolved, That the present deplorable civil war has been forced upon the country by the disunionists of the Southern States, now in revolt against the Constitutional Government, and in arms around the Capitol; that, in this national emergency, Congress, banishing all feeling of mere passion or resentment, will recollect only its duty to the whole country; that this war is not prosecuted upon our part in any spirit of oppression, nor for any purpose of conquest or subjugation, nor for the purpose of authorizing or interfering with the rights or established institutions of those States, but to defend and maintain the supremacy of the Constitution and all laws made in pursuance thereof, and to preserve the Union, with all the dignity, equality, and rights of the several States, unimpaired; that as soon as these objects are accomplished, the war ought to cease.

This was passed, after a long debate, by a vote of thirty to five.

On the 27th of July he delivered another memorable speech, in which he arraigned his former associates in the Senate as traitors, and by unanswerable arguments and an exhaustless statement of facts, convicted them by their own record. In his remarks on voting for the tariff, in August, he argued that it was no time to discuss details, and freely voted for the bill in order to sustain the Government.

On the 31st of January, 1862, he made an able speech on the conduct of Senator Bright, and voted for the expulsion of the man, who, four years before, had administered to him the Senatorial oath.

Meanwhile, affairs in the Border States were becoming more and more complicated. From the outset of the rebellion, the Secessionists had been rampant in Tennessee. The State had been sold to the rebels by Governor Harris and his myrmidons. Mob law prevailed, and ruffians, with all the malignity of hate and the ferocity of brutes, had inaugurated a reign of terror, and citizens who remained true to the Union, were subjected to every possible indignity and persecution. This had been carried so far, and the State had received so little protection and assistance from the General Government, that many of the Unionists had become submissionists to rebel rule for the sole purpose of saving their lives. The course of Senator Johnson in Congress, in 1860, had entailed upon him the wrath of the leading and most bitter Secessionists. In December, he had been burned in effigy at Memphis; and on his return to Tennessee in April, 1861, at the close of the session of Congress, he was assailed at various places along his route, was threatened with lynching, and repeatedly insulted by mobs of infuriated men. A price was set upon his head, and personal violence threatened if he remained in the State.

In June, 1861, while on his way to Washington to attend the special session of Congress, he received an ovation from the loyal citizens of Cincinnati, and in an able speech, defined his position, announcing his unalterable determination to stand by the Union. While in Washington, he urged upon the President and Secretary of War the importance and the justice of aiding and protecting the Unionists of East Tennessee. Returning to the West, in September, he addressed Union meetings at Newport, Ky., and at other places, and devoted himself zealously to arousing those Unionists who had fallen into or been forced into a state of apathy by the aspect of war.

Meanwhile Kentucky had been invaded, and the rebels were overrunning Tennessee, — plundering, burning, and murdering. In the Eastern portion of that State, they confiscated Mr. Johnson's slaves, went to his home, drove his sick wife with her child into the street, and turned their house, built by his own hands, into a hospital and barracks.

In February, 1862, General Grant entered Tennessee, and captured Forts Henry and Donelson. The subsequent advance of General Buell's forces compelled the withdrawal of the main body of the rebels from Western and Middle Tennessee. The larger portion of the State having been thus recovered and in the occupation of the Federal forces, President Lincoln appointed Andrew Johnson Military Governor, with the rank of Brigadier-General of Volunteers. This appointment was confirmed by the Senate, March 5th, and Governor Johnson left his seat in that body to enter upon the duties of his new position.

It is difficult to conceive of a more fitting appointment than this. On the floor of the Senate, amidst the mountains of East Tennessee, and in the cities and towns of the State, he had openly denounced treason and boldly proclaimed that traitors should be hung. He had borne many personal indignities, had been outlawed by outlaws who had set a price on his head, his family had been mercilessly persecuted, and his friends and neighbors had been driven from their homes. Neither threats nor bullets could intimidate him. Fearless but just, resolute but compassionate, he was the man of all men to "rule with a rod of iron" over traitors, to bring order out of anarchy, and to restore confidence where fear had had sway. Governor Johnson reached Nashville on the 12th of March, in company with Horace Maynard, Emerson Etheredge, and others who had been political exiles. He was enthusiastically received by the long suffering Unionists, and, in response to a serenade, addressed the assemblage, setting forth the views of the administration and shadowing his purposed policy. From his long and thorough acquaintance with Tennesseans, he knew the men with whom he had to deal. In a few days he published an "Appeal to the People," in which the subjects of secession, the state of affairs which then existed, and the promise of the future, were treated in a clear and comprehensive manner. This paper will be found in full in the following pages. Later in March, Governor Johnson ordered the Mayor and City Council of Nashville to take the oath of allegiance. Upon their declining so to do, their places were declared vacant, other officials were appointed, and they were subsequently incarcerated in the penitentiary. The press throughout the State was placed under proper supervision, and it was soon understood that spoken or written treason would subject the offenders to justice. In April the editor of the "Nashville Banner" was arrested and his paper suppressed. Judge Guild, of the Chancery Court, was also imprisoned on a charge of treason.

On the 12th of May an important convention was held at Nashville, to consider the subject of the restoration of the State to the Union. The meeting was numerously attended by citizens from all parts of the State, and Governor Johnson made one of his impassioned and characteristic addresses. The Unionists continuing to suffer from the depredations of guerrillas, Governor Johnson issued the following proclamation: —

EXECUTIVE OFFICE, NASHVILLE, TENN.,
May 9, 1862.

Whereas, Certain persons, unfriendly and hostile to the Government of the United States, have banded themselves together, and are now going at large through many of the counties of this State, arresting, maltreating, and plundering Union citizens wherever found:

Now therefore, I, Andrew Johnson, Governor of the State of Tennessee, by virtue of the power and authority in me vested, do hereby proclaim that in every instance in which a Union man is arrested and maltreated by the marauding bands aforesaid, five or more rebels, from the most prominent in the immediate neighborhood, shall be arrested, imprisoned, and otherwise dealt with as the nature of the case may require; and further, in all cases where the property of citizens loyal to the Government of the United States is taken or destroyed, full and ample remuneration shall be made to them out of the property of such rebels in the vicinity as have sympathized with, and given aid, comfort, information, or encouragement to the parties committing such depredations.

This order will be executed in letter and spirit. All citizens are hereby warned, under heavy penalties, from entertaining, receiving, or encouraging such persons so banded together, or in any wise connected therewith.

By the Governor: ANDREW JOHNSON.

EDWARD H. EAST,
Secretary of State.

An election for judge of the Circuit Court of Nashville having been ordered, Turner S. Foster, a well-known Secessionist, was chosen. The Governor, too much of a law-abiding citizen to ignore an election ordered by himself, gave Foster his commission as judge; but fearing that he might abuse the power thus vested in him, ordered his arrest and sent him to the penitentiary on the same day. Early in June he issued an order that all persons guilty of uttering disloyal sentiments who should refuse to take the oath, and give bonds in $1000 for their future good behavior, should be sent South, and be treated as spies if again found within the Federal lines. During this month Union meetings were held in various districts of the State, at all of which Governor Johnson appeared and took an active part.

Later in the same month six prominent clergymen of Nashville, who not only entertained treasonable sentiments but boldly preached them from their pulpits, were summoned before the Governor, and desired to take the oath. They requested five days to decide as to their course, which request was granted. At the expiration of that time they declined to "turn from the error of their ways," whereupon five of them were sent to prison, and the sixth, on account of illness, paroled.

The next four months proved a dark and perilous period for the citizens of Nashville and the safety of the Provisional Government. In addition to the guerrillas under Forrest, which had infested the State, the confederate forces under Kirby Smith, Anderson, Marshall, and Bragg, moved northward through Tennessee, to invade Kentucky. At different times Nashville was wholly isolated, its communications cut off in every direction, and the city in a state of siege. Provisions became scarce, and prices ruled enormously high; the laws were with difficulty enforced, and much suffering prevailed. Through all these trying times Governor Johnson remained hopeful and self-reliant, inspiring confidence in all around him, and reviving courage by his calmness and determination. Among the inhabitants of Nashville were many whose fathers, husbands, brothers, and sons were in arms against the Government, leaving their families to be cared for by the authorities. To remedy this, Governor

Johnson addressed the following circular to such of the avowed Secessionists of the city as were able pecuniarily to respond : —

STATE OF TENNESSEE, EXECUTIVE DEPARTMENT,
Nashville, August 18, 1862.

SIR, — There are many wives and helpless children in the city of Nashville and county of Davidson, who have been reduced to poverty and wretchedness in consequence of their husbands and fathers having been forced into the armies of this unholy and nefarious rebellion. Their necessities have become so manifest, and their demands for the necessaries of life so urgent, that the laws of justice and humanity would be violated unless something was done to relieve their suffering and destitute condition.

You are therefore requested to contribute the sum of dollars, which you will pay over within the next five days to James Whitworth, Esq., Judge of the County Court, to be by him distributed among these destitute families in such manner as may be prescribed.

Respectfully, &c.
ANDREW JOHNSON,
Military Governor.

Attest :
EDWARD H. EAST,
Secretary of State.

The amounts so assessed varied from fifty to three hundred dollars.

In September General Buell evacuated his position in Southern Tennessee, falling back on Nashville, and then proposed to abandon that city. Governor Johnson earnestly protested against such a course, asserting that the city should be defended to the last extremity, and then destroyed to prevent its falling into the hands of the enemy. He was so disgusted with General Buell's movements that he addressed a letter to President Lincoln on the subject, and recommended his removal. General Thomas, who was placed in command of the city, heartily seconded Governor Johnson's determination, and the city was strongly fortified. Afterwards General Negley was assigned to the command, and under him the more important operations were conducted. Governor Johnson encouraged and aided General Negley in all his operations, and was active throughout the siege. He had no thought of retreating or of surrendering. "I am no military man," he said; "but any one who talks of surrendering, I will shoot."

After several attacks upon the city which were gallantly repulsed by General Negley, the rebels were forced to retire, as General Rosecrans, who had relieved General Buell, was advancing from the direction of Bowling Green. Early in November the forces under command of the latter General entered the city, and found its defenders on half rations, but brave and determined still. In October Governor Johnson's family rejoined him, after a series of perilous adventures on their journey from Bristol, in the northeastern part of the State.

During the same month President Lincoln recommended an election for members of Congress in several districts in Tennessee, but the military operations then in progress prevented the accomplishment of this design until December, when Governor

Johnson issued a proclamation for elections in the Ninth and Tenth Districts. He had from the first opposed the idea of allowing rebel sympathizers to vote on any of the acts necessary to the restoration of the State, and closed his proclamation thus: "No person will be considered an elector qualified to vote, who, in addition to the other qualifications required by law, does not give satisfactory evidence to the judges holding the election of his loyalty to the Government of the United States."

On the 13th of December Governor Johnson issued an order nearly identical with his circular of August 18, assessing the property of the Secessionists to the amount of sixty thousand dollars, for the support of the poor, the widows, and the orphans, made so by the war.

In the spring of 1863, and again in the fall, he visited Washington, to confer with President Lincoln on the restoration of Tennessee to the Union. The military operations during the year succeeded in freeing the State of all organized bodies of rebels, and it was thought the time had arrived for the fulfilment of their hopes. Conventions were held at different places in the State, at which Governor Johnson and other leading men spoke in reference to the all-absorbing topic. The people, who had so long been subject to the tyranny of rebel thieves and murderers, were overjoyed at their deliverance, but needed instruction as to the method to be used for the accomplishment of the great and good work.

Governor Johnson pithily and tersely stated the case as follows: —

"Tennessee is not out of the Union, never has been, and never will be out. The bonds of the Constitution and the Federal power will always prevent that. This Government is perpetual; provision is made for reforming the Government and amending the Constitution, and admitting States into the Union; not for letting them out of it.

. . . .

"Where are we now? There is a rebellion; this was anticipated, as I said. The rebel army is driven back. Here lies your State; a sick man in his bed, emaciated and exhausted, paralyzed in all his powers, and unable to walk alone. The physician comes. Don't quarrel about antecedents, but administer to his wants, and cure him as quickly as possible. The United States sends an agent, or a military governor, whichever you please to call him, to aid you in restoring your Government. Whenever you desire, in good faith, to restore civil authority, you can do so, and a proclamation for an election will be issued as speedily as it is practicable to hold one. One by one all the agencies of your State Government will be set in motion. A legislature will be elected; judges will be appointed temporarily, until you can elect them at the polls; and so of sheriffs, county court judges, justices, and other officers, until the way is fairly open for the people, and all the parts of civil government resume their ordinary functions. This is no nice, intricate, metaphysical question. It is a plain, common-sense matter, and there is nothing in the way but obstinacy."

On the 8th and 21st of January, 1864, Governor Johnson addressed meetings at Nashville, and on the 26th of the same month issued a proclamation for a State election. April 12th he addressed the people of Tennessee, at Knoxville, and again on the 16th of the same month, at which latter time the citizens of the State, in mass meeting assembled, declared in favor of emancipation, and for a convention to alter the Constitution so as to make Tennessee a free State.

On the 6th of June Governor Johnson was unanimously nominated by the National Union Convention, assembled at Baltimore, as the candidate for the Vice-Presidency of the United States, Abraham Lincoln having been renominated for the Presidency. When this intelligence reached Nashville, a mass meeting was held, and Governor Johnson invited to address them. He was greeted with the greatest enthusiasm. In the course of his remarks he spoke upon the topics of slavery and emancipation. Alluding to the nation as being "in the throes of a mighty revolution," he said: —

"While society is in this disordered state, and we are seeking security, let us fix the foundations of the Government on principles of eternal justice, which will endure for all time. There are those in our midst who are for perpetuating the institution of slavery. Let me say to you, Tennesseans, and men from the Northern States, that slavery is dead. It was not murdered by me. I told you long ago what the result would be, if you endeavored to go out of the Union to save slavery, and that the result would be bloodshed, rapine, devastated fields, plundered villages and cities; and therefore I urged you to remain in the Union. In trying to save slavery you killed it, and lost your own freedom. Your slavery is dead, but I did not murder it. As Macbeth said to Banquo's bloody ghost, —

'Never shake thy gory locks at me,
Thou canst not say I did it.'

"Slavery is dead, and you must pardon me if I do not mourn over its dead body; you can bury it out of sight. In restoring the State, leave out that disturbing and dangerous element, and use only those parts of the machinery which will move in harmony.

"Now, in regard to emancipation, I want to say to the blacks that liberty means liberty to work and enjoy the fruits of your labor. Idleness is not freedom. I desire that all men shall have a fair start and an equal chance in the race of life, and let him succeed who has the most merit. This, I think, is a principle of Heaven. I am for emancipation for two reasons: first, because it is right in itself; and, second, because in the emancipation of the slaves we break down an odious and dangerous aristocracy. I think that we are freeing more whites than blacks in Tennessee. I want to see slavery broken up, and when its barriers are thrown down, I want to see industrious, thrifty emigrants pouring in from all parts of the country."

In formally accepting the nomination of the Convention, Governor Johnson wrote as follows: —

"NASHVILLE, Tenn., *July* 2, 1864.

"HON. WILLIAM DENNISON, *Chairman, and others, Committee of the National Union Convention:*

"GENTLEMEN, — Your communication of the 9th ult., informing me of my nomination for the Vice-Presidency of the United States by the National Convention held at Baltimore, and enclosing a copy of the resolutions adopted by that body, was not received until the 25th ult.

"A reply on my part had been previously made to the action of the Convention in presenting my name, in a speech delivered in this city on the evening succeeding the day of the adjournment of the Convention, in which I indicated my acceptance of the distinguished honor conferred by that body, and defined the grounds upon which that acceptance was based, substantially saying what I now have to say. From the comments made upon that speech by the various presses of the country to which my attention has been directed, I considered it to be regarded as a full acceptance.

"In view, however, of the desire expressed in your communication, I will more fully allude to a few points that have been heretofore presented.

"My opinions on the leading questions at present agitating and distracting the public mind, and especially in reference to the rebellion now being waged against the Government and authority of the United States, I presume are generally understood. Before the Southern people assumed a belligerent attitude, (and repeatedly since,) I took occasion most frankly to declare the views I then entertained in relation to the wicked purposes of the Southern politicians. They have since undergone but little, if any, change. Time and subsequent events have rather confirmed than diminished my confidence in their correctness.

"At the beginning of this great struggle I entertained the same opinion of it I do now, and in my place in the Senate I denounced it as treason, worthy the punishment of death, and warned the Government and people of the impending danger. But my voice was not heard or counsel heeded until it was too late to avert the storm. It still continued to gather over us without molestation from the authorities at Washington, until at length it broke with all its fury upon the country. And now, if we would save the Government from being overwhelmed by it, we must meet it in the true spirit of patriotism, and bring traitors to the punishment due their crime, and, *by force of arms*, crush out and subdue the last vestige of rebel authority in every State. I felt then, as now, that the destruction of the Government was deliberately determined upon by wicked and designing conspirators, whose lives and fortunes were pledged to carry it out; and that no compromise, short of an unconditional recognition of the independence of the Southern States could have been, or could now be proposed, which they would accept. The clamor for "Southern Rights," as the rebel journals were pleased to designate their rallying cry, was not to secure their assumed rights *in the Union and under the Constitution*, but to disrupt the Government, and establish an independent organization, based upon Slavery, which they could at all times control.

"The separation of the Government has for years past been the cherished purpose of the Southern leaders. Baffled in 1832 by the stern, patriotic heroism of Andrew Jackson, they sullenly acquiesced, only to mature their diabolical schemes, and await the recurrence of a more favorable opportunity to execute them. Then the pretext was the tariff, and Jackson, after foiling their schemes of nullification and disunion, with prophetic perspicacity warned the country against the renewal of their efforts to dismember the Government.

"In a letter, dated May 1, 1833, to the Rev. A. J. Crawford, after demonstrating the heartless insincerity of the Southern nullifiers, he said: 'Therefore the tariff was only a pretext, and disunion and a Southern Confederacy the real object. The next pretext will be the negro, or Slavery question.'

"Time has fully verified this prediction, and we have now not only 'the negro, or Slavery question,' as the pretext, but the real cause of the rebellion, and both must go down together. It is vain to attempt to reconstruct the Union with the distracting element of Slavery in it. Experience has demonstrated its incompatibility with free and republican governments, and it would be unwise and unjust longer to continue it as one of the institutions of the country. While it remained subordinate to the Constitution and laws of the United States, I yielded to it my support; but when it became rebellious, and attempted to rise above the Government, and control its action, I threw my humble influence against it.

"The authority of the Government is supreme, and will admit of no rivalry. No institution can rise above it, whether it be Slavery or any other organized power. In our happy form of government all must be subordinate to the will of the people, when reflected through the Constitution and laws made pursuant thereto — State or Federal. This great principle lies at the foundation of every government, and cannot be disregarded without the destruction of the government itself. In the support and practice of correct principles we can never reach wrong results; and by rigorously adhering to this great fundamental truth, the end will be the preservation of the Union, and the overthrow of an institution which has made war upon, and attempted the destruction of the Government itself.

"The mode by which this great change — the emancipation of the slave — can be effected, is properly found in the power to amend the Constitution of the United States. This plan is effectual and of no doubtful authority; and while it does not contravene the timely exercise of the war power by the President in his Emancipation Proclamation, it comes stamped with the authority of the people themselves, acting in accordance with the written rule of the supreme law of the land, and must therefore give more general satisfaction and quietude to the distracted public mind.

"By recurring to the principles contained in the resolutions so unanimously adopted by the Convention, I find that they substantially accord with my public acts and opinions heretofore made known and expressed, and are therefore most cordially indorsed and approved, and the nomination, having been conferred without any solicitation on my part, is with the greater pleasure accepted.

"In accepting the nomination I might here close, but I cannot forego the opportunity of saying to my old friends of the Democratic party *proper*, with whom I have so long and pleasantly been associated, that the hour has now come when that great party can justly vindicate its devotion to true Democratic policy and measures of expediency. The war is a war of great principles. It involves the supremacy and life of the

Government itself. If the rebellion triumphs, free government — North and South — fails. If, on the other hand, the Government is successful, — as I do not doubt, — its destiny is fixed, its basis permanent and enduring, and its career of honor and glory just begun. In a great contest like this for the existence of free government, the path of duty is patriotism and principle. Minor considerations and questions of administrative policy should give way to the higher duty *of first preserving the Government;* and then there will be time enough to wrangle over the men and measures pertaining to its administration.

"This is not the hour for strife and division among ourselves. Such differences of opinion only encourage the enemy, prolong the war, and waste the country. Unity of action and concentration of power should be our watchword and rallying cry. This accomplished, the time will rapidly approach when their armies in the field — that great power of the rebellion — will be broken and crushed by our gallant officers and brave soldiers; and ere long they will return to their homes and firesides to resume again the avocations of peace, with the proud consciousness that they have aided in the noble work of re-establishing upon a surer and more permanent basis the great temple of American Freedom.

"I am, gentlemen, with sentiments of high regard,

"Yours, truly,

"ANDREW JOHNSON."

On the 4th of October Governor Johnson addressed a meeting at Logansport, Indiana, and on the 24th of the same month spoke to the colored people at Nashville, denouncing the aristocracy, and promising that their condition should be improved and their rights guaranteed and protected. This speech, and the circumstances attending it, are reported as follows, by a correspondent of the "Cincinnati Gazette": —

I have said the speech of Governor Johnson, delivered to the colored population of Nashville on Monday night, was one of the most remarkable to which it was ever my fortune to listen. The time, the place, the circumstances, the audience, the man, all combined to make a powerful impression upon a spectator's mind.

The time was the fourth year of the rebellion, — the eve of a great political contest which was to determine for all time whether freedom or slavery in America should be overthrown.

The place was the proud city of the slaveholders, and immediately in front of the haughty Capitol of Tennessee.

The circumstances were such as exist only amid the throes and struggles of a mighty revolution.

The audience were men and women who only three years ago were abject, miserable slaves, for whom there was apparently no future and no hope.

The man was he who in a few days was certain to be chosen to the second highest office within the gift of the American people.

And this man, whose views and those of the President, soon to be rechosen, are known to be in exact accord, and who, from the position he holds, represents, more than any other man save Lincoln, the power and majesty of the Republic, — this man, standing before that audience of trembling, crouching bondsmen, — tore in pieces the last lingering excuse for outrage and wrong; threw from him the dishonored and dishonorable fragments, and planting himself squarely upon the principles of justice and eternal right, declared that so far as he was concerned there should henceforth be no compromise with slavery anywhere; but that the hour had come when worth and merit, without regard to color, should be the standard by which to judge the value of a man.

Governor Johnson had already commenced speaking when I succeeded in forcing my way through the dense crowd of men and women who surrounded him, and stood within a few feet of him. I have said that he spoke from the steps leading up from the street (Cedar) to the State-House yard. In front the street was filled up by a mass of human beings, so closely compacted together that they seemed to compose one vast body, no part of which could move without moving the whole. The State-House yard itself, and the great stone wall which separates it from the street, were also thronged. Over this vast crowd the torches and transparencies, closely gathered together near the speaker, cast a ruddy glow; and, as far as the light extended, the crowd could be seen stretching either way up and down the street.

I had heard cheers and shouts long before I could distinguish the words of the speaker; but when at last I succeeded in getting close to the spot where he stood, a dead silence prevailed, unbroken save by the speaker's voice. I listened closely, and these, as far as my memory serves me, were the wonderful words: —

"COLORED MEN OF NASHVILLE, — You have all heard of the President's Proclamation, by which he announced to the world that the slaves in a large portion of the seceded States were thenceforth and forever free. For certain reasons, which seemed wise to the President, the benefits of that Proclamation did not extend to you or to your native State. Many of you consequently were left in bondage. The taskmaster's scourge was not yet broken, and the fetters still galled your limbs. Gradually this iniquity has been passing away; but the hour has come when the last vestiges of it must be removed. Consequently, I, too, without reference to the President or any other person, have a proclamation to make; and, standing here upon the steps of the Capitol, with the past history of the State to witness, the present condition to guide, and its future to encourage me, I, Andrew Johnson, do hereby proclaim freedom, full, broad, and unconditional, to every man in Tennessee!"

It was one of those moments when the speaker seems inspired, and when his audience, catching the inspiration, rises to his level and becomes one with him. Strangely as some of the words of this immortal utterance sounded to those uncultivated ears, I feel convinced that not one of them was misunderstood. With breathless attention those sons of bondage hung upon each syllable; each individual seemed carved in stone until the last word of the grand climax was reached; and then the scene which followed beggars all description. One simultaneous roar of approval and delight burst from three thousand throats. Flags, banners, torches, and transparencies were waved wildly over the throng, or flung aloft in the ecstasy of joy. Drums, fifes, and trumpets added to the uproar, and the mighty tumult of this great mass of human beings rejoicing for their race, woke up the slumbering echoes of the capitol, vibrated throughout the length and breadth of the city, rolled over the sluggish waters of the Cumberland, and rang out far into the night beyond.

I am not attempting to repeat the Governor's speech. I had neither note-book nor pencil when I listened to him; and if I had both of them I could not have used them in the midst of that closely wedged crowd. I wish only to *describe* a few of the points in his speech which made the deepest impression on my mind.

Who has not heard of the great estate of Mack Cockrill, situated near the city of Nashville, — an estate whose acres are numbered by the thousand, whose slaves were once counted by the score? Mack Cockrill being a great slave-owner, was of course a leading rebel, and in the very wantonness of wealth, wrung from the sweat and toil and stolen wages of others, gave fabulous sums at the outset of the war to aid Jeff. Davis in overturning the Government.

Who has not heard of the princely estates of Gen. W. D. Harding, who, by means of his property alone, outweighed in influence any other man in Tennessee, no matter what were that other's worth, or wisdom, or ability. Harding, too, early espoused the cause of treason, and made it his boast that he had contributed, and directly induced others to contribute, millions of dollars in aid of that unholy cause.

These estates suggested to Governor Johnson one of the most forcible points of his speech: —

"I am no agrarian," said he. "I wish to see secured to every man, rich or poor, the fruits of his honest industry, effort, or toil. I want each man to feel that what he has gained by his own skill, or talent, or exertion, is rightfully his, and his alone. But if, through an iniquitous system, a vast amount of wealth has been accumulated in the hands of one man, or a few men, then that result is wrong, and the sooner we can right it the better for all concerned. It is wrong that Mack Cockrill and W. D. Harding, by means of forced and unpaid labor, should have monopolized so large a share of the lands and wealth of Tennessee; and I say if their immense plantations were divided up and parcelled out amongst a number of free, industrious, and honest farmers, it would give more good citizens to the Commonwealth, increase the wages of our mechanics, enrich the markets of our city, enliven all the arteries of trade, improve society, and conduce to the greatness and glory of the State."

And thus the Governor discussed the profoundest problems of politics and social life in the presence of the despised blacks of Nashville; in their hearing denounced the grasping and bloated monopoly of their masters; and used the overgrown estates of Harding and Cockrill to illustrate his doctrines, in the presence of Harding's and Cockrill's slaves.

That portion of the Governor's speech in which he described and denounced the aristocracy of Nashville, I cannot hope to render properly; but there was one point which I must not overlook.

"The representatives of this corrupt, (and if you will permit me almost to swear a little,) this damnable aristocracy, taunt us with our desire to see justice done, and charge us with favoring negro equality. Of all living men they should be the last to mouth that phrase; and, even when uttered in their hearing, it should cause their cheeks to tinge and burn with shame. Negro equality, indeed! Why, pass, any day, along the sidewalks of High Street where these aristocrats more particularly dwell,— these aristocrats, whose sons are now in the bands of guerillas and cut-throats who prowl and rob and murder around our city, — pass by their dwellings, I say, and you will see as many mulatto as negro children, the former bearing an unmistakable resemblance to their aristocratic owners!

"Colored men of Tennessee! This, too, shall cease! Your wives and daughters shall no longer be dragged into a concubinage, compared to which polygamy is a virtue, to satisfy the brutal lusts of slaveholders and overseers! Henceforth the sanctity of God's holy law of marriage shall be respected in your persons, and the great State of Tennessee shall no more give her sanction to your degradation and your shame!"

"Thank God! thank God!" came from the lips of a thousand women, who in their own persons had experienced the hellish iniquity of the man-seller's code. "Thank God!" fervently echoed the fathers, husbands, brothers of these women.

"And if the law protects you in the possession of your wives and children, if the law shields those whom you hold dear from the unlawful grasp of lust, will you endeavor to be true to yourselves, and shun, as it were death itself, the path of lewdness, crime, and vice?"

"We will! we will!" cried the assembled thousands; and joining in a sublime and tearful enthusiasm, another mighty shout went up to heaven.

"Looking at this vast crowd of colored people," continued the Governor, "and reflecting through what a storm of persecution and obloquy they are compelled to pass, I am almost induced to wish that, as in the days of old, a Moses might arise who should lead them safely to their promised land of freedom and happiness."

"You are our Moses," shouted several voices, and the exclamation was caught up and cheered until the Capitol rung again.

"God," continued the speaker, "no doubt has prepared somewhere an instrument for the great work he designs to perform in behalf of this outraged people, and in due time your leader will come forth; your Moses will be revealed to you."

"We want no Moses but you!" again shouted the crowd.

"Well, then," replied the speaker, "humble and unworthy as I am, if no other better shall be found, I will indeed be your Moses, and lead you through the Red Sea of war and bondage to a fairer future of liberty and peace. I speak now as one who feels the world his country, and all who love equal rights his friends. I speak, too, as a citizen of Tennessee. I am here on my own soil; and here I mean to stay and fight this great battle of truth and justice to a triumphant end. Rebellion and slavery shall, by God's good help, no longer pollute our State. Loyal men, whether white or black, shall alone control her destinies; and when this strife in which we are all engaged is past, I trust, I know, we shall have a better state of things, and shall all rejoice that honest labor reaps the fruit of its own industry, and that every man has a fair chance in the race of life."

It is impossible to describe the enthusiasm which followed these words. Joy beamed in every countenance. Tears and laughter followed each other in quick succession. The great throng moved and swayed back and forth in the intensity of emotion, and shout after shout rent the air.

A man might have exchanged an ordinary immortality to have made such a speech to such an audience, and been much the gainer.

It was a speech significant of one of the loftiest positions to which mankind, struggling upward toward universal freedom, has as yet attained.

The great Tribune descended from the steps of the Capitol. As if by magic the dense throng parted to let him through. And all that night long his name was mingled with the curses and execrations of the traitor and oppressor, and with the blessings of the oppressed and poor.

The result of the Presidential election on the 14th of November, 1864, is well known. All of the States voting save three, gave immense majorities for Lincoln and Johnson, thus indorsing the former administration of Mr. Lincoln and promising renewed and continued support.

On the 4th of March, 1865, the ceremonies of inauguration were performed at Washington, in the presence of an immense concourse of people. Vice-President Johnson was duly qualified, and assumed the duties of President of the Senate. The affairs of the nation were progressing in the most auspicious manner. The military operations of Generals Grant and Sherman attracted and absorbed the attention of the nation. President Lincoln, who was at the front with the Lieutenant-General, had sent despatch after despatch containing words of good cheer, culminating with the news of the evacuation of Richmond and Petersburg, and the occupation of those cities by the Federal troops. The country was wild with delight, and throughout the loyal States the people gathered together to give expression to their satisfaction. At the meeting in Washington on the 3d of April, Vice-President Johnson spoke as follows: —

"As I have been introduced, I will make one or two remarks, for I feel that no one would be justified in attempting to make an address on such an occasion, when the excitement is justly at so great a height.

"We are now, my friends, winding up a rebellion, — a great effort that has been made by bad men to overthrow the Government of the United States, — a Government founded upon free principles, and cemented by the best blood of the Revolution. [Cheers.] You must indulge me in making one single remark in connection with myself. At the time that the traitors in the Senate of the United States plotted against the Government, and entered into a conspiracy more foul, more execrable, and more odious than that of Catiline against the Romans, I happened to be a member of that body, and, as to loyalty stood solitary and alone among the Senators from the Southern States.

"I was then and there called upon to know what I could do with such traitors, and I want to repeat my reply here. I said, if we had an Andrew Jackson he would hang them as high as Haman; but as he is no more, and sleeps in his grave in his own beloved State, where traitors and treason have even insulted his tomb and the very earth that covers his remains, humble as I am, when you ask me what I would do, my reply is, I would arrest them — I would try them — I would convict them, and I would hang them.

"As humble as I am and have been, I have pursued but one, undeviating course. All that I have — life, limb, and property — have been put at the disposal of the country in this great struggle. I have been in camp, I have been in the field, I have been everywhere where this great rebellion was; I have pursued it until I believe I can now see its termination. Since the world began, there never has been a rebellion of such gigantic proportions, so infamous in character, so diabolical in motive, so entirely disregardful of the laws of civilized war. It has introduced the most savage mode of warfare ever practised upon the earth.

"I will repeat here a remark, for which I have been in no small degree censured. What is it, allow me to ask, that has sustained the nation in this great struggle? The cry has been, you know, that our Government was not strong enough for a time of rebellion; that in such a time she would have to contend against internal weakness as well as internal foes. We have now given the world evidence that such is not the fact; and when the rebellion shall have been crushed out, and the nation shall once again have settled down in peace, our Government will rest upon a more enduring basis than ever before.

"But, my friends, in what has the great strength of this Government consisted. Has it been in one-man power? Has it been in some autocrat, or in some one man who held absolute government? No! I thank God I have it in my power to proclaim the great truth, that this Government has derived its strength from the American people. They have issued the edict; they have exercised the power that has resulted in the overthrow of the rebellion, and there is not another government upon the face of the earth that could have withstood the shock.

"We can now congratulate ourselves that we possess the strongest, the freest, and the best Government the world ever saw. Thank God that we have lived through this trial, and that, looking in your intelligent faces here to-day, I can announce to you the great fact that Petersburg, the outpost to the strong citadel, has been occupied by our brave and gallant officers and our untiring, invincible soldiers. And not content with that, they have captured the citadel itself, — the stronghold of traitors. Richmond is ours, and is now occupied by the forces of the United States! Her gates have been entered, and the glorious Stars and Stripes, the emblem of Union, of power, and of supremacy, now float over the enemy's capitol!

"In the language of another, let that old flag rise higher and higher, until it meets the sun in his coming, and let the parting day linger to play upon its ample folds. It is the flag of your country, it is your flag, it is my flag, and it bids defiance to all the nations of the earth, and the encroachments of all the powers combined. It is not my intention to make any imprudent remarks or allusions, but the hour will come when those nations that exhibited toward us such insolence and improper interference in the midst of our adversity, and, as they supposed, of our weakness, will learn that this is a Government of the people possessing power enough to make itself felt and respected.

"In the midst of our rejóicing, we must not forget to drop a tear for those gallant fellows who have shed their blood that their Government must triumph. We cannot forget them when we view the many bloody battle-fields of the war, the new-made graves, our maimed friends and relatives, who have left their limbs, as it were, on the enemy's soil, and others who have been consigned to their long narrow houses, with no winding-sheet save their blankets saturated with their blood.

"One word more, and I have done. It is this: I am in favor of leniency; but, in my opinion, evil-doers should be punished. [Cries of 'That 's so.'] Treason is the highest crime known in the catalogue of crimes, and for him that is guilty of it — for him that is willing to lift his impious hand against the authority of the nation — I would say death is too easy a punishment. My notion is that treason must be made odious and traitors must be punished and impoverished, their social power broken, though they must be made to feel the penalty of their crime. You, my friends, have traitors in your very midst, and treason needs rebuke and punishment here as well as elsewhere. It is not the men in the field who are the greatest traitors. It is the men who have encouraged them to imperil their lives, while they themselves have remained at home, expending their means and exerting all their power to overthrow the Government. Hence I say this: 'The halter to intelligent, influential traitors.' But to the honest boy, to the deluded man, who has been deceived into the rebel ranks, I would extend leniency; I would say, 'Return to your allegiance, renew your support to the Government, and become a good citizen;' but the leaders I would hang. I hold, too, that wealthy traitors should be made to remunerate those men who have suffered as a consequence of their crime, — Union men who have lost their property, who have been driven from their homes, beggars and wanderers among strangers. It is well to talk about these things here to-day, in addressing the well-informed persons who compose this audience. You can, to a very great extent, aid in moulding public opinion, and in giving it a proper direction. Let us commence the work. We have put down these traitors in arms; let us put them down in law, in public judgment, and in the morals of the world."

The fall of Richmond was followed by the surrender of Lee's army on the 9th of April. Five days after, on the evening of the 14th, the bullet of the assassin struck down the head of the Nation, but it did not still the pulsations of its heart nor paralyze the action of its limbs. As the dreadful intelligence flashed over the electric wire, throughout the length and breadth of the land, the whole country stood for a moment, speechless and breathless, appalled by the dastardly outrage. The first thought of the Nation was for the safety of its Government. Self-perpetuating, the Government received, but scarcely felt, a shock which would have overthrown the dynasties of the Old World. The wires were yet trembling with the burden of the sad message, "Abraham Lincoln died this morning at twenty-two minutes after seven o'clock," when they were again called to proclaim that "Andrew Johnson was sworn into office as President of the United States, by Chief Justice Chase, to-day at eleven o'clock."

The formal ceremonies were brief but dignified, promptly performed, but invested with an unusual solemnity by the sad event which had rendered them necessary. Immediately on the death of President Lincoln, Hon. James Speed, Attorney-General of the United States, waited upon Vice-President Johnson with the following official communication:—

"WASHINGTON CITY, *April* 15, 1865.

"ANDREW JOHNSON, *Vice-President of the United States.*

"SIR, — ABRAHAM LINCOLN, President of the United States, was shot by an assassin last evening at Ford's Theatre, in this city, and died at the hour of twenty-two minutes after seven o'clock. About the same time at which the President was shot, an assassin entered the sick chamber of Hon. W. H. Seward, Secretary of State, and stabbed him in several places in the throat, neck, and face, severely, if no tmortally, wounding him. Other members of the Secretary's family were dangerously wounded by the assassin, while making his escape.

"By the death of President Lincoln the office of President has devolved, under the Constitution, upon you. The emergency of the Government demands that you should immediately qualify according to the requirements of the Constitution, and enter upon the duties of President of the United States. If you will please make known your pleasure, such arrangements as you deem proper will be made.

"Your obedient servants,

"HUGH MCCULLOCH, *Secretary of the Treasury;* EDWIN M. STANTON, *Secretary of War;* GIDEON WELLES, *Secretary of the Navy;* WILLIAM DENNISON, *Postmaster-General;* J. P. USHER, *Secretary of the Interior;* JAMES SPEED, *Attorney-General.*"

. . . .

Mr. Johnson suggested ten o'clock as the hour, and his apartments at the Kirkwood House as the place, where, at the hour designated, the ceremony was performed.

After the oath had been administered, President Johnson delivered the following address: —

"GENTLEMEN, — I must be permitted to say that I have been almost overwhelmed by the announcement of the sad event which has so recently occurred. I feel incompetent to perform duties so important and responsible as those which have been so unexpectedly thrown upon me. As to an indication of any policy which may be pursued by me in the administration of the Government, I have to say, that that must be left for development as the administration progresses. The message or declaration must be made by the acts as they transpire. The only assurance that I can now give of the future, is by reference to the past. The course which I have taken in the past, in connection with this rebellion, must be regarded as a guarantee of the future. My past public life, which has been long and laborious, has been founded, as I in good conscience believe, upon a great principle of right, which lies at the basis of all things. The best energies of my life have been spent in endeavoring to establish and perpetuate the principles of free government, and I believe that the Government, in passing through its present trials, will settle down upon principles consonant with popular rights more permanent and enduring than heretofore. I must be permitted to say, if I understand the feelings of my own heart, I have long labored to ameliorate and alleviate the condition of the great mass of the American people. Toil, and an honest advocacy of the great principles of free government, have been my lot. The duties have been mine — the consequences are God's. This has been the foundation of my political creed. I feel that in the end the Government will triumph. and that these great principles will be permanently established.

In conclusion, gentlemen, let me say that I want your encouragement and countenance. I shall ask and rely upon you and others in carrying the Government through its present perils. I feel, in making this request, that it will be heartily responded to by you, and all other patriots and lovers of the rights and interests of a free people."

SPEECH ON THE VETO-POWER.

DELIVERED IN THE HOUSE OF REPRESENTATIVES OF THE UNITED STATES, AUGUST 2, 1848.

MR. CHAIRMAN: — I have for some days attempted to obtain possession of the floor when the House has been in Committee of the Whole on the state of the Union, and having at length succeeded, I may not confine myself to the pending question, but diverge to others of a more general character, as other gentlemen have done who have preceded me in debate. I make the admission frankly that I shall introduce some general topics of discussion in the course of my argument, if anything that I shall say may be dignified with the appellation of an argument. However, as an hour is but a very limited time in which to speak on such varied and important questions as present themselves to my mind, I shall directly address myself to those questions, and if I cannot embody all my views, I may be able to present the outline, the bones, the general contour of those subjects, and leave to those who may feel sufficient interest in them to listen to my remarks to fill up the outlines and clothe the bones with suitable muscles and flesh.

For the last two or three days, and I may say

weeks, the more immediate subjects of discussion have been twofold. The first was the veto-power; and the next was the origin, progress, and consequences of the war with Mexico. To these questions, then, I shall confine myself. And, in relation to the veto-power, I confess I feel great diffidence in approaching a subject of so much importance; for at one period of my life I entertained some doubts as to the exercise of the veto-power myself. But from the most thorough investigation, I have become entirely satisfied as to the propriety of the creation and establishment of this power by the Constitution.

In the discussion of the veto-power, and tracing it from its origin to the present time, I may be charged with something of ultraism; for, upon a more complete examination, I find it to be of plebeian origin.

Where did the veto-power originate? It was established to enable the people to resist and repel encroachments on their rights. The veto-power had its origin in old Rome 3507 *Anno Mundi*; and before Christ 497; and from the building of the city of Rome 255; which would make, since its origin, 2345 years. These dates will show that the people of Rome had been submitting to gradual encroachments two hundred and fifty-five years, until further submission was insupportable. At this period the levies and laws of the Roman Senate were so enormous and oppressive that the people were compelled to employ means to resist their further encroachment. The people *en masse* retired to a mountain three miles distant from Rome, called Monsacer, and were there addressed by Junius Lucius and Sicinius Bellerus with masculine eloquence, — always the child of nature, — which induced the people to compel the Roman Senate to yield the power to them to establish five tribunes from among themselves, which, in process of time, were increased to ten, who should be clothed with the veto-power. These tribunes were placed at the Senate-door, and all laws passed by the Roman Senate were presented to them for their approval or rejection. If they approved a law, it was signed with the letter T; but if not approved, they used the word veto, which signifies "I forbid." This is the origin of the veto-power; and so long as it was exercised by tribunes or officers immediately responsible to the people for their election or appointment, the end that the people designed was successfully accomplished — that is, resistance to encroachments on their rights. And so long as this power was preserved in its original purity and simplicity, it was exercised to the advancement of the people's rights and interests.

Augustus, 706 years from the building of the city of Rome, or four hundred and fifty-one years after the establishment of the veto-power by the people, so managed as to have the power in practice conferred upon himself; and here is the first union of the veto-power and royalty. The tribunes were still elected, and existed nominally, but in fact they exercised no tribunitian power. The tribunes, in fact, continued to exist until the reign of Constantine, which was nine hundred and thirty-three years from the building of the city, or six hundred and seventy-eight years from the creation of the veto, when the office of tribune was completely merged in royalty, and abolished.

We may now pass on from this period of time to the exercise of the veto-power in modern Europe; and, from the days of Augustus, we shall see that the exercise of this power has passed to the opposite end of the line, — that is, from the people to the Crown.

In England, by a resolution of parliament, this power was conferred upon the King, and has not been exercised by him since 1692, which makes one hundred and fifty-six years; and from this an argument is drawn to prove that even the King of England is afraid to exercise the veto-power, and therefore it is dangerous, and should never be exercised in a democracy or a republic.

The King of England is not immediately responsible to the people for the exercise of this power, or responsible to them for the position he holds. He ascends the throne in the course of hereditary succession; and, when the power is exercised by him, in most instances it is to resist popular will, instead of carrying it out; hence the great fear of exercising the veto-power in England, lest the popular will should become so strong that it would overturn the throne; and consequently the King resorts to the liberal bestowment of the immense patronage at his disposal to defeat those measures, on their passage, which would require the exercise of the veto-power, as necessary to protect the other prerogatives of the Crown.

The Constituent Assembly of France conferred the veto-power on the King in 1789, but the very first exercise of it proved his ruin; it was in opposition to popular will, and in protection of the prerogatives of the Crown. The same power was also vested with the King of Norway, and in this instance it was exercised twice to sustain the family upon the throne, until at last the popular will be came so strong that it resulted in his overthrow.

I might go into detail, or more at length, in the cases enumerated, and even refer to others, but time will not permit.

I will now pass to a point of time when this power returns to its original source, — the people.

The patriots and sages of the Revolution, who were perfectly familiar with the veto-power as it existed in the colonies and the mother-country, after effecting our separation from Great Britain, were called upon to form a Constitution, and in that Constitution we find the veto-power established, and to be exercised by the people. This Constitution was submitted to the States, and, after mature and deliberate consideration by them, it was adopted.

On the 4th of March, 1789, George Washington, the father of his country, delegate to and president of the Convention that framed the Constitution, was inaugurated President of the United States, and, for the first time under the Constitution, the veto-power was exercised, — or, according to our opponents of this day, the "one-man" or "despotic power," and that, too, upon the ground of convenience and economy, and the second time upon constitutional grounds. And in this connection, although Mr. Jefferson never exercised the power while President, we can adduce proof which shows that he approved of the incorporation of the power into our Constitution, and of its exercise afterwards. In his letter to Mr. Madison, written when he was in Paris, dated December 20, 1787, he takes decided ground in favor of the veto.

In his opinion, as written out whilst Secretary of State during General Washington's administration, he urged its exercise, upon the ground that its omission might be construed into a non-user, or an official negligence. We find, then, that these two men, whose patriotism and purity of purpose no mortal man can doubt, were in favor of the veto-power, as established in the Constitution.

James Madison, the third Republican President, and, as he is called by some, "the great Apostle of Liberty," who was a member of the Convention that framed the great chart of American liberty, and afterwards President of the United States, and that, too, while all was fresh and green on his memory of the oppressions and outrages that had been committed by the British Government, under every pretence whatever, exercised this power six times during his eight years' administration.

Next, we come to Mr. Monroe; and, during his administration, it will be remembered that it was called "the era of good-will and conciliation of all parties"; who, it may be said, came into power almost without opposition, and under whose administration parties were almost merged, — a man that no one will charge with possessing the first element of the tyrant or the despot, and of whom it might be said, that he was a war-hating and peace-loving man; he ventured to exercise this power once.

We then pass over Mr. J. Q. Adams's administration to that of Andrew Jackson; and, notwithstanding he has been denounced as arbitrary and tyrannical, — that his will was iron and his nerves were steel, — even he, in the use of this power, always exercised it in defence of the people's interests, and in resisting encroachments on their rights. By this man it was exercised nine times, and the people said, "Well done, thou good and faithful servant."

We will pass by the administration of Mr. Van Buren to that of John Tyler, called by some — but not by me — in derision, "the Accidency President," who exercised this power four times; and under his administration is the only instance in which a law was passed over a veto, by two thirds of the two Houses of Congress, since the origin of the government, and that an unimportant law. Next comes Mr. Polk's administration, and since he came into power it has been exercised three times.

Thus it will be seen, that from the origin of the government to the present time this power has been exercised twenty-five times. The whole number of laws passed, from the organization of the government, and approved, is about seven thousand; which would make one veto to every two hundred and eighty acts, — a very small proportion; and I think I may appeal with confidence to all those who are conversant with legislation here, whether it would not have been better for the people and the country if five thousand out of the seven thousand had been vetoed. I have been thus particular in giving the origin and exercise of the veto-power to prove, that whenever it has been exercised in compliance with the popular will, by a tribune or president, or by any other name you may think proper to give him, so that he is immediately responsible to the people, it operates well. And to show further, that whenever this power is retained in the hands of the people, men entertaining certain principles, without any regard to their party name, make war upon this power when at this end of the line; but whenever it is transferred to the other end, and placed in the hands of irresponsible persons, they become its defenders and advocates. And this brings me up directly to one of the issues between the parties in this government.

By an examination of the Constitution, we find the veto-power lodged in another department of the government, as well as with the Executives; and that department is irresponsible to the people. I mean that the Judiciary, who are appointed to office during life, — or, tantamount thereto, during good behavior, — exercise the veto-power absolutely. They are men, and subject to all the prejudices and influences of other men, according to their construction of the Constitution. They can veto every act of Congress, after its approval by the President, and that veto is final. But against the exercise of this power by this department of the government the Federal party make no complaint; but think it a perfectly safe place for the lodgment of the power, as it is beyond the reach of the people; which will at once show to every reflecting and intelligent mind the sincerity of the Opposition in making war on the exercise of the veto-power, when exercised by that department of the Government immediately responsible to the people.

I cannot, Mr. Chairman, though pressed for time, dismiss the subject without noticing the figure or simile of the snag-boat used by the gentleman from Ohio.[1] In this illustration he represents the Con-

[1] Mr. Schenck.

stitution as the Mississippi, and the veto-power as a "snag"; and he comes forward making great preparation with his snag-boat, throwing out his grappling-irons, raising the steam, the wheels revolving, determined to extract this principle, the veto, from the Constitution.

This is an illustration of what I have just before said, that where the people, either directly or indirectly, can exert their power through the Constitution by an officer chosen by themselves, the snag-boat of Federal power is brought forward to tear it out by the roots. But I do not look upon the veto power as a "snag" on the Mississippi, to obstruct the navigation to our commerce; but as a breakwater, to use the figure, placed on the people's sea or Constitution, to arrest the mighty current of Federal power, heavily setting in, or to break the dashing waves of encroachments upon their liberties and their interests. The veto, as exercised by the Executives, is conservative, and enables the people, through their tribunitian officer, the President, to arrest or suspend for the time being unconstitutional, hasty, and improvident legislation, until the people, the sovereigns in this country, have time and opportunity to consider of its propriety. But the member from Ohio seems determined to tear out that portion of the Constitution where the people can be heard and felt.

But in that other department of government where they have no voice, they are compelled to submit to its absolute exercise, unless they resort to a revolution or to an amendment of the Constitution.

For myself, I will take the instrument as it is handed down by Washington and his compeers; and if it is tyranny to exercise this power as it has been, — approved by every Republican President from Washington's inauguration down to the present time, not even excepting General Harrison, who was brought into power by the Whigs, out of that chaotic state of things which existed in 1840, I am willing to abide by it, and await the ultimate decision of the people on the subject. If the gentleman from Ohio could succeed with his Federal snag-boat in extracting the people's power, the veto, from the Constitution, the harmony of our beautiful though complex form of government would be lost, — the equilibrium would be gone, and some of the departments would absorb the others, or become liquids, and result in the concentration of all power in one department.

Time will not permit, if I were disposed and capable, of going into an analysis of the power of this Government. I have not the time to take it down and examine each element, and then set it up again. I must content myself with what I have hastily and crudely said, and pass on to the next proposition I propose to discuss.

SPEECH ON THE HOMESTEAD BILL.

DELIVERED IN THE SENATE OF THE UNITED STATES, MAY 20, 1858.

The Senate having under consideration the bill to grant to any person who is the head of a family, and a citizen of the United States, a homestead of one hundred and sixty acres of land out of the public domain, upon the condition of occupancy and cultivation of the same for the period of five years, MR. JOHNSON said: —

MR. PRESIDENT: — The immediate proposition before the Senate is an amendment offered by the honorable Senator from North Carolina,[1] which provides that there shall be a land-warrant issued to each head of a family, by the Secretary of the Interior, and distributed among those who do not emigrate to the public domain and take possession of and cultivate the land for the term of years specified in the bill. I have something to say in reference to that amendment, but I will not say it in this connection. I will take it up in its order. I propose, in the first place, to explain briefly the provisions of the bill.

The first section provides for granting one hundred and sixty acres of land to every head of a family who will emigrate to any of the public do-

[1] Mr. Clingman.

main and settle upon it, and cultivate it for a term of five years. Upon those facts being made known to the register of the land-office, the emigrant is to be entitled to obtain a patent. The second section provides that he shall make an affidavit, and show to the satisfaction of the officer that his entry is made in good faith, and that his intention is to cultivate the soil and become an actual settler. The sixth section of the bill provides that any person who is now an inhabitant of the United States, but not a citizen, if he makes application, and in the course of five years becomes a citizen of the United States, shall be placed on a footing of equality with the native-born citizens of the country in this respect. The third section provides that those entries shall be confined to land that has been in market, and subjected to private entry; and that the persons entering the land shall be confined to each alternate section.

These are substantially the leading provisions of this bill. It does not proceed upon the idea, as some suppose, of making a donation or gift of the public land to the settler. It proceeds upon the principle of consideration; and I conceive, and I think many others do, that the individual who emigrates to the West, and reclaims and reduces to cultivation one hundred and sixty acres of the public domain, subjecting himself to all the privations and hardships of such a life, pays the highest consideration for his land.

But, before I say more on this portion of the

subject, I desire to premise a little by giving the history of this homestead proposition. Some persons from my own region of the country, or, in other words, from the South, have thrown out the intimation that this is a proposition which partakes, to some extent, of the nature of the Emigrant Aid Society, and is to operate injuriously to the Southern States. For the purpose of making the starting-point right, I want to go back and show when this proposition was first introduced into the Congress of the United States. I am not sure but that the Presiding Officer[1] remembers well the history of this measure.

In 1846, on the 27th day of March, long before we had any emigrant aid societies, long before we had the compromises of 1850 in reference to the slavery question, long before we had any agitation on the subject of slavery in 1854, long before we had any agitation upon it in 1858, this proposition made its advent into the House of Representatives. It met with considerable opposition. It scarcely received serious consideration for a length of time; but the measure was pressed until the public mind took hold of it; and it was still pressed until the 12th day of May, 1852, when it passed that body by a two-thirds vote. Thus we see that its origin and its consummation, so far as the House of Representatives was concerned, had nothing to do with North or South, but proceeded upon that

[1] Mr. Foot of Vermont in the chair.

great principle which interests every man in this country, and which, in the end, secures and provides for him a home. By putting these dates together, it will be perceived that it was just six years five months and fifteen days from the introduction of this bill until its passage by the House of Representatives.

I shall not detain the Senate by any lengthy remarks on the general principles of the bill; for I do not intend to be prolix, or to consume much of the Senate's time. What is the origin of the great idea of a homestead of land? We find, on turning to the first law-writer, — and I think one of the best, for we are informed that he wrote by inspiration, — that he advances the first idea on this subject. Moses made use of the following language: —

"The land shall not be sold forever; for the land is mine — for ye are strangers and sojourners with me." — *Leviticus*, chapter xxv. verse 23.

We begin, then, with Moses. The next writer to whom I will call the attention of the Senate is Vattel — one of the ablest, if not the ablest writer upon the laws of nations. He lays down this great principle: [1]

"Of all the arts, tillage or agriculture is the most useful and necessary. It is the nursing-father of the State. The cultivation of the earth causes it to produce an infinite increase; it forms the surest resource, and the most solid fund of rich commerce for the people who enjoy a happy climate.

"This affair, then, deserves the utmost attention from gov-

[1] Vattel, Book I. ch. 7.

ernment. The sovereign ought to neglect no means of rendering the land under his obedience as well cultivated as possible. He ought not to allow either communities or private persons to acquire large tracts of land to leave uncultivated. These rights of common, which deprive the proprietor of the free liberty of disposing of his lands, — that will not allow him to farm them, and cause them to be cultivated in the most advantageous manner, — these rights, I say, are contrary to the welfare of the state, and ought to be suppressed or reduced to a just bound. The property introduced among the citizens does not prevent the nation's having a right to take the most effectual measures to cause the whole country to produce the greatest and most advantageous revenue possible.

"The government ought carefully to avoid everything capable of discouraging husbandmen, or of diverting them from the labors of agriculture. Those taxes, those excessive and ill-proportioned impositions, the burden of which falls almost entirely upon the cultivators, and the vexations they suffer from the commissioners who levy them, take from the unhappy peasant the means of cultivating the earth, and depopulate the country. Spain is the most fertile, and the worst cultivated country in Europe. The Church possesses too much land, and the undertakers of royal magazines, who are authorized to purchase at low prices all the corn they find in possession of a peasant, above what is necessary for the subsistence of his wife and family, so greatly discourage the husbandman, that he sows no more corn than is necessary for the support of his own household. Whence arises the greatest scarcity in a country capable of feeding its neighbors.

"Another abuse injurious to agriculture is, the contempt cast upon husbandmen. The inhabitants of cities, even the most servile artist and the most lazy citizen, consider him who cultivates the soil with a disdainful eye; they humble and discourage him; they dare to despise a profession that feeds the human race — the natural employment of man. A stay-maker places far beneath him the beloved employment of the first consuls and dictators of Rome.

"China has wisely prevented this abuse. Agriculture is there held in honor; and to preserve this happy manner of thinking, every year, on a solemn day, the Emperor himself, followed by the whole court, sets his hands to the plow and sows a small piece of land. Hence China is the best cultivated country in the world. It nourishes an innumerable multitude of people that at first appears to the traveller too great for the space they possess.

"The cultivation of the soil is not only to be recommended by the government on account of the extraordinary advantages that flow from it, but from its being an obligation imposed by nature on mankind. The whole earth is appointed for the nourishment of its inhabitants, but it would be incapable of doing it was it uncultivated. Every nation is then obliged by a law of nature to cultivate the ground that has fallen to its share, and it has no right to expect or require assistance from others, any further than the land in its possession is incapable of furnishing it with necessaries. Those people, like the ancient Germans and modern Tartars, who, having fertile countries, disdain to cultivate the earth, and rather choose to live by rapine, are wanting to themselves, and deserve to be exterminated as savage and rapacious beasts. There are others who avoid agriculture, who would only live by hunting and flocks. This might doubtless be allowed in the first ages of the world, when the earth produced more than was sufficient to feed its few inhabitants; but at present, when the human race is so greatly multiplied, it would not subsist if all nations resolved to live in this manner. Those who still retain this idle life, usurp more extensive territories than they would have occasion for were they to use honest labor, and have, therefore, no reason to complain if other nations, more laborious and too closely confined, come to possess a part. Thus, though the conquest of the civilized empires of Peru and Mexico was a notorious usurpation, the establishment of many colonies in North America may, on their confining themselves within just bounds, be extremely lawful. The people of those vast countries rather overran than inhabited them."

I propose next to cite the authority of General Jackson, who was believed to be not only a friend to the South but a friend to the Union. He inculcated this great doctrine in his message of 1832:—

"It cannot be doubted that the speedy settlement of those lands constitutes the true interest of the Republic. The wealth and strength of a country are its population, and the best part of the population are cultivators of the soil. Independent farmers are everywhere the basis of society, and the true friends of liberty." . . . . .

"It seems to me to be our true policy that the public lands shall cease, as soon as practicable, to be a source of revenue; and that they be sold to settlers in limited parcels, at prices barely sufficient to reimburse the United States the expense of the present system, and the cost arising from our Indian contracts." . . . . .

"It is desirable, however, that the right of the soil, and the future disposition of it, be surrendered to the States respectively in which it lies.

"The adventurous and hardy population of the West, besides contributing their equal share of taxation under the impost system, have, in the progress of our Government, for the lands they occupy, paid into the treasury a large proportion of forty million dollars, and of the revenue received therefrom but a small portion has been expended among them. When, to the disadvantage of their situation in this respect, we add the consideration that it is their labor alone that gives real value to the lands, and that the proceeds arising from these sales are chiefly distributed among States that had not originally any claim to them, and which have enjoyed the undivided emoluments arising from the sales of their own lands, it cannot be expected that the new States will remain longer contented with the present policy, after the payment of the public debt. To avert the consequences which may be apprehended from this cause, to stop forever all partial and interested legislation on this subject, and to afford every American citizen of enterprise the opportunity of securing an independent freehold, it seems to me, therefore, best to abandon the idea of raising a future revenue out of the public lands."

Thus we have standing before us, in advocacy of this great principle, the first writer of laws, Moses; next we have Vattel; and in the third place we have General Jackson.

Now, let us see whether there has been any homestead policy in the United States. By turning to our statutes, we find that the first Homestead Bill ever introduced into the Congress of the United States was in 1791. I know that it is said by some, and it is sometimes cantingly and slurringly reiterated in the newspapers, that this is a demagogical movement, and that some person has introduced and advocates this policy purely for the purpose of pleasing the people. I want to see who some of these demagogues are; and, before I read the section of this statute, I will refer, in connection with Jackson and these other distinguished individuals, to the fact that Mr. Jefferson, the philosopher and statesman, recognized and appreciated this great doctrine. In 1791, the first bill passed by the Congress of the United States recognizing the homestead principle, is in the following words: —

"That four hundred acres of land be given" —

that is the language of the statute. We do not assume in this bill to give land. We assume that a consideration passes; but here was a law that was based on the idea that four hundred acres of land were to be given

— "to each of those persons who, in the year 1783, were heads of families at Vincennes, or the Illinois country, or the Mississippi, and who, since that time, have removed from one of the said places to the other; but the Governor of the Territory northwest of the Ohio is hereby directed to cause the same to be laid out for them at their own expense," &c.

Another section of the same act provides, —

"That the heads of families at Vincennes, or in the Illinois country, in the year 1783, who afterwards removed without the limits of said Territory, are nevertheless entitled to the donation of four hundred acres of land made by the resolve of Congress," &c.

That act recognized the principle embraced in the Homestead Bill. If this is the idea of a demagogue, if it is the idea of one catering or pandering to the public sentiment to catch votes, it was introduced into Congress in 1791, and received the approval of Washington, the father of his country. I presume that if he lived at this day, and were to approve the measure, as he did in 1791, he would be branded, and put in the category of those persons who are denominated demagogues. Under his administration there was another bill passed of a similar import, recognizing and carrying out the great homestead principle. Thus we find that this policy, so far as legislation is concerned, commenced with Washington, and received his approval as early as 1791. From General Washington's administration there are forty-four precedents running through every administration of this Government, down to the present time, in which this principle has been recognized and indorsed.

We discover from this historical review that this is no new idea, that it is no recent invention, that it is no new movement for the purpose of making votes; but it is a principle wellnigh as old as the Government itself, which was indorsed and approved by Washington himself.

This would seem, Mr. President, to settle the question of power. I know it has been argued by some that Congress had not the power to make donations of land; but even the statute, to which I have referred, makes use of the word "give" without consideration. It was considered constitutional by the early fathers to give away land. We proceed in this bill upon the principle that there is a consideration. If I were disposed to look for precedents, even for the donations of the public lands, I could instance the bounty-land act, I could take you through other acts donating land, showing that the principle has been recognized again and again, and that there is not now a question as to its constitutionality.

I believe there is a clear difference in the power of the Federal Government in reference to its appropriations of money and its appropriations of the public land. The Congress of the United States has power to lay and collect taxes, duties, imposts, and excises, to pay the debts and provide for the common defence and general welfare. I believe it has the power to lay and collect duties for these legitimate purposes; but when taxes have been laid, collected, and paid into the treasury, I do not think it has that general scope or that latitude in the appropriation of money that it has over the public lands. Once converted into revenue, Congress can only appropriate the revenue to the specific objects of the Constitution. It may derive revenue from the public lands, and being revenue, it can only be appropriated to the purposes for which revenue is raised under the Constitution.

But when we turn to another provision of the Constitution, we find that Congress has power "to dispose of and make all needful rules and regulations respecting the territory or other property belonging to the United States." Congress has, in the organization of all the Territories and in the admission of new States, recognized most clearly the principle of appropriating the public lands for the benefit of schools, colleges, and academies. It has granted the sixteenth and thirty-sixth sections in every township for school purposes; it has granted lands for public buildings and various other improvements. I am very clear on this point, that in the disposition of the public lands they should be applied to national purposes. If we grant the public lands to actual settlers, so as to induce them to settle upon and cultivate them, can there be anything more national in its character? What is the great object of acquiring territory? Is it not for settlement and cultivation? We may acquire territory by the exercise of the treaty-making power. We may be engaged in a war, and as terms or conditions of peace we may make large acquisitions of territory to the United States. But what is the great idea and principle on which you acquire territory? Is it not to settle and cultivate it?

I am aware that the argument is used, if you can dispose of the public lands for this purpose or that purpose, cannot you sell the public lands and apply the proceeds to the same purpose? I think there is a clear distinction between the two cases. It is equally clear to me that, if the Federal Government can set apart the public lands for school purposes in the new States, it can appropriate lands to enable the parent to sustain his child whilst enjoying the benefits conferred upon him by the Government in the shape of education. The argument is as sound in the one case as it is in the other. If we can grant lands in the one case, we can in the other. If, without making a contract in advance, you can grant your public lands as gratuities, as donations to men who go out and fight the battles of their country, after the services have been rendered, is it not strange, passing strange, that you cannot grant land to those who till the soil and make provision to sustain your army while it is fighting the battles of the country? It seems to me that the argument is clear. I do not intend to argue the constitutional question, for I think there can be really no doubt on that point. I do not believe any one at this day will seriously make any point on that ground against this bill. Is its purpose a national one? The great object is to induce persons to cultivate the land, and thereby make the soil productive. By doing this, you induce hundreds of persons throughout the United States, who are now producing but little, to come in contact with the soil and add to the productive capacity of the country, and thereby promote the national weal.

I come now to the amendment offered by the Senator from North Carolina. I have not looked over the *Globe* this morning to read his remarks of yesterday; but if I understood him correctly, he advocated the proposition of issuing a warrant for a hundred and sixty acres of land to each head of a family in the United States. I am inclined to think the Senator is not serious in this proposition. It has been offered on some occasions heretofore, and rejected by very decided votes. Let us compare it with the proposition of the bill. The idea of the honorable Senator seems to be that this bill was designed to force or compel, to some extent, the citizens of other States to go to the new States. Why, sir, there is no compulsory process in the bill. It leaves each man at his own discretion, at his own free will, either to go or to stay, just as it suits his inclinations.

The Senator seems to think too — and the same idea was advanced by his predecessor — that at this time such a measure would have a tendency to diminish the revenue. He intimates that the nation is now bankrupt, that we are borrowing money, that the receipts from customs have been greatly diminished, and that therefore it would be dangerous to pass this bill, because it would have a tendency to diminish the revenue. Let us compare the Senator's proposition and that of the bill, in this respect. His amendment is to issue warrants to each head of a family. The population of the United States is now estimated at about twenty-eight millions. Let us assume, for the sake of illustration, that there are three million heads of families in the United States. His proposition, then, is to issue and throw upon the market three millions of warrants, each warrant entitling the holder to one hundred and sixty acres of land. If that were done, and those warrants were thrown upon the market, what would they sell for? Little or nothing. If such land-warrants were thrown broadcast over the country, who would enter another acre of land at $1.25? Would not the warrants pass into the hands of land speculators and monopolists at a merely nominal price? Would they bring more than a quarter of a dollar an acre?

If you were to throw three millions of land-warrants into the market at one time, would they bring anything? Then the effect of that proposition would be to do but little good to those to whom the warrants were issued, and by throwing them into the market, it would cut off the revenue from public lands entirely, for no one would enter land for cash as long as warrants could be bought. That proposition, then, is to aid and feed speculation. I do not say that is the motive or intention, but it is the tendency and effect of the Senator's proposition to throw a large portion of the public lands into the hands of speculators, and to cut them off from the treasury as a source of revenue.

But what does this bill propose? Will it diminish the receipts into the treasury from the public lands? The bill provides that the entries under it shall be confined to the alternate sections, and that the person who obtains the benefit of the bill must be an actual settler and cultivator. In proportion as you settle and cultivate any portion of the public lands, do you not enhance the value of the remaining sections, and bring them into the market much sooner, and obtain a better price for them than you would without this bill? What is the principle upon which you have proceeded in all the railroad grants you have made? They have been defended upon the ground that by granting alternate sections for railroads, you thereby brought the remaining lands into the market, and enabled the Government to realize its means at a much earlier period, making the remainder of the public lands more valuable than they were before. This bill proceeds upon the same idea. You have granted an immense amount of lands to railroads on this principle, and now why not do something for the people?

I say, that instead of wasting the public lands, instead of reducing the receipts into the treasury, this bill would increase them. In the first place, it will enhance the value of the reserved quarter-sections. This may be illustrated by an example. In 1848 we had nine million quarter-sections; in 1858 we have about seven millions. Let us suppose that our population is twenty-eight millions, and that under the operation of this bill one million heads of families who are now producing but very little, and who have no land to cultivate, and very scanty means of subsistence, shall each have a quarter-section of land, what will the effect be? At present these persons pay little or nothing for the support of the Federal Government, under the operation of our tariff system, for the reason that they have not got much to buy with. How much does the land yield to the Government while it is lying in a state of nature, uncultivated? Nothing at all. At the rate we have been selling the public lands, about three million dollars' worth a year, estimating them at $1.25 an acre, it will take a fraction less than seven hundred years to dispose of the public domain.

I will take a case that will demonstrate as clearly as the simplest sum in arithmetic that this is a revenue measure. Let us take a million families who can now hardly procure the necessaries of life, and place them each on a quarter-section of land, — how long will it be before their condition will be improved so as to make them able to contribute something to the support of the Government? Now, here is soil producing nothing, here are hands producing but little. Transfer the man from the point where he is producing nothing, bring him in contact with a hundred and sixty acres of productive soil, and how long will it be before that man changes his condition? As soon as he gets upon the land he begins to make his improvements, he clears out his field, and the work of production is commenced. In a short time he has a crop, he has stock and other things that result from bringing his physical labor in contact with the soil. He has the products of his labor and his land, and he is enabled to exchange them for articles of consumption. He is enabled to buy more than he did before, and thus he contributes more to the support of his Government, while, at the same time, he becomes a better man, a more reliable man for all governmental purposes, because he is interested in the country in which he lives.

To illustrate the matter further, let us take a family of seven persons in number who now have no home, no abiding place that they can call their own, and transfer them to a tract of one hundred and sixty acres of land which they are to possess and cultivate. Is there a Senator here who does not believe, that, by changing their position from the one place to the other, they would produce at least a dollar more than they did before? I will begin at a point scarcely visible, — a single dollar. Is there a man here or anywhere else who does not know the fact to be, that you increase a man's ability to buy when he produces more, by bringing his labor in contact with the soil. The result of that contact is production; he produces something that he can convert and exchange for the necessities of his family. Suppose the increase was only a dollar a head for a million of families, each family consisting of seven persons. By transferring a million of families from their present dependent condition to the enjoyment and cultivation of the public domain, supposing it would only increase their ability to buy foreign imports to the extent of a dollar each, you would create a demand for seven millions' worth of imports. Our rates of duties, under the tariff act of 1846, are about thirty per cent., and thus, at the almost invisible beginning of a single dollar a head, you, in this way, increase the pecuniary and financial means of the Government to the extent of $2,100,000.

This would be the result, supposing that there would only be an addition of one dollar per head to the ability of each family by being taken from a condition of poverty and placed upon one hundred and sixty acres of land. This is the result, supposing them to have seven dollars more, with which to buy articles of consumption, than they had when they had no home, no soil to cultivate, no stimulant, no inducement to labor. If you suppose the effect would be to increase their ability two dollars per head, you would increase their consumption to the amount of $14,000,000, which, at thirty per cent. duty, would yield $4,200,000. If you supposed it increased the ability of a family four dollars per head, the total amount would be $28,000,000, which would yield a revenue of $8,400,000. I think that this would be far below the truth, and if you gave a family one hundred and sixty acres of land to cultivate, the effect would be to increase the ability of that family so as to buy fifty-six dollars' worth more than they bought before, — eight dollars a head. That would be a small increase to a family who had a home, compared with the condition of that family when it had none. The effect of that would be to run up the amount they buy to $56,000,000, which, at a duty of thirty per cent., would yield the sum of $16,800,000.

I show you, then, that, by taking one million families, consisting of seven persons each, and putting them each upon a quarter-section of land, making the soil productive, if you thereby only added to their capacity to buy goods to the amount of fifty-six dollars per family, you would derive a revenue of nearly seventeen million dollars. When you have done this, how much of the public lands would you have disposed of? Only one million quarter-sections, and you would have nearly six million quarter-sections left. By disposing of one sixth of your public domain in this way, upon this little miniature estimate, you bring into the coffers of the Federal Government by this bill $16,800,000 annually.

Does this look like diminishing the revenue? Does it not rather show that this bill is a revenue measure? I think it is most clearly a revenue measure. Not only is this the case in a money point of view, so far as the imports are concerned, but, by settling the alternate sections with actual cultivators, you make the remaining sections more valuable to the Government, and you bring them sooner into market. In continuation of this idea, I will read a portion of the argument which I made upon this subject when I first introduced the bill into the other House. I read from the report of my speech on that occasion: —

"Mr. J. said, it will be remembered by the House that he had already shown, that by giving an individual a quarter-section of the land, the Government would receive back, in the shape of a revenue, in every seven years, more than the Government price of the land; and, upon this principle, the Government would, in fact, be realizing two hundred and ten dollars every subsequent term of seven years. The whole number of acres of public land belonging to the United States at this time, or up to the 30th of September, 1848, is one billion four hundred and forty-two millions two hundred and sixteen thousand one hundred and sixty-eight acres. This amount, estimated at $1.25 per acre, will make $1,802,770,000. To dispose of $3,000,000 worth per annum, which is more than an average sum, would require seven hundred years, or a fraction less, to dispose of the entire domain. It will now be perceived at once, that the Government would derive an immense advantage by giving the land to the cultivator, instead of keeping it on hand this length of time. We find by this process the Government would derive from each quarter-section in six hundred years, (throwing off the large excess of nearly one hundred years,) $17,000, — seven going into six hundred eighty-five times. This, then, shows on the one hand what the Government would gain by giving the land away. . . . . . He said that this *exposê* ought to satisfy every one, that instead of violating the plighted faith of the Government, it was enlarging and making more valuable, and enabling the Government to derive a much larger amount of revenue to meet all its liabilities, and thereby preserving its faith inviolate."

I do not think there can be any question as to the revenue part of this proposition. We show that by granting a million quarter-sections you derive more revenue upon the public lands than you do by your entire land system, as it now stands. In 1850, it was estimated that each head of a family consumed $100 worth of home manufactures. If we increase the ability of the cultivator and occupier of the soil fifty-six dollars in the family, of course it is reasonable to presume that he would consume a correspondingly increased proportion of home manufactures. Can that proposition be controverted? I think not. Then we see on the one hand, that we should derive more revenue from granting the land, on the principle laid down in the bill, and also that we should open a market for articles manufactured in our own country. Then, taking both views of the subject, we see that it is an advantage to the manufacturing interest, and that it is also an advantage to the Government, so far as imports are concerned. I should like to know, then, where can the objection be, upon the score of revenue.

But, Mr. President, the question of dollars and cents is of no consideration to me. The money view of this subject does not influence my mind by the weight of a feather. I think it is clear, though; and this view has been presented to prove to Senators that this bill will not diminish, but, on the contrary, will increase the revenue.

But this is not the most important view of the subject. When you look at our country as it is, you see that it is very desirable that the great mass of the people should be interested in the country. By this bill you provide a man with a home, you increase the revenue, you increase the consumption of home manufactures, and you make him a better man, and you give him an interest in the country. His condition is better. There is no man so reliable as he who is interested in the welfare of his country; and who are more interested in the welfare of their country than those who have homes? When a man has a home, he has a deeper, a more abiding interest in the country, and he is more reliable in all things that pertain to the Government. He is more reliable when he goes to the ballot-box; he is more reliable in sustaining in every way the stability of our free institutions.

It seems to me that this, without the other consideration, would be a sufficient inducement. When we see the population that is accumulating about some of our cities, I think it behooves every man who is a statesman, a patriot, and a philanthropist, to turn his attention to this subject. I have lately seen some statistics with reference to the city of New York, in which it is assumed that one sixth of the population are paupers; that two sixths of the population are barely able to sustain themselves; leaving one pauper to be sustained by three persons in every six in the city of New York. Does not that present a frightful state of things? Suppose the population of that city to be one million: you would have in the single city of New York one hundred and sixty-six thousand paupers.

I do not look upon the growth of cities and the accumulation of population about cities, as being the most desirable objects in this country. I do not believe that a large portion of this population, even if you were to offer them homesteads, would ever go to them. I have no idea that they would; for a man who has spent most of his life about a city, and has sunk into a pauperized condition, is not the man to go West, reclaim one hundred and sixty acres of land, and reduce it to cultivation. He will not go there on that condition. Though we are satisfied of this, may not our policy be such as to prevent, as far as practicable, the further accumulation of such an unproductive population about our cities? Let us try to prevent their future accumulation; let these live, have their day, and pass away,—they will ultimately pass away,—but let our policy be such as to induce men to become mechanics and agriculturists. Interest them in the country; pin them to the soil; and they become more reliable and sustain themselves, and you do away with much of the pauperism in the country. The population of the United States being twenty-eight millions, if the same proportion of paupers as in the city of New York existed throughout the country, you would have four million six hundred and sixty-six thousand paupers in the United States. Do we want all our population to become of that character? Do we want cities to take control of this Government? Unless the proper steps be taken, unless the proper direction be given to the future affairs of this Government, the cities are to take charge of it and control it. The rural population, the mechanical and agricultural portions of this community, are the very salt of it. They constitute the "mud-sills," to use a term recently introduced here. They constitute the foundation upon which the Government rests; and hence we see the state of things before us. Should we not give the settlement of our public lands and the population of our country that direction which will beget and create the best portion of the population? Is it not fearful to think of four million six hundred and sixty-six thousand paupers in the United States, at the rate they have them in the city of New York? Mr. Jefferson never said a truer thing than when he declared that large cities were eye-sores in the body-politic: in democracies they are consuming cancers.

I know the idea of some is to build up great populous cities, and that thereby the interests of the country are to be promoted. Sir, a city not only sinks into pauperism, but into vice and immorality of every description that can be enumerated; and I would not vote for any policy that I believed would build up cities upon this principle. Build up your villages, build up your rural districts, and you will have men who rely upon their own industry, who rely upon their own efforts, who rely upon their own ingenuity, who rely upon their own economy and application to business for a support; and these are the people whom you have to depend upon. Why, Mr. President, how was it in ancient Rome? I know there has been a great deal said in denunciation of agrarianism and the Gracchi. It has been said that a doctrine something like this led to the decline of the Roman empire; but the Gracchi never had their day until a cancerous influence had destroyed the very vitals of Rome; and it was the destruction of Rome that brought forth Tiberius Gracchus. It was to prevent land monopoly, not agrarianism, in the common acceptation of the term, — which is dividing out lands that had been acquired by individuals. They sought to take back and put in the possession of the great mass of the people that portion of the public domain which had been assumed by the capitalists, who had no title to it in fact. The Gracchi tried to carry out this policy,— to restore that which had been taken from the people. The population had sunk into the condition of large proprietors on the one hand, and dependants on the other; and when this dependent condition was brought about, as we find from Niebuhr's History, the middle class of the community was all gone; it had left the country; there was nothing but an aristocracy on the one hand, and dependants upon that aristocracy on the other; and when this got to be the case, the Roman empire went down.

Having this illustrious example before us, we should be warned by it. Our true policy is to build up the middle class, to sustain the villages, to populate the rural districts, and let the power of this Government remain with the middle class. I want no miserable city rabble on the one hand; I want no pampered, bloated, corrupted aristocracy on the other. I want the middle portion of society to be built up and sustained, and to let them have the control of the Government. I am as much opposed to agrarianism as any Senator on this floor, or any individual in the United States; and this bill does not partake in the slightest degree of agrarianism; but, on the contrary, it commences with men at the precise point where agrarianism ends, and it carries them up in an ascending line, while that carries them down. It gives them an interest in their country, an interest in public affairs; and when you are involved in war, in insurrection, or rebellion, or danger of any kind, they are the men who are to sustain you. If you should have occasion to call volunteers into the service of the country, you will have a population of men having homes, having wives and children to care for, who will defend their hearth-stones when invaded. What a sacred thing it is to a man to feel that he has a hearth-stone to defend, a home, and a wife and children to care for, and to rest satisfied that they have an abiding place. Such a man is interested individually in repelling invasion; he is interested individually in having good government.

I know there are many, and even some in the Democratic ranks, whose nerves are a little timid in regard to trusting the people with too much power. Sir, the people are the safest, the best, and the most reliable lodgment of power, if you have a population of this kind. Keep up the middle class; lop off an aristocracy on the one hand, and a rabble on the other; let the middle class maintain the ascendency, let them have the power, and your Government is always secure. Then you need not fear the people. I know, as I have just remarked, that some are timid in regard to trusting the people; but there can be no danger from a people who are interested in their Government, who have homes to defend, and wives and children to care for. Even if we test this proposition by that idea of self-interest which is said to govern and control man, I ask you if a man, who has an interest in his country, is not more reliable than one who has none? Is not a man who is adding to the wealth of his country more reliable than one who is simply a consumer and has no interest in it? If we suppose a man to be governed only by the principle of self-interest, is he not more reliable when he has a stake in the country, and is it not his interest to promote and advance his own condition? Is it not the interest of the great mass to have everything done rightly in reference to Government? The great mass of the people hold no office; they expect nothing from the Government. The only way they feel, and know, and understand the operations of the Government is in the exactions it makes from them. When they are receiving from the Government protection in common, it is their interest to do right in all governmental affairs; and that being their interest, they are to be relied upon, even if you suppose men to be actuated altogether by the principle of self-interest. It is the interest of the middle class to do right in all governmental affairs; and hence they are to be relied upon. Instead of requiring you to keep up your armies, your mounted men, and your footmen on the frontier, if you will let the people go and possess this public land on the conditions proposed in this bill, you will have an army on the frontier composed of men who will defend their own firesides, who will take care of their own homes, and will defend the other portions of the country, if need be, in time of war.

I would remark in this connection, that the public lands have paid for themselves. According to the report of Mr. Stuart of Virginia, the Secretary of the Interior in 1850, it was shown that then the public lands had paid for themselves, and sixty millions over. We have received into the treasury since that time about thirty-two million dollars from the public lands. They have, therefore, already paid the Government more than they cost, and there can be no objection to this bill on the ground that the public lands have been bought with the common treasure of the whole country. Besides, this bill provides that each individual making an entry shall pay all the expenses attending it.

We see, then, Mr. President, the effect this policy is to have on population. Let me ask here, — looking to our popular elections, looking to the proper lodgment of power, — is it not time that we had adopted a policy which would give us men interested in the affairs of the country to control and sway our elections? It seems to me that this cannot long be debated; the point is too clear. The agricultural and mechanical portion of the community are to be relied upon for the preservation and continuance of this Government. The great mass of the people, the great middle class, are honest. They toil for their support, accepting no favor from Government. They live by labor. They do not live by consumption, but by production ; and we should consume as small a portion of their production as it is possible for us to consume, leaving the producer to appropriate to his own use and benefit as much of the product of his own labor as it is possible in the nature of things to do. The great mass of the people need advocates — men who are honest and capable, who are willing to defend them. How much legislation is done for classes, and how little care seems to be exercised for the great mass of the people. When we are among our constituents, it is very easy to make appeals to the people and professions of patriotism, and then — I do not mean to be personal or invidious — it is very easy, when we are removed from them a short distance, to forget the people and legislate for classes, neglecting the interest of the great mass. The mechanics and agriculturists are honest, industrious, and economical. Let it not be supposed that I am against learning or education, but I might speak of the man in the rural districts in the language of Pope, —

> " Unlearned, he knew no schoolman's subtle art,
> No language but the language of the heart;
> By nature honest, by experience wise;
> Healthy by temperance and exercise."

This is the kind of men whom we must rely upon. Let your public lands be settled ; let them be filled up; let honest men become cultivators and tillers of the soil. I do not claim to be prophetic, but I have sometimes thought that if we would properly direct our legislation in reference to our public lands and our other public policy, the time would come when this would be the greatest government on the face of the earth. Go to the great valley of the Mississippi; take the western slope of the mountains to the Pacific Ocean; take the whole area of this country, and we find that we have over three million square miles. Throw off one fourth as unfit for cultivation, reducing the area of the United States to fifteen hundred million acres, and by appropriating three acres to a person, it will sustain a population of over five hundred million people; and I have no doubt, if this continent was strained to its utmost capacity, it could sustain the entire population of the world. Let us go on and carry out our destiny; interest men in the soil; let your vacant land be divided equally so that men can have homes; let them live by their own industry; and the time will come when this will be the greatest nation on the face of the earth. Let agriculture and the mechanic arts maintain the ascendency, and other professions and pursuits be subordinate to them, for on these two all others rest.

Since the crucifixion of our Saviour, emigration has been westward; and the poetic idea might have started long before it did, —

"Westward the star of empire takes its way."

It has been taking its way westward. The United States are filling up. We are going on to the Pacific coast. Let me raise the inquiry here, when, in the history of mankind, in the progress of nations, was there any nation that ever reached the point we now occupy? When was there a nation in its progress, in its settlement, in its advance in all that constitutes and makes a nation great, that occupied the position we now occupy? When was there any nation that could look to the East and behold the tide of emigration coming, and, at the same time, turn around and look to the mighty West, and behold the tide of emigration approaching from that direction. The waves of emigration have usually been running in one direction, but we find the tide of emigration now changed, and we are occupying a central position on the globe. Emigration is coming to us from the East and from the West; and when our vacant territory shall be filled up, when it shall reach a population of one hundred and fifty or five hundred millions, who can say what will be our destiny?

When our railroad system shall progress on proper principles, extending from one extreme of the country to the other, like so many arteries; when our telegraphic wires shall be stretched along them as the nerves in the human frame, and they shall run in parallel lines, and be crossed at right angles, until the whole globe, as it were, and especially this great centre, shall be covered like a net-work with these arteries and nerves; when the face of the globe shall flash with intelligence like the face of man; we, occupying this important point, may find our institutions so perfected, science so advanced, that instead of receiving immigration, instead of receiving nations from abroad, this will be the great sensorium from which our notions of religion, our notions of government, our improvements in works of every description shall radiate as from a common centre, and revolutionize the world.

Who dares say that this is not our destiny, if we will only permit it to be fulfilled? Then let us go on with this great work of interesting men in becoming connected with the soil; interesting them in remaining in your mechanic shops; prevent their accumulation in the streets of your cities; and in doing this, you will dispense with the necessity for all your pauper system. By doing this you enable each community to take care of its own poor. By doing this you destroy and break down the great propensity that exists with men to hang and loiter and perish about the cities of the Union, as is done now in the older countries.

It is well enough, Mr. President, to see where our public lands have been going. There seems to be a great scruple now in reference to the appropriation of lands for the benefit of the people; but the Federal Government has been very liberal heretofore in granting lands to the States for railroad purposes. We can pass law after law, making grant after grant of the public lands to corporations, without alarming any one here. We have already granted to railroad monopolies, to corporations, twenty-four million two hundred and forty-seven thousand acres. Those grants hardly meet with opposition in Congress; but it seems to be very wrong, in the estimation of some, to grant lands to the people on the conditions proposed in the bill before us. We find, furthermore, that there have been granted to the States, as swamp-lands, — and some of these lands will turn out to be the most productive on the globe, — forty million one hundred and thirty-three thousand five hundred and sixty-five acres.

In relation to the public lands, and the grants which have been made by the Government, I have obtained from the Commissioner of the General Land-Office several tables, which I now submit.

Estimate of the Quantities of Land which will inure to the States under Grants for Railroads, up to June 30, 1857.

States.	Acres.	Date of Law.
Illinois	2,595,053	September 20, 1850.
Missouri	1,815,435	June 10, 1852; Feb. 9, 1853.
Arkansas	1,465,297	February 9, 1853.
Michigan	3,096,000	June 3, 1856.
Wisconsin	1,622,800	June 3, 1856.
Iowa	3,456,000	May 15, 1856.
Louisiana	1,102,560	June 3 and Aug. 11, 1856.
Mississippi	950,400	August 11, 1856.
Alabama	1,913,390	May 17, June 3, and Aug. 11, 1856; March 3, 1857
Florida	1,814,400	May 17, 1856.
Minnesota	4,416,000	March 3, 1857.
Total	24,247,335	

Statement showing the Quantity of Swamp-land approved to the several States, up to 30th. June, 1857.

States.	Acres.
Ohio	25,650.71
Indiana	1,250,937.51
Illinois	1,369,140.72
Missouri	3,615,966.57
Alabama	2,595.51
Mississippi	2,834,796.11
Louisiana	7,601,535.46
Michigan	5,465,232.41
Arkansas	5,920,024.94
Florida	10,396,982.47
Wisconsin	1,650,712.10
Total	40,133,564.51

Estimate of unsold and unappropriated Lands in each of the States and Territories, including surveyed and unsurveyed, offered and unoffered Lands, on the 30th June, 1856.

States and Territories.	Acres.	Number of quarter-sections.
Ohio	43,553.34	272
Indiana	36,307.41	227
Illinois	511,662.85	3,198
Missouri	13,365,319.81	83,533
Alabama	9,459,367.74	59,121
Mississippi	5,519,390.69	34,496
Louisiana	5,933,373.83	37,083
Michigan	10,056,298.06	62,852
Arkansas	15,609,542.84	97,560
Florida	18,067,072.75	112,919
Iowa	6,237,661.03	38,985
Wisconsin	15,222,549.50	95,141
California	113,682,436.00	710,515
Minnesota Territory	82,502,608.33	515,641
Oregon "	118,913,241.31	743,208
Washington "	76,444,055.25	477,775
New Mexico "	155,210,804.00	970,067
Utah "	134,243,733.00	839,023
Nebraska "	206,984,747.00	1,293,655
Kansas "	76,361,058.00	477,256
Indian "	42,892,800.00	268,080
Total	1,107,297,572.74	6,920,607

The table giving the estimated quantity of all our public lands, shows the feasibility of the plan in favor of which I have been speaking. I know that some gentlemen from the Southern States object to this bill because they fear that it will carry emigrants from the free States into those States. Well, sir, on this point I have drawn some conclusions from figures, which I will present to the Senate. In the State of Alabama there are now undisposed of fifty-nine thousand one hundred and twenty-one quarter-sections of land. I ask my Southern friends, would it not be better if a man in the State of Alabama would select a quarter-section there, and take the two hundred dollars it would have cost him, and expend it there, even though it might be inferior land, than to compel him to pay $1.25 an acre, and emigrate from the State of Alabama to a place where he could get better land? If you compel him to pay the higher price, it becomes his interest to leave his native State; but by permitting him to take the land and expend on its improvement what he would otherwise have to pay, and what it would cost him to move, the chances are that he will remain where he is. In the State of Mississippi here are thirty-four thousand four hundred and ninety-six quarter-sections; in Louisiana, thirty-seven thousand; in Arkansas, ninety-seven thousand; in Florida, one hundred and twelve thousand. Altogether, the quarter-sections of public lands belonging to the Government amount to six million nine hundred and twenty thousand. How feasible the plan is. I have shown, too, that it would take over six hundred years to dispose of the public lands at the rate we have been disposing of them, and that if you take one million quarter-sections and have them settled and cultivated, you will obtain more revenue, and you will enhance the remaining public lands more than the value of those the Government gives.

I live in a Southern State; and, if I know myself, I am as good a Southern man as any one who lives within the borders of the South. It seems to be feared that by this bill we compel men to go on the lands. I want to compel no man to go. I want to leave each and every man to be controlled by his own inclination, by his own interest, and not to force him; but is it statesmanlike, is it philanthropic, is it Christian, to keep a man in a State, and refuse to let him go, because, if he does go, he will help to populate some other portion of the country? If a man lives in the county in which I live, and he can, by crossing the line into another county, better his condition, I say let him go. If, by crossing the boundary of my State and going into another, he can better his condition, I say let him go. If a man can go from Tennessee into Illinois, or Louisiana, or Mississippi, or Arkansas, or any other State, and better his condition, let him go. I care not where he goes, so that he locates himself in this great area of freedom, becomes attached to our institutions, and interested in the prosperity and welfare of the country. I care not where he goes, so that he is under the protection of our Stars and Stripes. I say, let him go where he can better the condition of himself, his wife, and children; let him go where he can receive the greatest remuneration for his toil and for his labor. What kind of a policy is it to say that a man shall be locked up where he was born, and shall be confined to the place of his birth?

Take the State of North Carolina, represented by the honorable Senator before me,[1] — and I have no doubt it is his intention to represent that people to their satisfaction, — would it have been proper to require the people of North Carolina, from her early settlement to the present time, to be confined within her boundaries? Would they not have looked upon it as a hard sentence? Would they not have looked upon it as oppressive and cruel? North Carolina has supplied the Western States with a large proportion of her population, for the reason that by going West they could better their condition. Who would prevent them from doing it? Who would say to the poor man in North Carolina, that has no land of his own to cultivate, that lives upon some barren angle, or some piny plain, or in some other State upon some stony ridge, that he must plough and dig the land appointed to him by his landlord, and that he is not to emigrate to any place where he can better his condition?

[1] Mr. Clingman.

What is his prospect? He has to live poor; he has to live hard; and, in the end, when he dies, poverty, want, is the only inheritance he can leave his children. There is no one who has a higher appreciation of North Carolina than I have; she is my native State. I found it to be my interest to emigrate, and I should have thought it cruel and hard if I had been told that I could not leave her boundary. Although North Carolina did not afford me the advantages of education, though I cannot speak in the language of the schoolmen, and call her my cherishing mother, yet, in the language of Cowper, "with all her faults, I love her still." She is still my mother; she is my native State; and I love her as such, and I love her people, too. But what an idea is it to present, as influencing the action of a statesman, that people may not emigrate from one State to another! Sir, I say let a man go anywhere within the boundaries of the United States where he can better his condition.

Mr. President, if I entertained the notions that some of my friends who oppose this bill do, I should be a more ardent advocate of its policy than I am now, if that were possible. My friend from Alabama[1] entertains some strange notions in reference to democracy and the people; and in his speech on the fisheries bill, he gave this proposition a kind of side-blow, a lick by indirection. I do not object to that; but if I entertained his opinions, I should be

[1] Mr. Clay.

a more determined and zealous advocate of the policy of this bill than I am now, if that were possible. In his speech upon the Lecompton Constitution, that Senator, in speaking of the powers of the convention which framed the Constitution, said: —

"In my opinion, they would have acted in stricter accordance with the spirit and genius of our institutions if they had not submitted it in whole or in part to the popular vote. Our governments are republics, not democracies. The people exercise their sovereignty not in person at the ballot-box, but through agents, delegates, or representatives. Our fathers founded republican governments in preference to democracies, not so much because it would be impracticable as because it would be unwise and inexpedient for the people themselves to assemble and adopt laws."

I have always thought the general idea had been that it was not practicable to do everything in a strict democratic sense, and that it was more convenient for the people to appear through their delegates. But the Senator said further: —

"They were satisfied, from reading and reflection, of the truth of Mr. Madison's observation about pure democracies, that they 'have ever been spectacles of turbulence and contention; have ever been found incompatible with personal security, or the rights of property; and have in general been as short in their lives as they have been violent in their deaths.' . . . . . .

. . . . . . "They knew that a large body of men is more liable to be controlled by passion or by interest than a single individual, and is more apt to sacrifice the rights of the minority, because it can be done with more impunity. Hence they endeavored to impose restraints upon themselves. Hence they committed the making of all their laws, organic or municipal, to their delegates or representatives, whose crimes they could punish, whose errors they could correct, and whose powers they could reclaim.

"The great security of our rights of life, liberty, and property, is in the responsibility of those who make and of those who execute the law. Establish as a principle that, to give sanction to law, it must be approved by a majority at the ballot-box, and you take away this security and surrender those rights to the most capricious, rapacious, and cruel of tyrants. I regret to see the growing spirit in Congress and throughout the country to democratize our government; to submit every question, whether pertaining to organic or municipal laws, to the vote of the people. This is sheer radicalism; it is the Red Republicanism of revolutionary France, which appealed to the sections on all occasions, and not the American Republicanism of our fathers. Their Republicanism was stable and conservative; this is mutable and revolutionary. Theirs afforded a shield for the minority; this gives a sword to the majority. Theirs defended the rights of the weak; this surrenders them to the power of the strong. God forbid that the demagogism of this day should prevail over the philanthropic and philosophic statesmanship of our fathers."

In the same speech, the Senator said, —

"Property is the foundation of every social fabric. To preserve, protect, and perpetuate rights of property, society is formed, and government is framed."

Now, if I entertained these notions, I should unquestionably go for the Homestead Bill. I am free to say, here, that I do not hold the doctrine advanced by the honorable gentleman from Alabama, to the extent that he goes. I believe the people are capable of self-government. I think they have demonstrated it most clearly; and I do not think the Senator's history of democracy states the case as it should be. I presume in the Senator's own State the people acted directly upon their Constitution at the ballot-box. That is the organic law. If they did not there, they have done so in most of the States of the Union; not, perhaps, in their original formation of their governments, but as the people have gone on and advanced in popular government. The honorable Senator seems to be opposed to democratizing, — in other words, he is opposed to popularizing our institutions; he is afraid to trust the control of things to the people at the ballot-box. Why, sir, the organic law which confers all the power upon your State legislatures, creates the different divisions, different departments of the State. The government is controlled at the ballot-box, and the doctrine set forth in the Constitution of Alabama is, that the people have a right to abolish and change their form of government when they think proper. The principle is clearly recognized; and on this my honorable friend and myself differ essentially. I find a similar doctrine laid down in a pamphlet which I have here: —

"In the convention that framed the Constitution of the United States, Gouverneur Morris said, that 'Property is the main object of society.' Mr. King said, 'Property is the primary object of society.' Mr. Butler contended strenuously that 'Property was the only just measurer of representation. This was the great object of government; the great cause of war; the great means of carrying it on.' Mr. Madison said, that 'In future times a great majority of the people will not only be without landed, but any other sort of property. These will either combine under the influence of their common situation, — in which case the right of property and the public liberty will not be secure in their hands, — or, what is more probable, they will become the tools of opulence and ambition.' Gouverneur Morris again said, 'Give the votes to the people who have no property, and they will sell them to the rich who will be able to buy them. We should not confine our attention to the present moment. The time is not far distant when this country will abound with mechanics and manufacturers, who will receive their bread from their employers. Will such men be the secure and faithful guardians of liberty?' Madison remarks, that those who opposed the property basis of representation, did so on the ground that the number of people was a fair index to the amount of property in any district."

These are not notions entertained by me; but they are important as the notions of some of our public men at the early formation of our Government. I entertain no such notions. If, however, the Senator from Alabama holds that property is the main object and basis of society, he, above all other men, ought to go for this bill, so as to place every man in the possession of a home and an interest in his country. The very doctrine that he lays down appeals to him trumpet-tongued, and asks him to place these men in a condition where they can be relied upon. His argument is unanswerable, if it be true, in favor of the Homestead Bill. It is taking men out of a dependent condition; it is preventing this Government from sinking into that condition that Rome did in her decline. I ask him now, if he entertains these opinions, as promulgated in his speech, to come up and join with us in the passage of this bill, and make every man, if possible, a property-holder, interested in his country; give him a basis to settle upon, and make him reliable at the ballot-box.

His speech is a fine production. I heard it with interest at the time it was delivered. I hold the opposite to him. Instead of the voice of the people being the voice of a demon, I go back to the old idea, and I favor the policy of popularizing all our free institutions. We are Democrats, occupying a position here from the South; we start together, but we turn our backs upon each other very soon. His policy would take the Government further from the people. I go in a direction to popularize it, and bring it nearer to the people. There is no better illustration of this than that old maxim, which is adopted in all our ordinary transactions, that "if you want a thing done, send somebody to do it; if you want it well done, go and do it yourself." It applies with great force in governmental affairs as in individual affairs; and if we can advance and make the workings and operation of our Government familiar to and understood by the people, the better for us. I say, when and wherever it is practicable, let the people transact their own business; bring them more in contact with their Government, and then you will arrest expenditure, you will arrest corruption, you will have a purer and better government.

I hold to the doctrine that man can be advanced;

that man can be elevated ; that man can be exalted in his character and condition We are told, on high authority, that he is made in the image of his God; that he is endowed with a certain amount of divinity. And I believe man can be elevated; man can become more and more endowed with divinity; and as he does he becomes more God-like in his character and capable of governing himself. Let us go on elevating our people, perfecting our institutions, until democracy shall reach such a point of perfection that we can exclaim with truth that the voice of the people is the voice of God.

As I said, I have entertained different notions from those inculcated by the honorable Senator. If I entertained his notions, then I should be for the Homestead. I hold in my hand a document, by which it was proclaimed in 1776, —

> "We hold these truths to be self-evident: that all men are created equal; that they are endowed by their Creator with certain inalienable rights; that among these are life, liberty, and the pursuit of happiness; that to secure these rights governments are instituted among men, deriving their just powers from the consent of the governed."

Is property laid down there as the great element and the great basis of society? It is only one; and Mr. Jefferson laid it down in the Declaration of Independence, that it was a self-evident truth that government was instituted — for what? To protect men in life, liberty, and the pursuit of happiness. That is what Mr. Jefferson said. And who indorsed it? The men who framed the Declaration of Independence, who did not go upon the idea that property was the only element of society. The doctrine established by those who proclaimed our independence, was, that life, liberty, and the pursuit of happiness were three great ends of government, and not property exclusively. When the declaration came forth from the old Congress Hall, it came forth as a column of fire and light. It declared that the security of life and liberty, and the pursuit of happiness, were the three great ends of government. Mr. Jefferson says, in his first Inaugural Address, which is the greatest paper that has ever been written in this Government, — and I commend it to the reading of those who say they are Democrats, by way of refreshing their memories, that they may understand what are correct Democratic principles, —

> "Sometimes it is said that man cannot be trusted with the government of himself. Can he, then, be trusted with the government of others? Or have we found angels in the form of kings to govern him. Let history answer this question."

Mr. Jefferson seems to think man can be trusted with the government of himself. In the Declaration of Independence he does not embrace property; in fact, it is not referred to. But I am willing to concede that it is one of the primary and elementary principles in government. Mr. Jefferson declares the great truth that man is to be trusted; that man is capable of governing himself, and that he has a right to govern himself. In the same Inaugural Address of Mr. Jefferson, we find the passage usually attributed to Washington's Farewell Address, which has got universal circulation, — that we should pursue our own policy; that we should promote our own institutions, maintaining friendly relations with all, entangling alliances with none. Let us carry out the doctrines of the Inaugural Address of Mr. Jefferson; let us carry out the great principles laid down in the Declaration of Independence, which this Homestead Bill embraces.

But I wish to call attention to some other authority on this subject. As contradistinguished from the views of the Senator from Alabama, I present the views of a recent writer[1] as in accordance with my own notions of Democracy: —

"The democratic party represents the great principle of progress. It is onward and outward in its movements. It has a heart for action, and motives for a world. It constitutes the principle of diffusion, and is to humanity what the centrifugal force is to the revolving orbs of a universe. What motion is to them, democracy is to principle. It is the soul in action. It conforms to the providence of God. It has confidence in man, and an abiding reliance in his high destiny. It seeks the largest liberty, the greatest good, and the surest happiness. It aims to build up the great interests of the many, to the least detriment of the few. It remembers the past, without neglecting the present. It establishes the present, without fearing to provide for the future. It cares for the weak, while it permits no injustice to the strong. It conquers the oppressor, and prepares the subjects of tyranny for freedom. It melts the bigot's

[1] Lamartine.

heart to meekness, and reconciles his mind to knowledge. It dispels the clouds of ignorance and superstition, and prepares the people for instruction and self-respect. It adds wisdom to legislation, and improved judgment to government. It favors enterprise that yields a reward to the many and an industry that is permanent. It is the pioneer of humanity — the conservator of nations. It fails only when it ceases to be true to itself. *Vox populi, vox Dei,* — has proved to be both a proverb, and a prediction.

"It is a mistake to suppose that democracy may not be advanced under different forms of government. Its own, it should be remembered, is the highest conventional form, that which precedes the lofty independence of the individual, spoken of by the Apostle to the Hebrews, who will need government but from the law which the Lord has placed in his heart.

"In one respect, all nations are governed upon the same principle; that is, each adopts the form which it has the understanding and the power to sustain. There is in all a greater or lesser power, and it requires no profound speculation to decide which will control. A tyrannical dictator may do more to advance the true interests of democracy than a moderate sovereign who is scrupulously guarded by an antiquated constitution; for the tyrant adds vigor to his opponents by his deeds of oppression.

"The frequent question as to what form of government is best, is often answered without any reference to condition or application of principles. There can be properly but one answer, and yet the application of that answer may lead to great diversity of views.

"When it is asserted that the democratic form of government is unquestionably the best, it must be considered that the answer not only designates the form preferred, but implies a confident belief in the advanced condition of the people who are to be the subjects of it. It premises the capacity for self-control, and a corresponding degree of knowledge in regard to the rights, balances, and necessities of society. It involves a discriminating appreciation of the varied duties of the man, the citizen, and the legislator. It presupposes a reasonable knowledge of the legitimate means and ends of government, enlarged views of humanity, and of the elements of national existence.

"The democratic form of government is the best, because its standard of moral requisition is the highest. It claims for man a universality of interest, liberty, and justice. It is Christianity with its mountain beacons and guides. It is the standard of Deity based on the eternal principles of truth, passing through and rising above the yielding clouds of ignorance, into the regions of infinite wisdom. As we live on, this 'pillar of the cloud by day, and the pillar of fire by night,' will not be taken from before the people, but stand immovable, immeasurable, and in the brightness of its glory continue to shed increasing light on a world and a universe.

"The great objects of knowledge and moral culture of the people are among its most prominent provisions. Practical religion and religious freedom are the sunshine of its growth and glory. It is the sublime and mighty standard spoken of by the Psalmist, who exclaims, in the beautiful language of poetical conception, —

"'The Lord is high above all nations, and his glory above the heavens. Who is like unto the Lord our God, who dwelleth on high; who humbleth himself to behold the things that are in heaven and in the earth? He raiseth up the poor out of the dust, and lifteth the needy out of the dunghill, that he may set him with princes, even with the princes of the people.'

"Democracy is a permanent element of progress, and is present everywhere, whatever may be the temporary form of the ruling power. Its inextinguishable fires first burst forth in an empire, and its welcome lights cheer the dark domains of despotism. While tyrants hate the patriot and exile him from their contracted dominions, the spirit of democracy invests him as a missionary of humanity, and inspires him with an eloquence which moves a world. Its lightning rays cannot be hidden; its presence cannot be banished. Dictators, kings, and emperors, are but its servants; and, as man becomes elevated to the dignity of self-knowledge and control, their administration ceases. Their rule indicates an imperfect state of society, and may be regarded as the moral props of the builder, necessary only to sustain a people in their different periods of growth. One cannot speak of them lightly, nor indulge in language that should seem to deny their fitness as the instruments of good in the hands of Providence. Their true position may be best gathered from the prediction which is based upon a knowledge of the past and present condition of man, — that all kingdoms and empires must cease whenever a people have a knowledge of their rights, and acquire the power of a practical application of principles. This is the work of time. It is the work of constant, repeated trial. The child that attempts to step an hundred times and falls; the new-fledged bird that tries its feeble wings again and again before it is able to sweep the circle of the sky with its kindred flock, indicate the simple law upon which all strength depends, whether it be the strength of an insect, or the strength of a nation.

" Because a people do not succeed in changing their form of government, even after repeated trials, we are not to infer that they are indulging in impracticable experiments, nor that they will be disappointed in ultimately realizing the great objects of their ambition. Indeed, all failures of this class are indicative of progressive endeavor. They imply an increasing knowledge of the true dignity of man, and a growing disposition to engage in new and more and more difficult endeavors. These endeavors are but the exercise of a nation, and without them, no people can ever command the elements of national existence and of self-control. But inquiries in regard to so extensive a subject should be shaped within more practical limits." . . . . . .

" The triumphs of democracy constitute the way-marks of the world. They demand no extraneous element of endurance for permanency, no fictitious splendor for embellishment, no

6

borrowed greatness for glory. Originating in the inexhaustible sources of power, moved by the spirit of love and liberty, and guided by the wisdom which comes from the instincts and experience of the immortal soul, as developed in the people, democracy exists in the imperishable principle of progress, and registers its achievements in the institutions of freedom, and in the blessings which characterize and beautify the realities of life. Its genius is to assert and advance the true dignity of mind, to elevate the motives and affections of man, and to extend, establish, protect, and equalize the common rights of humanity.

"Condorcet, although an aristocrat by genius and by birth, became a democrat from philosophy."

A few years since a Whig member of the United States Senate sneeringly asked Senator Allen, of Ohio, the question, "What is democracy?" The following was the prompt reply:

"Democracy is a sentiment not to be appalled, corrupted, or compromised. It knows no baseness; it cowers to no danger; it oppresses no weakness; destructive only of despotism, it is the sole conservator of liberty, labor, and property. It is the sentiment of freedom, of equal rights, of equal obligations — the law of nature pervading the law of the land."

"'What, sir,' asked Patrick Henry, in the Virginia Convention of 1778, 'is the genius of democracy? Let me read that clause of the Bill of Rights of Virginia, which relates to this (third clause): That government is or ought to be instituted for the common benefit, protection, and security of the people, nation, or community; of all the various modes and forms of government, that is best which is capable of producing the greatest degree of happiness and safety, and is most effectually secured against the dangers of mal-administration; and that whenever any government shall be found inadequate or contrary to those principles, or contrary to those purposes, a majority of the community hath an indubitable, inalienable, and indefeasible right to reform, alter, or abolish it, in such manner as shall be judged the most conducive to the public weal.'"[1]

In the same convention Judge Marshall said, —

"What are the favorite maxims of democracy? A strict observance of justice and public faith, and a steady adherence to virtue; -- these, sir, are the principles of a good government."[2]

"'Democracy,' says the late Mr. Legaré, of South Carolina, in an article published in the 'New York Review,' 'in the high and only true sense of that much-abused word, is the destiny of nations, because it is the spirit of Christianity.'"[3]

I have referred to the remarks of the Senator from Alabama to show that if his doctrines were true, he should go for the passage of the Homestead Bill, because, in order to sustain the Government on the principles laid down by him, every man should be a property-holder. I want it understood that I enter a disclaimer to the doctrine presented by him, and merely present his argument to show why he, above all others, ought to go for the Homestead policy. I refer to Mr. Legaré, Judge Marshall, and the author of the "History of Democracy," as laying down my notions of democracy, as contradistinguished from those laid down by the distinguished Senator from Alabama. We are both members from the Democratic party. I claim to be a Democrat, East, West, North, or South, or anywhere else. I have nothing to disguise. I have referred to the Declaration of Independence, and to Mr.

1 Elliot's *Debates*, Vol. III. p. 77. 2 Ibid. p. 223.
3 Ibid. Vol. V. p. 297.

Jefferson's Inaugural Address, for the purpose of showing that democracy means something very different from what was laid down by the distinguished Senator from Alabama. I furthermore refer to these important documents to show that property is not the leading element of government and of society. Mr. Jefferson lays down, as truths to be self-evident, that life, liberty, and the pursuit of happiness are the leading essentials of government.

But it is not my purpose to dwell longer on that; and I wish to pass to the speech of the Senator from South Carolina.[1] I disagree in much that was said by that distinguished Senator; and I wish to show that he ought to go for the Homestead policy, so as to interest every man in the country. If property is the leading and principal element on which society rests; if property is the main object for which government was created, the gentlemen who are the foremost, the most zealous, and most distinguished advocates of that doctrine should sustain the Homestead policy. The honorable Senator from South Carolina, in his speech on the Lecompton Constitution, by innuendo or indirection, had a hit at the Homestead — a side-blow. He said: —

"Your people are awaking. They are coming here. They are thundering at our doors for homesteads, one hundred and sixty acres of land for nothing; and Southern Senators are supporting them. Nay, they are assembling, as I have said, with arms in their hands, and demanding work at $1000 a year for six hours a day. Have you heard that the ghosts of

1 Mr. Hammond.

Mendoza and Torquemada are stalking in the streets of your great cities? That the Inquisition is at hand?"

If this be true, as assumed by the distinguished Senator from South Carolina, is it not an argument why men should be placed in a condition where they will not clamor, where they will not raise mobs to threaten Government, and demand homesteads? Interest these men in the country; give them homes, or let them take homes; let them become producers; let them become better citizens; let them be more reliable at the ballot-box. I want to take them on their ground, their principle, that property is the main element of society and of government; and if their doctrine be true, the argument is still stronger in favor of the Homestead than the position I assume. But the distinguished Senator from South Carolina goes on: —

"In all social systems there must be a class to do the menial duties, to perform the drudgery of life. That is, a class requiring but a low order of intellect, and but little skill. Its requisites are vigor, docility, fidelity. Such a class you must have, or you would not have that other class which leads progress, civilization, and refinement. It constitutes the very mud-sill of society and of political government; and you might as well attempt to build a house in the air, as to build either the one or the other, except on this mud-sill.

"'The poor ye always have with you'; for the man who lives by daily labor, and scarcely lives at that, and who has to put out his labor in the market, and take the best he can get for it — in short, your whole hireling class of manual laborers and 'operatives,' as you call them, are essentially slaves. The difference between us is, that our slaves are hired for life and well compensated; there is no starvation, no begging, no want of employment among our people; and not too much employment either. Yours are hired by the day, not cared for, and scantily compensated, which may be proved in the most painful manner, at any hour, in any street in any of your large towns. Why, you meet more beggars in one day, in any single street of the city of New York, than you would meet in a lifetime in the whole South. We do not think that whites should be slaves either by law or necessity."

In this portion of the Senator's remarks I concur. I do not think whites should be slaves; and if slavery is to exist in this country, I prefer black slavery to white slavery. But what I want to get at is, to show that my worthy friend from South Carolina should defend the Homestead policy, and the impolicy of making the invidious remarks that have been made here in reference to a portion of the population of the United States. Mr. President, so far as I am concerned, I feel that I can afford to speak what are my sentiments. I am no aspirant for anything on the face of God Almighty's earth. I have reached the summit of my ambition. The acme of all my hopes has been attained, and I would not give the position I occupy here to-day for any other in the United States. Hence, I say, I can afford to speak what I believe to be true.

In one sense of the term we are all slaves. A man is a slave to his ambition; he is a slave to his avarice; he is a slave to his necessities; and, in enumerations of this kind, you can scarcely find any man, high or low in society, but who, in some sense, is a slave; but they are not slaves in the sense we mean at the South, and it will not do to assume that every man who toils for his living is a slave. If that be so, all are slaves; for all must toil more or less, mentally or physically. But in the other sense of the term, we are not slaves. Will it do to assume that the man who labors with his hands, every man who is an operative in a manufacturing establishment or a shop, is a slave? No, sir; that will not do. Will it do to assume that every man who does not own slaves, but has to live by his own labor, is a slave? That will not do. If this were true, it would be very unfortunate for a good many of us, and especially so for me. I am a laborer with my hands, and I never considered myself a slave, in the acceptation of the term slave in the South. I do own some; I acquired them by my industry, by the labor of my hands. In that sense of the term I should have been a slave while I was earning them with the labor of my hands.

Mr. Hammond. Will the Senator define a slave?

Mr. Johnson. What we understand to be a slave in the South, is a person who is held to service during his or her natural life, subject to, and under the control of, a master who has the right to appropriate the products of his or her labor to his own use. The necessities of life, and the various positions in which a man may be placed, operated upon by avarice, gain, or ambition, may cause him to labor; but that does not make a slave. How many men are there in society who go out and work with their own hands, who reap in the field, and mow in a meadow, who hoe corn, who work in the shops? Are they slaves? If we were to go back and follow out this idea, that every operative and laborer is a slave, we should find that we have had a great many distinguished slaves since the world commenced. Socrates, who first conceived the idea of the immortality of the soul, Pagan as he was, labored with his own hands; — yes, wielded the chisel and the mallet, giving polish and finish to the stone; he afterwards turned to be a fashioner and constructor of the mind. Paul, the great expounder, himself was a tent-maker, and worked with his hands: was he a slave? Archimedes, who declared that, if he had a place on which to rest the fulcrum, with the power of his lever he could move the world: was he a slave? Adam, our great father and head, the lord of the world, was a tailor by trade: I wonder if he was a slave?

When we talk about laborers and operatives, look at the columns that adorn this chamber, and see their finish and style. We are lost in admiration at the architecture of your buildings, and their massive columns. We can speak with admiration. What would it have been but for hands to construct it? Was the artisan who worked upon it a slave? Let us go to the South and see how the matter stands there. Is every man that is not a slaveholder to be denominated a slave because he labors? Why indulge in such a notion? The argument cuts at both ends of the line, and this kind of doctrine does us infinite harm in the South. There are operatives there; there are laborers there; there are mechanics there. Are they slaves? Who is it in the South that gives us title and security to the institution of slavery? Who is it, let me ask every Southerner around me? Suppose, for instance, we take the State of South Carolina, — and there are many things about her and her people that I admire, — we find that the 384,984 slaves in South Carolina are owned by how many whites? They are owned by 25,556. Take the State of Tennessee, with a population of 800,000, — 239,000 slaves are owned by 33,864 persons. The slaves in the State of Alabama are owned by 29,295 whites. The whole number of slaveholders in all the slave States, when summed up, makes 347,000, owning three and a half million slaves. The white population in South Carolina is 274,000; the slaves greater than the whites. The aggregate population of the State is 668,507.

The operatives in South Carolina are 68,549. Now, take the 25,000 slave-owners out, and a large proportion of the people of South Carolina work with their hands. Will it do to assume that, in the State of South Carolina, the State of Tennessee, the State of Alabama, and the other slaveholding States, all those who do not own slaves are slaves themselves? Will this assumption do? What does it do at home in our own States? It has a tendency to raise prejudice, to engender opposition to the institution of slavery itself. Yet our own folks will do it.

Mr. MASON. Will the Senator from Tennessee allow me to interrupt him for a moment?

Mr. JOHNSON. Yes, sir.

Mr. MASON. The Senator is making an exhibition of the very few slaveholders in the Southern States, in proportion to the white population, according to the census. That is an exhibition which has been made before by Senators who sit on the other side of the Chamber. They have brought before the American people what they allege to be the fact, shown by the census, that of the white population in the Southern States, there are very few who are slaveholders. The Senator from Tennessee is now doing the same thing. I understand him to say there are but some — I do not remember exactly the number, but I think three hundred thousand or a fraction more — of the whites in the slaveholding States, who own three million slaves; but he made no further exposition. I ask the Senator to state the additional fact that the holders of the slaves are the heads of families of the white population; and neither that Senator nor those whose example he has followed on the other side, has stated the fact that the white population in the Southern States, as in the other States, embraces men, women, and children. He has exhibited only the number of slaveholders who are heads of families.

Mr. Johnson. The Senator says I have not made an exhibit of the fact. The Senator interrupted me before I had concluded. I gave way as a matter of courtesy to him. Perhaps his speech would have had no place, if he had waited to hear me a few moments longer.

Mr. Mason. I shall wait. I thought the Senator had passed that point.

Mr. Johnson. I was stating the fact, that according to the census-tables three hundred and forty-seven thousand white persons owned the whole number of slaves in the Southern States. I was about to state that the families holding these slaves might average six or eight or ten persons, all of whom are interested in the products of slave-labor, and many of these slaves are held by minors and by females. I was not alluding to the matter for the purpose the Senator from Virginia seems to have intimated, and I should have been much obliged to him if he had waited until he heard my application of these figures. I was going to show that expressions like those to which I have alluded, operate against us in the South, and I was following the example of no one. I was taking these facts from the census-tables, which were published by order of Congress, to show the bad policy and injustice of declaring that the laboring portion of our population were slaves and menials. Such declarations should not be applied to the people either North or South. I wished to say in that connection, that, in my opinion, if a few men at the North and at the South, who entertain extreme views on the subject of slavery, and desire to keep up agitation, were out of the way, the great mass of the people, North and South, would go on prosperously and harmoniously under our institutions.

. . . .

Sir, carry out the Homestead policy, attach the people to the soil, induce them to love the Government, and you will have the North reconciled to the South, and the South to the North, and we shall not have invidious doctrines preached to stir up bad feelings in either section. I know that in my own State, and in the other Southern States, the men who do not own slaves are among the first to take care of the institution. They will submit to no encroachment from abroad, no interference from other sections.

I have said, Mr. President, much more than I intended to say, and, I fear, in rather a desultory manner, but I hope I have made myself understood. I heard that some gentleman was going to offer an amendment to this bill, providing that the Government should furnish every man with a slave. So far as I am concerned, if it suited him, and his inclination led him that way, I wish to God every head of a family in the United States had one to take the drudgery and menial service off his family.

I would have no objection to that; but this intimation was intended as a slur upon my proposition. I want that to be determined by the people of the respective States, and not by the Congress of the United States. I do not want this body to interfere by innuendo or by amendment, prescribing that the people shall have this or the other. I desire to leave that to be determined by the people of the respective States, and not by the Congress of the United States.

I hope, Mr. President, that this bill will be passed. I think it involves the very first principles of the Government: it is founded upon statesmanship, humanity, philanthropy, and even upon Christianity itself. I know the argument has been made, why permit one portion of the people to go and take some of this land and not another? The law is in general terms; it places it in the power of every man who will go to take a portion of the land. The Senator from Alabama suggests to me that a person, in order to get the benefit of this bill, must prove that he is not the owner of other land. An amendment was yesterday inserted in the bill striking out that provision. Then it places all on an equality to go and take. Why should this not be done? It was conceded yesterday that the land was owned by the people. There are over three million heads of families in the United States; and if every man who is the head of a family were to take a quarter-section of public land, there would still be nearly four million quarter-sections left. If some people go and take quarter-sections, it does not interfere with the rights of others, for he who goes takes only a part of that which is his, and takes nothing that belongs to anybody else. The domain belongs to the whole people; the equity is in the great mass of the people; the Government holds the fee and passes the title, but the beneficial interest is in the people. There are, as I have said, two quarter-sections of land for every head of a family in the United States, and we merely propose to permit a head of a family to take one half of that which belongs to him.

I believe the passage of this bill will strengthen the bonds of the Union. It will give us a better voting population, and just in proportion as men become interested in property, they will become reconciled to all the institutions of property in the country, in whatever shape they may exist. Take the institution of slavery, for instance: would you rather trust it to the mercies of a people liable to be ruled by the mobs of which my honorable friend from South Carolina spoke, or would you prefer an honest set of landholders? Which would be the most reliable? Which would guarantee the greatest security to our institutions, when they come to the test of the ballot-box?

Mr. President, I hope the Senate will pass this bill. I think it will be the beginning of a new state of things — a new era.

So far as I am concerned, — I say it not in any spirit of boasting or egotism, — if this bill were passed, and the system it inaugurates carried out, of granting a reasonable quantity of land for a man's family, and looking far into the future I could see resulting from it — a stable, an industrious, a hardy, a Christian, a philanthropic community, I should feel that the great object of my little mission was fulfilled. All that I desire is the honor and the credit of being one of the American Congress to consummate and to carry out this great scheme that is to elevate our race and to make our institutions more permanent. I want no reputation as some have insinuated. You may talk about Jacobinism, Red Republicanism, and so on. I pass by such insinuations as the idle wind which I regard not.

I know the motives that prompt me to action. I can go back to that period in my own history when I could not say that I had a home. This being so, when I cast my eyes from one extreme of the United States to the other, and behold the great number that are homeless, I feel for them. I believe this bill would put them in possession of homes; and I want to see them realizing that sweet conception when each man can proclaim, "I have a home; an abiding place for my wife and for my children; I am not the tenant of another; I am my own ruler; and I will move according to my own will, and not at the dictation of another."

Yes, Mr. President, if I should never be heard of again on the surface of God's habitable globe, the proud satisfaction of having contributed my little aid to the consummation of this great measure is all the reward I desire.

The people need friends. They have a great deal to bear. They make all; they do all; but how little they participate in the legislation of the country? All, or nearly all, of our legislation is for corporations, for monopolies, for classes, and individuals; but the great mass who produce while we consume, are little cared for; their rights and interests are neglected and overlooked. Let us, as patriots, as statesmen, let us as Christians, consummate this great measure which will exert an influence throughout the civilized world in fulfilling our destiny. I thank the Senate for their attention.

THE CONSTITUTIONALITY AND RIGHTFULNESS OF SECESSION.

SPEECH DELIVERED IN THE SENATE OF THE UNITED STATES, ON TUESDAY AND WEDNESDAY, DECEMBER 18 AND 19, 1860.

The question pending being the Joint Resolution introduced by Mr. Johnson, on Thursday, the 13th of December, 1860, proposing amendments to the Constitution of United States.[1]

Mr. PRESIDENT: By the joint resolution now before the Senate, three amendments to the Constitution of the United States are proposed. One proposes to change the mode of election of President and Vice-President of the United States from the electoral college to a vote substantially and directly by the people. The second proposes that the Senators of the United States shall be elected by the people, once in six years, instead of by the Legislatures of the respective States. The third provides that the Supreme Court shall be divided into three classes, — the term of the first class to expire in four years from the time that the classification is made; of the second class in eight years; and of the third class in twelve years; and as these vacancies occur they are to be filled by persons chosen, one half from the slave States and the other half from the non-slaveholding States,

[1] See Appendix, p. 1.

thereby taking the judges of the Supreme Court from the respective divisions of the country.

Mr. President, if these amendments had been made, and the Constitution had been in the shape now proposed, I think the difficulties that are now upon the country would have been obviated. It would have been required that either the President or the Vice-President should be taken from the South, and that would have destroyed, to some extent, the sectional character of our recent election.

The next provision of the amendment would require the votes cast for President and Vice-President to be cast by districts; and if we are to take as an indication the returns to the House of Representatives of a majority of twenty-seven against the incoming Administration, it is pretty conclusive that a President differing in politics and sentiments from the one who has been recently elected would have been chosen. Each district would have voted directly for the President and Vice-President of the United States. The individual having a majority of the votes in that district would be considered as receiving one electoral vote, just as we count the votes for one member of Congress. Hence, if all the votes in the respective districts had been cast on the same principle, we should in the next Congress have a majority of twenty-seven in opposition to the incoming Administration in the House of Representatives; for they would have given us a majority in the electoral colleges. It seems to me, if these propositions were adopted and made a part of the Constitution, that, to a very great extent, the difficulty and complaint that are now manifested in different portions of the country would be obviated, and especially so with some improvement or modification of the law which provides for the restoration of fugitives from labor.

It is not my purpose, sir, to discuss these propositions to amend the Constitution in detail to-day, and I shall say but little more in reference to them and to their practical operation; but, as we are now, as it were, involved in revolution, (for there is a revolution, in fact, upon the country,) I think it behooves every man, and especially every one occupying a public place, to indicate, in some manner, his opinions and sentiments in reference to the questions that agitate and distract the public mind. I shall be frank on this occasion in giving my views and taking my position, as I have always been upon questions that involve the public interest. I believe it is the imperative duty of Congress to make some effort to save the country from impending dissolution; and he that is unwilling to make an effort to preserve the Union, or, in other words, to preserve the Constitution, and the Union as an incident resulting from the preservation of the Constitution, is unworthy of public confidence, and the respect and gratitude of the American people.

In most that I shall say on this occasion, I shall

not differ very essentially from my Southern friends. The difference will consist in the mode and manner by which this great end is to be accomplished. Some of our Southern friends think that secession is the mode by which these ends can be accomplished; that if the Union cannot be preserved in its spirit, by secession they will get those rights secured and perpetuated that they have failed to obtain within the Union.

I am opposed to secession. I believe it is no remedy for the evils complained of. Instead of acting with that division of my Southern friends who take ground for secession, I shall take other grounds, while I try to accomplish the same end. I think that this battle ought to be fought not outside, but inside of the Union, and upon the battlements of the Constitution itself. I am unwilling voluntarily to walk out of the Union which has been the result of a Constitution made by the patriots of the Revolution. They formed the Constitution; and this Union that is so much spoken of, and which all of us are so desirous to preserve, grows out of the Constitution; and I repeat, I am not willing to walk out of a Union growing out of the Constitution that was formed by the patriots and the soldiers of the Revolution. So far as I am concerned, and I believe I may speak with some degree of confidence for the people of my State, we intend to fight that battle inside and not outside of the Union; and if anybody must go out of the

Union, it must be those who violate it. We do not intend to go out. It is our Constitution; it is our Union, growing out of the Constitution; and we do not intend to be driven from it or out of the Union. Those who have violated the Constitution either in the passage of what are denominated personal-liberty bills, or by their refusal to execute the fugitive-slave law, — they having violated the instrument that binds us together, — must go out, and not we. If we violate the Constitution by going out ourselves, I do not think we can go before the country with the same force of position that we shall if we stand inside of the Constitution, demanding a compliance with its provisions and its guarantees; or if need be, as I think it is, demanding additional securities. We should make that demand inside of the Constitution, and in the manner and mode pointed out by the instrument itself. Then we keep ourselves in the right; we put our adversary in the wrong; and though it may take a little longer, we take the right means to accomplish an end that is right in itself.

I know that sometimes we talk about compromises. I am not a compromiser, nor a conservative, in the usual acceptation of those terms. I have been generally considered radical, and I do not come forward to-day in anything that I shall say or propose, asking for anything to be done upon the principle of compromise. If we ask for anything, it should be for that which is right and reasonable in itself. If it be right, those of whom we ask it, upon the great principle of right, are bound to grant it. Compromise! I know in the common acceptation of the term it is to agree upon certain propositions in which some things are conceded on one side and others conceded on the other. I shall go for enactments by Congress or for amendments to the Constitution, upon the principle that they are right, and upon no other ground. I am not for compromising right with wrong. If we have no right, we ought not to demand it. If we are in the wrong, they should not grant us what we ask. I approach this momentous subject on the great principles of right, asking for nothing and demanding nothing but what is right in itself, and what every right-minded man and a right-minded community and a right-minded people, who wish for the preservation of this Government, will be disposed to grant.

In fighting this battle, I shall do it upon the basis laid down by a portion of the people of my own State, in a large and very intelligent meeting. A committee of the most intelligent men in the country reported this resolution: —

"*Resolved*, That we deeply sympathize with our sister Southern States, and freely admit that there is good cause for dissatisfaction and complaint on their part, on account of the recent election of sectional candidates to the Presidency and Vice-Presidency of the United States; yet we, as a portion of the people of a slaveholding community, are not for seceding or breaking up the Union of these States until every fair and honorable means has been exhausted in trying to obtain, on the part of the non-slaveholding States, a compliance with the spirit and letter of the Constitution and all its guarantees; and when this shall have been done, and the States now in open rebellion against the laws of the United States, in refusing to execute the fugitive-slave law, shall persist in their present unconstitutional course, and the Federal Government shall fail or refuse to execute the laws in good faith, it (the Government) will not have accomplished the great design of its creation, and will therefore, in fact, be a practical dissolution, and all the States, as parties, be released from the compact which formed the Union."

The people of Tennessee, irrespective of party, go on and declare further: —

"That in the opinion of this meeting no State has the constitutional right to secede from the Union without the consent of the other States which ratified the compact. The compact, when ratified, formed the Union without making any provision whatever for its dissolution. It (the compact) was adopted by the States *in toto and forever*, '*without reservation or condition;*' hence a secession of one or more States from the Union, without the consent of the others ratifying the compact, would be revolution, leading in the end to civil, and perhaps servile war. While we deny the right of a State, constitutionally, to secede from the Union, we admit the great and inherent right of revolution, abiding and remaining with every people, but a right which should not be exercised, except in extreme cases, and in the last resort, when grievances are without redress, and oppression has become intolerable."

They declare further: —

"That in our opinion, we can more successfully resist the aggression of Black Republicanism by remaining within the Union, than we can by going out of it; and more especially so, while there is a majority of both branches in the National Legislature opposed to it, and the Supreme Court of the United States is on the side of law and the Constitution."

They go on, and declare further: —

"That we are not willing to abandon our Northern friends who have stood by the Constitution of the United States, and in standing by it have vindicated our rights, and in their vindication have been struck down; and now, in their extremity, we cannot and will not desert them by seceding, or otherwise breaking up the Union."

This is the basis upon which a portion of the people of Tennessee, irrespective of party, propose to fight this battle. We believe that our true position is inside of the Union. We deny the doctrine of secession; we deny that a State has the power, of its own volition, to withdraw from the Confederacy. We are not willing to do an unconstitutional act, to induce or to coerce others to comply with the Constitution of the United States. We prefer complying with the Constitution, and fighting our battle, and making our demand inside of the Union.

I know, Mr. President, that there are some who believe — and we see that some of the States are acting on that principle — that a State has the right to secede; that, of its own will, it has a right to withdraw from the Confederacy. I am inclined to think, and I know it is so in fact, that in many portions of the country this opinion has resulted from the resolutions of your own State, sir,[1] of 1798 and 1799. I propose to-day to examine that subject, for I know from the examination of it that there has been a false impression made upon my own mind in reference to those resolutions, and the power proposed to be exercised by a State in seceding upon its own will. When we come to examine those resolutions, we find that the third reads as follows :

> "That this Assembly doth explicitly and peremptorily declare that it views the powers of the Federal Government, as resulting from the compact, to which the States are parties, as limited by the plain sense and intention of the instrument constituting that compact, as no further valid than they are authorized by the grants enumerated in that compact; and that in case of a deliberate, palpable, and dangerous exercise of other powers, not granted by the said compact, the States who are parties thereto have the right, and are in duty bound, to interpose for arresting the progress of the evil, and for maintaining within their respective limits the authorities, rights, and liberties appertaining to them."

The phraseology of the Kentucky Resolution is somewhat broader and more extensive. It declares that a State has the right to judge of the infraction of the Constitution, as well as the mode and measure of redress. This is what is declared by that resolution which is repeated by so many in speeches and publications made through the country. Now, let Mr. Madison speak for himself as to what he meant by that resolution. Mr. Madison, in his report upon those resolutions, goes on and states ex-

[1] Mr. Mason, of Virginia, in the chair.

pressly that in the resolution the word "States" is used, notwithstanding the word "respective" is used. Mr. Madison says: —

"It appears to your committee to be a plain principle, founded in common sense, illustrated by common practice, and essential to the nature of compacts, that, where resort can be had to no tribunal superior to the authority of parties, the parties themselves must be the rightful judges, in the last resort, whether the bargain made has been pursued or violated. The Constitution of the United States was formed by the sanction of the States, given by each in its sovereign capacity. It adds to the stability and dignity, as well as to the authority of the Constitution, that it rests on this legitimate and solid foundation. The States, then, being the parties to the constitutional compact, and in their sovereign capacity, it follows of necessity, that there can be no tribunal above their authority, to decide, in the last resort, whether the compact made by them be violated; and, consequently, that, as the parties to it, they must themselves [that is the States] decide, in the last resort, such questions as may be of sufficient magnitude to require their interposition."

"The States" are referred to through the report. He further remarks: —

"But the resolution has done more than guard against misconstruction, by expressly referring to cases of a *deliberate*, *palpable*, and *dangerous* nature. It specifies the object of the interposition, which it contemplates to be solely that of arresting the progress of the *evil* of usurpation, and of maintaining the authorities, rights, and liberties appertaining to the States, as parties to the Constitution."

Now we find, by the examination of this subject, that Mr. Madison, in his report, explains it, and repudiates the idea that a State, as a party to the compact, has a right to judge of an infraction of the Constitution or any other grievance, and, upon its own volition, withdraw from the Confederacy. I will here read a letter of Mr. Madison to Nicholas P. Trist, in explanation of this very proposition: —

"MONTPELIER, *December* 23, 1832.

"DEAR SIR: I have received yours of the 19th, inclosing some South Carolina papers. There are in one of them some interesting views of the doctrine of secession, among which is one that had occurred to me, and which for the first time I have seen in print, namely: that if one State can at will withdraw from the others, the others can withdraw from her, and turn her, *nolentem volentem*, out of the Union.

"Until of late there is not a State that would have abhorred such a doctrine more than South Carolina, or more dreaded an application of it to herself. The same may be said of the doctrine of nullification, which she now preaches as the only doctrine by which the Union can be saved.

"I partake of the wonder that the men you name should view secession in the light mentioned. The essential difference between a free government and a government not free is, that the former is founded in compact, the parties to which are mutually and equally bound by it. Neither of them, therefore, can have a greater right to break off from the bargain than the other or others have to hold him to it; and certainly there is nothing in the Virginia Resolutions of 1798 adverse to this principle, which is that of common sense and common justice.

"The fallacy which draws a different conclusion from them lies in confounding a single party with the parties to the constitutional compact of the United States. The latter, having made the compact, may do what they will with it. The former, as one of the parties, owes fidelity to it till released by consent or absolved by an intolerable abuse of the power created. In the Virginia Resolutions and report the plural number (States) is in every instance used whenever reference is made to the authority which presided over the Government."

He says the plural is used; that "States" is the word that is used; and when we turn to the resolution we find it just as Mr. Madison represents it, thereby excluding the idea that a State can separately and alone determine the question, and have the right to secede from the Union.

"As I am now known to have drawn those documents, I may say, as I do with a distinct recollection, that it was intentional. It was in fact required by the course of reasoning employed on the occasion. The Kentucky Resolutions, being less guarded, have been more easily perverted. The pretext for the liberty taken with those of Virginia is tne word 'respective' prefixed to the 'rights,' &c., to be secured within the States. Could the abuse of the expression have been foreseen or suspected, the form of it would doubtless have been varied. But what can be more consistent with common sense than that all having the rights, &c., should unite in contending for the security of them to each?

"It is remarkable how closely the nullifiers, who make the name of Mr. Jefferson the pedestal for their colossal heresy, shut their eyes and lips whenever his authority is ever so clearly and emphatically against them. You have noticed what he says in his letters to Monroe and Carrington (pp. 43 and 203, vol. 2) with respect to the power of the old Congress to coerce delinquent States; and his reason for preferring for the purpose a naval to a military force; and, moreover, his remark that it was not necessary to find a right to coerce in the Federal articles, that being inherent in the nature of a compact. It is high time that the claim to secede at will should be put down by the public opinion, and I am glad to see the task commenced by one who understands the subject.

"I know nothing of what is passing at Richmond more than what is seen in the newspapers. You were right in your foresight of the effect of passages in the late proclamation. They have proven a leaven for much fermentation there, and created an alarm against the danger of consolidation balancing that of disunion.

"With cordial salutations, JAMES MADISON.

"NICHOLAS P. TRIST."

I have another letter of Mr. Madison, written in 1833, sustaining and carrying out the same interpretation of the resolutions of 1798 and 1799. I desire to read some extracts from that letter. Mr. Madison says: —

"Much use has been made of the term 'respective' in the third resolution of Virginia, which asserts the right of the *States*, in cases of sufficient magnitude, to interpose 'for maintaining within their *respective* limits the authorities,' &c., appertaining to them; the term 'respective' being construed to mean a constitutional right in *each State*, *separately*, to decide on and resist by force encroachments within its limits. A foresight or apprehension of the misconstruction might easily have guarded against it. But, to say nothing of the distinction between ordinary and extreme cases, it is observable that in this, as in other instances throughout the resolutions, the plural number (*States*) is used in referring to them; that a concurrence and coöperation of all might well be contemplated in interpositions for effecting the objects within reach; and that the language of the closing resolution corresponds with this view of the third. The course of reasoning in the report on the resolutions required the distinction between *a State* and *the States*.

"It surely does not follow, from the fact of the States, or rather the people embodied in them, having, as parties to the constitutional compact, no tribunal above them, that, in controverted meanings of the compact, a minority of the parties can rightfully decide against the majority, still less that a single party can decide against the rest, and as little that it can at will withdraw itself altogether from its compact with the rest.

"The characteristic distinction between free governments and governments not free, is that the former are founded on compact, not between the government and those for whom it acts, but among the parties creating the government. Each of these being equal, neither can have more right to say that the compact has been violated and dissolved than every other has to deny the fact, and to insist on the execution of the bargain. An inference from the doctrine that a single State has a right to secede at will from the rest, is that the rest would have an equal right to secede from it; in other words to turn it, against its will, out of its union with them. Such a doctrine would not, till of late, have been palatable anywhere, and nowhere less so than where it is now most contended for."

When these letters are put together they are clear and conclusive. Take the resolutions; take the report; take Mr. Madison's expositions of them in 1832 and 1833; his letter to Mr. Trist; his letter to Mr. Webster; his letter to Mr. Rives; and when all are summed up, this doctrine of a State, either assuming her highest political attitude or otherwise, having the right, of her own will, to dissolve all connection with this Confederacy, is an absurdity, and contrary to the plain intent and meaning of the Constitution of the United States. I hold that the Constitution of the United States makes no provision, as said by the President of the United States, for its own destruction. It makes no provision for breaking up the Government, and no State has the constitutional right to secede and withdraw from the Union.

In July, 1788, when the Constitution of the United States was before the convention of New York for ratification, Mr. Madison was in the city of New York. Mr. Hamilton, who was in the convention, wrote a letter to Mr. Madison to know if New York could be admitted into the Union, with certain reservations or conditions. One of those reservations or conditions was, as Mr. Hamilton says in his letter, that they should have the privilege of receding within five or seven years if certain alterations and amendments were not made to the Constitution of the United States. Mr. Madison, in reply to that letter, makes use of the following emphatic language, which still further corroborates and carries out the idea that the Constitution makes no provision for breaking up the Government, and that no State has a right to secede. Mr. Madison says:—

"NEW YORK, *Sunday Evening.*

"MY DEAR SIR: Yours of yesterday is this instant come to hand, and I have but a few minutes to answer it. I am sorry that your situation obliges you to listen to propositions of the nature you describe. My opinion is, that a reservation of a right to withdraw if amendments be not decided on under the form of the Constitution within a certain time, is a *conditional* ratification; that it does not make New York a member of the new Union, and consequently that she could not be received on that plan. Compacts must be reciprocal — this principle would not in such a case be preserved. The Constitution requires an adoption *in toto* and *forever*."

This is the language of James Madison.

"It has been so adopted by the other States. An adoption for a limited time would be as defective as an adoption of some of the articles only. In short, any *condition* whatever must vitiate the ratification. What the new Congress, by virtue of the power to admit new States, may be *able* and disposed to do in such case, I do not inquire, as I suppose that is not the material point at present. I have not a moment to add more than my fervent wishes for your success and happiness. The idea of reserving a right to withdraw was started at Richmond, and considered as a conditional ratification, which was itself abandoned as worse than a rejection.

"Yours, JAMES MADISON, JR."

I know it is claimed, and I see it stated in some of the newspapers, that Virginia and some of the other States made a reservation, upon the ratification of the Constitution, that certain conditions were annexed; that they came in upon certain conditions, and therefore they had a right, in consequence of those conditions, to do this or the other thing. When we examine the journal of the convention, we find that no mention is made of any reservation on the ratification of the Constitution by the State of Virginia. We find that Mr. Madison says, in his letter to Mr. Hamilton, that this idea was first mooted at Richmond, and was abandoned as worse than a rejection. His letter was written after the ratification of the Constitution of the United States by the State of Virginia: hence he spoke with a knowledge of the fact that no reservation was made; but if it had been made by one of the parties, and not sanctioned by the other parties to the compact, what would it have amounted to? Then we see that Mr. Madison repudiates the doctrine that a State has the right to secede. We see that his resolutions admit of no such construction. We see that Mr. Madison, in his letter to Mr. Hamilton, puts the interpretation that this Constitution was adopted *in toto* and forever, without reservation and without condition.

I know that the inquiry may be made, how is a State, then, to have redress? There is but one way, and that is expressed by the people of Tennessee. You have entered into this compact; it was mutual; it was reciprocal; and you of your own volition have no right to withdraw and break the compact, without the consent of the other parties. What remedy, then, has the State? It has a remedy that remains and abides with every people upon the face of the earth. When grievances are without a remedy, or without redress, when oppression becomes intolerable, they have the great, the inherent right of revolution.

Sir, if the doctrine of secession is to be carried out upon the mere whim of a State, this Government is at an end. I am as much opposed to a strong, or what may be called by some a consolidated Government, as it is possible for a man to be; but while I am greatly opposed to that, I want a Government strong enough to preserve its own existence; that will not fall to pieces by its own weight or whenever a little dissatisfaction takes place in one of its members. If the States have the right to secede at will and pleasure, for real or imaginary evils or oppressions, I repeat again, this Government is at an end; it is not stronger than a rope of sand; its own weight will crumble it to pieces, and it cannot exist. Notwithstanding this doctrine may suit some who are engaged in this perilous and impending crisis that is now upon us, duty to my country, duty to my State, and duty to my kind, require me to avow a doctrine that I believe will result in the preservation of the Government, and to repudiate one that I believe will result in its overthrow, and the consequent disasters to the people of the United States.

If a State can secede at will and pleasure, and this doctrine is maintained, why, I ask, on the other hand, as argued by Mr. Madison in one of his letters, cannot a majority of the States combine and reject a State out of the Confederacy? Have a majority of these States, under the compact that they have made with each other, the right to combine and reject any one of the States from the Confederacy? They have no such right; the compact is reciprocal. It was ratified without reservation or condition, and it was ratified "*in toto* and forever"; such is the language of James Madison; and there is but one way to get out of it without the consent of the parties, and that is, by revolution.

I know that some touch the subject with trembling and fear. They say, here is a State that, perhaps by this time, has seceded, or if not, she is on the road to secession, and we must touch this subject very delicately; and that if the State secedes, conceding the power of the Constitution to her to secede, you must talk very delicately upon the subject of coercion. I do not believe the Federal Government has the power to coerce a State; for by the eleventh amendment of the Constitution of the United States it is expressly provided that you cannot even put one of the States of this Confederacy before one of the courts of the country as a party. As a State, the Federal Government has no power to coerce it; but it is a member of the compact to which it agreed in common with the other States, and this Government has the right to pass laws, and to enforce those laws upon individuals within the limits of each State. While the one proposition is clear, the other is equally so. This Government can, by the Constitution of the country and by the laws enacted in conformity with the Constitution, operate upon individuals, and has the right and the power, not to coerce a State, but to enforce and execute the law upon individuals within the limits of a State.

I know that the term, "to coerce a State," is used in an *ad captandum* manner. It is a sovereignty that is to be crushed! How is a State in the Union? What is her connection with it? All the connection she has with the other States is that which is agreed upon in the compact between the States. I do not know whether you may consider it in the Union or out of the Union, or whether you simply consider it a connection or a disconnection with the other States; but to the extent that a State nullifies or sets aside any law or any provision of the Constitution, to that extent it has dissolved its connection, and no more. I think the States that have passed their personal-liberty bills, in violation of the Constitution of the United States, coming in conflict with the fugitive-slave law, to that extent have dissolved their connection, and to that extent it is revolution. But because some of the free States have passed laws violative of the Constitution; because they have, to some extent, dissolved their connection with this Government, does that justify us of the South in following that bad example? Because they have passed personal-liberty bills, and have, to that extent, violated the compact which is reciprocal, shall we turn round, on the other hand, and violate the Constitution by coercing them to a compliance with it? Will we do so?

Then I come back to the starting-point: let us stand in the Union and upon the Constitution; and if anybody is to leave this Union, or violate its guaranties, it shall be those who have taken the initiative, and passed their personal-liberty bills. I am in the Union, and intend to stay in it. I intend to hold on to the Union, and the guaranties under which this Union has grown; and I do not intend to be driven from it, nor out of it, by their unconstitutional enactments.

Then, Mr. President, suppose, for instance, that a fugitive is arrested in the State of Vermont to-morrow, and under the personal-liberty bill of that State, or the law — I do not remember its precise title now — which prevents, or is intended to prevent, the faithful execution of the fugitive-slave law, Vermont undertakes to rescue him, and prevent the enforcement of the law: what is it? It is nullification; it is resistance to the laws of the United States made in conformity with the Constitution; it is rebellion; and it is the duty of the President of the United States to enforce the law, at all hazards and to the last extremity. And, if the Federal Government fails or refuses to execute the laws made in conformity with the Constitution, and those States persist in their violation and let those unconstitutional acts remain upon their statute-books, and carry them into practice; if the Government, on the one hand, fails to execute the laws of the United States, and those States, by their enactments, violate them on the other, the Government is at an end, and the parties are all released from the compact.

Mr. Collamer explained that the Vermont legislation, to which allusion had been made, was anterior to the passage of the fugitive-slave law; and, besides, the laws of Vermont were referred to a board of revision, by which, as well as by the courts of that State, no enactment would be sanctioned that was in conflict with the Constitution of the United States.

Mr. Johnson continued: I do not think the honorable Senator's explanation is entirely satisfactory, inasmuch as, though one law was anterior, another was passed in 1858. The Senator is a lawyer; he has presided in the courts of his State; and he has been a long time in the councils of the country; and therefore I had reason to expect a direct answer.

I think it will be determined by the courts and by the judgment of the country, that the acts passed in 1850 and 1858 by the Legislature of Vermont are a violation, a gross, palpable violation of the Constitution of the United States. It is clear and conclusive to my mind, that a State passing an unconstitutional act intended to impede or to prevent the execution of a law passed by the Congress of the United States which is constitutional, is thereby placed, so far as the initiative is concerned, in a state of rebellion. It is an open act of nullification. I am not aware that there has been any attempt in Vermont to wrest any persons out of the hands of the officers of the United States, or to imprison or to fine any person under the operation of this law; but the passage of such an act is to initiate rebellion. I think it comes in conflict directly with the spirit and letter of the Constitution of the United States, and to that extent is an act of nullification, and places the State in open rebellion to the United States.

I have stated that there is no power conferred upon the Congress of the United States, by the Constitution, to coerce a State in its sovereign capacity; that there is no power on the part of the Congress of the United States even to bring a State into the supreme tribunal of the country. You cannot put a State at the bar of the Supreme Court of the United States. The Congress of the United States has the power to pass laws to operate upon individuals within the limits of a State, by which all the functions of this Government can be executed and carried out; and if Vermont, either by an act of secession, which I take to be unconstitutional, or without having first seceded from the Union of the States by open force, in conformity with the laws of the State, should resist or attempt to resist the execution of the laws of the United States, it would be a practical rebellion, an overt act; and this Government has the authority under the Constitution to enforce the laws of the United States, and it has the authority to call to its aid such means as are deemed necessary and proper for the execution of the laws, even if it were to lead to the calling out of the militia, or calling into service the Army and Navy of the United States to execute the laws. This principle applies to every State placing herself in an attitude of opposition to the execution of the laws of the United States.

I do not think it necessary, in order to preserve this Union, or to keep a State within its sphere, that the Congress of the United States should have the power to coerce a State. All that is necessary is for the Government to have the power to execute and to carry out all the powers conferred upon it by the Constitution, whether they apply to the State or otherwise. This, I think, the Government clearly has the power to do; and so long as the Government executes all the laws in good faith, denying the right of a State constitutionally to secede, so long the State is in the Union, and subject to all the provisions of the Constitution and the laws passed in conformity with it. For example: the power is conferred on the Federal Government to carry the mails through the several States; to establish post-offices and post-roads; to establish courts in the respective States; to lay and collect taxes, and so on. The various powers are enumerated, and each and every one of these powers the Federal Government has the constitutional authority to execute within the limits of the States. It is not an invasion of a State for the Federal Government to execute its laws, to take care of its public property, and to enforce the collection of its revenue; but if, in the execution of the laws; if, in the enforcement of the Constitution, it meets with resistance, it is the duty of the Government, and it has the authority, to put down resistance, and effectually to execute the laws as contemplated by the Constitution of the country.

But this is a diversion from the line of my argument. I was going on to show that, according to the opinions of the fathers, not only of the country but of the Constitution itself, no State, of its own volition, has the right to withdraw from the Confederacy after having entered into the compact. I have referred to the last letter Mr. Madison wrote upon this subject, — at least it is the last one that I have been able to find, — in which he summed up this subject in a conclusive and masterly manner. In his letter to Mr. Webster of March 15, 1833, upon the receipt of Mr. Webster's speech, after the excitement had subsided to some extent and the country had taken its stand, Mr. Madison said: —

"The Constitution of the United States being established by a competent authority, by that of the sovereign people of the several States who were parties to it, it remains only to inquire what the Constitution is; and here it speaks for itself. It organizes a Government into the usual legislative, executive, and judiciary departments; invests it with specified powers, leaving others to the parties to the Constitution. It makes the Government, like other governments, to operate directly on the people; places at its command the needful physical means of executing its powers; and finally proclaims its supremacy, and that of the laws made in pursuance of it, over the constitutions and laws of the States, the powers of the Government being exercised, as in other elective and responsible governments, under the control of its constituents, people, and the legislatures of the States, and subject to the revolutionary rights of the people in extreme cases.

"Such is the Constitution of the United States *de jure* and *de facto;* and the name, whatever it be, that may be given to it, can make it nothing more or less than what it is."

This is clear and conclusive, so far as Mr. Madison goes on the subject. I have already shown that in 1789, in making his report upon the Virginia Resolutions, he gave the true interpretation to those resolutions, and explained what was meant by the word "respective" before "States." In his letter, in 1832, to Mr Rives, and in his letter of 1832 to Mr. Trist, having had time to reflect on the operation of the various provisions of the Constitution upon the country, in the decline of life, when he had seen the experiment fairly made, when his mind was matured upon every single point and provision in the Constitution, he, at that late period, sums up the doctrine and comes to the conclusion that I am contending for on the present occasion.

In addition to this, Mr. Jefferson, who prior to the formation of the Constitution was in Paris, writing letters on the subject of the formation of a stable Government here, saw the great defect in the Federal head under the old Articles of Confederation, and he pointed with the unerring finger of philosophy to what is now in the Constitution, as what was wanting in the old Articles of Confederation. Mr. Jefferson, in his letter to Colonel Monroe, dated Paris, August 11, 1786, speaks thus: —

"There never will be money in the treasury till the Confederacy shows its teeth. The States must see the rod; perhaps it must be felt by some one of them. I am persuaded all of them would rejoice to see every one obliged to furnish its contributions. It is not the difficulty of furnishing them which beggars the treasury, but the fear that others will not furnish as much. Every rational citizen must wish to see an effective instrument of coercion, and should fear to see it on any other element than the water."

Here Mr. Jefferson, seeing the difficulty, that under the old Articles of Confederation the Federal Government had not the power to execute its laws, that it could not collect revenue, points to what should be in the Constitution of the United States when formed. Mr. Jefferson, upon the same idea which was in his mind, and which was afterwards embodied in the Constitution, said, in a letter to E. Carrington, dated Paris, August 4, 1787:—

"I confess I do not go as far in the reforms thought necessary, as some of my correspondents in America; but if the convention should adopt such propositions, I shall suppose them necessary. My general plan would be, to make the States one as to everything connected with foreign nations, and several as to everything purely domestic. But, with all the imperfections of our present Government, it is without comparison the best existing, or that ever did exist. Its greatest defect is the imperfect manner in which matters of commerce have been provided for. It has been so often said, as to be generally believed, that Congress have no power by the Confederation to enforce anything — for example, contributions of money. It was not necessary to give them that power expressly; they have it by the law of nature. When *two parties make a compact, there results to each a power of compelling the other to execute it.*"

Even if it was not expressed in the Constitution,

the power to preserve itself and maintain its authority would be possessed by the Federal Government upon the great principle that it must have the power to preserve its own existence. But we find that, in plain and express terms, this authority is delegated. The very powers that Mr. Jefferson pointed out as being wanting in the old Government, under the Articles of Confederation, are granted by the Constitution of the United States to the present Government by express delegation. Congress has the power to lay and collect taxes; Congress has the power to pass laws to restore fugitives from labor escaping from one State into another; Congress has the power to establish post-offices and post-roads; Congress has the power to establish courts in the different States; and having these powers, it has the authority to do everything necessary to sustain the collection of the revenue, the enforcement of the judicial system, and the carrying of the mails. Because Congress, having the power, undertakes to execute its laws, it will not do to say that the Government is placed in the position of an aggressor. Not so. It is only acting within the scope of the Constitution, and in compliance with its delegated powers. But a State that resists the exercise of those powers becomes the aggressor, and places itself in a rebellious or nullifying attitude. It is the duty of this Government to execute its laws in good faith. When the Federal Government shall fail to execute all the laws that are made in strict conformity with the Constitution, when our sister States shall pass laws violative of that Constitution, and obstruct the laws of Congress passed in conformity with it, then, and not till then, will this Government have failed to accomplish the great objects of its creation. Then it will be at an end, and all the parties to the compact will be released.

But I wish to go a little further into the authorities as to the power of a State to secede from the Union, and to quote an opinion of Judge Marshall, given at a very early day. I know it is very common to denounce him as a Federalist, but I care not where the truth comes from; wherever a sound argument may be found to sustain a proposition that is right in itself, I am willing to adopt it; and I have put myself to the trouble to hunt up these unquestionable authorities on this subject, knowing that they would have more influence before the country, and before my constituents, than anything that I could say. Though I am not a lawyer, though I have not made the law my study and my pursuit, I claim to have some little common sense and understanding as to the application of general principles. I find that Judge Marshall, in speaking on the question of the right of a State upon its own volition to go out of the Confederacy, in the case of Cohens *vs.* Virginia, said:—

"It is very true, that whenever hostility to the existing system"—that is, the system of our Government—"shall become universal, it will be also irresistible. The people made the Constitution, and the people can unmake it."

I care not whether he speaks here of the people in the aggregate or not. The application of the principle is just as clear, whether you say the people, through the States, made the Constitution, or leave out the qualifying words "through the States."

"It is the creature of their will, and lives only by their will. But this supreme and irresistible power to make and unmake resides only in the whole body of the people; not in any subdivision of them. The attempt of any of the parts to exercise it is usurpation, and ought to be repelled by those to whom the people have delegated their power of repelling it." [1]

Now, whether you apply that, in a general sense, to the people in the aggregate, or to the States occupying the same relation to the Federal Government that the people do to the States, the principle is just the same; and if you speak of States ratifying and making the Constitution of the United States, one State — one of the community that made the Constitution — has no right, without the consent of the other States, to withdraw from the compact, and set the Constitution at naught. It is the principle that I seek; and the principle applies as well to a community of States as it does to a community of individuals. Admitting that this Federal Government was made by a community

[1] *Wheaton's Reports*, Vol. VI. p. 389.

of States, can one of that community of States, of its own will, without the consent of the rest, where the compact is reciprocal, set it aside, and withdraw itself from the operation of the Government? I have given you the opinion of Judge Marshall, one of the most distinguished jurists that ever presided in this country, though he is called by some a Federalist. His mind was clear; he lived in that day when the Constitution should be understood, and when it was understood — in the days of Madison and Jefferson; and this is his opinion upon that subject, as far back as 1821.

In this connection, I would call the attention of the Senate to General Jackson's views upon this subject; and I would also call their attention to Mr. Webster's views, if it were necessary, for he is conceded, by some at least, to be one of the most able expounders of the Constitution of the United States. General Jackson, though not celebrated for his legal attainments, was celebrated for his sagacity, his strong common sense, his great intuitive power of reaching correct conclusions, and understanding correct principles. In 1833, General Jackson, in his proclamation, takes identically the same ground; and declares, first, that a State has no power of itself to nullify a law of Congress within its limits; and next, that, notwithstanding a State may claim to have seceded, it has no constitutional power to withdraw itself from the Union of the States, and thereby set at naught the laws and the Constitution. He argues this question forcibly and clearly; and comes to the unerring conclusion, according to my judgment, that no State has the constitutional power to withdraw itself from this Confederacy without the consent of the other States; and it may do good to reproduce his views on the subject. He says, in his famous proclamation, speaking of the nullification ordinance of South Carolina: —

"And whereas the said ordinance prescribes to the people of South Carolina a course of conduct in direct violation of their duty as citizens of the United States, contrary to the laws of their country, subversive of its Constitution, and having for its object the destruction of the Union, — that Union which, coeval with our political existence, led our fathers, without any other ties to unite them than those of patriotism and a common cause, through a sanguinary struggle to a glorious independence, — that sacred Union, hitherto inviolate, which, perfected by our happy Constitution, has brought us, by the favor of Heaven, to a state of prosperity at home, and high consideration abroad, rarely, if ever, equalled in the history of nations. To preserve this bond of our political existence from destruction; to maintain inviolate this state of national honor and prosperity, and to justify the confidence my fellow-citizens have reposed in me, I, ANDREW JACKSON, *President of the United States*, have thought proper to issue this my proclamation, stating my views of the Constitution and the laws applicable to the measures adopted by the convention of South Carolina, and to the reasons they have put forth to sustain them, declaring the course which duty will require me to pursue, and, appealing to the understanding and patriotism of the people, warn them of the consequences that must inevitably result from an observance of the dictates of the convention."

He argues the question at length: —

"This right to secede is deduced from the nature of the Constitution, which, they say, is a compact between sovereign States, who have preserved their whole sovereignty, and therefore are subject to no superior; that because they made the compact they can break it when, in their opinion, it has been departed from by the other States. Fallacious as this course of reasoning is, it enlists State pride, and finds advocates in the honest prejudices of those who have not studied the nature of our Government sufficiently to see the radical error on which it rests." . . . . .

"The people of the United States formed the Constitution, acting through the State Legislatures in making the compact, to meet and discuss its provisions, and acting in separate conventions when they ratified those provisions; but the terms used in its construction show it to be a Government in which the people of all the States collectively are represented. We are ONE PEOPLE in the choice of the President and Vice-President. Hence the States have no other agency than to direct the mode in which the votes shall be given. The candidates having the majority of all the votes are chosen. The electors of a majority of the States may have given their votes for one candidate, and yet another may be chosen. The people, then, and not the States, are represented in the executive branch."

. . . .

"The Constitution of the United States, then, forms a Government, not a league; and whether it be formed by compact between the States, or in any other manner, its character is the same. It is a Government in which all the people are represented; which operates directly on the people individually, not upon the States — they retained all the power they did not grant. But each State having expressly parted with so many powers as to constitute, jointly with the other States, a single nation, cannot, from that

10

period, possess any right to secede; because such *secession does not break a league but destroys the unity of a nation*; and any injury to that unity is not only a breach, which would result from the contravention of a compact, but it is an offence against the whole Union. To say that any State may, at pleasure, secede from the Union, is to say that the United States are not a nation; because it would be a solecism to contend that any part of a nation might dissolve its connection with the other parts, to their injury or ruin, without committing any offence. Secession, like any other revolutionary act, may be morally justified by the extremity of oppression; but to call it a constitutional right, is confounding the meaning of terms, and can only be done through gross error, or to deceive those who are willing to assert a right but would pause before they made a revolution, or incurred the penalties consequent on a failure.

"Because the Union was formed by compact, it is said the parties to that compact may, when they feel themselves aggrieved, depart from it; but it is precisely because it is a compact that they cannot. A compact is an agreement or binding obligation. It may by its terms have a sanction or penalty for its breach, or it may not. If it contains no sanction, it may be broken, with no other consequence than moral guilt; if it have a sanction, then the breach insures the designated or implied penalty. A league between independent nations, generally, has no sanction other than a moral one; or if it should contain a penalty, as there is no common superior, it cannot be enforced. A Government, on the contrary, always has a sanction expressed or implied; and, in our case, it is both necessarily implied and expressly given. An attempt, by force of arms, to destroy a Government, is an offence by whatever means the constitutional compact may have been formed, and such Government has the right, by the law of self-defence, to pass acts for punishing the offender, unless that right is modified, restrained, or resumed by the constitutional act. In our system, although it is modified in the case of treason, yet authority is expressly given to pass all laws necessary to carry its powers into effect, and under this grant, provision has been made for punishing acts which obstruct the due administration of the laws." . . . "It treats, as we have seen, on the alleged undivided sovereignty of the States, and on their having formed, in this sovereign capacity, a compact which is called the Constitution, from which, because they made it, they have the right to secede. Both of these positions are erroneous, and some of the arguments to prove them so have been anticipated.

"The States, severally, have not retained their entire sovereignty. It has been shown that in becoming parts of a nation, not members of a league, they surrendered many of their essential parts of sovereignty. The right to make treaties, declare war, levy taxes, exercise exclusive judicial and legislative powers, were all of them functions of sovereign power. The States, then, for all these purposes, were no longer sovereign. The allegiance of their citizens was transferred, in the first instance, to the Government of the United States: they became American citizens, and owed obedience to the Constitution of the United States, and to laws made in conformity with the powers it vested in Congress. This last position has not been, and cannot be, denied. How, then, can that State be said to be sovereign and independent whose citizens owe obedience to laws not made by it, and whose magistrates are sworn to disregard those laws when they come in conflict with those passed by another? What shows conclusively that the States cannot be said to have reserved an undivided sovereignty is, that they expressly ceded the right to punish treason, not treason against their separate power, but treason against the United States. Treason is an offence against *sovereignty*, and sovereignty must reside with the power to punish it. But the reserved rights of the States are not less sacred because they have, for their common interest, made the General Government the depository of those powers." . . . . .

"So obvious are the reasons which forbid this secession, that it is necessary only to allude to them. The Union was formed for the benefit of all. It was produced by mutual sacrifices of interest and opinions. Can these sacrifices be recalled? Can the States, who magnanimously surrendered their title to the territories of the West, recall the grant? Will the inhabitants of the inland States agree to pay the duties that may be imposed without their assent by those on the Atlantic or the Gulf for their own benefit? Shall there be a free port in one State, and onerous duties in another? No man believes that any right exists in a single State to involve all the others in these and countless other evils, contrary to the engagement solemnly made. Every one must see that the other States, in self-defence, must oppose it at all hazards."

Having travelled thus far, the question arises, in what sense are we to construe the Constitution of the United States? I assume what is assumed in one of Mr. Madison's letters, that the Constitution was formed for perpetuity; that it never was intended to be broken up. It was commenced, it is true, as an experiment; but the founders of the Constitution intended that this experiment should go on; and by way of making it perpetual, they provided for its amendment. They provided that this instrument could be amended and improved, from time to time, as the changing circumstances, as the changing pursuits, as the changing notions of men might require; but they made no provision whatever for its destruction. The old Articles of Confederation were formed for the purpose of making "a perpetual union." In 1787, when the convention concluded their deliberations and adopted the Constitution, what do they say in the very preamble of that Constitution? Having in their mind the idea that was shadowed forth in the old Articles of Confederation, that the Union was to be perpetual, they say, at the commencement, that it is to make "a more perfect union" than the union under the old Articles of Confederation, which they called "perpetual."

What furthermore do we find? The Constitution of the United States contains a provision that it is to be submitted to the States respectively for their ratification; but on nine States ratifying it, it shall be the Constitution for them. In that way the Government was created; and in that way provision was made to perfect it. What more do we find? The Constitution, as I have just remarked, provides for its own amendment, its improvement, its perpetuation, by pointing out and by prescribing the mode and manner in which improvements shall be made. That still preserves the idea that it is to be perpetual. We find, in addition, a provision that Congress shall have power to admit new States.

Hence, in travelling along through the instrument, we find how the Government is created, how it is to be perpetuated, and how it may be enlarged in reference to the number of States constituting the Confederacy; but do we find any provision for winding it up, except on that great inherent principle that it may be wound up by the States — not by a State, but by the States which brought it into existence — and by no other means? That is a means of taking down the Government that the Constitution could not provide for. It is above the Constitution; it is beyond any provision that can be made by mortal man.

Now, to expose the absurdity of the pretension that there is a right to secede, let me press this argument a little further. The Constitution has been formed; it has been made perfect, or, in other words, means have been provided by which it can be made perfect. It was intended to be perpetual. In reference to the execution of the laws under it, what do we find? As early as 1795, Congress passed an excise law, taxing distilleries throughout the country, and what were called the whiskey boys of Pennsylvania resisted the law. The Government wanted means. It taxed distilleries. The people of Pennsylvania resisted it. What is the difference between a portion of the people resisting a constitutional law, and all of the people of a State doing so? But because you can apply the term coercion in one case to a State, and in the other call it simply the execution of the law against individuals, you say there is a great distinction! We do not assume the power to coerce a State, but we assume that Congress has power to lay and collect taxes, and Congress has the right to enforce that law when obstructions and impediments are opposed to its enforcement. The people of Pennsylvania did object; they did resist and oppose the legal authorities of the country. Was that law enforced? Was it called coercion at that day to enforce it? Suppose all the people of the State of Pennsylvania had resisted; would not the law have applied with just the same force, and would it not have been just as constitutional to execute it against all the people of the State, as it was to execute it upon a part of their citizens?

George Washington, in his annual message to the Congress of the United States, referred to the subject; and it will be seen what George Washington considered to be his duty in the execution of the laws of the United States upon the citizens of the States: —

"Thus the painful alternative could not be discarded. I ordered the militia to march, after once more admonishing the insurgents, in my proclamation of the 25th of September last.

"It was a task too difficult, to ascertain with precision the lowest degree of force competent to the quelling of the insurrection. From a respect, indeed, to economy, and the ease of my fellow-citizens belonging to the militia, it would have gratified me to accomplish such an estimate. My very reluctance to ascribe too much importance to the opposition, had its extent been accurately seen, would have been a decided inducement to the smallest efficient numbers. In this uncertainty, therefore, I put in motion fifteen thousand men, as being an army which, according to all human calculation, would be prompt and adequate in every view, and might, perhaps, by rendering resistance desperate, prevent the effusion of blood. Quotas had been assigned to the States of New Jersey, Pennsylvania, Maryland, and Virginia; the Governor of Pennsylvania having declared, on this occasion, an opinion which justified a requisition to the other States.

"As commander-in-chief of the militia, when called into the actual service of the United States, I have visited the places of general rendezvous, to obtain more exact information, and to direct a plan for ulterior movements. Had there been room for persuasion that the laws were secure from obstruction; that the civil magistrate was able to bring to justice such of the most culpable as have not embraced the proffered terms of amnesty, and may be deemed fit objects of example; that the friends to peace and good government were not in need of that aid and countenance which they ought always to receive, and, I trust, ever will receive, against the vicious and turbulent; I should have caught with avidity the opportunity of restoring the militia to their families and homes. But succeeding intelligence has tended to manifest the necessity of what has been done; it being now confessed by those who were not inclined to exaggerate the ill conduct of the insurgents, that their malevolence was not pointed merely to a particular law, but that a spirit inimical to all order has actuated many of the offenders. If the state of things had afforded reason for the continuance of my presence with the army, it would not have been withholden. But every appearance assuring such an issue as will redound to the reputation and strength of the United States, I have judged it most proper to resume my duties at the seat of Government, leaving the chief command with the Governor of Virginia." . . .

"While there is cause to lament that occurrences of this

nature should have disgraced the name or interrupted the tranquillity of any part of our community, or should have diverted to a new application any portion of the public resources, there are not wanting real and substantial consolations for the misfortune. It has demonstrated that our prosperity rests on solid foundations, by furnishing an additional proof that my fellow-citizens understand the true principles of government and liberty; that they feel their *inseparable union*; that, notwithstanding all the devices which have been used to sway them from their interest and duty, they are now as ready to maintain the authority of the laws against licentious invasions as they were to defend their rights against usurpation. It has been a spectacle, displaying to the highest advantage the value of republican government, to behold the most and the least wealthy of our citizens standing in the same ranks as private soldiers, preëminently distinguished by being the army of the Constitution, undeterred by a march of three hundred miles over rugged mountains, by the approach of an inclement season, or by any other discouragement. Nor ought I to omit to acknowledge the efficacious and patriotic coöperation which I have experienced from the Chief Magistrates of the States to which my requisitions have been addressed."[1]

President Washington thought there was power in this Government to execute its laws; he considered the militia the army of the Constitution; and he refers to this Union as being inseparable. This is the way that the laws were executed by the Father of his Country, the man who sat as president of the convention that made the Constitution. Here was resistance interposed — opposition to the execution of the laws; and George Washington, then President of the United States, went in person at

1 *American State Papers*, Miscellaneous, Vol. I. p. 85.

the head of the militia; and it showed his sagacity, his correct comprehension of men, and the effect that an immediate movement of that kind would have upon them. He ordered fifteen thousand of his countrymen to the scene of action, and went there in person, and stayed there till he was satisfied that the insurrection was quelled. That is the manner in which George Washington put down rebellion. That is the manner in which he executed the laws.

Here, then, we find General Washington executing the law, in 1795, against a portion of the citizens of Pennsylvania who rebelled; and, I repeat the question, where is the difference between executing the law upon a part and upon the whole? Suppose the whole of Pennsylvania had rebelled and resisted the excise law; had refused to pay taxes on distilleries; was it not as competent and as constitutional for General Washington to have executed the law against the whole as against a part? Is there any difference? Governmental affairs must be practical as well as our own domestic affairs. You may make nice metaphysical distinctions between the practical operations of Government and its theory; you may refine upon what is a State, and point out a difference between a State and a portion of a State; but what is it when you reduce it to practical operation, and square it by common sense?

In 1832, resistance was interposed to laws of

the United States in another State. An ordinance was passed by South Carolina, assuming to act as a sovereign State, to nullify a law of the United States. In 1833, the distinguished man who filled the executive chair, who now lies in his silent grave, loved and respected for his virtue, his honor, his integrity, his patriotism, his undoubted courage, and his devotion to his kind, with an eye single to the promotion of his country's best interests, issued the proclamation, extracts from which I have already presented. He was sworn to support the Constitution, and to see that the laws were faithfully executed; and he fulfilled the obligation. He took all the steps necessary to secure the execution of the law, and he would have executed it by the power of the Government if the point of time had arrived when it was necessary to resort to power. We can see that he acted upon principles similar to those acted upon by General Washington. He took the precaution of ordering a force there sufficient for the purpose of enabling him to say effectually to the rebellious, and those who were interposing opposition to the execution of the laws, "The laws which we made according to the Constitution, the laws that provide for the collection of the revenue to sustain this Government, must be enforced, and the revenue must be collected. It is a part of the compact; it is a part of the engagement you have undertaken to perform, and you of your own will have no power or authority to set it aside." The duties were collected; the law was enforced; and the Government went on. In his proclamation he made a powerful appeal. He told them what would be done; and it would have been done, as certain as God rules on high, if the time had arrived which made it necessary.

Then we see where General Washington stood, and where General Jackson stood. Now, how does the present case stand? The time has come when men should speak out. Duties are mine; consequences are God's. I intend to discharge my duty, and I intend to avow my understanding of the Constitution and the laws of the country. Have we no authority or power to execute the laws in the State of South Carolina as well as in Vermont and Pennsylvania? I think we have. As I before said, although a State may, by an ordinance, or by a resolve, or by an act of any other kind, declare that they absolve their citizens from all allegiance to this Government, it does not release them from the compact. The compact is reciprocal; and they, in coming into it, undertook to perform certain duties and abide by the laws made in conformity with the compact. Now, sir, what is the Government to do in South Carolina? If South Carolina undertakes to drive the Federal courts out of that State, the Federal Government has the right to hold those courts there. She may attempt to exclude the mails, yet the Federal Government has the right to establish post-offices and post-roads and to carry the mails there. She may resist the collection of revenue at Charleston, or any other point that the Government has provided for its collection; but the Government has the right to collect it and to enforce the law. She may undertake to take possession of the property belonging to the Government which was originally ceded by the State, but the Federal Government has the right to provide the means for retaining possession of that property. If she makes an advance either to dispossess the Government of that which it has purchased, or to resist the execution of the revenue laws, or of our judicial system, or the carrying of the mails, or the exercise of any other power conferred on the Federal Government, she puts herself in the wrong, and it will be the duty of the Government to see that the laws are faithfully executed. By reference to the records, it will be seen that, on

"December 19, 1805, South Carolina granted all the right, title, and claim of the State to all the lands reserved for Fort Moultrie, on Sullivan's Island, not exceeding five acres, with all the forts, fortifications, &c., thereon; canal, &c.; the high lands, and part of the marsh, belonging to Fort Johnson, not exceeding twenty acres; the land on which Fort Pinckney is built, and three acres around it; a portion of the sandbank on the southeasternmost point of Charleston, not exceeding two acres; not exceeding four acres for a battery, or fort, &c., on Blythe's Point, at the mouth of Sampit River; Mustard Island, in Beaufort River, opposite Paris's Island; not exceeding seven acres of land on St. Helena Island, for a principal fort; the whole on condition that the United States should, within three years, repair forts, &c.; the United States to compensate individuals for property; the lands, &c., to be free from taxes to the State."

Here is a clear deed of cession. The Federal Government has complied with all the conditions, and has, in its own right, the land on which these forts are constructed. The conditions of the cession have been complied with; and the Government has had possession from that period to the present time. There are its forts; there is its arsenal; there are its dock-yards; there is the property of the Government; and now, under the Constitution, and under the laws made in pursuance thereof, has South Carolina the authority and the right to expel the Federal Government from its own property that has been given to it by her own act, and of which it is now in possession? By resisting the execution of the laws, by attempting to dispossess the Federal Government, does she not put herself in the wrong? Does she not violate the laws of the United States? Does she not violate the Constitution? Does she not put herself, within the meaning and purview of the Constitution, in the attitude of levying war against the United States? The Constitution defines and declares what is treason. Let us talk about things by their right names. I know that some hotspur or madcap may declare that these are not times for a government of law; that we are in a revolution. I know that Patrick Henry once said, "If this be treason, make the most of it." If anything can be treason in the scope and purview of the Constitution, is not levying war upon the United States treason? Is not an attempt to take its property treason? Is not an attempt to expel its soldiers treason? Is not an attempt to resist the collection of the revenue, or to expel your mails, or to drive your courts from her borders, treason? It is treason, and nothing but treason; and if one State, upon its own volition, can go out of this Confederacy without regard to the effect it is to have upon the remaining parties to the compact, what is your Government worth? What will it come to? In what will it end? It is no Government at all upon such a construction.

But it is declared and assumed that, if a State secedes, she is no longer a member of the Union, and that, therefore, the laws and the Constitution of the United States are no longer operative within her limits, and she is not guilty if she violates them. This is a matter of opinion. I have tried to show what this doctrine of secession is, and there is but one concurring and unerring conclusion reached by all the great and distinguished men of the country, from the origin of the Government down to the present time. Madison, who is called the Father of the Constitution, denies the doctrine. Washington, who was the Father of his Country, denies the doctrine. Jefferson, Jackson, Clay, and Webster, all deny the doctrine; and yet all at once it is discovered and ascertained that a State, of its own volition, can go out of this Confederacy, without regard to consequences, without regard to the injury and woe that may be inflicted on the remaining members from the act!

Suppose this doctrine to be true, Mr. President, that a State can withdraw from this Confederacy; and suppose South Carolina has seceded, and is now out of the Confederacy: in what an attitude does she place herself? There might be circumstances under which the States ratifying the compact might tolerate the secession of a State, she taking the consequences of the act. But there might be other circumstances under which the States could not allow one to secede. Why do I say so? Some suppose — and it is a well-founded supposition — that by the secession of a State all the remaining States might be involved in disastrous consequences; they might be involved in war; and by the secession of one State, the existence of the remaining States might be involved. Then, without regard to the Constitution, dare the other States permit one to secede when it endangers and involves all the remaining States? The question arises in this connection, whether the States are in a condition to tolerate or will tolerate the secession of South Carolina. That is a matter to be determined by the circumstances; that is a matter to be determined by the emergency; that is a matter to be determined when it comes up. It is a question which must be left open to be determined by the surrounding circumstances, when the occasion arises.

But conceding, for argument's sake, the doctrine of secession, and admitting that the State of South Carolina is now upon your coast, a foreign Power, absolved from all connection with the Federal Government, out of the Union: what then? There was a doctrine inculcated in 1823, by Mr. Monroe, that this Government, keeping in view the safety of the people and the existence of our institutions, would permit no European Power to plant any more colonies on this continent. Now, suppose that South Carolina is outside of the Confederacy, and this Government is in possession of the fact that she is forming an alliance with a foreign Power — with France, with England, with Russia, with Austria, or with all of the principal Powers of Europe; that there is to be a great naval station established there; an immense rendezvous for their army, with a view to ulterior objects, with a view of making advances upon the rest of these States: let me ask the Senate, let me ask the country, if they dare permit it? Under and in compliance with the great law of self-preservation, we dare not let her do it; and if she were a sovereign Power to-day, outside of the Confederacy, and were forming an alliance that we deemed inimical to our institutions and the existence of our Government, we should have a right to conquer and hold her as a province, — a term which is used with so much scorn.

Mr. President, I have referred to the manner in which this Government was formed. I have referred to the provision of the Constitution which provides for the admission of new States. Now, let me ask, can any one believe that, in the creation of this Government, its founders intended that it should have the power to acquire territory and form it into States, and then permit them to go out of the Union? Let us take a case. How long has it been since your armies were in Mexico? How long since your brave men were exposed to the diseases, the privations, the sufferings, which are incident to a campaign of that kind? How long since they were bearing your eagles in a foreign land, many of them falling at the point of the bayonet, consigned to their long, narrow home, with no winding-sheet but their blankets saturated with their blood? How many victories did they win? How many laurels did they acquire? How many trophies did they bring back? The country is full of them. What did it cost you? One hundred and twenty million dollars. What did you pay for the country you acquired, besides? Fifteen million dollars. Peace was made; territory was acquired; and, in a few years, from that territory California erected herself into a free and independent State, and, under the provisions of the Constitution, we admitted her as a member of this Confederacy. After having expended $120,000,000 in the war; after having lost many of our bravest and most gallant men; after having paid $15,000,000 to Mexico for the territory, and admitted it into the Union as a State, now that the people of California have got into the Confederacy and can stand alone, according to this modern doctrine, your Government was just made to let them in, and then to let them step out. Is not the conclusion illogical? Is it not absurd to say, that, now that California is in, she, on her own volition, — without regard to the consideration paid for her, without regard to the policy which dictated her acquisition by the United States, — can walk out and bid you defiance? Is it not an absurdity, if you take the reason and object of Government?

But we need not stop here; let us go to Texas. Texas was engaged in a revolution with Mexico. She succeeded in the assertion and establishment of her independence; and she became a sovereign and independent Power outside of this Union. She applied for admission, and she was admitted into this family of States. After she was in, she was oppressed by the debts of her war which resulted in her separation from Mexico; she was harassed by the Indians upon her border; and in 1850, by way of relief to Texas, what did we do? There was an extent of territory that lies north, if my memory serves me right, embracing what is now called the Territory of New Mexico. Texas had it not in her power to protect the citizens that were there. It was a dead limb, paralyzed, lifeless. The Federal

Government came along as a kind physician, saying, "We will take this dead limb from your body, and vitalize it, by giving protection to the people, and incorporating it into a territorial government; and, in addition to that, we will give you $10,000,000, and you may retain your own public lands"; and the other States were taxed in common to pay the $10,000,000. Now, after all this is done, Texas, forsooth, upon her own volition, is to say, "I will walk out of this Union!" Were there no other parties to that compact? We are told the compact is reciprocal. Did we take in California, did we take in Texas, just to benefit them? No; but to add to this great family of States; and it is apparent, from the fact of their coming in, that the compact is reciprocal; and having entered into the compact, they have no right to withdraw without the consent of the remaining States.

Again: take the case of Louisiana. What did we pay for her in 1803, and for what was she wanted? Just to get Louisiana into the Confederacy! Just for the benefit of that particular locality! Was not the mighty West looked to? Was is not to secure the free navigation of the Mississippi River, the mouth of which was then in possession of France, shortly before of Spain, passing about between those two Powers? Yes, the navigation of that river was wanted. Simply for Louisiana? No, but for all the States. The United States paid $15,000,000, and France ceded the country to the United States. It remained in a territorial condition for a while, sustained and protected by the strong arm of the Federal Government. We acquired the territory and the navigation of the river; and the money was paid for the benefit of all the States, and not of Louisiana exclusively. And now that this great valley is filled up; now that the navigation of the Mississippi is one hundred times more important than it was then; now, after the United States have paid the money, have acquired the title to Louisiana, and have incorporated her into the Confederacy, it is proposed that she shall go out of the Union! In 1815, when her shores were invaded; when her city was about to be sacked; when her booty and her beauty were about to fall a prey to British aggression, the brave men of Tennessee, and of Kentucky, and of the surrounding States, rushed into her borders and upon her shores, and, under the lead of their own gallant Jackson, drove the invading forces away. And now, after all this; after the money has been paid; after the free navigation of the river has been obtained, — not for the benefit of Louisiana alone, but for her in common with all the States, — Louisiana says to the other States, "We will go out of this Confederacy; we do not care if you did fight our battles; we do not care if you did acquire the free navigation of this river from France; we will go out if we think proper, and constitute ourselves an independent Power, and bid defiance to the other States." It is an absurdity; it is a contradiction; it is illogical; it is not deducible from the structure of the Government itself.

It may be that, at this moment, there is not a citizen in the State of Louisiana who would think of obstructing the free navigation of the river; but are not nations controlled by their interests in varying circumstances? It strikes me so; and hereafter, when a conflict of interest arises; when difficulty may spring up between two separate Powers, Louisiana, having the control of the mouth of the river, might feel disposed to tax our citizens going down there. It is a power that I am not willing to concede to be exercised at the discretion of any authority outside of this Government. So sensitive have been the people of my State upon the free navigation of that river, that as far back as 1796, now sixty-four years ago, in their Bill of Rights, before they passed under the jurisdiction of the United States, they declared, —

"That an equal participation of the free navigation of the Mississippi is one of the inherent rights of the citizens of this State; it cannot, therefore, be conceded to any prince, potentate, Power, person, or persons whatever."

This shows the estimate that the people fixed on this stream sixty-four years ago; and now we are told, if Louisiana does go out, it is not her intention at this time to tax the people above. Who can tell what may be the intention of Louisiana hereafter? Are we willing to place the rights, the travel, and the commerce of our citizens at the discretion of any Power outside of this Government? I will not.

How long has it been since Florida lay on our coasts, an annoyance to us? And now she has got entirely feverish about being an independent and separate Government, while she has not as many qualified voters as there are in one congressional district of any other State. What condition did Florida occupy in 1811? She was in the possession of Spain. What did the United States think about having adjacent territory outside of their jurisdiction? Let us turn to the authorities, and see what proposition they were willing to act upon. I find, in the statutes of the United States, this joint resolution: —

"Taking into view the peculiar situation of Spain, and of her American provinces, and considering the influence which the destiny of the territory adjoining the Southern border of the United States may have upon their security, tranquillity, and commerce: Therefore,

"*Resolved by the Senate and House of Representatives of the United States of America in Congress assembled*, That the United States, under the peculiar circumstances of the existing crisis, cannot, without serious inquietude, see any part of the said territory pass into the hands of any foreign Power; and that a due regard to their own safety compels them to provide, under certain contingencies, for the temporary occupation of the said territory. They, at the same time, declare that the said territory shall, in their hands, remain subject to future negotiation."

What principle is set forth there? Florida was in the possession of Spain. English spies were harbored in her territory. Spain was inimical to the United States; and in view of the great principle of self-preservation, the Congress of the United States passed a resolution declaring that if Spain attempted to transfer Florida into the hands of any other Power, the United States would take possession of it. Yet Congress were gracious and condescending enough to say that it should remain open to future negotiation. That is to say, "Hereafter, if we can make a negotiation that will suit us, we will make it; if we do not, we will keep the territory"; that is all. There was the territory lying upon our border, outside of the jurisdiction of the United States; and we declared, by an act of Congress, that no foreign Power should possess it.

We went still further and appropriated $100,000, and authorized the President to enter and take possession of it with the means placed in his hands. Afterwards, we negotiated with Spain, and gave $6,000,000 for the territory; and we established a territorial government for it. What next? We undertook to drive out the Seminole Indians, and we had a war in which this Government lost more than it lost in all the other wars it was engaged in; and we paid the sum of $25,000,000 to get the Seminoles out of the swamps, so that the territory could be inhabited by white men. We paid for it, we took possession of it; and I remember, when I was in the other House, and Florida was knocking at the door for admission, how extremely anxious her then able Delegate was to be admitted. He now sits before me.[1] I remember how important he thought it was then to come under the protecting wing of the United States as one of the stars of our Confederacy. But now the territory is paid for, England is driven out, $25,000,000 have been expended; and they want no longer the protection of this Government, but will go out without consulting the other States, without reference to the effect upon the remaining parties to the compact. Where will she go? Will she attach herself to Spain again? Will she pass back under the jurisdiction of the Seminoles? After having been nurtured and protected and fostered by all these States, now, without regard to them, is she to be allowed, at her own volition, to withdraw from the Union? I say she has no constitutional right to do it; and when she does it, it is an act of aggression. If she succeeds, it will only be a successful revolution. If she does not succeed, she must take the penalties and terrors of the law.

But, sir, there is another question that suggests itself in this connection. Kansas, during the last Congress, applied for admission into this Union. She assumed to be a State, and the difficulty in the way was a provision in her constitution, and the manner of its adoption. We did not let Kansas in. We did not question her being a State; but on ac-

[1] Mr. Yulee.

count of the manner of forming her constitution and its provisions, we kept Kansas out. What is Kansas now? Is she a State, or is she a Territory? Does she revert back to her territorial condition of pupilage? Or, having been a State, and having applied for admission and been refused, is she standing out a State? You hold her as a Territory; you hold her as a province. You prescribe the mode of electing the members of her Legislature, and pay them out of your own treasury. Yes, she is a province controlled by Federal authority, and her laws are made in conformity with the acts of Congress. Is she not a Territory? I think she is.

Suppose the State of California withdraws from the Union. We admitted her. She was territory acquired by the United States, by our blood and our treasure. Now, suppose she withdraws from the Confederacy: does she pass back into a territorial condition, remain a dependency upon the Federal Government, or does she stand out as a separate government? Let me take Louisiana, for which we paid $15,000,000. That was a Territory for a number of years — yes, a province. It is only another name for a province. It is a possession held under the jurisdiction of the United States. We admitted Louisiana into the Union as a State. Suppose we had refused to admit her: would she not still have remained a Territory? Would she not have remained under the protection of the United States? But now, if she has the power to withdraw from the Union, does she not pass back into the condition in which she was before we admitted her into the Union? In what condition does she place herself? When those States which were at first Territories cease their connection with this Government, do they pass back into the territorial condition? When Florida is going out, when Louisiana is going out, and these other States that were originally Territories go out of the Union, in what condition do they place themselves? Are they Territories or States? Are they merely on probation to become members of this Confederacy, or are they States outside of the Confederacy?

I have referred to the acts of Congress for acquiring Florida as setting forth a principle. Let me read another of those acts: —

"An Act to enable the President of the United States, under certain contingencies, to take possession of the country lying east of the river Perdido, and south of the State of Georgia and the Mississippi Territory, and for other purposes.

"*Be it enacted by the Senate and House of Representatives of the United States of America in Congress assembled,* That the President of the United States be, and he is hereby, authorized to take possession of and occupy all or any part of the territory lying east of the river Perdido, and south of the State of Georgia and the Mississippi Territory, in case an arrangement has been or shall be made with the local authorities of the said territory for the delivering up the possession of the same, or any part thereof, to the United States, or in the event of an attempt to occupy the said territory or any part thereof by any foreign Government; and he may, for the purpose of taking possession and occupying the territory aforesaid, in order to maintain therein the authority of the United States, employ any part of the army and navy of the United States which he may deem necessary."

What is the principle avowed here? That from the geographical relations of this territory to the United States, from its importance to the safety and security of the institutions of the United States, we authorized the President to expend $100,000 to get a foothold there, and especially to take possession of it if it were likely to pass to any foreign Power. We see the doctrine and principle there established and acted upon by our Government.

This principle was again avowed by distinguished men at Ostend. A paper was drawn up there by Mr. Buchanan, Mr. Soulé of Louisiana, and Mr. Mason of Virginia, our ministers to the three principal Courts in Europe. They met at Ostend and drew up a paper in which they laid down certain doctrines in strict conformity with the act of Congress that I have just read. They say in that paper, signed by James Buchanan, J. Y. Mason, and Pierre Soulé: —

"Then, 1. It must be clear to every reflecting mind, that, from the peculiarity of its geographical position, and the considerations attendant on it, Cuba is as necessary to the North American Republic as any of its present members, and that it belongs naturally to that great family of States of which the Union is the providential nursery.

"From its locality it commands the mouth of the Mississippi, and the immense and annually increasing trade which must seek this avenue to the ocean.

"On the numerous navigable streams, measuring an aggregate course of some thirty thousand miles, which disembogue themselves through this magnificent river into the Gulf of Mexico, the increase of the population within the last ten years amounts to more than that of the entire Union at the time Louisiana was annexed to it.

"The natural and main outlet to the products of this entire population, the highway of their direct intercourse with the Atlantic and Pacific States, can never be secure, but must ever be endangered while Cuba is a dependency of a distant power in whose possession it has proved to be a source of constant annoyance and embarrassment to their interests." . . . .

"The system of immigration and labor lately organized within its limits, and the tyranny and oppression which characterize its immediate rulers, threaten an insurrection at any moment which may result in direful consequences to the American people.

"Cuba has thus become to us an unceasing danger, and a permanent cause of anxiety and alarm." . . . .

"Self-preservation is the first law of nature, with States as well as with individuals. All nations have, at different periods, acted upon this maxim. Although it has been made the pretext for committing flagrant injustice, as in the partition of Poland, and other similar cases which history records, yet the principle itself, though often abused, has always been recognized." . . . . "Our past history forbids that we should acquire the Island of Cuba without the consent of Spain, unless justified by the great law of self-preservation. We must, in any event, preserve our own conscious rectitude, and our own self-respect."

Mark you, we are never to acquire Cuba unless it is necessary to our self-preservation.

"While pursuing this course we can afford to disregard the censures of the world, to which we have been so often and so unjustly exposed.

"After we shall have offered Spain a price for Cuba far beyond its present value, and this shall have been refused, it will then be time to consider the question does Cuba, in the possession of Spain, seriously endanger our internal peace and the existence of our cherished Union?

"Should this question be answered in the affirmative, then, by every law, human and divine, we shall be justified in wresting it from Spain, if we possess the power; and this upon the very same principle that would justify an individual in tearing down the burning house of his neighbor, if there were no other means of preventing the flames from destroying his own home."

Now, this is all pretty sound doctrine. I am for all of it.

"Under such circumstances we ought neither to count the cost nor regard the odds which Spain might enlist against us. We forbear to enter into the question, whether the present condition of the island would justify such a measure? We should, however, be recreant to our duty, be unworthy of our gallant forefathers, and commit base treason against our posterity, should we permit Cuba to be Africanized and become a second St. Domingo, with all its attendant horrors to the white race, and suffer the flames to extend to our own neighboring shore, seriously to endanger or actually to consume the fair fabric of our Union."

We find in this document, signed by our three ministers, and approved by the American people, the doctrine laid down clearly that if the United States believed that Cuba was to be transferred by Spain to England, or to France, or to some other Power inimical to the United States, the safety of the American people, the safety of our institutions, the existence of the Government, being imperilled, we should have a right, without regard to money or blood, to acquire it.

Where does this carry us? We find that this doctrine was not only laid down, but practised, in the case of Florida. Suppose Louisiana was now out of the Confederacy, holding the key to the Gulf, the outlet to the commerce of the great West: under the doctrine laid down by these ministers, and practised by the Congress of the United States, would not this Government have the right, in obedience to the great principle of self-preservation, and for the safety of our institutions, to seize it and pass it under the jurisdiction of the United States, and hold it as a province subject to the laws of the United States? I say it would. The same principle will apply to Florida. The same principle would apply to South Carolina. I regret that she occupies the position that she has assumed, but I am arguing a principle, and do not refer to her out of any disrespect. If South Carolina were outside of the Confederacy, an independent Power, having no connection with the United States, and our institutions were likely to be endangered, and the existence of the Government imperilled by her remaining a separate and independent Power, or by her forming associations and alliances with some foreign Power, I say we should have a right, on the principle laid down by Mr. Mason, Mr. Buchanan, and Mr. Soulé, and upon the principle practised by the Congress of the United States in the case of Florida, to seize her, pass her under the jurisdiction of the United States, and hold her as a province.

Mr. President, I have spoken of the possibility of a State standing in the position of South Carolina making alliances with a foreign Power. What do we see now? Ex-Governor Manning, of that State, in a speech made not long since at Columbia, made these declarations: —

> "Cotton is king, and would enable us in peace to rule the nations of the world, or successfully to encounter them in war. The millions in France and England engaged in its manufacture, are an effectual guarantee of the friendship of those nations. If necessary, their armies would stand to guard its uninterrupted and peaceful cultivation, and their men-of-war would line our coasts to guard it in its transit from our ports."

Ah! are we prepared, in the face of doctrines like these, to permit a State that has been a member of our Confederacy to go out, and erect herself into an independent Power, when she points to the time when she will become a dependant of Great Britain, or when she will want the protection of France? What is the doctrine laid down by Mr. Buchanan and Mr. Mason and Mr. Soulé? If Cuba is to pass into the hands of an unfriendly Power, or any Power inimical to the United States, we have a right to seize and to hold her. Where is the difference between the two cases?

If South Carolina is outside of the Confederacy as an independent Power, disconnected from this Government, and we find her forming alliances to protect her, I ask what becomes of that great principle, the law of self-preservation? Does it not apply with equal force? We are told, upon pretty high authority, that Great Britain is operating in the United States; that she is exerting a powerful influence. I find that, in a paper issued from the executive office, Little Rock, Arkansas, and addressed to the militia of the State of Arkansas, the following language is used: —

"It is my opinion, that the settled and secret policy of the British Government is to disturb the domestic tranquillity of the United States; that its object is to break up and destroy our Government, get rid of a powerful rival, extend the area of the British dominions on this Continent, and become the chief and controlling Power in America."

I will not read it all. He gives many reasons why it is so. He says: —

"I believe that such a conspiracy exists against our Federal Government, and that, if all the secret facts and transactions connected with it, and the names of the secret agents and emissaries of the British Government, distributed throughout the United States, could be ascertained, well authenticated, and made public, the patriotic people of the United States would be filled with astonishment; and having discovered the *real author and instigator* of the mischief, all discord between the free States and the slave States would at once be allayed, if not entirely cease, and that then they would become fraternally and more firmly united; and that the united indignation of the patriotic citizens of the whole Union against the British Government and its agents and emissaries would be so great that war would be declared against the British Government in less than twelve months."

The Governor of the State of Arkansas says, that if all the secret workings of Great Britain in this country could be ascertained, war would be declared in less than twelve months against the Government of Great Britain. What further does he say: —

"Entertaining these opinions, I deem it my duty to the people of the State of Arkansas, to warn them to go to work *in earnest* and make *permanent and thorough preparations*, so that they may at all times be ready to protect themselves and our State against evils which I believe the British Government intends shall not be temporary and trifling, but continuous and aggravated, 'irrepressible' and terrible."

This is signed by "Elias N. Conway, Governor of the State of Arkansas, and commander-in-chief of the army of said State, and of the militia thereof." But ex-Governor Manning, of South Carolina, declares that cotton is king, and that the armies of Great Britain, and the fleets of France, and their men-of-war, would protect them: the one in the peaceful production of cotton, and the other in its exportation to the ports of the world. What sort of times are we falling on? Where are we going? Are these the threats that we are to be met with? Is the United States to be told by one of the States attempting to absolve itself from its allegiance, without authority, and in fact in violation of the Constitution of the United States, that, being disconnected with the Confederacy, it will, upon our coast, form an alliance with France and with England, which will protect her more securely than the protection which she now receives from the United States? The question recurs, have we not an existence, have we not institutions, to preserve; and, in compliance with the great law of self-preservation, can we permit one of these States to take the protection of a foreign Power that is inimical and dangerous to the peaceful relations of this Government? I do not believe that we can. I repeat, for fear it may be misunderstood, that there are certain circumstances and conditions under which the remaining States, parties to the compact, might tolerate the secession of one State; and there are other circumstances and other conditions under which they dare not do it, in view of the great principle of self-preservation of which I have been speaking. When any State takes such an attitude, what will be our course of policy? The case must be determined by the existing circumstances at the time.

But it is expected and said by some that South Carolina, in making this movement, intends to carry the other States along with her; that they will be drawn into it. Now, Mr. President, is that the way for one sister, for one rebellious State, to talk to others? Is that the language in which they should be addressed? I ask my friend from California to read an extract from the message of Governor Gist, of South Carolina. He will do me a favor by so doing; and then we shall see the basis upon which we stand, and the attitude in which we are to be placed. Not only is South Carolina to go out of the Union in violation of the Constitution, impeding and resisting the execution of the laws, but the other States are to be dragged along with her, and we are all to be involved in one common ruin.

Mr. LATHAM read the following extract from the message of Governor Gist to the Legislature of South Carolina: —

"The introduction of slaves from other States which may not become members of the Southern Confederacy, and particularly the border States, should be prohibited by legislative enactment; and by this means they will be brought to see that their safety depends upon a withdrawal from their enemies and an union with their friends and natural allies. If they should continue their union with the non-slaveholding States, let them keep their slave property in their own borders, and the only alternative left them will be emancipation by their own act, or by the action of their own confederates. We cannot consent to relieve them from their embarrassing situation by permitting them to realize the money value for their slaves by selling them to us, and thus prepare them, without any loss of property, to accommodate themselves to the Northern free-soil idea. But should they unite their destiny with us, and become stars in the Southern galaxy, — members of a great Southern Confederation, — we will receive them with open arms and an enthusiastic greeting." . . . . .

"All hope, therefore, of concerted action by a Southern convention being lost, there is but one course left for South Carolina to pursue consistent with her honor, interest, and safety, and that is, to look neither to the right or the left, but go straight forward to the consummation of her purpose. It is too late now to receive propositions for a conference; and the State would be wanting in self-respect, after having deliberately decided on her own course, to entertain any proposition looking to a continuance of the present Union. We can get no better or safer guaranty than the present Constitution; and that has proved impotent to protect us against the fanaticism of the North. The institution of slavery must be under the exclusive control of those directly interested in its preservation, and not left to the mercy of those that believe it to be their duty to destroy it."

Mr. JOHNSON continued: — If my friend will read an extract from the speech of Mr. KEITT of South Carolina, it will show the determination and policy to be pursued. It is done with all respect to him; for he is a man upon whom I look as a perfect and entire gentleman, from all my acquaintance with him; but I merely want to quote from his speech to get at the policy they wish to pursue.

Mr. LATHAM read as follows: —

"Hon. L. M. KEITT was serenaded at Columbia on Monday evening; and in response to the compliment he spoke at considerable length in favor of separate State action. He said South Carolina could not take one step backward now without receiving the curses of posterity. South Carolina, single and alone, was bound to go out of this accursed Union: he would take her out if but three men went with him, and if slaves took her back it would be to her graveyard. Mr. Buchanan was pledged to secession, and he meant to hold him to it. The policy of the State should be prudent and bold. His advice was, move on, side by side. He requested union and harmony among those embarked in the same great cause; but yield not a day too long, and when the time comes let it come speedily. Take your destinies in your own hands, and shatter this accursed Union. South Carolina could do it alone. But if she could not, she could at least throw her arms around the pillars of the Constitution, and involve all the States in a common ruin. Mr. KEITT was greatly applauded throughout his address."

Mr. Johnson continued: — Mr. President, I have referred to these extracts to show the policy intended to be pursued by our seceding sister. What is the first threat thrown out? It is an intimidation to the border States, alluding especially, I suppose, to Virginia, Maryland, Kentucky, and Missouri. They constitute the first tier of the border slave States. The next tier would be North Carolina and Tennessee and Arkansas. We in the South have complained of and condemned the position assumed by the Abolitionists. We have complained that their intention is to hem slavery in, so that, like the scorpion when surrounded by fire, if it did not die from the intense heat of the scorching flames, it would perish from its own poisonous sting. Now, our sister, without consulting her sisters, without caring for their interest or their consent, says that she will move forward; that she will destroy the Government under which we have lived, and that hereafter, when she forms a government or a constitution, unless the border States come in, she will pass laws prohibiting the importation of slaves into her State from those States, and thereby obstruct the slave-trade among the States, and throw the institution back upon the border States, so that they will be compelled to emancipate their slaves upon the principle laid down by the Abolition party. That is the rod held over us!

I tell our sisters in the South that so far as Tennessee is concerned, she will not be dragged into a Southern or any other confederacy until she has had time to consider; and then she will go when she believes it to be her interest, and not before. I tell our Northern friends, who are resisting the execution of the laws made in conformity with the Constitution, that we will not be driven on the other hand into their confederacy, and we will not go into it unless it suits us, and they give us such guaranties as we deem right and proper. We say to you of the South, we are not to be frightened and coerced. Oh, when one talks about coercing a State, how maddening and insulting to the State; but when you want to bring the other States to terms, how easy to point out a means by which to coerce them! But, sir, we do not intend to be coerced.

We are told that certain States will go out and tear this accursed Constitution into fragments, and drag the pillars of this mighty edifice down upon us, and involve us all in one common ruin. Will the border States submit to such a threat? No. But if they do not come into the movement, the pillars of this stupendous fabric of human freedom and greatness and goodness are to be pulled down, and all will be involved in one common ruin. Such is the threatening language used. "You shall come into our confederacy, or we will coerce you to the emancipation of your slaves." That is the language which is held towards us.

There are many ideas afloat about this threatened dissolution, and it is time to speak out. The question arises, in reference to the protection and preservation of the institution of slavery, whether dissolution is a remedy or will give to it protection. I avow here, to-day, that if I were an Abolitionist, and wanted to accomplish the overthrow and abolition of the institution of slavery in the Southern States, the first step that I would take would be to break the bonds of this Union, and dissolve this Government. I believe the continuance of slavery depends upon the preservation of this Union, and a compliance with all the guaranties of the Constitution. I believe an interference with it will break up the Union; and I believe a dissolution of the Union will, in the end, though it may be some time to come, overthrow the institution of slavery. Hence we find so many in the North who desire the dissolution of these States as the most certain and direct and effectual means of overthrowing the institution of slavery.

What protection would it be to us to dissolve this Union? What protection would it be to us to convert this nation into two hostile Powers, the one warring with the other? Whose property is at stake? Whose interest is endangered? Is it not the property of the border States? Suppose Canada were moved down upon our border, and the two separated sections, then different nations, were hostile: what would the institution of slavery be worth on the border? Every man who has common sense will see that the institution would take up its march and retreat, as certainly and as unerringly as general laws can operate. Yes; it would commence to retreat the very moment this Union was divided into two hostile Powers, and you made the line between the slaveholding and non-slaveholding States the line of division.

Then, what remedy do we get for the institution of slavery? Must we keep up a standing army? Must we keep up forts bristling with arms along the whole border? This is a question to be considered, one that involves the future; and no step should be taken without mature reflection. Before this Union is dissolved and broken up, we in Tennessee, as one of the slave States, want to be consulted; we want to know what protection we are to have; whether we are simply to be made outposts and guards to protect the property of others, at the same time that we sacrifice and lose our own. We want to understand this question.

Again: if there is one division of the States, will there not be more than one? I heard a Senator say, the other day, that he would rather see this Government separated into thirty-three fractional parts than to see it consolidated; but when you once begin to divide, when the first division is made, who can tell when the next will be made? When these States are all turned loose, and a different condition of things is presented, with complex and abstruse interests to be considered and weighed and understood, what combinations may take place no one can tell. I am opposed to the consolidation of government, and I am as much for the reserved rights of States as any one; but, rather than see this Union divided into thirty-three petty governments, with a little prince in one, a potentate in another, a little aristocracy in a third, a little democracy in a fourth, and a republic somewhere else; a citizen not being able to pass from one State to another without a passport or a commission from his government; with quarrelling and warring amongst the little petty powers, which would result in anarchy; I would rather see this Government to-day — I proclaim it here in my place — converted into a consolidated government. It would be better for the American people; it would be better for our kind; it would be better for humanity; better for Christianity; better for all that tends to elevate and ennoble man, than breaking up this splendid, this magnificent, this stupendous fabric of human government, the most perfect that the world ever saw, and which has succeeded thus far without a parallel in the history of the world.

When you come to break up and turn loose the different elements, there is no telling what combinations may take place in the future. It may occur, for instance, to the Middle States that they will not get so good a government by going a little further South as by remaining where we are.

It may occur to North Carolina, to Tennessee, to Kentucky, to Virginia, to Maryland, to Missouri — and perhaps Illinois might fall in, too — that, by erecting themselves into a central, independent republic, disconnected either with the North or the South, they could stand as a peace-maker — could stand as a great breakwater, resisting the heated and surging waves of the South, and the fanatical Abolitionism of the North. They might think that they could stand there and lift themselves up above the two extremes, with the sincere hope that the time would arrive when the extremes would come together, and reunite once more, and we could reconstruct this greatest and best Government the world has ever seen. Or it might so turn out, our institution of slavery being exposed upon the northern line, that by looking to Pennsylvania, to New York, and to some of the other States, instead of having them as hostile Powers upon our frontiers, they might come to this central republic, and give us such constitutional guaranties, and such assurances that they would be executed, that it might be to our interest to form an alliance with them, and have a protection on our frontier.

I throw these out as considerations. There will be various projects and various combinations made. Memphis is now connected with Norfolk, in the Old Dominion; Memphis is connected with Baltimore within two days. Here is a coast that lets us out to the commerce of the world. When we look around in the four States of Tennessee, Kentucky, Virginia, and Maryland, there are things about which our memories, our attachments, and our associations linger with pride and with pleasure. Go down into the Old Dominion; there is the place where, in 1781, Cornwallis surrendered his sword to the immortal Washington. In the bosom of her soil are deposited her greatest and best sons. Move along in that trail, and there we find Jefferson and Madison and Monroe, and a long list of worthies.

We come next to old North Carolina, my native State, God bless her! She is my mother. Though she was not my cherishing mother, to use the language of the classics, she is the mother whom I love, and I cling to her with undying affection, as a son should cling to an affectionate mother. We find Macon, who was associated with our early history, deposited in her soil. Go to King's Mountain, on her borders, and you there find the place on which the battle was fought that turned the tide of the Revolution. Yes, within her borders the signal battle was fought that turned the tide which resulted in the surrender of Cornwallis at Yorktown, in the Old Dominion.

Travel on a little further, and we get back to Tennessee. I shall be as modest as I can in reference to her, but she has some associations that make her dear to the people of the United States.

In Tennessee we have our own illustrious Jackson. There he sleeps — that Jackson who issued his proclamation in 1833, and saved this Government. We have our Polk and our Grundy, and a long list of others who are worthy of remembrance.

And who lie in Kentucky? Your Hardings, your Boones, your Roanes, your Clays, are among the dead; your CRITTENDEN among the living. All are identified and associated with the history of the country.

Maryland has her Carroll of Carrollton, and a long list of worthies, who are embalmed in the hearts of the American people. And you are talking about breaking up this Republic, with this cluster of associations, these ties of affection, around you. May we not expect that some means may be devised by which it can be held together?

Here, too, in the centre of the Republic, is the seat of Government, which was founded by Washington, and bears his immortal name. Who dare appropriate it exclusively? It is within the borders of the States I have enumerated, in whose limits are found the graves of Washington, of Jackson, of Polk, of Clay. From them is it supposed that we will be torn away? No, sir; we will cherish these endearing associations with the hope, if this Republic shall be broken, that we may speak words of peace and reconciliation to a distracted, a divided, I may add, a maddened people. Angry waves may be lashed into fury on the one hand; on the other blustering winds may rage; but we stand immovable upon our basis, as on our own native mountains — presenting their craggy brows, their unexplored caverns, their summits "rock-ribbed, and ancient as the sun,"— we stand speaking peace, association, and concert to a distracted Republic.

But, Mr. President, will it not be well, before we break up this great Government, to inquire what kind of a government this new government in the South is to be, with which we are threatened unless we involve our destinies with this rash and precipitate movement? What intimation is there in reference to its character? Before my State and those States of which I have been speaking, go into a Southern or Northern confederacy, ought they not to have some idea of the kind of government that is to be formed? What are the intimations in the South in reference to the formation of a new government? The language of some speakers is that they want a Southern government obliterating all State lines — a government of consolidation. It is alarming and distressing to entertain the proposition here. What ruin and disaster would follow, if we are to have a consolidated government here! But the idea is afloat and current in the South that a Southern government is to be established, in the language of some of the speakers in the State of Georgia, "obliterating all State lines." Is that the kind of entertainment to which the people are to be invited? Is that the kind of government under which we are to pass; and are we to be forced to emancipate our slaves unless we go into it? Another suggestion in reference to a Southern government is, that we shall have a Southern Confederacy of great strength and power, with a constitutional provision preventing any State from changing its domestic institutions without the consent of three-fourths, or some great number to be fixed upon. Is that the kind of government under which we want to pass? I avow here, that, so far as I am concerned, I will never enter, with my consent, any government, North or South, less republican, less democratic, than the one under which we now live.

Where are we drifting? What kind of breakers are ahead? Have we a glimpse through the fog that envelops the rock on which the vessel of state is drifting? Should we not consider maturely, in giving up this old Government, what kind of government is to succeed it? Ought we not to have time to think? Are we not entitled to respect and consideration? In one of the leading Georgia papers we find some queer suggestions; and, as the miners would say, these may be considered as mere surface-indications, that develop what is below. We ought to know the kind of government that is to be established. When we read the allusions made in various papers, and by various speakers, we find that there is one party who are willing to give up this form of government; to change its character; and, in fact, to pass under a monarchical form of government. I hope that my friend will read the extracts which I will hand him.

Mr. LATHAM read the following extracts: —

"If the Federal system is a failure, the question may well be asked, *is not the whole republican system a failure?* Very many wise, thinking men say so. We formed the Federal Government because the separate States, it was thought, were not strong enough to stand alone, and because they were likely to prove disadvantageous, if not dangerous, each to the other, in their distinct organization, and with their varying interests. When we break up, will the disadvantages and dangers of separate States be such as to require the formation of a new confederacy of those which are, at present, supposed to be homogeneous? If we do form a new confederacy, when the old is gone, *it would seem to be neither wise, prudent, nor statesmanlike to frame it after the pattern of the old.* New safeguards and guaranties must necessarily be required, and none but a heedless maniac would seek to avoid looking this matter squarely in the face.

"It is true that we might make a constitution for the fifteen Southern States, which would secure the rights of all, *at present*, from harm, or, at least, which would require a *clear violation of its letter*, so plain that the world could discern it, when unconstitutional action was consummated. But then, in the course of years, as men changed, times changed, interests changed, business changed, productions changed, a violation of the *spirit* might occur, which would not be clearly a violation of the letter. It may be said that the constitution might provide for its own change as times changed. Well, that was the design when our present Constitution was formed, and, still, we say, it was a failure. How more carefully could a new one be arranged? Men will say that we of the South *are one*, and that we shall get along well enough. But they who say it know neither history nor human nature. When the Union was formed, twelve of the thirteen States were slaveholding; and if the cotton-gin had not been invented there would not probably to-day have been an African slave in North America.

"But how about the State organizations? This is an important consideration, for whether we consult with the other Southern States or not, it is certain that each State must act for itself, in the first instance. When any State goes out of the present Federal Union, it then becomes a *foreign Power* as to all the other States, as well as to the world. Whether it will unite again with any of the States, or stand alone, is for it to determine. The new confederacy must then be made by those States which desire it; and if Georgia, or any other State, does not find the proposed terms of federation agreeable, she can maintain her own separate form of government, or at least try it. Well, what form of government shall we have? This is more easily asked than answered.

"*Some of the wisest and best citizens propose a* HEREDITARY CONSTITUTIONAL MONARCHY; but, however good that may be in itself, the most important point to discover is, whether or not the people are prepared for it. It is thought, again, by others, that we shall be able to go on for *a generation or two*, in a new confederacy, with additional safeguards; such, for instance, as an *Executive for life*, *a vastly restricted suffrage*, *Senators elected for life, or for a long period*, say *twenty-one years*, and the most popular branch of the assembly elected for *seven years*, the judiciary absolutely independent, and for life, or good behavior. The frequency of elections, and the universality of suffrage, with the attendant arousing of the people's passions, and the necessary sequence of demagogues being elevated to high station, are thought by many to be *the great causes* of trouble among us.

"We throw out these suggestions that the people may think of them, and act as their interests require. Our own opinion is, that the South might be the greatest nation on the earth, and might maintain, on the basis of African slavery, not only a splendid government, but a *secure republican* government. *But still our fears are that through anarchy we shall reach the despotism of military chieftains, and finally be raised again to a monarchy*."[1]

"LET US REASON TOGETHER. — Permit a humble individual to lay before you a few thoughts that are burnt into his heart of hearts by their very truth.

"The first great thought is this: The institution known as the 'Federal Government,' established by the people of the United States of America, is a *failure*. This is a fact which cannot be gainsayed. It has *never* been in the power of the 'Federal Government' to enforce all its own laws within its own territory; it has, therefore, been measurably a failure from the beginning; but its first convincing evidence of weakness was in allowing one branch of its organization to pass an unconstitutional law (the Missouri Compromise). Its next evidence of decrepitude was its inability to enforce a constitutional law, (the fugitive-slave law,) the whole fabric being shaken to its foundation by the only attempt of enforcement made by its chief officer (President Pierce). I need not enlarge in this direction. The 'Federal Government' *is a failure*.

"What then? The States, of course, revert to their original position, each sovereign within itself. There can be no other just conclusion. This, then, being our position, the question for sober, thinking, earnest men is, what shall we do for the future? I take it for granted that no man in his senses would advocate the remaining in so many petty sovereignties. We should be worse than Mexicanized by

[1] Augusta (Georgia) *Chronicle and Sentinel*, Dec. 8, 1860.

that process. What, then, shall we do? In the first place, I would say, let us look around and see if there is a government of an enlightened nation that has not yet proven a failure, but which is now, and has ever been, productive of happiness to all its law-abiding people. If such a government can be found — a government whose first and only object is the *good*, the REAL GOOD (not *fancied good*, an *ignis fatuus* which I fear both our fathers and ourselves have too much run after in this country) of all its people, — if such a government exists, let us examine it carefully; if it has apparent errors, (as what human institution has not?) let us avoid them. Its beneficial arrangements let us adopt. Let us not be turned aside by its name, nor be lured by its pretensions. Try it by its works, and adopt or condemn it by its fruits. *No more experiments.* 'I speak as to wise men; judge ye what I say.'

"I am one of a few who ever dared to think that republicanism was a failure from its inception, and I have never shrunk from giving my opinion when it was worth while. I have never wished to see this Union disrupted; but if it must be, then I raise my voice for a return to a

"CONSTITUTIONAL MONARCHY."[1]

"COLUMBIA, South Carolina, *December* 5, 1860.

"Yesterday the debate in the House of Representatives was unusually warm. The parties arrayed against each other in the matter of organizing an army, and the manner of appointing the commanding officers, used scathing language, and debate ran high throughout the session. So far as I am able to judge, both the opposing parties are led on by bitter prejudices. The Joint Military Committee, with two or three exceptions, have pertinaciously clung to the idea that a standing army of paid volunteers, to be raised at once, to have the power of choosing their officers, up to captain, and to require all above to be appointed by the

1 Columbus (Georgia) *Times*.

Governor, is the organization for the times. Mr. Cunningham, of the House, who is put forward by the committee to take all the responsibility of extreme sentiments, has openly avowed his hatred of democracy in the camp. He considered the common soldier as incapable of an elective choice. He and others of his party wage a bitter war against democracy, and indicate an utter want of faith in the ability of the people to make proper choice in elections.

"The party opposed to this, the predominant party, is ostensibly led in the House by Mr. McGowan of Abbeville, and Mr. Moore of Anderson. These gentlemen have a hard fight of it. They represent the democratic sentiments of the rural districts, and are in opposition to the Charleston clique, who are urged on by Edward Rhett, Thomas Y. Simmons, and B. H. Rhett, Jr., of the 'Charleston Mercury.' The tendencies of these gentlemen are all towards a dictatorship, or monarchical form of government; at least it appears so to my mind, and I find myself not alone in the opinion. They fight heart and soul for an increase of gubernatorial power; and one of their number, as I have already stated, openly avows his desire to make the Governor a military chieftain, with sovereign power."[1]

Mr. JOHNSON continued: — Mr. President, I have merely called attention to these surface indications for the purpose of sustaining the assumption that even the people in the Southern States ought to consider what kind of government they are going to pass under, before they change the present one. We have been told that the present Constitution would be adopted by the new confederacy, and in a short time everything would be organized under it. But we find here other indications, and we are told from another quarter that another character of

[1] *Correspondence of the "Baltimore American."*

government is preferable. We know that, North and South, there is a portion of our fellow-citizens who are opposed to a government based on the intelligence and will of the people. We know that power is always stealing from the many to the few. We know that it is always vigilant and on the alert; and now that we are in a revolution, and great changes are to be made, should we not, as faithful sentinels, as men who are made the guardians of the interests of the Government, look at these indications and call the attention of the country to them? Is it not better to

> "bear those ills we have,
> Than fly to others that we know not of"?

We see, by these indications, that it is contemplated to establish a monarchy. We see it announced that this Government has been a failure from the beginning. Now, in the midst of a revolution, while the people are confused, while chaos reigns, it is supposed by some that we can be induced to return to a constitutional or absolute monarchy. Who can tell that we may not have some Louis Napoleon among us, who may be ready to make a *coup d'etat*, and enthrone himself upon the rights and upon the liberties of the people? Who can tell what kind of government may grow up? Hence the importance, in advance, of considering maturely and deliberately before we give up the old one.

I repeat again that the people of Tennessee will

never pass under another government that is less republican, less democratic in all its bearings, than the one under which we now live, I care not whether it is formed in the North or the South. We will occupy an isolated, a separate, and distinct position, before we will do it. We will pass into that fractional condition to which I have alluded before we will pass under an absolute or a constitutional monarchy. I do not say this is the design North or South, or perhaps of any but a very small portion ; but it shows that there are some who, if they could find a favorable opportunity, would fix the description of government I have alluded to on the great mass of the people. Sir, I will stand by the Constitution of the country as it is, and by all its guaranties. I am not for breaking up this great Confederacy. I am for holding on to it as it is, with the mode and manner pointed out in the instrument for its own amendment. It was good enough for Washington, for Adams, for Jefferson, and for Jackson. It is good enough for us. I intend to stand by it, and to insist on a compliance with all its guaranties, North and South.

Notwithstanding we want to occupy the position of a breakwater between the Northern and the Southern extremes, and bring all together if we can, I tell our Northern friends that the constitutional guaranties must be carried out ; for the time may come when, after we have exhausted all honorable and fair means, if this Government still fails to execute the laws, and protect us in our rights, it will be at an end. Gentlemen of the North need not deceive themselves in that particular; but we intend to act in the Union and under the Constitution, and not out of it. We do not intend that you shall drive us out of this house that was reared by the hands of our fathers. It is our house. It is the constitutional house. We have a right here; and because you come forward and violate the ordinances of this house, I do not intend to go out; and if you persist in the violation of the ordinances of the house, we intend to eject you from the building, and retain the possession ourselves. We want, if we can, to stay the heated, and I am compelled to say, according to my judgment, the rash and precipitate action of some of our Southern friends, that indicates red-hot madness. I want to say to those in the North, comply with the Constitution and preserve its guaranties, and in so doing save this glorious Union and all that pertains to it. I intend to stand by the Constitution as it is, insisting upon a compliance with all its guaranties. I intend to stand by it as the sheet-anchor of the Government; and I trust and hope, though it seems to be now in the very vortex of ruin, though it seems to be running between Charybdis and Scylla, the rock on the one hand and the whirlpool on the other, that it will be preserved, and will remain a beacon to guide, and an example to be imitated by all the nations of the earth. Yes, I intend to hold on to it as the chief ark of our safety, as the palladium of our civil and our religious liberty. I intend to cling to it as the shipwrecked mariner clings to the last plank, when the night and the tempest close around him. It is the last hope of human freedom. Although denounced as an experiment by some who want to see a constitutional monarchy, it has been a successful experiment. I trust and I hope it will be continued; that this great work may go on.

Why should we go out of the Union? Have we anything to fear? What are we alarmed about? We say that you of the North have violated the Constitution, that you have trampled under foot its guaranties; but we intend to go to you in a proper way, and ask you to redress the wrong, and to comply with the Constitution. We believe the time will come when you will do it, and we do not intend to break up the Government until the fact is ascertained that you will not do it. What is the complaint; what is the grievance that presses on our sister, South Carolina, now? Is it that she wants to carry slavery into the Territories; that she wants protection to slavery there? How long has it been since, upon this very floor, her own Senators voted that it was not necessary to make a statute now for the protection of slavery in the Territories? No longer ago than the last session. They declared, in the resolutions adopted by the Senate, that when it was necessary they had the power to do it; but that it was not necessary then. Are you going out for a grievance that has not occurred, and which your own Senators then said had not occurred? Is it because you want to carry slaves to the Territories? You were told that you had all the protection needed; that the courts had decided in your behalf, under the Constitution; and that, under the decisions of the courts, the law must be executed.

We voted for the passage of resolutions that Con gress had the power to protect slavery, and that Congress ought to protect slavery when necessary and wherever protection was needed. Was there not a majority on this floor for it; and if it was necessary then, could we not have passed a bill for that purpose without passing a resolution saying that it should be protected wherever necessary? I was here; I know what the substance of the proposition was; and the whole of it was simply to declare the principle, that we had the power, and that it was the duty of Congress, to protect slavery when necessary, in the Territories or wherever else protection was needed. Was it necessary then? If it was, we had the power, and why did we not pass the law?

The Journal of the Senate records that on the 25th of May last,

"On motion by Mr. Brown, to amend the resolution by striking out all after the word 'resolved,' and in lieu thereof inserting:

"That, experience having already shown that the Constitution and the common law, unaided by statutory enactments, do not afford adequate and sufficient protection to slave property; some of the Territories having failed, others having refused, to pass such enactments, it has become the duty of Congress to interpose and pass such laws as will afford to slave property in the Territories that protection which is given to other kinds of property.

"It was determined in the negative — yeas 3, nays 42.

"On motion by Mr. Brown, the yeas and nays being desired by one fifth of the Senators present. Those who voted in the affirmative are:

"Messrs. Brown, Johnson of Arkansas, and Mallory.

"Those who voted in the negative are:

"Messrs. Benjamin, Bigler, Bragg, Bright, Chesnut, Clark, Clay, Clingman, Crittenden, Davis, Dixon, Doolittle, Fitzpatrick, Foot, Foster, Green, Grimes, Gwin, Hamlin, Harlan, Hemphill, Hunter, Iverson, Johnson of Tennessee, Lane, Latham, Mason, Nicholson, Pearce, Polk, Powell, Pugh, Rice, Sebastian, Slidell, Ten Eyck, Thomson, Toombs, Trumbull, Wigfall, Wilson, and Yulee."

I say, therefore, that the want of protection to slavery in the Territories cannot be considered a grievance now. That is not the reason why she is going out, and going to break up the Confederacy. What is it, then? Is there any issue between South Carolina and the Federal Government? Has the Federal Government failed to comply with, and to carry out, the obligations that it owes to South Carolina? In what has the Federal Government failed? In what has it neglected the interests of South Carolina? What law has it undertaken to enforce upon South Carolina that is unconstitutional and oppressive?

If there are grievances, why cannot we all go together, and write them down, and point them out to our Northern friends after we have agreed on what those grievances are, and say, "Here is what we demand; here our wrongs are enumerated; upon these terms we have agreed; and now, after we have given you a reasonable time to consider these additional guaranties in order to protect ourselves against these wrongs, if you refuse them, then, having made an honorable effort, having exhausted all other means, we may declare the association to be broken up, and we may go into an act of revolution." We can then say to them, "You have refused to give us guaranties that we think are needed for the protection of our institutions and for the protection of our other interests." When they do this, I will go as far as he who goes the furthest.

I tell them here to-day, if they do not do it, Tennessee will be found standing as firm and unyielding in her demands for those guaranties, in the way a State should stand, as any other State in this Confederacy. She is not quite so belligerent now. She is not making quite so much noise. She is not as blustering as Sempronius was in the council in Addison's play of "Cato," who declared that his "voice was still for war." There was another character there, Lucius, who was called upon to state what his opinions were; and he replied that he must confess his thoughts were turned on peace; but when the extremity came, Lucius, who was deliberative, who was calm, and whose thoughts were upon peace, was found true to the interests of his country.

He proved himself to be a man and a soldier; while the other was a traitor and a coward. We will do our duty; we will stand upon principle, and defend it to the last extremity.

We do not think, though, that we have just cause for going out of the Union now. We have just cause of complaint; but we are for remaining in the Union, and fighting the battle like men. We do not intend to be cowardly, and turn our backs on our own camps. We intend to stay and fight the battle here upon this consecrated ground. Why should we retreat? Because Mr. Lincoln has been elected President of the United States? Is this any cause why we should retreat? Does not every man, Senator or otherwise, know, that if Mr. Breckinridge had been elected we should not be to-day for dissolving the Union? Then what is the issue? It is because we have not got our man. If we had got our man, we should not have been for breaking up the Union; but as Mr. Lincoln is elected, we are for breaking up the Union! I say no. Let us show ourselves men, and men of courage.

How has Mr. Lincoln been elected, and how have Mr. Breckinridge and Mr. Douglas been defeated? By the votes of the American people, cast according to the Constitution and the forms of law, though it has been upon a sectional issue. It is not the first time in our history that two candidates have been elected from the same section of country. General Jackson and Mr. Calhoun were elected on the same ticket; but nobody considered that cause of dissolution. They were from the South. I oppose the sectional spirit that has produced the election of Lincoln and Hamlin, yet it has been done according to the Constitution and according to the forms of law. I believe we have the power in our own hands, and I am not willing to shrink from the responsibility of exercising that power.

How has Lincoln been elected, and upon what basis does he stand? A minority President by nearly a million votes; but had the election taken place upon the plan proposed in my amendment of the Constitution, by districts, he would have been this day defeated. But it has been done according to the Constitution and according to law. I am for abiding by the Constitution; and in abiding by it I want to maintain and retain my place here, and put down Mr. Lincoln and drive back his advances upon Southern institutions, if he designs to make any. Have we not got the brakes in our hands? Have we not got the power? We have. Let South Carolina send her Senators back; let all the Senators come; and on the fourth of March next we shall have a majority of six in this body against him. This successful sectional candidate, who is in a minority of a million, or nearly so, on the popular vote, cannot make his Cabinet on the fourth of March next, unless this Senate will permit him.

Am I to be so great a coward as to retreat from duty? I will stand here and meet the encroachments upon the institutions of my country at the threshold; and as a man, as one that loves my country and my constituents, I will stand here and resist all encroachments and advances. Here is the place to stand. Shall I desert the citadel, and let the enemy come in and take possession? No. Can Mr. Lincoln send a foreign minister, or even a consul, abroad, unless he receives the sanction of the Senate? Can he appoint a postmaster whose salary is over a thousand dollars a year without the consent of the Senate? Shall we desert our posts, shrink from our responsibilities, and permit Mr. Lincoln to come with nis cohorts, as we consider them, from the North, to carry off everything? Are we so cowardly that now that we are defeated, not conquered, we shall do this? Yes, we are defeated according to the forms of law and the Constitution; but the real victory is ours, — the moral force is with us. Are we agoing to desert that noble and that patriotic band who have stood by us at the North, who have stood by us upon principle, and upon the Constitution? They stood by us and fought the battle upon principle; and now that we have been defeated, not conquered, are we to turn our backs upon them and leave them to their fate? I, for one, will not. I intend to stand by them. How many votes did we get in the North? We got more votes in the North against Lincoln than the entire Southern States cast. Are they not able and faithful allies? They are; and now, on account of this temporary defeat, are we to turn our backs upon them and leave them to their fate?

We find, when all the North is summed up, that Mr. Lincoln's majority there is only about two hundred thousand on the popular vote; and when that is added to the other vote cast throughout the Union, he stands to-day in a minority of nearly a million votes. What, then, is necessary to be done? To stand to our posts like men, and act upon principle; stand for the country; and in four years from this day, Lincoln and his administration will be turned out, the worst-defeated and broken-down party that ever came into power. It is an inevitable result from the combination of elements that now exist. What cause, then, is there to break up the Union? What reason is there for deserting our posts and destroying this greatest and best Government that was ever spoken into existence?

I voted against him; I spoke against him; I spent my money to defeat him; — but still I love my country; I love the Constitution; I intend to insist upon its guaranties. There, and there alone, I intend to plant myself, with the confident hope and belief that if the Union remains together, in less than four years the now triumphant party will be overthrown. In less time, I have the hope and belief that we shall unite and agree upon our grievances here and demand their redress, not as suppliants at the footstool of power, but as parties to a great compact; we shall say that we want additional guaranties, and that they are necessary to the preservation of this Union; and then, when they are refused deliberately and calmly, if we cannot do better, let the South go together, and let the North go together, and let us have a division of this Government without the shedding of blood, if such a thing be possible; let us have a division of the property; let us have a division of the Navy; let us have a division of the Army, and of the public lands. Let it be done in peace, and in a spirit that should characterize and distinguish this people. I believe we can obtain all our guaranties. I believe there is too much good sense, too much intelligence, too much patriotism, too much capability, too much virtue, in the great mass of people to permit this Government to be overthrown.

I have an abiding faith, I have an unshaken confidence in man's capability to govern himself. I will not give up this Government that is now called an experiment, which some are prepared to abandon for a constitutional monarchy. No; I intend to stand by it, and I entreat every man throughout the nation, who is a patriot, and who has seen, and is compelled to admit, the success of this great experiment, to come forward, not in heat, not in fanaticism, not in haste, not in precipitancy, but in deliberation, in full view of all that is before us, in the spirit of brotherly love and fraternal affection, and rally around the altar of our common country, and lay the Constitution upon it as our last libation, and swear by our God and all that is sacred and holy, that the Constitution shall be saved, and the Union preserved. Yes, in the language of the departed Jackson, let us exclaim that the Union, "the Federal Union, it must be preserved."

Are we likely, when we get to ourselves, North and South, to sink into brotherly love? Are we likely to be so harmonious in that condition as some suppose? I am sometimes impressed with the force of Mr. Jefferson's remark, that we may as well keep the North to quarrel with, for if we have no North to quarrel with, we shall quarrel among ourselves. We are a sort of quarrelsome, pugnacious people; and if we cannot get a quarrel from one quarter, we shall have it from another; and I would rather quarrel a little now with the North than be quarrelling with ourselves. What did a Senator say here in the American Senate, only a few days ago, because the Governor of a Southern State was refusing to convene the Legislature to hasten this movement that was going on throughout the South, and because he objected to that course of conduct? The question was asked if there was not some Texan Brutus that would rise up and rid the country of the hoary-headed traitor! This is the language that a Senator used. This is the way we begin to speak of Southern Governors. Yes; to remove an obstacle in our way, we must have a modern Brutus who will go to the capital of a State and assassinate a Governor to accelerate the movement. If we are so unscrupulous in reference to ourselves, and in reference to the means we are willing to employ to consummate this dissolution, then it does not look very much like harmony among ourselves after we get out of it.

Mr. President, I have said much more than I anticipated when I commenced; and I have spoken more at length than a regard for my own health and strength would have allowed; but if there is any effort of mine that would preserve this Government till there is time to think, till there is time to consider, even if it cannot be preserved any longer; if that end could be secured by making a sacrifice of my existence and offering up my blood, I would be willing to consent to it. Let us pause in this mad career; let us hesitate. Let us consider well what we are doing before we make a movement. I believe that, to a certain extent, dissolution is going to take place. I say to the North, you ought to come up in the spirit which should characterize and control the North on this question; and you ought to give those indications of good faith that will approach what the South demands. It will be no sacrifice on your part. It is no suppliancy on ours, but simply a demand of right. What concession is there in doing right? Then, come forward. We have it in our power — yes, this Congress here to-day has it in its power to save this Union, even after South Carolina has gone out. Will they not do it? You can do it. Who is willing to take the dreadful alternative without making an honorable effort to save this Government? This Congress has it in its power to-day to arrest this thing, at least for a season, until there is time to consider about it, until we can act discreetly and prudently, and I believe arrest it altogether.

Shall we give all this up to the Vandals and the Goths? Shall we shrink from our duty, and desert the Government as a sinking ship, or shall we stand by it? I, for one, will stand here until the high behest of my constituents demands of me to desert my post; and instead of laying hold of the columns of this fabric and pulling it down, though I may not be much of a prop, I will stand with my shoulder supporting the edifice as long as human effort can do it.

In saying what I have said on this occasion, Mr. President, I have had in view the duty that I owe to my constituents, to my children, to myself. Without regard to consequences, I have taken my position; and when the tug comes, when Greek shall meet Greek, and our rights are refused after all honorable means have been exhausted, then it is that I will perish in the last breach; yes, in the language of the patriot Emmet, "I will dispute every inch of ground; I will burn every blade of grass; and the last intrenchment of Freedom shall be my grave." Then, let us stand by the Constitution; and in preserving the Constitution we shall save the Union; and in saving the Union we save this the greatest Government on earth.

I thank the Senate for their kind attention.

SPEECH ON THE STATE OF THE UNION.

DELIVERED IN THE SENATE OF THE UNITED STATES, FEBRUARY 5TH AND 6TH, 1861.

The Senate having under consideration the message of the President communicating resolutions of the Legislature of Virginia, —

Mr. JOHNSON remarked: — Mr. President, on the 19th of December I made a speech in the Senate, with reference to the present crisis, which I believed my duty to my State and to myself required. In making that speech, my intention — and I think I succeeded in it — was to establish myself upon the principles of the Constitution and the doctrines inculcated by Washington, Jefferson, Madison, Monroe, and Jackson. Having examined the positions of those distinguished fathers of the Republic, and compared them with the Constitution, I came to the conclusion that they were right; and upon them I planted myself, and made the speech to which I have referred, in vindication of the Union and the Constitution, and against the doctrine of nullification or secession, which I look upon as a great political heresy. As far back as 1833, when I was a young man, before I made my advent into public life, when the controversy arose between the Federal Government and the State of South Carolina, and it became necessary for Andrew Jackson, then President of the United States, to issue his proclamation, exhorting that people to obey the law and comply with the requirements of the Constitution, I planted myself upon the principles then announced by him. I believed that the positions taken then by General Jackson, and those who came to his support, were the true doctrines of the Constitution, and the only doctrines upon which this Government could be preserved. I have been uniformly, from that period to the present time, opposed to the doctrine of secession, or of nullification, which is somewhat of a hermaphrodite, but approximates to the doctrine of secession. I repeat, that I then viewed it as a heresy and as an element which, if maintained, would result in the destruction of this Government. I maintain the same position to-day.

I oppose this heresy for another reason: not only as being destructive of the existing Government, but as being destructive of all future confederacies that may be established as a consequence of a disruption of the present one; and I availed myself of the former occasion on which I spoke, to enter my protest against it, and to do something to extinguish a political heresy that ought never to be incorporated upon this or any other

Government which may be subsequently established. I look upon it as the prolific mother of political sin; as a fundamental error; as a heresy that is intolerable in contrast with the existence of the Government itself. I look upon it as being productive of anarchy; and anarchy is the next step to despotism. The developments that we have recently seen in carrying this doctrine into practice, admonish us, I think, that this will be the result.

But, Mr. President, since I made that speech, on the 19th of December, I have been the peculiar object of attack. I have been denounced, because I happened to be the first man south of Mason and Dixon's line who entered a protest or made an argument in the Senate against this political error. From what I saw here on the evening when I concluded my speech — although some may have thought that it intimidated and discouraged me — I was inspired with confidence; I felt that I had struck Treason a blow. I thought then, and I know now, that men who were engaged in treason felt the blows that I dealt out on that occasion. As I have been made the peculiar object of attack, not only in the Senate, but out of the Senate, my purpose on this occasion is to meet some of these attacks, and to say some things in addition to what I then said against this movement.

REPLY TO MR. BENJAMIN.

Yesterday the last of the Senators who represent what are called the seceding States, retired, and a drama was enacted. The piece was well performed; the actors were perfect in their parts; it was got up to order; I will not say that the mourning auxiliaries had been selected in advance. One of the retiring Senators, in justifying the course that his State had taken, made a very specious and plausible argument in reference to the doctrine of secession. I allude to the Senator from Louisiana.[1] He argued that the sovereignty of that State had never passed to the United States; that the Government held it in trust; that no conveyance was made; that sovereignty could not be transferred; that out of the gracious pleasure and good-will which the First Consul of France entertained toward the American people, the transfer was made of the property without consideration, and the sovereignty was in abeyance or trust, and therefore his State had violated no faith, and had a right to do precisely what she has done. With elaborate preparation and seeming sincerity, with sweet tones, euphonious utterances, mellifluous voice, and the greatest earnestness, he called our attention to the treaty to sustain his assumption. But when we examine the subject, Mr. President, how do the facts stand? I like fairness: I will not say that the Senator, in making quotations from the treaty and commenting upon them, was intentionally unfair; nor can I say that the Senator from Louisiana, with all his acumen, his habits of industry, and his great research, had not read and understood

[1] Mr. Benjamin.

all the provisions of the treaty. In doing so, I should reflect upon his character; it might be construed as a reflection upon his want of research, for which he has such a distinguished reputation. The omission to read important portions of the treaty I will not attribute to any intention to mislead; I will simply call the attention of the Senate and the country to his remarks, and then to the treaty. The Senator, after premising, went on to say: —

> "I have said that the Government assumed to act as trustee or guardian of the people of the ceded province, and covenanted to transfer to them the sovereignty thus held in trust for their use and benefit, as soon as they were capable of exercising it. What is the express language of the treaty?"

He then read the third article of the treaty of cession of Louisiana, which provides merely for their incorporation into the United States; their protection in the enjoyment of their religion, &c.; and thus he commented on it: —

> "And, sir, as if to mark the true nature of the cession in a manner too significant to admit of misconstruction, the treaty stipulates no price; and the sole consideration for the conveyance, as stated on its face, is the desire to afford a strong proof of the friendship of France for the United States. By the terms of a separate convention stipulating the payment of a sum of money, the precaution is again observed of stating that the payment is to be made, not as a consideration, or a price, or a condition precedent of the cession, but it is carefully distinguished as being a consequence of the cession."

Now, Mr. President, to make this matter more intelligible, and better understood by the country, it seems to me it would have been better to read the first article of the treaty, which commences thus: —

"The President of the United States of America, and the First Consul of the French Republic, in the name of the French people, desiring to remove all source of misunderstanding relative to objects of discussion," &c.

After reciting the other treaties pending between France and the United States and Spain, they go on in the first article as follows: —

"And whereas, in pursuance of the treaty, and particularly the third article, the French Republic has an incontestable title to the domain and to the possession of the said territory, [that is, of Louisiana,] the First Consul of the French Republic, desiring to give to the United States a strong proof of his friendship, doth hereby cede to the said United States, in the name of the French Republic, forever and in full sovereignty, the said territory, with all its rights and appurtenances, as fully and in the same manner as they have been acquired by the French Republic, in virtue of the above-mentioned treaty concluded with his Catholic Majesty."

Now, sir, is there not a clear and distinct and explicit conveyance of sovereignty, of property, of jurisdiction, of everything that resided in the First Consul of France, to the people of the United States? Clearly and distinctly the jurisdiction and control of that Government were transmitted absolutely by the treaty. Why not have read that part of the treaty first?

The second article is in these words: —

16

"ART. 2. In the cession made by the preceding article, are included the adjacent islands belonging to Louisiana, all public lots and squares, vacant lands, and all public buildings, fortifications, barracks, and other edifices, which are not private property. The archives, papers, and documents relative to the domain and sovereignty of Louisiana and its dependencies, will be left in the possession of the commissaries of the United States, and copies will be afterwards given in due form to the magistrates and municipal officers of such of the said papers and documents as may be necessary to them."

We see, then, in the first article, that property and sovereignty were all conveyed together, in clear and distinct terms. If there was a power residing anywhere to control the people and the property of Louisiana, it was in the First Consul of France, who conveyed absolutely the sovereignty and right of property to the people of the United States. Then we come to the third article, which the Senator read yesterday: —

"ART. 3. The inhabitants of the ceded territory shall be incorporated in the Union of the United States, and admitted as soon as possible, according to the principles of the Federal Constitution, to the enjoyment of all the rights, advantages, and immunities of citizens of the United States; and, in the mean time, they shall be maintained and protected in the free enjoyment of their liberty, property, and the religion which they profess."

There is some order in that; one thing fits the other. There is the conveyance of sovereignty and property. There is a minute enumeration in the second article; and in the third article it is provided that as soon as possible, according to the principles of the Federal Constitution, they shall be incorporated into the Union, and protected in the enjoyment of the religion which they may profess. We see, then, how the thing stands. Have not all these things been complied with? But, by way of exonerating Louisiana from censure for her recent act of attempted secession, it is urged that, when this treaty was made, there was no consideration; but that, out of the good-will that the First Consul had towards the American people, the sovereignty was given to us in trust; that we took the property in trust; that we took everything in trust. Sir, the Federal Government took the property, and the sovereignty with it, in trust for all the States. The retiring Senator's speech — whether it was intended or not, I do not undertake to say — is calculated to make the false impression that some time afterwards, perhaps in some other treaty remote from that, some money was paid by the United States to France, out of the good-will that this Government had towards them. And yet, sir, on the same day — the 30th of April, 1803 — on which the other treaty was made and signed, the following convention between the United States of America and the French Republic was made: —

"The President of the United States of America, and the First Consul of the French Republic, in the name of the French people, in consequence of the treaty of cession of Louisiana, which has been signed this day, wishing to regulate definitely everything which has relation to the said cession," &c.

This, be it observed, was made on the same day, and was, perhaps, written out before the other treaty was signed. And what does the first article say? It says expressly: —

> "ART. 1. The Government of the United States engages to pay to the French Government, in the manner specified in the following article, the sum of sixty million francs, independent of the sum which shall be fixed by another convention, for the payment of debts due by France to the citizens of the United States."

What becomes of the specious plea that we took it simply in trust, and that no consideration was paid? Turn over to the American State Papers; look at Mr. Livingston's letters, upon which these treaties were predicated; read his correspondence with Mr. Madison, who was Secretary of State; and you will find that France demanded the sum of 100,000,000f. independent of what they owed the citizens of the United States; but after long negotiations, the First Consul of the French concluded to take 60,000,000f.; and the first two articles of the treaty which I have read are based upon the 60,000,000f. paid by this Government in consideration of the sovereignty and territory, all of which was to be held in trust by the United States for all the States.

This was given to us out of the pure good-will that Napoleon at that time had towards the United States! Sir, he had great hate for Great Britain; and by the promptings of that hate he was disposed to cede this territory to some other Power. He feared that Great Britain, whose navy was superior to his own, would take it. He desired to obtain money to carry on his wars and sustain his Government. These considerations, and not love or partiality or friendship for the United States, led him to make the cession. Then what becomes of the Senator's special pleading? From the Senator's remarks, it may have been concluded that we got it as a gratuity. But after examining the State Papers and the correspondence, and looking at the tedious and labored negotiation previous to the making of the treaty, it is clear that at the time the first treaty was made, on the very same day, the consideration was fixed; and yet the Senators tell us that at some other time a treaty was made not referring to any amount of money agreed to be paid at this particular time, and that therefore they are excusable and justifiable in going out of the Confederacy of these States.

And then an appeal was made. It was a very affecting scene. Louisiana was gone; and what was the reason? Great oppression and great wrong. She could not get her rights in the Union, and consequently she has sought them out of it. What are the wrongs of Louisiana? What was the cause for all the sympathy expressed on the one hand, and the tears shed on the other? Louisiana was presented to the country in a most pathetic and sympathetic attitude. Her wrongs were without number; their enormity was almost without estimate; they could scarcely be fathomed by human sympathy. It was not unlike the oration of Mark Antony over the dead body of Cæsar. Weeping friends grouped picturesquely in the foreground; the bloody robe, the ghastly wounds, were conjured to the imagination; and who was there that did not expect to hear the exclamation, "If you have tears, prepare to shed them now"?

Sir, what are the great wrongs that have been inflicted upon Louisiana? Prior to 1803 Louisiana was transferred from Spain to France, and from France back to Spain, — both property and sovereignty, — almost with the same facility as a chattel from one person to another. On the 30th of April, 1803, when this treaty was made, what was the condition of Louisiana? It was then a province of the First Consul of France, subject to be disposed of at his discretion. The United States came forward and paid to the First Consul of France 60,000,000f. for the territory. The treaty was made; the territory was transferred; and in 1806, in express compliance with the treaty, as soon as practicable according to the terms of the Federal Constitution, Louisiana was admitted into the Union as a State. We bought her; we paid for her; we admitted her into the Union upon terms of equality with the other States. Was there any oppression, any great wrong, any grievance in that?

In 1815 — war having been declared in 1812 —

Louisiana was attacked; the city of New Orleans was about to be sacked and laid prostrate in the dust; "Beauty and Booty" were the watchwords. She was oppressed then, was she not? Kentucky, your own gallant State, sir, (and, thank God! she is standing erect now,) and Tennessee, (which, as I honestly believe, will ever stand by her side in this struggle for the Constitution and the Union,) in conjunction with the other States, met Packenham and his myrmidons upon the plains of New Orleans, and there dealt out death and desolation to her invading foe. What soil did we invade? What city did we propose to sack? Whose property did we propose to destroy? Was not Louisiana there gallantly, nobly, bravely, and patriotically defended, by the people of the United States, from the inroads and from the sacking of a British foe? Is that defence one of her oppressions? Is that one of the great wrongs that have been inflicted upon Louisiana?

What more has been done by this Government? How much protection has she received upon her sugar? In order to give that protection, the poorest man throughout the United States is taxed for every spoonful that he uses to sweeten his coffee. How many millions, under the operation of a protection upon sugar, have been contributed to the wealth and prosperity of Louisiana since she has been in this Confederacy? Estimate them. Is this another of her wrongs? Is this another of her grievances? Is this another of the oppressions that the United States have inflicted upon Louisiana?

Sum them all up, and what are the wrongs, what the grievances which justify Louisiana in taking leave of the United States? We have defended her soil and her citizens; we have paid the price asked for her by the French Government; she has been protected in the production of her sugar, and in the enjoyment of every right that a sovereign State could ask at the hands of the Federal Government. And how has she treated the United States? What is her position? Upon her own volition, without consultation with her sister States, without even consulting with Tennessee and Kentucky, who defended her when she was in peril, she proposes to secede from the Union. She does more: in violation of the Constitution of the United States, in despite of the plighted faith that exists between all the States, she takes our arsenals, our forts, our custom-house, our mint, with about a million dollars. Gracious God! to what are we coming? Is it thus that the Constitution of the United States is to be violated? Forts, arsenals, custom-houses, and property belonging to all the people of all the States, have been ruthlessly seized, and their undisturbed possession is the sum total of the great wrongs that have been inflicted upon Louisiana by the United States!

Mr. President, when I look at the conduct of some of the States, I am reminded of the fable of King Log and the frogs. They got tired of the log that lay in their midst, upon which they could bask in the sun, or from which they could dive to the depth beneath, without interference. And these seceding States have got tired of the Federal Government, which has been so profitable to them, and loathe the blessings which they enjoy. Seemingly, its inability to take care of itself created their opposition to it. It seems, the inability of the United States to defend and take care of its own property has been an invitation to them to take possession of it; and, like the frogs, they seek a substitute for their log. They prayed to Jupiter, the supreme deity, to send them another king; and he answered their prayer by sending them a stork, who soon devoured his subject frogs. There are storks, too, in the seceding States. South Carolina has her stork king, and so has Louisiana. In the heavy appropriations they are making to maintain armies, and in all their preparations for war, for which there is no cause, they will find they have brought down storks upon them that will devour them.

What do we find, Mr. President, since this movement commenced? In about forty-six days, since the first State went out until the last one disappeared, — the 26th of January, — they have taken from the United States, this harmless old ruler, sixteen forts and one thousand and ninety-two guns, without any resistance, amounting to $6,513,000. They are very much alarmed at the power of this Government. Thus the Government oppresses them, — thus this Government oppresses Louisiana, pertinaciously persisting in allowing those States to take all the guns, all the forts, all the arsenals, all the dock-yards, all the custom-houses, and all the mints. Thus they are so cruelly oppressed. Is it not a farce? Is it not the greatest outrage and the greatest folly that was ever consummated since man was spoken into existence? But these are the grievances of Louisiana. I shall say nothing against Louisiana. Tennessee and Kentucky have given demonstrations most noticeable, that when she needed friends, when she needed aid, they were at her bidding.

But with Louisiana there was another very important acquisition. We acquired the exclusive and entire control of the navigation of the Mississippi River. We find that Louisiana, in her ordinance of secession, makes the negative declaration that she has the control of the navigation of that great stream, by stating that the navigation of the river shall be free to those States that remain on friendly terms with her, with the proviso that moderate contributions are to be levied to defray such expenses as they may deem expedient from time to time. That is the substance of it. Sir, look at the facts. All the States, through their Federal Government, treated for Louisiana. The treaty was made. All the States, by the contribution of their money, paid for Louisiana and the navigation of the Mississippi River. Where, and from what source, does Louisiana now derive the power or the authority to secede from this Union and set up exclusive control of the navigation of that great stream which is owned by all the States, which was paid for by the money of all the States, and upon whose borders the blood of many citizens of the States has been shed?

This is one of the aggrieved, the oppressed States! Mr. President, is it not apparent that these grievances and oppressions are mere pretences? A large portion of the South (and that portion of it I am willing to stand by to the very last extremity) believe that aggressions have been made upon them by the other States, in reference to the institution of slavery. A large portion of the South believe that something ought to be done in the shape of what has been offered by the distinguished Senator from Kentucky, or something very similar. They think and feel that that ought to be done. But, sir, there is another portion who do not care for those propositions to bring about reconciliation, but who, on the contrary, have been alarmed lest something should be done to reconcile and satisfy the public mind, before this diabolical work of secession could be consummated. Yes, sir, they have been afraid; and the occasion has been used to justify and to carry into practice a doctrine which will be not only the destruction of this Government, but the destruction of all other governments that may be originated embracing the same principle. Why not, then, meet it like men? We know there is a portion of the South who are for secession, who are for breaking up this Government, without regard to slavery or anything else, as I shall show before I have done.

The Senator from Louisiana,[1] in a speech that he made some days since, took occasion to allude to some authority that I had introduced from General Washington, the first President who executed the laws of the United States against armed resistance ; and it occurred to him that, by way of giving his argument force, it was necessary to remark that I was not a lawyer, and that therefore I had not examined the subject with that minuteness and with that care and familiarity that I should have done ; and hence that I had introduced authority which had no application to the question under consideration. The proof that he gave to show that I had not examined the subject carefully was contained in the very extract that I had quoted, and which he said declared that General Washington had been informed by the marshal that he could not execute the laws ; and from the fact of the marshal being incapable of executing them, General Washington was called upon to employ the means, under the Constitution and the laws, which were necessary to their enforcement. It may have been necessary for the distinguished Senator to inform the Senate and the country that I was not a lawyer ; but it was not necessary to inform anybody that read his speech and had the slightest information or

[1] Mr. Benjamin.

sagacity, that he was a lawyer, and that he was making a lawyer's speech upon the case before him; not an argument upon the great principles of the Government. The speech was a complete lawyer's speech, the authorities were summed up simply to make out the case on his side; and he left out all those that would disprove his position.

That Senator yesterday seemed to be very serious in regard to the practical operation of the doctrine of secession. I felt sorry myself, somewhat. I am always reluctant to part with a gentleman with whom I have been associated, and nothing had transpired to disturb between us those courteous relations which should always exist between persons associated on this floor. I thought the scene was pretty well got up, and was acted out admirably. The plot was executed to the very letter. You would have thought that his people in Louisiana were borne down and seriously oppressed by remaining in this Union of States. Now, I have an extract before me, from a speech delivered by that gentleman since the election of Abraham Lincoln, while the distinguished Senator was on the western slope of the Rocky Mountains, at the city of San Francisco. He was called upon to make an address; and I will read an extract from it, which I find in the "New York Times," the editors of which paper said they had the speech before them; and I have consulted a gentleman here who was in California at the time, and he tells me that the report is correct. In that speech — after the Senator had spoken some time with his accustomed eloquence — he uttered this language: —

> "Those who prate of, and strive to dissolve this glorious Confederacy of States, are like those silly savages who let fly their arrows at the sun in the vain hope of piercing it! And still the sun rolls on, unheeding, in its eternal pathway, shedding light and animation upon all the world."

Even after Lincoln was elected, the Senator from Louisiana is reported to have said, in the State of California, and in the city of San Francisco, that this great Union could not be destroyed. Those great and intolerable oppressions, of which we have since heard from him, did not seem to be flitting across his vision and playing upon his mind with that vividness and clearness which were displayed here yesterday. He said, in California, that this great Union would go on in its course, notwithstanding the puny efforts of the silly savages that were letting fly their arrows with the vain hope of piercing it. What has changed the Senator's mind on coming from that side of the continent to this? What light has broken in upon him? Has he been struck on his way, like Paul, when he was journeying from Tarsus to Damascus? Has some supernatural power disclosed to him that his State and his people will be ruined if they remain in the Union? Where do we find the distinguished Senator only at the last session? On the 22d of May last, when he made his celebrated reply to the Senator from Illinois,[1] the Senator from Louis-

[1] Mr. Douglas.

iana, alluding to the contest for the Senate between Mr. LINCOLN and Mr. DOUGLAS, said: —

"In that contest, the two candidates for the Senate of the United States, in the State of Illinois, went before their people. They agreed to discuss the issues; they put questions to each other for answer; and I must say here — for I must be just to all — that I have been surprised, in the examination that I made again, within the last few days, of this discussion between Mr. Lincoln and Mr. Douglas, to find that, on several points, Mr. Lincoln is a far more conservative man, unless he has since changed his opinion, than I had supposed him to be. There was no dodging on his part. Mr. Douglas started with his questions. Here they are, with Mr. Lincoln's answers."

The impression evidently made on the public mind then, before the presidential election, was that Lincoln, the rank Abolitionist now, was more conservative than Mr. Douglas; and he said further, after reading the questions put by Mr. Lincoln, and his answers to them, —

"It is impossible, Mr. President, however we may differ in opinion with the man, not to admire the perfect candor and frankness with which the answers were given; no equivocation; no evasion."

Since that speech was made, since the Senator has travelled from California to this place, the grievances, the oppressions of Louisiana, have become so great that she is justified in going out of the Union, taking into her possession the custom-house, the mint, the navigation of the Mississippi River, the forts, and arsenals. Where are we? "O Consistency, thou art a jewel much to be admired, but rarely to be found."

Mr. President, I never do things by halves. I am against this doctrine entirely. I commenced making war upon it, — a war for the Constitution and the Union, — and I intend to sink or swim upon it. In the remarks that I made on the 19th of December, I discussed at some length the alleged right of secession. I repudiated the whole doctrine. I introduced authorities to show its unsoundness, and made deductions from those authorities which have not been answered to this day; but by innuendo and indirection, without reference to the person who used the authorities, attempts have been made to answer the speech. Let those who can, answer the speech, answer the authorities, answer the conclusions which have been deduced from them. I was more than gratified, shortly afterwards, when one of the distinguished Senators from Virginia[1] delivered a speech upon this floor, which it was apparent to all had been studied closely; which had been digested thoroughly; which, in the language of another, had been conned and set down in a note-book, and got by rote; not only the sentences constructed, but the language measured. In the plan which he proposed as one upon which the Government can be continued and administered, in his judgment, he brought his mind seemingly, irresistibly, to the conclusion that this doctrine of secession was a heresy. What does he

[1] Mr. Hunter.

say in that able, that methodical, that well-digested speech? He goes over the whole ground. He has been reasoning on it; he has been examining the principle of secession; he has arrived at the conclusion to which it leads; and he is seemingly involuntarily, but irresistibly, forced to admit that it will not do to acknowledge this doctrine of secession, for he says: —

"I have presented this scheme, Mr. President, as one which, in my opinion, would adjust the differences between the two social systems, and which would protect each from the assault of the other. If this were done, so that we were made mutually safe, I, for one, would be willing to regulate the right of secession, which I hold to be a right not given in the Constitution, but resulting from the nature of the compact. I would provide that before a State seceded, it should summon a convention of the States in the section to which it belonged, and submit to them a statement of its grievances and wrongs. Should a majority of the States in such a convention decide the complaint to be well founded, then the State ought to be permitted to secede in peace. For, whenever a majority of States in an entire section shall declare that good cause for secession exists, then who can dispute that it ought to take place? Should they say, however, that no good cause existed, then the moral force of such a decision, on the part of the confederates, of those who are bound to the complaining State by identical and homogeneous interests, would prevent it from prosecuting the claim any further."

Sir, I quoted the Old Dominion extensively before. I took the foundation of this doctrine and traced it along step by step, and showed that there was no such notion tolerated by the fathers of the

Republic as the right of secession. Now, who comes up to my relief? When the States are seceding, the distinguished Senator from Virginia says, in so many words, that he admits the error, and the force of the principle that a State ought not to be permitted to go out of the Confederacy without the consent of the remaining members. He says, however, that the right to secede results from the nature of the compact. Sir, I have read Mr. Jefferson, and I am as much inclined to rely on the former distinguished men of the State of Virginia as I am on the latter. In the old Articles of Confederation, when the revenue required for the support of the Federal Government was apportioned among the States, and each State had to raise its portion, the great difficulty was, that there were no means by which the States could be compelled to contribute their amount; there were no means of forcing the State to compliance; and yet Mr. Jefferson, in view of that very difficulty, said in 1786 : —

"It has been often said that the decisions of Congress are impotent, because the Confederation provides no compulsory power. But when two or more nations enter into compact, it is not usual for them to say what shall be done to the party who infringes it. Decency forbids this, and it is as unnecessary as indecent; because the right of compulsion naturally results to the party injured by the breach. When any one State in the American Union refuses obedience to the Confederation by which they have bound themselves, the rest have a natural right to compel it to obedience."

The Senator from Virginia says a State has the

right to secede from the Union, and that it is a right resulting from the nature of the compact; but Mr. Jefferson said that even under the old Articles of Confederation, no State had a right to refuse obedience to the Confederacy, and that there was a right to enforce its compliance, —

> "Congress would probably exercise long patience before they would recur to force; but if the case ultimately required it, they would use that recurrence. Should this case ever arise, they will probably coerce by a naval force, as being more easy, less dangerous to liberty, and less likely to produce much bloodshed."[1]

When was this? I have stated that it was under the old Articles of Confederation, when there was no power to compel a State even to contribute her proportion of the revenues; but in that view of the case, Mr. Jefferson said that the injured party had a right to enforce compliance with the compact from the offending State, and that this was a right deducible from the laws of nature. The present Constitution was afterwards formed; and to avoid this difficulty in raising revenue, the power was conferred upon the Congress of the United States "to lay and collect taxes, duties, imposts, and excises," and the Constitution created a direct relation between the citizen and the Federal Government in that matter, and to that extent that relation is just as direct and complete between the Federal Government and the citizen as is the relation between the

[1] *Jefferson's Works*, Vol. IX. p. 291.

State and the citizen in other matters. Hence we find that, by an amendment to the Constitution of the United States, the citizens cannot even make a State a party to a suit, and bring her into the Federal courts. They wanted to avoid the difficulty of coercing a State, and the Constitution conferred on the Federal Government the power to operate directly upon the citizen, instead of operating on the States. It being the right of the Government to enforce obedience from the citizen in those matters of which it has jurisdiction, the question comes up as to the exercise of this right. It may not always be expedient. It must depend upon discretion, as was eloquently said by the Senator from Kentucky[1] on one occasion. It is a matter of discretion, even as Mr. Jefferson laid it down before this provision existed in the Constitution, before the Government had power to collect its revenue as it now has. I know that when, on a former occasion, I undertook to show, as I thought I did show, clearly and distinctly, the difference between the existence and the exercise of this power, words were put into my mouth that I did not utter, and positions answered which I had never assumed. It was said that I took the bold ground of coercing a State. I expressly disclaimed it. I stated in my speech, that, by the Constitution, we could not put a State into court; but I said there were certain relations created by the Constitution between the Federal Government and the citizen, and that we

[1] Mr. Crittenden.

could enforce those laws against the citizen. I took up the fugitive-slave law; I took up the revenue law; I took up the judicial system; I took up the post-office system; and I might have taken up the power to coin money and to punish counterfeiters, or the power to pass laws to punish mail robbers. I showed that under these we had power, not to punish a State, but to punish individuals as violators of the law. Who will deny it; who can deny it, that acknowledges the existence of the Government? This point, I think, was settled in the decision of the Supreme Court in the case of Ableman *vs.* Booth. When the decision of the Supreme Court is in our favor, we are very much for it; but sometimes we are not so well reconciled to it when it is against us. In that case the court decided, —

"But, as we have already said, questions of this kind must always depend upon the Constitution and laws of the United States, and not of a State. The Constitution was not formed merely to guard the States against danger from foreign nations, but mainly to secure union and harmony at home; for if this object could be obtained, there would be but little danger from abroad; and to accomplish this purpose, it was felt by the statesmen who framed the Constitution, and by the people who adopted it, that it was necessary that many of the rights of sovereignty which the States then possessed should be ceded to the General Government; and that, in the sphere of action assigned to it, it should be supreme, and strong enough to execute its own laws by its own tribunals, without interruption from a State or from State authorities. And it was evident that anything short of this would be inadequate to the main objects for which the Government was established; and that local interests, local passions or prejudices, incited and fostered by individuals for sinister purposes, would lead to acts of aggression and injustice by one State upon the rights of another, which would ultimately terminate in violence and force, unless there was a common arbiter between them, armed with power enough to protect and guard the rights of all, by appropriate laws, to be carried into execution peacefully by its judicial tribunals."[1]

When the fugitive-slave law was executed in the city of Boston, by the aid of military force, was that understood to be coercing a State, or was it simply understood to be an enforcement of the law upon those who, it was assumed, had violated it? In this same decision the Supreme Court declare that the fugitive-slave law, in all its details, is constitutional, and therefore should be enforced. Who is prepared to say that the decision of the court shall not be carried out? Who is prepared to say that the fugitive-slave law shall not be enforced? Do you coerce a State when you simply enforce the law? If one man robs the mail and you seek to arrest him, and he resists, and you employ force, do you call that coercion? If a man counterfeits your coin, and is arrested and convicted, and punishment is resisted, cannot you execute the law? It is true that sometimes so many may become infected with disobedience, outrages and violations of law may be participated in by so many, that they get beyond the control of the ordinary operations of law; the disaffection may swell to such proportions as to

[1] *Howard's Supreme Court Reports*, Vol. XXI. p. 516.

be too great for the Government to control; and then it becomes a matter of discretion, not a matter of constitutional right.

In this connection I desire to introduce an authority from Virginia, for I do delight in authority from the Old Dominion; and from the indications that are now visible — although it is possible that before the setting of the sun I may receive news that will convert my present hopes and my present exhilarated feelings into despair — she is going to make a stand for the Union and the Constitution. I delight in calling upon her for authority. The doctrine that I am trying to inculcate here to-day was the doctrine of Virginia in 1814; and I ask my friend from California to read an extract which I have from the "Richmond Enquirer" of the 1st of November, 1814.

Mr. LATHAM read, as follows: —

"THE TRUE QUESTION. — *The Union is in Danger.* Turn to the convention of Hartford, and learn to tremble at the madness of its authors. How far will those madmen advance? Though they may conceal from *you* the project of disunion, though a few of them may have even concealed it from themselves, yet who will pretend to set bounds to the rage of disaffection? One false step after another may lead them to resistance to the laws, to a treasonable neutrality, to a war against the Government of the United States. In truth, the first act of resistance to the law is *treason* to the United States. Are you ready for this state of things? Will you support the men who would plunge you into this ruin?

"No man, no association of men, no State or set of States *has a right* to withdraw itself from this Union, of its own accord. The same power which knit us together can only unknit. The same formality which forged the links of the Union is necessary to dissolve it. The *majority of States* which form the Union must consent to the withdrawal of *any one* branch of it. Until *that* consent has been obtained, any attempt to dissolve the *Union*, or obstruct the efficacy of its constitutional laws, is treason — treason to all intents and purposes.

"Any other doctrine, such as that which has been lately held forth by the 'Federal Republican,' that any one State may withdraw itself from the Union, is an abominable heresy — which strips its author of every possible pretension to the name or character of a *Federalist.*

"We call, therefore, upon the Government of the Union to exert its energies, when the season shall demand it — and seize the first traitor who shall spring out of the hotbed of the convention of Hartford. This illustrious Union, which has been cemented by the blood of our forefathers, the pride of America and the wonder of the world, must not be tamely sacrificed to the heated brains or the aspiring hearts of a few malcontents. The Union must be saved, when any one shall dare to assail it.

"Countrymen of the East! we call upon you to keep a vigilant eye upon those wretched men who would plunge us into civil war and irretrievable disgrace. Whatever be the temporary calamities which may assail us, let us swear, upon the altar of our country, to SAVE THE UNION."

Mr. JOHNSON continued: — Mr. President, I subscribe most heartily to the sentiment presented by the "Richmond Enquirer" of November 1, 1814. Then it was declared by that high authority that the Union was to be saved; that those persons who were putting themselves in opposition to the law were traitors, and that their treason should be punished as such. Now, sir, what is treason? The Constitution of the United States defines it, and narrows it down to a very small compass. The Constitution declares that "treason against the United States shall consist only in levying war against them, or in adhering to their enemies, giving them aid and comfort." Who are levying war upon the United States? Who are adhering to the enemies of the United States, giving them aid and comfort? Does it require a man to take the lantern of Diogenes, and make a diligent search to find those who have been engaged in levying war against the United States? Will it require any very great research or observation to discover the adherents of those who are making war against the United States, and giving them aid and comfort? If there are any such in the United States, they ought to be punished according to law and the Constitution. [Applause in the galleries, which was suppressed by the Presiding officer, Mr. Fitch in the chair.] Mr. Ritchie, speaking for the Old Dominion, used language that was unmistakable: "The treason springing out of the hot-bed of the Hartford Convention should be punished." It was all right to talk about treason *then;* it was all right to punish traitors in *that* direction. For myself, I care not whether treason be committed North or South; he that is guilty of treason deserves a traitor's fate.

But, Mr. President, when we come to examine the views of some of those who have been engaged in this work, we find that the beginning of their desire to break up the Government dates beyond, and goes very far back of, any recent agitation of the slavery question. There are some men who want to break up this Government anyhow; who want a separation of the Union. There are some who have got tired of a government *by the people.* They fear the people. Take the State of South Carolina. Although she has had Senators on this floor who have acted a portion of the time with the Democratic party, and sometimes with no party, there is, in that State, an ancient and a fixed opposition to a government by the people. They have an early prejudice against this thing called democracy — a government of the people. They entertained the idea of secession at a very early day; it is no new idea with them; it has not arisen out of the slavery question and its recent agitation. Even to this day, the people, the freemen of South Carolina, have never been permitted to vote for President and Vice-President of the United States. They have never enjoyed that great luxury of freemen, of having a voice in the selection of their Chief Magistrate.

I have before me an old volume. In the frontispiece I find a picture of "William Moultrie, Esq., late Governor of South Carolina, and Major-General in the American Revolutionary War." The book is entitled, "Memoirs of the American Revolution, so far as it related to the States of North and South Carolina and Georgia"; and the author is William Moultrie. The Articles of Confederation, it will be remembered, were adopted July 9, 1778. South Carolina was one of the members of the Confederacy — a party to the compact. Charleston was besieged during the Revolutionary War, in 1779, by the British. The defence of the town had been kept up for a considerable length of time, and at last General Moultrie sent a message to the British commander, desiring to know "on what terms he would be disposed to grant a capitulation." The answer of General Prevost was submitted to the Governor, who summoned a council of war, and the result was the following message to the British commander: —

CHARLESTOWN, *May* 12, 1779.

SIR: I cannot possibly agree to so dishonorable a proposal as is contained in your favor of yesterday; but if you will appoint an officer to confer on terms, I will send one to meet him, at such time and place as you fix on.

I have the honor to be, &c.,

WILLIAM MOULTRIE.

Brigadier-General PREVOST.

This is to be found on pages 431 and 432 of Moultrie's Memoirs. On the latter page he says, —

"When the question was carried for giving up the town upon a neutrality, I will not say who was for the question; but this I well remember, that Mr. John Edwards, one of the Privy Council, a worthy citizen, and a very respectable merchant of Charlestown, was so affected as to weep, and said, 'What! are we to give up the town at last!'"

He says that he endeavored to get a message carried from the Governor and Council to General Prevost. Those to whom he applied begged to be excused; but finally he pressed them into a compliance. The message was, —

"To propose a neutrality during the war between Great Britain and America, and the question whether the State shall belong to Great Britain, or remain one of the United States, be determined by the treaty of peace between those two Powers."

The Governor, it seems, proposed a neutrality; proposed to withdraw from the Confederacy, to desist from resistance to Great Britain, and leave it to the two Powers, in making a treaty, to say whether they should remain a colony of Great Britain or be one of the United States. *At this early day South Carolina was willing to go back and be subjected to the Crown of Great Britain under King George III.*

Mr. Wigfall. I ask the Senator merely to permit me to correct him as to a fact.

Mr. Johnson. I do not yield the floor.

Mr. Wigfall. I do not intend to interrupt you ——

Mr. Johnson. I do not yield the floor.

The Presiding Officer.[1] The Senator from Tennessee is entitled to the floor.

Mr. Wigfall. The Articles of Confederation were formed in 1781; that is all.

Mr. Johnson. I have them before me: "Articles of Confederation and Perpetual Union"; and they end: "Done at Philadelphia, in the State of Pennsylvania, the 9th day of July, in the year of our Lord 1778."

[1] Mr. Fitch.

Mr. Wigfall. They were ratified in 1781. If you will read history and inform yourself, you will not fall into so many errors: 1781 is the time; I know it.

Mr. Johnson. I will just refer to the document.

Mr. Wigfall. While the Senator is looking over it, I will merely observe that I made the correction out of kindness to him.

Mr. Johnson. I always prefer having correct ideas, and selecting my own sources of information. [Laughter.]

Mr. Wigfall. The year 1781 was the time the Articles of Confederation were ratified. You were simply mistaken; that is all.

Mr. Johnson. I do not accept the correction, nor have I very much respect for the motive that prompted it. Let that be as it may, however, it does not change the great historical fact that at that day, instead of holding out with the other colonies who were members of the Confederacy and engaged in the war, South Carolina was willing to enter into an agreement of neutrality, and go back under the protection of King George III.

I have another document that I wish to read from; a book called "The Remembrancer, or Impartial Repository of Public Events for the year 1780." In that year the people of Charleston, a large number of them, in view of the difficulties then upon the country, prepared an address, which I ask my friend from California, who reads so much better than I do, to read for me.

Mr. LATHAM read as follows: —

To their Excellencies, SIR HENRY CLINTON, *Knight of the Bath, General of his Majesty's forces, and* MARIOT ARBURTHNOT, *Esq., Vice-Admiral of the Blue, his Majesty's Commissioners to restore peace and good government in the several colonies in rebellion in North America:*

The humble address of divers inhabitants of Charlestown: —

The inhabitants of Charlestown, by the articles of capitulation, are declared prisoners of war on parole; but we, the underwritten, having every inducement to return to our allegiance, and ardently hoping speedily to be readmitted to the character and condition of British subjects, take this opportunity of tendering to your Excellencies our warmest congratulations on the restoration of this capital and province to their political connection with the Crown and Government of Great Britain; an event which will add lustre to your Excellencies' characters, and, we trust, entitle you to the most distinguishing mark of the royal favor. Although the right of taxing America in Parliament excited considerable ferment in the minds of the people of this province, yet it may, with a religious adherence to truth, be affirmed that they did not entertain the most distant thought of dissolving the union that so happily subsisted between them and their parent country; and when, in the progress of that fatal controversy, the doctrine of independency (which originated in the more northern colonies) made its appearance among us, our nature revolted at the idea, and we look back with the most painful regret on those convulsions that gave existence to a power of subverting a constitution for which we always had, and ever shall retain, the most profound veneration, and substituting in its stead a rank democracy, which, however carefully digested in theory, on being reduced into practice has exhibited a system of tyrannic domination only to be found among the uncivilized part of mankind or in the history of the dark and barbarous ages of antiquity.

We sincerely lament that, after the repeal of those statutes which gave rise to the troubles in America, the overtures made by his Majesty's Commissioners, from time to time, were not regarded by our late rulers. To this fatal inattention are to be attributed those calamities which have involved our country in a state of misery and ruin from which, however, we trust it will soon emerge, by the wisdom and clemency of his Majesty's auspicious Government, and the influences of prudential laws, adapted to the nature of the evils we labor under; and that the people will be restored to those privileges, in the enjoyment whereof their former felicity consisted.

Animated with these hopes, we entreat your Excellencies' interposition in assuring his Majesty that we shall glory in every occasion of manifesting that zeal and affection for his person and Government with which gratitude can inspire a free and joyful people.

Charlestown, June 5, 1780.

[Signed by two hundred and ten of the principal inhabitants.] — *The Remembrancer*, Part. II. 1780, p. 84.

Mr. Johnson continued: — It will be seen, from these two documents, what the early notions of the people of South Carolina were. There never was, and I doubt very much whether, with a large portion of them, there ever will be, any idea of the people governing themselves. They had, at that early day, a great aversion to a *government by the people.* It was repudiated; and in the document which has just been read, signed by two hundred and ten citizens of Charleston, they proposed to pass back under the British Government. This carries out the previous proposition to remain with Great Britain by treaty stipulation, and not go through the Revolutionary struggle with the colonies with whom they had formed a confederation.

Again: in 1833, under the pretence of resistance to the operation of our revenue system and to a protective tariff, they endeavored to break up the Government. They were overruled then. Their pride was wounded by that failure; and their determination was fixed, whenever it was in their power, to break up this Government and go out of the Union. This feeling, I have no doubt, has existed there from that period to the present time. When we turn to the debates which recently took place in the South Carolina Convention, we find that Mr. Maxcy Gregg, Mr. Rhett, and others, said that their reason for going out of the Union now dates as far back as forty years; some of them said thirty years, and some twenty. Mr. Gregg said, in the South Carolina Convention, on the 21st of December last, —

"If we undertake to set forth all the causes, do we not dishonor the memory of all the statesmen of South Carolina, now departed, who commenced forty years ago a war against the tariff and against internal improvements, saying nothing of the United States Bank, and other measures, which may now be regarded as obsolete."

Mr. Rhett, on the 24th of December, said, —

"The secession of South Carolina is not an event of a day. It is not anything produced by Mr. Lincoln's election, or by the non-execution of the fugitive-slave law. It has been a matter which has been gathering head for thirty years."

Hence we see that there is a design with some to break up this Government without reference to the slavery question; and the slavery question is by them made a pretence for destroying this Union. They have at length passed their ordinance of secession; they assume to be out of the Union; they declare that they are no longer a member of the Confederacy. Now what are the other States called upon to do? Are the other States called upon to make South Carolina an exemplar? Are those slave States who believe that freemen should govern and that freemen can take care of slave property, to be "precipitated into a revolution" by following the example of South Carolina? Will they do it? What protection, what security will Tennessee, will Kentucky, will Virginia, will Maryland, or any other State, receive from South Carolina by following her example? What protection can she give them? On the contrary, she indulges in a threat towards them — a threat that if they do not imitate her example and come into a new confederacy upon her terms, they are to be put under the ban, and their slave property to be subjected to restraint and restriction. What protection can South Carolina give Tennessee? Any? None upon the face of the earth.

Some of the men who are engaged in the work of disruption and dissolution want Tennessee and Kentucky and Virginia to furnish them with men and money in the event of their becoming engaged in a war for the conquest of Mexico. The Tennesseeans and Kentuckians and Virginians are very desirable when their men and their money are wanted; but what protection does South Carolina give Tennessee? If negro property is endangered in Tennessee, *we* have to defend it and take care of it — not South Carolina, which has been an apple of discord in this Confederacy from my earliest recollection to the present time, complaining of everything, satisfied with nothing. I do not intend to be invidious, but I have sometimes thought that it would be a comfort if Massachusetts and South Carolina could be chained together as the Siamese twins, separated from the continent, and taken out to some remote and secluded part of the ocean, and there fast anchored, to be washed by the waves, and to be cooled by the winds; and after they had been kept there a sufficient length of time, the people of the United States might entertain the proposition of taking them back. [Laughter.] They have been a source of dissatisfaction pretty much ever since they entered the Union; and some experiment of this sort, I think, would operate beneficially upon them; but as they are here, we must try to do the best we can with them.

REPLY TO MR. LANE.

So much, Mr. President, for South Carolina and Louisiana in this struggle. I do not think they are setting examples very worthy of imitation. But, sir, the speech that I made on the 19th of December seems to have produced some little stir; and among other distinguished Senators, the Senator from Oregon[1] felt it his duty, late in the evening, to make a reply to me. I do not see why it was called for from the Senator from Oregon. I did not know that I had said anything that was offensive to him; it was not my intention to do so; it was an inadvertence, if I did. I felt that I had just come out of a campaign in which I had labored hard, and in which I had expended my money and my time in vindicating him and the present Vice-President, who was a candidate for the Presidency, from the charge of favoring secession and disunion. Through the dust and heat, through the mud and rain, I traversed my State, meeting the charge of the Opposition that secession was at the bottom of this movement; that there was a fixed design and plan to break up this Government; that it started at Charleston, and was consummated at Baltimore; and the charge was made that my worthy friend — if I may be permitted to call him such; I thought I was his friend then — was the embodiment of disunion and secession. I met the charge. I denied it. I repudiated it. I tried to convince the people — and I think I did succeed in convincing some of them — that the charge was untrue; and that he and Mr. Breckinridge were the two best Union men in the country. I did not see what there was in my

[1] Mr. Lane.

speech that should extort reply from him, who resided away North. I had not come in conflict with anything that he had said or done. When he was striking these blows at me without cause, I thought it was, at least, unkind. I may not have defended him to his entire satisfaction. It so turned out that we were unfortunate; we were defeated; but I was willing to stand like a man; to stand upon the Constitution and the Union, and, if I must fall, fall decently. After I had gone through the canvass; after I had defended the Senator, and sustained him with my voice and my vote, I thought it was strange that he should attack me in the manner he did. I felt like replying to him, on the spur of the occasion; but it was late in the evening, and by the time he had concluded, the Senate was tired out, and I declined going on. I preferred to let it pass, and submit to all the wrong and injury inflicted upon me. In his speech upon that occasion, the Senator from Oregon made use of the following language: —

"He [alluding to myself] has spoken very handsomely of the gallant conduct of that glorious band, the Northern Democracy of the country, who, though in a minority at home, have struggled for the rights of their Southern brethren — for the equality and rights of all the States. I belong to that portion of the people of this country; and I will say to that honorable gentleman that while they struggle for the constitutional rights of the other States of the Union, as they have always done, and as they will continue to do, there is one thing that they will not do: they will not march under his banner to strike down a gallant, chivalrous, and generous people, contending for rights that have been refused them by the other States of this Union. They will not march with him under his bloody banner, or Mr. Lincoln's, to invade the soil of the gallant State of South Carolina when she may withdraw from a Confederacy that has refused her that equality to which she is entitled, as a member of the Union, under the Constitution. On the contrary, when he or any other gentleman raises that banner and attempts to subjugate that gallant people, instead of marching with him, we will meet him there, ready to repel him and his forces. He shall not bring with him the Northern Democracy to strike down a people contending for rights that have been refused them in a Union that ought to recognize the equality of every member of the Confederacy."

I do not know that I used any argument that should have caused a reply like that. Did anybody hear me use the term "bloody banner"? Did anybody hear me talk about marching down upon South Carolina? Did anybody hear me speak about coercing a State? No.

Mr. LANE. Will the Senator allow me a word?

Mr. JOHNSON. I would rather go on, sir. Why, then, answer positions I did not assume, or attribute to me language that I did not use? Was it in the speech? No. Why, then, use language and assign a position to me which, if not intended, was calculated to make a false impression? What called it forth? What reason was there for it? I saw the consternation which was created. I looked at some of their faces. I knew that I had stirred up animosity, and it was important that somebody from another quarter should make the attack. If the attack had been upon what I said or upon the position I had assumed, I should have no cause to complain; and I do not complain now. Sir, though not very old, I have lived down some men. I have survived many misrepresentations. I feel that I have a conscience and a heart that will lead me to do it again. But when I had said nothing, when I had done nothing, to be struck by him whom I have vindicated, I might well have exclaimed, "That was the unkindest cut of all."

Again: the Senator said, —

"If it should come unfortunately upon this country, inaugurated by a tyrant, who would like to conquer and hold American citizens as vassals, then I will say to that coward who would do it, 'You will walk over your humble servant's body first.' I shall never coöperate with any portion of this country, North or South, that would strike down a people contending for their rights."

I march down upon South Carolina! Did I propose any such thing? No. War is not the natural element of my mind; and, as I stated in that speech, my thoughts were turned on peace, and not on war. I want no strife. I want no war. In the language of a denomination that is numerous in the country, I may say I hate war and love peace. I belong to the peace party. I thought, when I was making that speech, that I was holding out the olive-branch of peace. I wanted to give quiet and reconciliation to a distracted and excited country. That was the object I had in view. War, I repeat, is not the natural element of my mind. I would rather wear upon my garments the dinge of the shop and the dust of the field, as badges of the pursuits of peace, than the gaudy epaulet upon my shoulder, or a sword dangling by my side, with its glittering scabbard, the insignia of strife, of war, of blood, of carnage; sometimes of honorable and glorious war. But, sir, I would rather see the people of the United States at war with every other Power upon the habitable globe, than to be at war with each other. If blood must be shed, let it not be shed by the people of these States, the one contending against the other.

But the Senator went on still further in that discussion. Why it was necessary to follow up his attack upon me, I cannot tell. Alluding to the Senator from Tennessee, he said, —

"He took occasion to give an account of the action of the Senate upon certain resolutions introduced here, setting forth the principles that were made the issue in the late contest, and that were overridden and trodden down. He called the attention of the Senate to a proposition introduced by the honorable Senator from Mississippi[1] to declare that now is the time for action; that a law ought to be passed at this time protecting property in the Territories. Though it was my opinion then that it would have been well to pass such a law, yet that Senator knew, and so did every other one, that it was impossible in this Congress to pass such a law. We might have passed such a bill through this body, but it could never have passed the other. Then it was our duty,

[1] Mr. Brown.

as it was our privilege, to set forth the principles on which this Government reposed, and which must be maintained, or the Government cannot exist. They were the principles upon which this great battle was fought, that resulted in the election of Mr. Lincoln."

Before I take up that proposition in connection with what I said before, I wish to say here that, had the Senator avowed the doctrine prior to the last presidential election that he avowed here in reply to me, expressing his secession and disunion sentiments, I give it as my opinion that he could not have obtained ten thousand votes in the State of Tennessee in the last election, and I think I know what I say. I give that, however, simply as my opinion.

But to come back to the point at which the Senator speaks of the resolutions introduced by the Senator from Mississippi.[1] I had referred to those resolutions to show that there was no occasion for this immediate secession without giving the people time to think or understand what was to be done. I thought so then, and I think so now; and I want to show what the Senator's views were then, and see what has brought about such a change upon his mind since. We find that while those resolutions were under consideration, Mr. CLINGMAN offered an amendment, to come in after the fourth resolution, to insert the following: —

"*Resolved*, That the existing condition of the Territories

[1] Mr. Davis.

of the United States does not require the intervention of Congress for the protection of property in slaves.

"On the question to agree to the amendment proposed by Mr. BROWN, to wit: Strike out of the amendment the word 'not,'

"It was determined in the negative — yeas five, nays forty-three."

Now, by striking out the word "not," it makes the resolution read, —

"*Resolved*, That the existing condition of the Territories of the United States does require the intervention of Congress for the protection of property in slaves."

Mr. BROWN of Mississippi moved to strike out the word "not," thereby making it read that the condition of the Territories does require the protection of Congress for slave property; and upon the yeas and nays being taken on that motion to strike out the word "not," there were — yeas five, nays forty-three.

"On motion of Mr. CLINGMAN,

"The yeas and nays being desired by one fifth of the Senators present, —

"Those who voted in the affirmative are: Messrs. Brown, Clay, Iverson, Johnson of Arkansas, Yulee.

"Those who voted in the negative are: Messrs. Benjamin, Bigler, Bingham, Bragg, Bright, Chandler, Chesnut, Clark, Clingman, Collamer, Crittenden, Davis, Dixon, Doolittle, Fitzpatrick, Foot, Green, Gwin, Hale, Hamlin, Hammond, Hemphill, Hunter, Johnson of Tennessee, Kennedy, Lane, Latham, Mallory, Mason, Nicholson, Pearce, Polk, Powell, Pugh, Rice, Sebastian, Slidell, Ten Eyck, Toombs, Trumbull, Wade, Wigfall, Wilson."

Thus, forty-three Senators recorded their vote

during the last session of Congress that it was not necessary to pass a law to protect slavery in the Territories. The Senator from Oregon, in connection with other Senators, under the solemn sanction of an oath, declared that it was not necessary to pass laws for the protection of slavery in the Territories. What right has South Carolina lost since the last session? What right has any State lost since the last session of Congress? You declared that it was not necessary to pass a law to protect them in the enjoyment of their property in the Territories; and now, forsooth, in the short space of two or three moons, you turn around and tell the country that States are justified in going out of the Union because Congress will not pass a law to protect them in the enjoyment of their property in the Territories, when you said it was not necessary! That is what I call driving the nail in. [Laughter.] I will remark, as I go along, that the eloquent and distinguished Senator who made his valedictory here yesterday, on retiring from the Senate, voted for that identical resolution. This protection was not necessary then. They said it was wholly unnecessary. But since that they have waked up to a sense of its necessity, and resolved to secede if it should not be granted. To this same proposition Mr. ALBERT G. BROWN offered an amendment. Mark you, this is the 25th day of May, 1860; and that is not long ago.

"On motion by Mr. BROWN, to amend the resolution by

striking out all after the word 'resolved,' and in lieu thereof, inserting:"

I wish I had the whole continent here to hear this paragraph: —

"That experience having already shown that the Constitution and the common law, unaided by statutory enactment, do not afford adequate and sufficient protection to slave property; some of the Territories having failed, others having refused to pass such enactments, it has become the duty of Congress to interpose and pass such laws as will afford to slave property in the Territories that protection which is given to other kinds of property."

That is a pretty clear proposition. Upon that, Mr. Brown made an argument, showing the number of slaves in the Territories, and the action of the Legislatures, and concluded that if the time ever would arrive, it was then before Congress, and they should pass a law on the subject. What was the vote upon that? How does it stand? We find, after an argument being made by Mr. Brown, showing that the necessity did exist, according to his argument, the vote upon the proposition stood thus: The question being taken by yeas and nays, it was determined in the negative — yeas three, nays forty-two.

Forty-two Senators voted that you did not need protection; that slavery was not in danger.

"The yeas and nays being desired by one fifth of the Senators present, —

"Those who voted in the affirmative are: Messrs. Brown, Johnson of Arkansas, Mallory."

There were only three. Who said it was not necessary? Who declared, under the solemn sanction of an oath, that protection was not needed?

"Those who voted in the negative, are: Messrs. Benjamin,"—

Ah! Yes; BENJAMIN! —

"Bigler, Bragg, Bright, Chesnut, Clark, Clay, Clingman, Crittenden, Davis, Dixon, Doolittle, Fitzpatrick, Foot, Foster, Green, Grimes, Gwin, Hamlin, Harlan, Hemphill, Hunter," —

HUNTER of Virginia, also! —

"Iverson, Johnson of Tennessee, Lane."

Ah! [Laughter.] Yes, LANE of Oregon voted on the 25th day of last May, that slavery did not need protection in the Territories. Now he will get up and tell the American people and the Senate that he is for a State seceding, and for breaking up the Government, because they cannot get what he swore they did not need. [Laughter.] That is what I call putting the nail through. [Laughter in the galleries.]

The PRESIDING OFFICER.[1] The galleries must preserve order.

Mr. JOHNSON continued: — Then, after voting that it was not necessary to have a proposition to protect slavery in the Territories, the original proposition, as amended, was adopted by a vote of thirty-five yeas to two nays; thus voting all the way through, even to the final action of the Senate,

[1] Mr. Fitch in the chair.

that no such protection was necessary. You have not got protection, your rights, your "equality"; and you tell me now by your position that I have done you injustice by defending you against the charge that you were in favor of a dissolution of the Union! Even if you approved it, it would only show that I was mistaken. I was deceived then; that was your fault; if deceived again, the fault will be mine. I assumed, on that occasion, in reference to the act of ratification of the Constitution by the State of Virginia, that so far as I was capable of examining it, Virginia had made no reservation, no condition, in her ratification of the Constitution of the United States. I had examined the question; I had looked at all the authorities that could be found upon the subject, and I could find no warrant for the assertion; but still the Senator from Oregon, in his reply to me, spoke with great familiarity of the proceedings of that convention ratifying the Constitution, as though he understood it; and with great confidence said it had made a reservation. I will read what he said: —

> "That gallant old State of Virginia, that glorious Old Dominion, made a condition upon which she adopted the Constitution. It became a portion of the compact. And not only Virginia, but New York, made the same condition when she adopted the Constitution; and Rhode Island also."

He spoke with great confidence in this reply to me. He then said: —

"Now, I would ask the honorable Senator from Tennessee, if the time has not arrived when these States ought to resume the powers conferred on a Federal Government; or if it has not, I should like to know when the time can come."

After declaring under the solemn sanction of an oath that no protection was needed, and nothing else has since transpired, he wants to know when the time will come, if it has not come, that they will be justified in breaking up this Confederacy? I saw a good deal of the confusion manifested here that evening; authorities were hunted up, paragraphs marked, and leaves turned down; all, I suppose, to facilitate the intended attack. Sometimes a man had a great deal better read and understand a question for himself before he hazards an opinion. I will not say that that is the case with the honorable Senator, for I should proceed upon the idea that he was laboring under the impression that he understood it exactly. It is not a very uncommon occurrence to be mistaken. Sometimes the mistake results from a want of examination; sometimes from an incapacity to understand the subject, and various other causes. So it is that it occurs very frequently we labor under false impressions. We find, when we come to examine this subject of the ratification of the Constitution by Virginia, that a committee was appointed in the convention of Virginia, and that that committee reported a set of resolutions. They reported one resolution in lieu of the preamble. That resolution is as follows: —

"*Resolved*, That previous to the ratification of the new Constitution of Government recommended by the late Federal Convention, a declaration of rights, asserting and securing from encroachment the great principles of civil and religious liberty, and the inalienable rights of the people, together with amendments to the most exceptionable parts of the said Constitution of Government, ought to be referred by this convention to the other States in the American Confederacy for their consideration." [1]

Here was a proposition making conditions; and upon a vote to adopt this amendment it was voted down — ayes eighty, noes eighty-eight. Then what follows? The committee reported an ordinance adopting the Constitution of the United States; but in their ordinance they go on and make a kind of preamble, or a whereas, a declaration as to their understanding — not conditions, not reservations — but a declaration of their understanding. What do they say?

"We, the delegates of the people of Virginia, duly elected in pursuance of a recommendation from the General Assembly, and now met in convention, having fully and freely investigated and discussed the proceedings of the Federal Convention, and being prepared as well as the most mature deliberations hath enabled us, to decide thereon," —

Now, mark you, —

"do, in the name and in the behalf of the people of Virginia, declare and make known, that the powers granted

[1] *Elliot's Debates*. Vol. III. p. 653.

under the Constitution, being derived from the people of the United States, be resumed by them whensoever the same shall be perverted to their injury or oppression."[1]

They declare, in behalf of Virginia, that the powers of the Constitution are derived from the people of the United States, to "be resumed by them whenever they shall be converted to their injury or oppression." Who is to resume them? The people of the United States. That idea was always inculcated by James Madison. What more do they say? This is not the ratifying clause. They say, —

"With these impressions," —

Not these conditions, not these reservations, —

"With these impressions, with a solemn appeal to the Searcher of hearts, for the purity of our intentions, and under the conviction that whatsoever imperfections may exist in the Constitution ought rather to be examined in the mode prescribed therein, than to bring the Union into danger by delay with a hope of obtaining amendments previous to the ratification,"

Now comes the ordinance of adoption; and what is it?

"We, the said delegates, in the name and behalf of the people of Virginia, do, by these presents, *assent to* and *ratify the Constitution*, recommended on the 17th day of September, 1787, by the Federal Convention, for the Government of the United States; hereby announcing to all whom it may concern that the said Constitution is binding upon the said people, according to an authentic copy hereunto annexed in the words following."[2]

[1] *Elliot's Debates*, Vol. III. p. 656. [2] Idem.

Is there any reservation or condition there? It seems to me that the sight of a man would be tolerably keen that could see a condition there. When was this? We find that Virginia adopted that on Tuesday, June 26, 1788. When did South Carolina come into the Union? Before Virginia did. If Virginia made a condition, South Carolina was already in. How many States were in? The covenant was formed and had been ratified by nine States before Virginia came into the Union. The idea of Virginia appending conditions after the Government was formed and the Constitution ratified by nine States!

But, to make this thing more clear, Mr. Madison, while in New York, received a letter from Mr. Hamilton, stating that he had some doubts as to the ratification of the Constitution by New York; that they wanted some conditions, and one condition was, that they might have the privilege to recede within five or seven years in the event certain amendments were not adopted to the Constitution. I should have remarked, before passing to this, that they adopted it, not wanting delay, and then went in the same committee to report a long list of amendments to be submitted, and some of them were ratified afterwards by the different States. Mr. Madison writes, in reply to Mr. Hamilton, and tells him, if the Constitution is adopted, it must be adopted *in toto*, without reservation or condition. I am inclined to think Mr. Madison had some idea of this ordinance. I think he understood it. Here is his letter. That ordinance was adopted in Virginia on June 26, 1787, and, in reply to Mr. Hamilton, in the following July, Mr. Madison said, —

> "The idea of reserving a right to withdraw was started at Richmond, and considered as a conditional ratification, which was itself abandoned as worse than a rejection."

Does not that show that I have put the correct interpretation upon it? James Madison understood it as being an abandonment. I would as soon rely upon *his* construction of the ordinance that brought Virginia into the Union as I would on that of the distinguished Senator from Oregon. I am inclined to think he was quite as familiar with the history of that transaction and with the whole subject as the Senator from Oregon, with all his familiarity and astuteness on the subject. So much in answer to that portion of the Senator's argument. We find, upon an examination, as I before remarked, that nine States had ratified the Constitution before Virginia came in. New York, North Carolina, and Rhode Island came in afterwards. Mr. Madison so understood it. The fathers of the Republic so understood it. The country so understand it. Common sense so understands it. Practicability so understands it. Everything that pertains to the preservation and salvation of the Government so understands it, as contradistinguished from the admission of this doctrine of secession.

But let us progress a little further. The Government was formed; the Constitution was ratified; and after the Constitution was ratified and the Government in existence, there is provision made, for what? "New States may be admitted by the Congress into this Union." These are the words of the Constitution. Congress has the power to prescribe the terms and conditions of admission of a new State into the Union; and in the discretion of Congress, they are admitted upon an equal footing with the other States. It being an express grant to admit, I say the Federal Government can exercise incidents that are necessary and proper to carry the admission of States into existence upon such a basis as they believe the good of the Government demands. I am not so sure but the admission of a new State is placed upon a different ground from that of one of the original States ratifying the Constitution. As the Senator seems to be so familiar with things of this sort, I will refer to the act admitting the State of Alabama:—

An act to enable the people of Alabama Territory to form a Constitution and State Government, and for the admission of such State into the Union on an equal footing with the original States. (Approved March 2, 1819.)

Be it enacted, &c., That the inhabitants of the Territory of Alabama be, and they are hereby, authorized to form for themselves a Constitution and State Government, and to assume such name as they may think proper; and that the said Territory, when formed into a State, shall be admitted into the Union upon the same footing with the original States, in all respects whatever.

Here is the ordinance of Alabama accepting the terms of the above act, passed 2d August, 1819: —

"This convention, for and in behalf of the people inhabiting this State, do accept the propositions offered by the act of Congress under which they are assembled; and this convention, for and in behalf of the people inhabiting this State, do ordain, agree, and declare." . . . . .

"And this ordinance is hereby declared irrevocable without the consent of the United States."

This act was declared irrevocable. They agreed to the conditions offered to them in the act of Congress with reference to the public lands and other subjects, and then the ordinance of coming into the Union was declared irrevocable without the consent of the United States. Congress then passed an act accepting them upon the terms they imposed. That was the compact. What has been done to Alabama? What great complaint has she? Why should she leave the Union in such hot haste?

So much for that, sir. In the remarks that I made when I last addressed the Senate, I referred to the Constitution of the State of Tennessee, which was adopted in 1796, and their Bill of Rights, in which they declare that they would never surrender or give up the navigation of the Mississippi to any people. The Senator from Oregon, on that occasion, in reply to me, used the following language: —

"Then he is concerned about the navigation of the Mississippi River. He says that the great State of Tennessee and he, himself, are concerned about the navigation of that river. I believe it is recognized as the law of nations, as the law of all civilized nations, that a great inland sea running through several Governments shall be open equally to all of them; and besides, as the honorable Senator from Louisiana said, there is no man in Louisiana that would think for a moment of depriving Tennessee of the right of navigating that great river. No, sir, nor Kentucky either, nor Indiana, nor Illinois, nor any other State whose waters flow into that mighty stream. No such thing would ever be done."

That was the Senator's declaration then, that nobody would question the right of those States to navigate that great inland sea. He seemed to show great familiarity with international law. I took it for granted that he had read Grotius and Wheaton upon international law, and all the other authorities on the subject, for he spoke about it with great familiarity, as if he understood it well. How does the matter stand, sir? Before the printer's ink that impressed his speech upon the paper is dry, we find an ordinance passed, as I remarked before, by the State of Louisiana, declaring negatively that she has the right to control the navigation of that river under her act of secession. If the Senator had put himself to the trouble, as I presume he did, or ought to have done, to examine this subject, he would have found that the navigation of the Mississippi River has been a subject of negotiation for years upon years. He would have found that the navigation of various rivers throughout the world has been the subject of long, angry, and contested negotiation. While upon this point, I desire to present to the Senate an extract from a leading authority on this subject. I read from Wheaton's "Elements of International Law": —

"The territory of the State includes the lakes, seas, and rivers entirely enclosed within its limits. The rivers which flow through the territory also form a part of the domain, from their sources to their mouths, or as far as they flow within the territory, including the bays or estuaries formed by their junction with the sea. Where a navigable river forms the boundary of coterminous States, the middle of the channel, or *thalweg*, is generally taken as the line of separation between the two States, the presumption of law being that the right of navigation is common to both; but this presumption may be destroyed by actual proof of prior occupancy and long undisturbed possession, giving to one of the riparian proprietors the exclusive title to the entire river.

"Things of which the use is inexhaustible, such as the sea and running water, cannot be so appropriated as to exclude others from using these elements in any manner which does not occasion a loss or inconvenience to the proprietor. This is what is called an *innocent use*. Thus we have seen that the jurisdiction possessed by one nation over sounds, straits, and other arms of the sea leading through its own territory to that of another, or to other seas common to all nations, does not exclude others from the right of innocent passage through these communications. The same principle is applicable to rivers flowing from one State through the territory of another into the sea, or into the territory of a third State. The right of navigating, for commercial purposes, a river, which flows through the territories of different States, is common to all the nations inhabiting the different parts of its banks; but this right of innocent passage being what the text writers call an *imperfect right*, its exercise is necessarily modified by the safety and convenience of the State affected by it, and can only be effectually secured by mutual convention regulating the mode of its exercise.

"It seems that this right draws after it the incidental right of using all the means which are necessary to the secure enjoyment of the principal right itself. Thus the Roman law, which considered navigable rivers as public or common property, declared that the right to the use of the shores was incident to that of the water; and that the right to navigate a river involved the right to moor vessels to its banks, to lade and unlade cargoes, &c. The public jurists apply this principle of the Roman civil law to the same case between nations, and infer the right to use the adjacent land for these purposes, as means necessary to the attainment of the end for which the free navigation of the water is permitted." [1]

Now, what are we told? That Louisiana, for which we paid $15,000,000, whose battles we fought, whose custom-houses, forts, arsenals, dock-yards, and hospitals we built, — in the exercise of the plenitude of her power, declares that she has control of the Mississippi, and such States may navigate that stream as are on friendly relations with her, she being the judge. Is not this what the dogma of secession leads us to? We see where it carries us; we see in what it will end — litigation, war, and bloodshed. As I remarked before, as we approach and advance in the investigation of the subject, we discover its enormities more and

[1] *Wheaton's Elements of International Law*, Part II. chap. 4, pp. 252–254.

more. I repeat, it is the prolific mother of anarchy, which is the next step to despotism itself. The Senator from Oregon seems not to be apprehensive at all; and yet, before his voice has done reverberating in the Hall, we have the open declaration that they intend to exercise the control of the navigation of the Mississippi. Would it not have been better for Louisiana ——

Mr. LANE. I think the Senator ought to allow me to say a word.

Mr. JOHNSON. I do not want to be interrupted. I certainly mean no discourtesy at all to the Senator.

Mr. LANE. I only wish to say, in the way of explanation, that the people of New Orleans have had police regulations by which they have collected taxes to improve their wharves ever since New Orleans belonged to this country.

Mr. JOHNSON. It is a very common thing in all cities where there are wharves, either on the river or ocean, to have what is commonly called a wharfage tax. We understand that. The navigation of the high seas and rivers is a different thing from paying wharfage and a little tax to defray the expense of keeping wharves and docks up. We understand all about that. That is a very different affair from placing batteries at this early day upon the banks of that great stream.

Mr. LANE. That was against the common enemy.

Mr. JOHNSON. I did not know we had any enemies in these States. I thought we were brothers, and were entitled to carry on free trade from one extremity of this Confederacy to the other. I did not know that the people of Indiana and Illinois and Kentucky and Tennessee, going along down that river, had got to be enemies. I suppose, however, when we look at these things our minds change and vary by varying circumstances. When we are candidates for the Presidency, we feel more like brothers; but when we have made the experiment, and signally failed, I suppose the enemy's line begins just at the line where our defeat was consummated. [Laughter and applause in the galleries.]

The PRESIDING OFFICER called to order.

Mr. JOHNSON continued: — How long has it been since we were prepared to go to war with the most formidable Power upon earth because she claimed the right of search? We would not concede to Great Britain the right of searching our ships on the high seas; and yet what do we now see? Batteries placed upon the banks of the Mississippi to enforce the right of search. Do we not see where it will lead? Do we not all know in what it will end?

I have no disposition to do the Senator from Oregon, or any other Senator, injustice. In this connection, I will say, as I have intimated before, that I thought his attack upon me unkind and uncalled for. Let that be as it may, it is not my disposition or my intention, on this occasion, to do him injustice. I intend to do him full justice. In the reply that he made to me — to which I yesterday referred — he gave the contradiction direct to what I stated in the presidential canvass, in answer to the charge that had been made that you, Mr. President, and the Senator from Oregon, were disunionists, were in favor of secession; and that you were used by what was called the seceding or disunion party for the purpose of disrupting and breaking up the Government. I met those charges — because I believed they were untrue, that they were not founded in fact — in various places, before large assemblies, and, I thought, successfully, at least to my own mind, exonerated you and the candidate for the Vice-Presidency from the charge. I confess it was somewhat mortifying to me, after the reply which the Senator made, to have to say to the people, and the country generally, that I vindicated him against a charge which was true; for, when we take up his speech here in reply to the remarks that I made on that occasion, none of which had the slightest reference to him, involving neither his position before the country, nor his consistency as a legislator, we find that he took bold ground, advocating and justifying secession, arguing, in fact, that it was constitutional. I felt, after that speech, that I was involved in inconsistency before my people, an inconsistency in which I ought not to have been involved.

But in the same speech in which the honorable

Senator involved me in these contradictions, he goes on to state, — and I will do him justice by reading his speech, for I do not want to misquote him, —

> "But, sir, understand me; I am not a disunionist. I am for the right, and I would have it in the Union; and if it cannot be obtained there, I would go out of the Union, and have that out of the Union that I could not obtain in it, though I was entitled to it."

Mr. President, I have called the attention of the Senate to the paragraph of the Senator's speech which I have just read, in which he disavows disunion sentiments; but when you take the preceding part of his speech, you find that he advocates the doctrine of disunion and secession almost from the beginning up to the sentence that I have read. It seems to me it is paradoxical; but that may be my misfortune, not his. He may be capable of reconciling the conflict, the seeming inconsistency of first advocating the doctrine of dissolution, secession, and disunion, and then at the same time exclaiming that he is no disunionist. I do not know how a Senator can be for the Union, and at the same time concede the right that a State has the authority to secede under the Constitution; that it is justified in seceding, and ought to secede; that when it demands rights in the Union that it cannot get, it should go out of the Union to obtain that which could not be obtained in it. But let all that pass. I wish to do him no injustice; therefore

I desired to call attention to his disclaimer of being a disunionist and a secessionist.

Mr. President, the Senator, in the sentence I have quoted, assumes that South Carolina, for instance, had the right to secede ; and he says also that South Carolina can obtain that out of the Union which she has failed to obtain in it. Let us raise the inquiry here : What is it, since she entered into this Confederacy of States, that South Carolina has desired or asked at the hands of the Federal Government, or demanded upon constitutional ground, that she has not obtained ? What great wrong, what great injury has been inflicted upon South Carolina by her continuance in this Union of States ? I know it is very easy, and even Senators have fallen into the habit of it, to repeat some phrases almost as a chorus to a song, such as, "If we cannot get our rights in the Union, we will go out of the Union and obtain those rights ; that we are for the equality of the States in the Union, and if we cannot get it we will go out of the Union," I suppose to bring about that equality. What is the point of controversy in the public mind at this time ? Let us look at the question as it is. We know that the issue which has been before the country to a very great extent, and which, in fact, has recently occupied the consideration of the public, is the territorial question. It is said that South Carolina has been refused her rights in the Union, with reference to that territorial question, and therefore she is going out of the Union to obtain that which she cannot get in it.

Now, Mr. President, when we come to examine this subject, how does the matter stand? I showed yesterday, in reference to the protection of slave property in the Territories of this Confederacy, that South Carolina, in connection with the distinguished Senator from Oregon, had voted expressly that no slavery code was needed; that no further protection was needed, so far as Congress was concerned. They decided it here in this body. South Carolina, by her own vote, on the 25th day of May last, decided that she needed no further protection in the Territories of the United States, so far as Congress was concerned. The Senator from Oregon voted with her. That vote seemed to be connected with and predicated upon the great fact that the Supreme Court of the United States had decided this question; that they had declared the Missouri Compromise — in other words, the law excluding slavery north of 36° 30′, and making it permissive south of 36° 30′ — unconstitutional and void; and, according to our forms of Government, it was in fact stricken from the statute-book by the decision of the court. They thereby said to the country, the supreme arbiter of the land, so made by the Constitution of the United States, has decided that the people have a right, without regard to the character or description of their property, to carry it into all the Territories of the United States, and that under the Constitution of the United States it is protected there. It was said, the court having decided that they had a right to go there with this institution of slavery, and the Constitution finding it there, it was recognized and protected by the Constitution of the United States.

In this connection, permit me to go outside of the Senate Chamber, and state what occurred in my own State. There, those who were the best friends of the distinguished Senator from Oregon, and who are ultra upon this subject, before thousands of the people of that State took the bold ground that they wanted no further protection from Congress; that the Constitution of the United States and the opinion of the Supreme Court were all the slavery code they desired; that the question was settled; that the power was complete; and that protection was ample.

In this connection, sir, we must recollect the decision made by the Senate upon the resolutions introduced by the Senator from Mississippi[1] on the 25th day of May last. On that day, under the solemn sanction of an oath, and all the formalities of legislation spread upon the journals, the yeas and nays being taken, we declared, after an argument on the subject, that no further protection was needed at that time. The Senate went on and stated, in the fifth resolution — I give the substance, I do not pretend to repeat the words — that if hereafter it should become necessary to have protection

[1] Mr. Davis.

of this kind, then Congress should give it; but they said it was unnecessary at that time. If South Carolina and the Senator from Oregon took this position then, what has transpired since that period of time that now justifies a State in withdrawing or seceding from this Union, on account of Congress not doing that which they declared was not necessary to be done?

But let us take the fact as it is. South Carolina, it is said, wanted protection in the Territories. I have shown that she said, herself, that further protection was not needed; but if it should be needed, then Congress should give it. But South Carolina, — the Kingdom of South Carolina, — in the plentitude of her power, and upon her own volition, without consultation with the other States of this Confederacy, has gone out of the Union, or assumed to go out. The next inquiry is: What does South Carolina now get, in the language of the distinguished Senator from Oregon, out of the Union that she did not get in the Union? Is there a man in South Carolina to-day that wants to carry a single slave into any Territory we have got in the United States that is now unoccupied by slave property? I am almost ready to hazard the assertion that there is not one. If he had not the power and the right to carry his slave property into a Territory while in the Union, has he obtained that right now by going out of the Union? Has anything been obtained by violating the Constitution of the United

States, by withdrawing from the sisterhood of States, that could not have been obtained in it? Can South Carolina now any more conveniently and practically carry slavery into the Territories than she could before she went out of the Union? Then what has she obtained? What has she got, even upon the doctrine laid down by the distinguished Senator from Oregon?

But it is argued, striding over the Constitution and violating that comity and faith which should exist amongst the States composing this Confederacy, that she had a right to secede; she had a right to carry slaves into the Territories; and therefore she will secede and go out of the Union. This reasoning on the part of South Carolina is about as sound as that of the madman, who assumed that he had dominion over the beasts of the forest, and therefore that he had a right to shear a wolf. His friends remonstrated with him, and, admitting his right to do so, inquired of him if he had considered the danger and the difficulty of the attempt. "No," said the madman, "I have not considered that; that is no part of my consideration; man has the dominion over the beasts of the forest, and therefore he has a right to shear a wolf; and as I have a right to do, so I will exercise it." His friends still remonstrated and expostulated, and asked him, not only, "Have you considered the danger, the difficulty, and the consequences resulting from such an attempt; but, what will the shearing be worth?"

"But," he replied, "I have the right, and therefore I will shear a wolf." South Carolina has the right, according to the doctrine of the seceders and disunionists of this country, to go out of the Union, and therefore she will go out of the Union.

And what, Mr. President, has South Carolina gained by going out? It has been just about as profitable an operation as the shearing of the wolf by the madman. Can she now carry slaves into the Territories? Does she even get any division of the Territories? None; she has lost all that. Does she establish a right? No; but by the exercise of this abstract right, as contended for by secessionists, what has she got? Oppression, taxation, a reign of terror over her people, as the result of their rashness in the exercise of this assumed right. In what condition is her people now? They have gone out of the Union to obtain their rights, to maintain their liberty, to get that out of the Union which they could not get in it! While they were in the Union, they were not taxed a million and some six or seven or eight hundred thousand dollars, in addition to their usual expenditures, to sustain standing armies and to meet other expenditures which are incurred by separation. But still she has the right to tax her people; she has the right to institute a reign of terror; she has the right to exclude her people from the ballot-box; and she has exercised the right, and these are the consequences. She has got her rights! She has gone out of the Union to be relieved from taxes, and has increased the burdens upon her people fourfold. All this is in the exercise of her right!

Mr. President, when we examine this subject, and follow it step by step, to see what is gained by this movement, human reason deplores the folly which it exhibits. The public mind seems to have been inflamed to madness, and in its delirium it overbears all restraint. To some it appears that our admirable system of civil liberty is crumbling to pieces; that the temple of Liberty is upheaved; that its columns are falling, and that nothing will remain but a general ruin; and in their consternation too many stand back appalled, and take no position for the relief of their country in the pending crisis. But, sir, the relation that we bear to the people of the United States requires every man, whether Senator or Representative, or even private citizen, to come forward as a patriot and lover of his country, and look at the condition of the country as it is. Without regard to the consequences upon myself, I have determined to meet this question, and to present my views to the country in such form as I believe to be right and proper.

Sir, let us look at the contest through which we are passing, and consider what South Carolina, and the other States who have undertaken to secede from the Confederacy, have gained. What is the great difficulty which has existed in the public mind? We know that, practically, the territorial question is settled. Then what is the cause for breaking up this great Union of States? Has the Union or the Constitution encroached upon the rights of South Carolina or any other State? Has this glorious Union, that was inaugurated by the adoption of the Constitution, which was framed by the patriots and sages of the Revolution, harmed South Carolina or any other State? No; it has offended none; it has protected all. What is the difficulty? We have some bad men in the South, — the truth I will speak, — and we have some bad men in the North, who want to dissolve this Union in order to gratify their unhallowed ambition. And what do we find here upon this floor and upon the floor of the other House of Congress? Words of crimination and recrimination are heard. Bad men North say provoking things in reference to the institutions of the South, and bad men and bad-tempered men of the South say provoking and insulting things in return; and so goes on a war of crimination and recrimination in reference to the two sections of the country, and the institutions peculiar to each. They become enraged and insulted, and then they are denunciatory of each other; and what is the result? The Abolitionists, and those who entertain their sentiments, abuse men of the South, and men of the South abuse them in return. They do not fight each other; but they both become offended and enraged. One is dissatisfied with the other; one is insulted by the other; and then, to seek revenge, to gratify themselves, they both agree to make war upon the Union that never offended or injured either. Is this right? What has this Union done? Why should these contending parties make war upon it because they have insulted and aggrieved each other? This glorious Union, that was spoken into existence by the fathers of the country, must be made war upon to gratify these animosities. Shall we, because we have said bitter things of each other which have been offensive, turn upon the Government, and seek its destruction, and entail all the disastrous consequences upon commerce, upon agriculture, upon the industrial pursuits of the country, that must result from the breaking up of a great Government like this? What is to be gained out of the Union that we cannot get in it? Anything? I have been zealously contending for — and intend to continue to contend for — every right, even to the ninth part of a hair, that I feel the State which I have the honor in part to represent is entitled to. I do not intend to demand anything but that which is right; and I will remark, in this connection, that there is a spirit in the country which, if it does not exist to a very great extent in this Hall, does exist in the great mass of the people North and South, to do what is right; and if the question could be taken away from politicians; if it could be taken away from the Congress of the United States, and referred to the great mass of the intelligent voting population of the United States, they would settle it without the slightest difficulty, and bid defiance to secessionists and disunionists. [Applause in the galleries.]

The VICE-PRESIDENT. There must be many persons in the galleries who have been warned again and again that order must be maintained. I hope not to have occasion to refer to the subject again.

Mr. JOHNSON. Mr. President, I have an abiding confidence in the people; and if it were so arranged to-day that the great mass of the American people could be assembled in an amphitheatre capacious enough to contain them all, and the propositions which have been presented here to preserve this Union, could be reduced to a tangible shape, and submitted to them, politicians being left out of view, the question being submitted to the great mass of the people, it being their interest to do right, they being lovers of their country, having to pay all, having to produce all, having to provide all, there would be but one single response, "Do that which will give satisfaction, ample and complete, to the various and conflicting sections of this glorious Republic."

But, sir, how are we situated? There are politicians here, and throughout the land, some of whom want to break up the Union, to promote their own personal aggrandizement; some, on the other hand, desire the Union destroyed that slavery may be extinguished. Then let me appeal to every patriot in the land, in view of this state of things, to come forward and take the Government out of the hands of the Goths and Vandals, wrest it from the Philistines, save the country, and hand it down to our children as it has been handed down to us.

I have already asked what is to be gained by the breaking up of this Confederacy. An appeal is made to the border slaveholding States to unite in what is commonly styled the Gulf Confederacy. If there is to be a division of this Republic, I would rather see the line run anywhere than between the slaveholding and the non-slaveholding States, and the division made on account of a hostility, on the one hand, to the institution of slavery, and a preference for it, on the other; *for whenever that line is drawn, it is the line of civil war; it is the line at which the overthrow of slavery begins; the line from which it commences to recede.* Let me ask the border States, if that state of things should occur, who is to protect them in the enjoyment of their slave property? Will South Carolina, that has gone madly out, protect them? Will Mississippi and Alabama and Louisiana, still further down towards the Gulf? Will they come to our rescue, and protect us? Shall we partake of their frenzy, adopt the mistaken policy into which they have fallen, and begin the work of the destruction of the institution in which we are equally interested with them? I have already said that I believe the dissolution of this Union will be the commencement of the overthrow and destruction of the institution of slavery. In a Northern confederacy, or in a Southern confederacy, or in a Middle confederacy, the border slaveholding States will have to take care of that particular species of property by their own strength, and by whatever influence they may exert in the organization in which they may be placed. The Gulf States cannot, they will not, protect us. We shall have to protect ourselves, and perchance to protect them. As I remarked yesterday, my own opinion is, that the great desire to embrace the border States, as they are called, in this particular and exclusive Southern confederacy, which it is proposed to get up, is not that they want us there out of pure good-will, but they want us there as a matter of interest; so that if they are involved in war, in making acquisitions of territory still further south, or war growing out of any other cause, they may have a *corps de reserve*, they may have a power behind, that can furnish them men and money, — men that have the hearts and the souls to fight and meet an enemy, come from what quarter he may.

What have we to gain by that? The fact that two taken from four leaves but two remaining, is not clearer to my mind than it is that the dissolution of the Union is the beginning of the destruction of slavery; and that if a division be accomplished, as some desire, directly between the slaveholding and the non-slaveholding States, the work will be commenced most effectually. Upon this point I propose to read a short extract from South Carolina herself. Mr. Boyce, late a member of the other House, a distinguished man, a man of talent, and I believe a good man, and who, I have no doubt, in his heart this day regrets most deeply and sincerely the course which South Carolina has taken, said, in 1851, when the same issue was presented, -

> "Secession, separate nationality, with all its burdens, is no remedy. It is no redress for the past; it is no security for the future. It is only a magnificent sacrifice to the present, without in any wise gaining in the future." . . . . . .
>
> "For the various reasons I have stated, I object in as strong terms as I can, to the secession of South Carolina. Such is the intensity of my conviction on this subject, that if secession should take place — of which I have no idea, for I cannot believe in the existence of such a stupendous madness — I shall consider the institution of slavery as doomed, and that the great God, in our blindness, has made us the instruments of its destruction."

He said then, that if South Carolina, in her madness, (but he did not believe she could,) should determine upon secession, he would look upon it that the great God had doomed the institution of slavery. This is the opinion of one of the most distinguished and, I conscientiously believe, best men of South Carolina.

But, sir, I pass on from the paragraph of the speech of the honorable Senator from Oregon to which I have referred; and as there seems to have been a sort of arrangement — at least it appears so to my mind — to make and keep up an attack on me, because I agreed with Mr. Boyce of South Carolina in this respect; because I agreed with many distinguished men; and because I advanced the doctrines of the fathers who formed the Republic, I shall take up these Senators in the order in which I was attacked. Without being egotistical, without being vain, when I feel that I have got truth on my side, when I feel that I am standing on principle, when I know that I have got facts and arguments that cannot be answered, I never inquire as to the difference of ability or experience between myself and those with whom I have to contend.

REPLY TO MR. DAVIS.

The next Senator in order that made an attack upon me on account of my previous speech was the distinguished Senator from Mississippi,[1] who took occasion to do so in making his valedictory address to the Senate after his State had passed her ordinance of secession. It has been the case not only with that Senator, but with others, that an attempt has been made by innuendo, by indirection, by some side remark, to convey the impression that a certain man has a tendency or bearing towards Black Republicanism or Abolitionism. Sometimes gentlemen who cannot establish such a charge, are yet willing to make it, not directly, but

[1] Mr. Davis.

by innuendo, to create a false impression on the public mind, —

> "Willing to wound, but yet afraid to strike."

If the charge can be successfully made, why not make it directly, instead of conveying it by innuendo? The Senator from Mississippi did not attempt to reply to my speech, did not answer my arguments, did not meet my authorities, did not controvert my facts; but after reaching a certain point in his own argument, he disposes of all that I had said in these very few words, —

> "I am here confronted with a question which I will not argue. The position which I have taken necessarily brings me to its consideration. Without arguing it, I will merely mention it. It is the right of a State to withdraw from the Union. The President says it is not a constitutional right. The Senator from Ohio,[1] and his *ally*, the Senator from Tennessee, argued it as no right at all."

Is that the way for a Senator, a distinguished Senator, an Ajax of his peculiar sect, — for when we come to examine this doctrine of secession, it is only broad enough to found a sect upon; it is not comprehensive enough, it has not scope enough, on which to found a great national party, — to notice the arguments of others? The Senator from Mississippi would not argue the right of secession. I say, that if any government be organized hereafter, in which this principle of secession is recognized, it will result in its destruction and

[1] Mr. Wade.

overthrow. But the Senator says that the Senator from Ohio,[1] and "his ally from Tennessee," regard secession as no right at all; and by that statement the whole argument is answered. What is the idea here? Let us talk plainly, though courteously and respectfully. What was the idea which this remark was calculated, if not intended, to convey? I am free to say, that I think it was intended, as well as calculated, to convey the impression that the Senator from Tennessee was an ally of Mr. Wade of Ohio, who was a Republican; and the whole speech of the Senator from Tennessee, the authorities, the facts, and the arguments, are all upturned by that single allusion. Thank God, there is too much good sense and intelligence in this country, to put down any man by an innuendo or side remark like that. But, sir, so far as the people whom I have the honor in part to represent are concerned, I stand above innuendoes of that kind. They have known me from my boyhood up. They understand my doctrines and my principles, in private and in public life. They have tried me in every position in which it was in their power to place a public servant, and they, to-day, will not say that Andrew Johnson ever deceived or betrayed them. In a public life of twenty-five years, they have never deserted or betrayed me; and, God willing, I will never desert or betray them. The great mass of

[1] Mr. Wade.

the people of Tennessee know that I am for them; they know that I have advocated those great principles and doctrines upon which the perpetuity of this Government depends; they know that I have perilled my all, pecuniarily and physically, in vindication of their rights and their interests. Little innuendoes, thrown off in snarling moods, fall harmless at my feet.

It was said that I was the *ally* of the Senator from Ohio. I turn to the doings of the committee of thirteen to show who were *allies* there. I do not inquire what a man's antecedents have been when there is a great struggle to preserve the existence of the Government; but my first inquiry is, are you for preserving this Government? are you for maintaining the Constitution upon which it rests? If Senator Wade, or Senator anybody else, is willing to come up to this great work, either by amending the Constitution of the United States, or passing laws that will preserve and perpetuate this great Union, I am his ally and he is mine; and I say to every Senator, to every member of the House of Representatives, to every man that loves his country throughout the length and breadth of this great Confederacy, if you are for preserving this Union on its great and fundamental principles, I am your ally, without reference to your antecedents, or to what may take place hereafter. I say to all such men, come forward, and, like gallant knights, let us lock our shields and make common cause for this glorious people. If I were to indulge in a similar kind of innuendo, by way of repartee, where would the Senator from Mississippi find himself? In the committee of thirteen, a resolution was introduced by the distinguished Senator from New York[1] — who, I must say, since this question has sprung up, has given every indication of a desire for reconciliation and for compromise, and of a disposition to preserve the Government, that a man occupying his position could do — to this effect: —

> "*Resolved*, That the following article be, and the same is hereby, proposed and submitted as an amendment to the Constitution of the United States, to be valid, to all intents and purposes, as a part of said Constitution, when ratified by the Legislatures of three fourths of the States:
>
> "1. No amendment shall be made to the Constitution which will authorize or give to Congress the power to abolish, or interfere, within any State, with the domestic institutions thereof, including that of persons held to labor or service by the laws of said State."

That was a proposition which was calculated, to a very great extent, to allay the apprehensions and the fears that have been entertained in the South in reference to the institution of slavery. Why do I say so? We know what the argument has been before the Southern mind. It has been: first, that the Northern anti-slavery party wanted to abolish slavery in the District of Columbia, as an entering wedge; next, to exclude it from the

[1] Mr. Seward.

Territories, following up the attack upon slavery; but these points were looked upon as of minor importance; they were looked upon as outposts, as the prelude to an interference with the institution within the States, which has been supposed to be the great end and the great consideration. Do you not know this to be the argument: that they were merely taking these positions as entering wedges to an interference with the institution of slavery in the States? Such is the real question, and such it will remain, the Territorial question being substantially settled. What does Mr. SEWARD, who has acquired so much notoriety by his "irrepressible conflict," say? He comes here and proposes an amendment to the Constitution, which puts an estoppel upon his "irrepressible conflict" doctrine. He is willing to make it *perpetual*, so that the institution cannot be interfered with in the States by any future amendment of the Constitution. That is Mr. Seward's measure. Upon the adoption of that resolution, I believe every member of the committee voted for it, save two. The Senator from Mississippi[1] voted for it; Mr. Seward voted for it; and Mr. Wade of Ohio voted for it. Whose ally is he? Here we find Wade and Seward and Davis, and the whole committee, with the exception of two, in favor of amending the Constitution so that the institution of slavery cannot be interfered with in the States,

[1] Mr. Davis.

making that provision irrepealable by any number of States that may come into the Confederacy. Who were "allies" then?

But, Mr. President, recurring to what I said yesterday, there are two parties in this country that want to break up the Government. Who are they? The nullifiers proper of the South, the secessionists, or disunionists — for I use them all as synonymous terms. There is a portion of them who, *per se*, desire the disruption of the Government for purposes of their own aggrandizement. I do not charge upon them that they want to break up the Government for the purpose of affecting slavery; yet I charge that the breaking up of the Government would have that effect; the result would be the same. Who else is for breaking up this Government? I refer to some bad men in the North. There is a set of men there who are called Abolitionists, and they want to break up the Government. They are disunionists; they are secessionists; they are nullifiers. Sir, the Abolitionists and the distinguished Senator from Mississippi and his party both stand in the same attitude, to attain the same end, a dissolution of this Union; the one party believing that it will result in their own aggrandizement South, and the other believing that it will result in the overthrow of the institution of slavery. Who are the disunionists of the North? Who are the "allies" of the distinguished Senator from Mississippi? We find that a resolution was adopted at the anniversary of the Massachusetts Anti-Slavery Society, convened in Boston, in these words: —

"*Resolved*, That the one great issue before the country is the dissolution of the Union, in comparison with which all other issues with the slave power are as dust in the balance; therefore we give ourselves to the work of annulling this covenant with death, as essential to our own innocency, and the speedy and everlasting overthrow of the slave system."

This resolution was passed by the Abolition anti-slavery society of Massachusetts. They think a dissolution of the Union would result in the destruction of slavery, and absolve them from this "covenant with death," and attest their innocency, as far as the Government is concerned. On that, we find that Mr. Wendell Phillips made the following remarks: —

"I entirely accord with the sentiments of that last resolution. I think all we have to do is to prepare the public mind by the daily and hourly presentation of the doctrine of disunion. Events which, fortunately for us, the Government itself, and other parties, are producing with unexampled rapidity, are our best aid."

Again: in reply to a remark made by Mr. Giddings, respecting the dissolution of the Union, the "Boston Liberator" says: —

"Mr. Giddings says truly, that the dissolution of the Union has long been held up as a scarecrow by the South; but when he adds that the friends of liberty never demanded it, his statement is untrue, unless he means to confine it to his political associates, who are but compromisers at last. We demand nothing short of a dissolution, absolute and immediate. The Union which was founded by our fathers was cemented by the blood of the slave, and effected through his immolation."

And still further: William Lloyd Garrison, at a Fourth of July celebration, at Framingham, Massachusetts, declared: —

"Let us then to-day, rejecting as wild and chimerical all suggestions, propositions, and contrivances for restraining slavery in its present limits, while extending constitutional protection to it in fifteen of the States, register our pledge anew before Heaven and the world, that we will do what in us lies to effect the eternal overthrow of this blood-stained Union; that thus our enslaved countrymen may find a sure deliverance, and we may no longer be answerable for their blood."

The Union is to be overthrown by way of getting clear of the "great sin of slavery." Mr. J. B. Swasey, on the same occasion, said: —

"In the olden times I was what was called an anti-slavery Whig; but, Mr. President, it has come to my mind, like a conviction, that it is utterly in vain to hope that we can live under such a Government as this, with our professions, and with our pretended love of freedom and right. Why, the thing is impossible. There cannot, in the nature of things, be any union between the principles of liberty and slavery. There never has been any union, except by the subjugation of the principles of liberty to those of despotism. For one, sir, I believe that the duty of every true man is to take the ground of secession."

Again: Wendell Phillips, in a speech at Boston on the 20th of January, argued that disunion was desirable, because it would abolish slavery. He also argued that the North would gain by disunion, and used the following language: —

> "Sacrifice everything for the Union? God forbid! Sacrifice everything to keep South Carolina in it? Rather build a bridge of gold, and pay her toll over it. Let her march off with banners and trumpets, and we will speed the parting guests. Let her not stand upon the order of her going, but go at once. Give her the forts and arsenals and sub-treasuries, and lend her jewels of silver and gold, and Egypt will rejoice that she has departed."

He looks upon disunion as the beginning of the destruction and overthrow of the institution of slavery. Then, when we come to talk about "allies," whose allies are these gentlemen? Whose allies are the Abolitionists of the North, if they are not the allies of the secessionists and disunionists of the South? Are they not all laboring and toiling to accomplish the same great end, the overthrow of this great nation of ours? Their object is the same. They are both employing, to some extent, the same means. Here is Wendell Phillips; here is Garrison; here is the anti-slavery society of Massachusetts; and all, in the very same point of view, the allies of the distinguished Senator from Mississippi and his coadjutors; all in favor of disrupting and breaking down this Union, with the view of destroying the institution of slavery itself. "Allies laboring to destroy the Government!" Who else are laboring to destroy it but the disunionists and secessionists of the

South, and Garrison and Phillips, and the long list that might be enumerated at the North? Here they stand, presenting an unbroken front, to destroy this glorious Union, which was made by our fathers.

Mr. President, I have alluded to this subject of "allies" in order to show who is engaged in this unholy and nefarious work of breaking up this Union. We find first the run-mad Abolitionists of the North. They are secessionists; they are for disunion; they are for dissolution. When we turn to the South we see the red-hot disunionists and secessionists engaged in the same work. I think it comes with a very bad grace from them to talk about the "allies" of others who are trying to save the Union and preserve the Constitution.

I went back yesterday and showed that South Carolina had held this doctrine of secession at a very early day, a very short time after she entered into the Articles of Confederation, and after she had entered the Union by which and through which the independence of the country was achieved. What else do we find at a very early day? Go to Massachusetts during the war of 1812, and the Hartford Convention, and there you will find men engaged in this treasonable and unhallowed work. Even in 1845, Massachusetts, in manifesting her great opposition to the annexation of Texas to the United States, passed a resolution resolving herself out of the Union. She seceded; she went off by her own act, because Texas was admitted into the Union. Thus we find South Carolina and Massachusetts taking the lead in this secession movement. We find the Abolitionists proper of the North shaking the right hand of fellowship with the disunionists of the South in this work of breaking up the Union; and yet we hear intimations here that Senators from the South who are not secessionists are Black Republican allies! If I were compelled to choose either, — I would not wish to be compelled to make a choice, — but if I were compelled to be either, having the privilege of choosing, I would rather be a black Republican than a red one. I think the one is much more tolerable than the other. If red republicanism is ever to make its way into this country, it is making its way in this disunion and secession movement that is now going on; for we see that right along with the sentiment of secession the reign of terror prevails. Everything is carried away by it, while the conservative men of the country are waiting for the excited tempest to pass. It is now sweeping over the country. Everything is carried by usurpation, and a reign of terror follows along in its wake.

I am charged with being "an ally" of the Senator from Ohio! I, who, from my earliest infancy, or from the time I first comprehended principle, down to the present time, have always stood battling for the same great principles that I contend for now! My people know me; they have tried me; and your little innuendoes and your little indirections will not alarm them, even if your infuriated seceding Southern men dare to intimate that I am an ally of Mr. Wade. The Senator charges me with being "an ally"; while he and the leaders of Abolitionism are uniting all their energies to break up this glorious Union. I an ally! Thank God, I am not in alliance with Giddings, with Phillips, with Garrison, and the long list of those who are engaged in the work of destruction, and in violating the Constitution of the United States.

So much, Mr. President, in regard to the argument about allies. I am every man's ally when he acts upon principle. I have laid down, as the cardinal point in my political creed, that, in all questions that involve principle, especially where there was doubt, I would pursue principle; and in the pursuit of a great principle I never could reach a wrong conclusion. If, in the pursuit of principle, in trying to reach a correct conclusion, I find myself by the side of another man who is pursuing the same principle, or acting upon the same line of policy, I extend to him my assistance, and I ask his in return.

But the Senator from Mississippi, in his reply to me, also said: —

"I was reading, a short time ago, an extract which referred to the time when 'we' — I suppose it means Tennessee —

would take the position which it was said to be an absurdity for South Carolina to hold; and Tennessee still was put, in the same speech, in the attitude of a great objector against the exercise of the right of secession. Is there anything in her history which thus places her? Tennessee, born of secession, rocked in the cradle of revolution, taking her position before she was matured, and claiming to be a State because she had violently severed her connection with North Carolina, and through an act of secession and revolution claimed then to be a State."

I suppose it was thought that this would be a poser; that it would be conclusive; and as Tennessee was "born of secession, rocked in the cradle of revolution," I was estopped; that my lips were hermetically sealed, so far as related to anything I could give utterance to in opposition to this heresy. When we come to examine the history of that subject, we find the Senator has fallen into just as great an error as he did in his allusion to allies. Tennessee had her birth not in secession — very far from it. The State of Frankland had its origin in that way. They attempted to separate themselves from the State of North Carolina. When was that? In 1784. Peace was made in 1783; but in 1784, — I read from Wheeler's "History of North Carolina," —

"In 1784, the General Assembly, in April, at Hillsboro' among other acts for the relief of the General Government, ceded her western lands, and authorized her delegation in Congress to execute a deed, provided Congress would accept this offer within two years.

"This act, patriotic and self-sacrificing, was worthy of the

State; and although not then accepted by Congress, was the real source of the civil commotion which we are about to record."

What was that civil commotion? The pioneers of that country had suffered great hardships, and they viewed with suspicion this act of 1784. On the 24th of August of that year, they held a convention at Jonesboro', and resolved to send a person to Congress to urge the acceptance of the offer of North Carolina. But I will read from this history:

"The General Assembly of North Carolina met at Newbern on the 22d October, 1784, and repealed the act of the former session, in consequence of which the convention at Jonesboro' broke up in confusion." . . . . .

"The spirit of the people was roused. On December 4, 1784, a convention of five delegates from each county met at Jonesboro'. John Sevier was made president of this convention. They formed a constitution for the State of Frankland, which was to be rejected or received by another body, 'fresh from the people,' to meet at Greenville in November, 1785. This body met at the time and place appointed; the constitution was ratified; Langdon Carter was Speaker of the Senate; William Cage, Speaker of the House of Commons. John Sevier was chosen Governor; David Campbell, Joshua Gist, and John Henderson, judges of the superior court. Other officers, civil and military, were appointed.

"The General Assembly of the State of Frankland, by a communication signed by both Speakers, informed Richard Caswell, Esq., Governor of North Carolina, that the people of the counties of Washington, Sullivan, and Greene, had declared themselves sovereign, and independent of the State of North Carolina.

"Governor Caswell was a soldier and a statesman. He was

not of a temper to brook such high-handed measures. He issued, on the 25th of April, 1785, his proclamation against this lawless thirst for power." . . . . .

"But the State of Frankland did not heed this warning, so properly expressed, and so dignified in its character and tone. It proceeded to erect new counties, levy taxes, appropriate money, form treaties with the Indians, and exercise all the power and prerogatives of a sovereign State." . . . . .

"The scarcity of money was severely felt. The salary of the Governor was £200 annually; a judge £150; the treasurer £40; to be paid from the treasury. The taxes were to be paid into the treasury, in the circulating medium of Frankland, such as they had, namely: good flax linen, ten hundred, at three shillings and six pence per yard; good clean beaver skins, six shillings each; racoon and fox skins, at one shilling and three pence; deer skins, six shillings; bacon, at six pence per pound; tallow, at six pence; good whiskey, at two shillings and six pence a gallon.

"This has given rise to some humor at the expense of the State of Frankland. It was referred to in debate in our House of Commons, 1827, by H. C. Jones, and in Congress some years ago by Hon. Daniel Webster; which was replied to by Hon. Hugh L. White. It was pleasantly stated that the salaries of the Governor and judges were paid in fox-skins, and the fees of the sheriff and constables in mink-skins, and that the Governor, the sheriffs, and constables were compelled to receive the skins at the established price.

"Even this primitive currency was, by the ingenuity of man, extensively counterfeited, by sewing racoon-tails to the opossum-skins, — opossum-skins being worthless and abundant, and racoon-skins were valued by law at one shilling and three pence." . . . . .

"The General Assembly of North Carolina, assembled at Newbern, in November, 1785, passed an act to bury in oblivion the conduct of Frankland, provided they returned to their allegiance, and appointed elections to be held in the different counties for members to the General Assembly of North Carolina, and also appointed civil and military officers to support those already appointed. The next year, 1786, presented a strange state of affairs; two empires extended at the same time over the same territory and over the same people.

"Courts were held by both Governments, military officers appointed by both, to exercise the same powers. John Tipton headed the party for North Carolina, and John Sevier the Frankland party." . . . . .

"The next year taxes were imposed by both administrations; but the people most *innocently* pretended that they did not know to whom to pay; so paid to neither. Thus deprived of one of the chief means of government, the affairs of Frankland were approaching to its end. Tipton and Sevier were both residents of Washington County. Sevier was a brave soldier; he had proved his valor on King's Mountain; but he was seduced by the allurements of office and ambition, —

'The sin whereby the angels fell.'

"He applied to Dr. Franklin for advice and support; to the Governor (Matthews) of Georgia, and to Virginia; from none did he receive any aid or advantage. He realized with fearful truth the fable of Gay, —

The child who many fathers share,
Hath rarely known a father's care.
He who on many doth depend
Will rarely ever find a friend.' "

All this shows, Mr. President, that the State of Frankland took its origin in 1784. A government was recognized, and it continued until September, 1787. The Legislature that year met at Greenville, the very town in which I live.

"In September, 1787, the Legislature of Frankland met for the last time at Greenville. John Menifee was Speaker of the Senate, and Charles Robinson Speaker of the House. They authorized the election of two Representatives to attend the Legislature of North Carolina, and one of the judges of Frankland was elected (David Campbell) and her Treasurer (Langdon Carter) the other.

"Had the party of Sevier accepted the liberal, fair, and just proposition of Governor Caswell, in 1785, as stated previously, how much pain and trouble would have been spared to this country, and how much personal suffering to himself? With all his virtues, honesty, and former public service, he was at this time a doomed man.

"On the return of the members from the General Assembly at Tarboro', in February, 1788, it was soon understood that Frankland was no more.

"An execution against the estate of General Sevier had been placed in the hands of the sheriff, and levied on his negroes on Nolichucky River. These were removed for safe-keeping to the house of Colonel Tipton.

"Brave in his character, obstinate and headstrong, Sevier raised one hundred and fifty men, and marched to Tipton's house, on Watauga River, eight miles east of Jonesboro'. Tipton had information of Sevier's design only time enough to obtain the aid of some fifteen friends, who were with him on Sevier's arrival.

"Sevier, with his troops and a small cannon, demanded an unconditional surrender of Tipton and all in his house. Tipton had barricaded the house; and in reply to the unceremonious demand, sent him word 'to fire, and be d—d.' He then sent a written summons to surrender. This letter Tipton forwarded forthwith to the colonel of the county, for aid. This aid, through Robert and Thomas Love, was promptly afforded. The house was watched closely. A man by the name of Webb was killed, a woman wounded in the shoulder, and a Mr. Vann. While, from extreme cold, Sevier's guards were at the fire, a large reinforcement from Sullivan County, under Maxwell and

Pemberton, passed the guard, and joined the beleaguered household. The moment the junction was formed they sallied out with shouts; a tremor seized the troops of Sevier, who fled in all directions at the first fire of Tipton. Pugh, the high sheriff of Washington, was mortally wounded, and many taken prisoners. Sevier himself escaped; his two sons, James and John, were prisoners." . . . . .

"Judge Spencer, one of the judges of the State of North Carolina, holding court at Jonesboro', issued a bench-warrant against Governor Sevier for high treason, (1788.)

"In October, Colonels Tipton, Love, and others, apprehended Sevier, at the house of Mrs. Brown, near Jonesboro'. Tipton was armed, and swore that he would kill Sevier; and Sevier really thought he would do so. Tipton was, however, with much exertion, pacified. Handcuffs were placed upon *Governor* Sevier, and he was carried to Jonesboro.' From thence he was carried, under strong guard, to Morganton, in Burke County, North Carolina, and delivered to William Morrison, the sheriff of Burke.

"As he passed through Burke, General Charles McDowell and General Joseph McDowell (the latter who was with him in the battle of King's Mountain, and fought by his side) became his securities for a few days, until he could see some friends. He returned punctually, and upon his own responsibility the sheriff allowed him time to procure bail. His two sons, with friends, came to Morganton privately, and under their escort he escaped.

"Thus the career of the first and *last Governor of Frankland* terminated. But with all his defects, John Sevier had many virtues. He was fearless to a fault, kind to his friends, and hospitable to all. This gave him great weight among the people; and although in the General Assembly of North Carolina, (Fayetteville,) in 1788, general oblivion and pardon were extended to all concerned in the late revolt, John Sevier was especially excepted in the act, and debarred from all offices of trust, honor, or profit.

"The next year (1789) so great a favorite with the people was Sevier, that he was elected from Greene, to represent that county in the Senate of the General Assembly of North Carolina. He appeared at Fayetteville at the time appointed for the meeting of the Legislature, (second Monday of November.)

"Such was the sense of his worth, or his contrition for the past, that the Legislature passed early an act repealing the section disqualifying him from any office; and on taking the oath of allegiance, he was allowed his seat. Thus were the difficulties settled.

"North Carolina had ever been willing to allow her daughter to set up for herself when of lawful age and under proper restrictions. Cherishing this feeling, she was never unjust towards her fair and lovely offspring.

"On the 25th of February, 1790, as authorized by a previous act of the General Assembly, passed in the year 1789, Samuel Johnston and Benjamin Hawkins, Senators in Congress, executed a deed to the United States in the words of the cession act; and on the 2d of April of that year, Congress accepted the deed, and Tennessee was born.

"By proclamation, dated September 1, 1790, Governor Martin announced that the Secretary of State for the United States had transmitted to him a copy of the act of Congress, accepting the cession of North Carolina for this district of the western territory, and the inhabitants of said district 'would take due notice thereof, and govern themselves accordingly.'"

John Sevier was brave and patriotic, a man loved by the people; but he had fallen into this error of secession or separation from the State of North Carolina that I have called your attention to here in the history of that State. We find that this doctrine of secession could not even be sustained by him, with his great popularity and with the attachment the people had for him. Instead of Tennessee having her origin or her birth in secession, the precise reverse is true. The State of Frankland had its birth in an attempt at disunion and was rocked to death in the cradle of secession; and its great defender and founder at that time, notwithstanding his great popularity and the attachment the people had for him, was lodged in irons. That is where secession carried him, with all his popularity, with all his patriotism, with all the attachment the people had for him. Yes, sir, this nefarious, this blighting, this withering doctrine of secession ended by placing that distinguished man in irons.

What next occurred? North Carolina passed a law for general pardon and oblivion for all those that had been engaged in this movement, with the exception of this great man, John Sevier. His name is even now venerated in the section of the country where I live; but, with all his talents and popularity, this infamous, this diabolical, this hell-born and hell-bound doctrine of secession carried him into chains. The State of Frankland had expired, rocked to death in the cradle of secession, and he went back to Greene County, and was elected a member of the Legislature of North Carolina. In passing this general oblivion and pardon, he was made an exception; and he was not permitted to take his seat in the Legislature until the exception was removed. It was removed, and he took his seat in the Legislature of North Carolina. Frankland had expired; it was no more; and yet we see the odious weight that was heaped upon him by this nefarious doctrine of secession.

Then what follows, Mr. President? When we turn to the history, we find that North Carolina then made her cession act, completed it in 1790, and ceded the territory to the United States. A territorial government was established. General Washington himself appointed the first officers in the Territory, which was then styled "the Territory southwest of the river Ohio." In 1794 the Council or Legislature of that Territory elected James White the first delegate to the Congress of the United States from the Territory southwest of the river Ohio — not Frankland or Franklin, for that is numbered with the things that were, but are not. Even with the popularity of the name of Dr. Franklin, it was consigned to oblivion. In 1794 the delegate to represent the Territory made his appearance here, and took his seat. In 1796 the constitution was formed; and then it was that Tennessee began her existence. The peace was made in 1783, and in 1796 Tennessee formed her constitution and applied for admission into this Union. Then it was that Tennessee was brought into existence. She did not pass through this ordeal of secession; this probation of disunion. She germinated upon proper principles. The Territory was first organized by Congress after the death of the organization called Frankland; and in 1796 the people of Tennessee formed their constitution, and were admitted into the Union as a State.

And, sir, who came into the Union with her when she was admitted as a State? Andrew Jackson. It may have been that his early knowledge of the country, it may have been that his early information upon the subject, made him understand and appreciate ever afterwards the value of the Union. When Tennessee was ushered into this family of States, as an equal member of the Confederacy, General Jackson took his seat as her Representative. The Senator from Mississippi said that Tennessee was "born in secession; rocked in the cradle of revolution." Sir, she has many fond recollections of the Revolution; but with all her revolutionary character, her people have never attempted secession. General Jackson first represented her in Congress when she came into the Union; she brought him to the notice of the people of the United States as a public man. In 1833, when an attempt somewhat similar to the present was made, he was President of the United States; and it is unnecessary for me to relate what his views of secession were then. It is not necessary for me to refer to the acts of General Jackson in 1833. And now, sir, not intending to disparage others, but to give utterance to my conscientious belief, I must say that if such a man as Andrew Jackson were President of the United States at the present time, before this moment steps would have been taken which would have preservea us a united people without the shedding of blood, without making war. I believe that if Andrew Jackson were President of the United States, this glorious Union of ours would still be intact. Perhaps it might be jarred a little in some places, but not sufficiently to disturb the harmony and general concord of the whole. That is my opinion. I do not say it to disparage others; but I believe that this would have been the case if he had been President, pursuing the policy which I feel certain he would have pursued in such an emergency.

Tennessee came into the Union in 1796. She was the third State that entered the Confederacy after the old thirteen ratified the Constitution. She was in this Union before Alabama, before Mississippi, before Louisiana, before Florida had an existence. There was a Union then, and she was in it. She has been in it ever since; and she has continued to contribute her money, her men, and her blood, to the defence of the flag of the Union; and though these other States may go out, I trust in God that she will still remain in the position she occupied before they were spoken into existence. We have been told that the Union is broken up — that it is already dissolved. Why, sir, according to the Constitution, nine States formed the Government; and provision was made for taking in new States. Taking in a State or taking out a State does not disturb the Union. It was a Union before the

State came in; it is a Union after it goes out. We got along very well before these States came in; and where is the great injury now to result to Tennessee because they propose to go out?

I took occasion, in my former remarks, to call the attention of the Senate, and of my constituents to the extent that I have the honor to represent them, to the kind of government that was likely to be formed by the seceding States, and the country they might acquire after they did secede. In relation to this, the Senator from Mississippi said, —

"But the Senator found somewhere, I believe in Georgia, a newspaper article which suggested the advantages of a constitutional monarchy. Does the Senator believe there is any considerable number of people in any of the States who favor the establishment of a constitutional monarchy?"

The Senator from Georgia[1] felt called upon to say something in the same connection. He said, —

"As allusion has been made by the Senator from Mississippi to an article which appeared in a paper in my own town, and about which a good deal of noise has been made, and which was referred to by the Senator from Tennessee, in his celebrated speech, the other day, as evidence that there was a party in the South in favor of a constitutional monarchy" —

He went on to state that that idea was suggested in some paper, he could not exactly tell how; but it was not by the editor, and it did not amount to much. I did not refer to a single paper; but I made various extracts from newspapers and speeches, simply as surface indications, as symptoms of what

[1] Mr. Iverson.

lay below, and what was intended to be the result. I referred to the "Charleston Mercury"; I referred to other papers; I referred to the speeches of distinguished men, some of them leaders in this movement. Is it not apparent, now, that unless the public mind is aroused, unless the people are put on the alert, there is a design to establish a government upon the principles of a close corporation? Can any one that has the least sagacity be so unobservant as not to see what is going on in the South? It is apparent to all. They seem to unite in setting out with the proposition that the new confederacy shall exclude every State which is not slaveholding, for the reason that those States which are interested in slaves should have the exclusive control and management of them. Here is a great family of States, some free and some slave, occupying, in one sense, the same relation to each other that individuals in the community do to one another. The proposition is started to form a government of States exclusively interested in slaves. That excludes all the free States. Is the argument good? Has not slavery been secure heretofore in the Union with non-slaveholding States; and will not our geographical and physical position be just the same after the present Union is dissolved? Where does the argument carry us? We must have a confederacy now composed of slave States exclusively. When we have excluded the free States, and we come to make a new government, does not the same argument apply that we must have a government to be controlled and administered by that description of persons among us who are exclusively interested in slaves? If you cannot trust a free State in the confederacy, can you trust a non-slaveholder in a slaveholding State to control the question of slavery? Where does your argument carry you? We see where they are drifting; and, as a faithful sentinel upon the watch-tower, I try to notify the people and sound the tocsin of alarm. If this idea be not carried out, it will be because the public feeling, the public opinion, is aroused against it.

I alluded yesterday to the fact that the freemen of the State of South Carolina have not been permitted to vote for a President since it was a State. There is a great terror and dread of the capacity of the people to govern themselves. In South Carolina, when the ordinance was passed to withdraw from the Union, did the convention trust the people to pass their judgment upon it. Were they consulted? Did they indorse it? Have they passed their judgment upon it to this day? Taking the language of Mr. Boyce as an index of their feeling, I have no more doubt than I have of my existence that if this reign of terror subsides, and the hearts of the people of South Carolina can be gotten at, it will be found that a majority of them disapprove and repudiate what has been done there. What do we find in the State of Georgia? There the proposition was moved to submit the ordinance to the people; and were the people consulted? The vote was 138 to 116, I think. It shows a great division. Did they submit it to the people? Oh no. I know something of the people of the State of Georgia; and I believe this day, if that seceding ordinance could be submitted to the voting population of Georgia, and the question be fully canvassed and fairly understood, they would repudiate and put it down. Go to Florida: were the people consulted there? Not at all. Look to Alabama; look to the arguments made there in the convention. It was said, our power is ample; we must consummate this thing, and not let the people pass upon it. Louisiana refused to refer the matter to the people. The people have not been consulted. A reign of terror has been instituted. States have been called upon to make large appropriations of money to buy arms and munitions of war; for what end? The idea has been: "we can, almost with the speed of lightning, run States out of the Union without consulting the people; and then, if they dare resist, we have got an army, we have got the money to awe them into submission." These gentlemen are very fearful of coercion, exceedingly alarmed at the word "coerce"; but when you attempt to interpose and stop *their* career, they do not know of any other term but coercion. Look at the despatch which Governor Pickens sent to Mississippi:—

CHARLESTON, *January*, 19, 1861.

Judge Magrath and myself have sent four telegraphs to you. Please urge Mississippi to send delegates to the Montgomery meeting of States, at as early a day as possible — say 4th of February — to *form immediately a strong provisional government.* It is the only thing to prevent war, and let that convention elect *immediately* a commander-in-chief for the seceding States. You may as well return, at least as far as Montgomery. F. W. PICKENS.

To Hon. A. BURT JACKSON.

South Carolina has a military establishment, with officers appointed, and the taxes necessary to support them now are grinding her people to the dust; but she expects in a very short time to transfer that military establishment, with her officers, to the Southern Confederacy that is to be established; and I suppose the great object in getting the leader appointed at once is that they may be able by military force to awe the people into submission. Have we not seen that nine regiments have been authorized to be raised in Mississippi, and a distinguished Senator, who occupied a seat on this floor a short time since, made the major-general? No doubt, when the scheme is consummated and carried out, when the military organization is complete, if the people offer to resist, they will be subdued and awed, or driven into submission at the point of the bayonet. Some of these gentry are very much afraid of the people.

Why, sir, a proposition was even started in my own State to raise sixteen regiments; for what? With whom are we at war? Is anybody attacking us? No. Do we want to coerce anybody? No. What do we want with sixteen regiments?

And it was proposed to appropriate $250,000 to sustain them. There is a wonderful alarm at the idea of coercing the seceding States; great dread in reference to the power of this Federal Government to secure obedience to its laws, and especially in reference to making war upon one of the States; but the public property can be taken, your flag can be fired upon, your ships driven out of port, your gallant officer, with a few men, penned up in a little fort to subsist as best they may. So far as the officer to whom I have just alluded is concerned, I will give utterance to the feelings of my heart when I express my profound approbation of his conduct. He was put there to defend the flag of his country. He was there not as an intruder. He was there in possession of the property owned by the United States, not to menace, not to insult, not to violate rights, but simply to defend the flag and honor of his country, and take care of the public property; and because he retired from a position where he could have been captured, where the American flag could have been struck and made to trail in the dust, and the Palmetto banner substituted, because he, obeying the impulses of a gallant and brave heart, took choice of another position; acting upon principles of humanity, not injuring others, but seeking to protect his own command from being sacrificed and destroyed, he is condemned and repudiated, and his action is sought to be converted into a menace of war. Has it come to this, that the Government of the United States cannot even take care of its own property, that your vessels must be fired upon, that your flag must be struck, and still you are alarmed at coercion; and because a gallant officer has taken possession of a fort where he cannot very well be coerced, a terrible cry is raised, and war is to be made?

I was speaking of the proposition brought forward in my own State to raise sixteen regiments. Sir, as far back as the battle of King's Mountain, and in every war in which the rights of the people have been invaded, Tennessee, God bless her, has stood by that glorious flag, which was carried by Washington and followed by the gallant patriots and soldiers of the Revolution, even as the blood trickled from their feet as they passed over the ice and snow; and under that flag, not only at home, but abroad, her sons have acquired honor and distinction, in connection with citizens of the other States of the Union. She is not yet prepared to band with outlaws, and make war upon that flag under which she has won laurels. Who are we going to fight? Who is invading Tennessee? Conventions are got up; a reign of terror is inaugurated; and if, by the influence of a subsidized and mendacious press, an ordinance taking the State out of the Confederacy can be extorted, those who make such propositions expect to have our army ready, to have their bands equipped, to have their pretorian divisions; then they will tell the people that they must carry the ordinance into effect, and join a Southern Confederacy, whether they will or not; they shall be lashed on to the car of South Carolina, who entertains no respect for them, but threatens their institution of slavery unless they comply with her terms. Will Tennessee take such a position as that? I cannot believe it; I never will believe it; and if an ordinance of secession should be passed by that State under these circumstances, and an attempt should be made to force the people out of the Union, as has been done in some other States, without first having submitted that ordinance to the people for their ratification or rejection, I tell the Senate and the American people that there are many in Tennessee whose dead bodies will have to be trampled over before it can be consummated. [Applause in the galleries.] The Senator from Mississippi referred to the flag of his country; and I will read what he said, so that I may not be accused of misrepresenting him: —

"It may be pardoned to me, sir, who, in my very boyhood, was given to the military service, and who have followed that flag under tropical suns, and over northern snows, if I here express the deep sorrow which always overwhelms me when I think of turning from the flag I have followed so long, for which I have suffered in ways it does not become me to speak of; feeling that henceforth it is not to be the banner I will hail with the rising sun, and greet as the sun goes down; the banner which, by day and by night, I am ready to follow.

But God, who knows the hearts of men, will judge between you and us, at whose door lies the responsibility of this."

There is no one in the United States who is more willing to do justice to the distinguished Senator from Mississippi than myself; and when I consider his early education; when I look at his gallant services, finding him first in the military school of the United States, educated by his Government, taught the science of war at the expense of his country — taught to love the principles of the Constitution; afterwards entering its service, fighting beneath the Stars and Stripes to which he has so handsomely alluded, winning laurels that are green and imperishable, and bearing upon his person scars that are honorable; some of which have been won at home; others of which have been won in a foreign clime, and upon other fields — I would be the last man to pluck a feather from his cap or a single gem from the chaplet that encircles his brow. But when I consider his early associations; when I remember that he was nurtured by this Government; that he fought for this Government; that he won honors under the flag of this Government, I cannot understand how he can be willing to hail another banner, and turn from that of his country, under which he has won laurels and received honors. This is a matter of taste, however; but it seems to me that, if I could not unsheathe my sword in vindication of the flag of my country, its glorious Stars and Stripes, I would return the sword to its scabbard; I would never sheathe it in the bosom of my mother; never! never! never! Sir, my own feelings in reference to that flag are such as must have filled the heart of that noble son of South Carolina, Joel R. Poinsett, when, nearly thirty years ago, in an address to the people of Charleston, he declared, —

"Wherever I have been, I have been proud of being a citizen of this Republic, and to the remotest corners of the earth have walked erect and secure under that banner which our opponents would tear down and trample under foot. I was in Mexico when the town was taken by assault. The house of the American ambassador was then, as it ought to be, the refuge of the distressed and persecuted; it was pointed out to the infuriated soldiery as a place filled with their enemies. They refused to attack. My only defence was the flag of my country, and it was thrown out at the instant that hundreds of muskets were levelled at us. Mr. Mason — a braver man never stood by his friend in the hour of danger — and myself placed ourselves beneath its waving folds; and the attack was suspended. We did not blanch, for we felt strong in the protecting arm of this mighty Republic. We told them that the flag that waved over us was the banner of that nation to whose example they owed their liberties, and to whose protection they were indebted for their safety. The scene changed as by enchantment; those men who were on the point of attacking and massacring the inhabitants cheered the flag of our country, and placed sentinels to protect it from outrage.

"Fellow-citizens, in such a moment as that, would it have been any protection to me and mine to have proclaimed myself a Carolinian? Should I have been here to tell you this tale if I had hung out the palmetto and single star? Be assured that, to be respected abroad, we must maintain our place in the Union."

Sir, I intend to stand by that flag, and by the Union of which it is the emblem. I agree with Mr. A. H. Stephens of Georgia, "that this Government of our fathers, with all its defects, comes nearer the objects of all good governments than any other on the face of the earth."

I have made allusions to the various Senators who have attacked me, in vindication of myself. I have been attacked on all hands by some five or six, and may be attacked again. All I ask is, that, in making these attacks, they meet my positions, answer my arguments, refute my facts. I care not for the number that may have attacked me; I care not how many may come hereafter. Feeling that I am in the right, that argument, that fact, that truth are on my side, I place them all at defiance. Come one, come all; for I feel, in the words of the great dramatic poet, —

> "Thrice is he armed that hath his quarrel just;
> And he but naked, though locked up in steel,
> Whose conscience with [treason] is corrupted."

I have been told, and I have heard it repeated, that this Union is gone. It has been said in this Chamber that it is in the cold sweat of death; that, in fact, it is really dead, and merely lying in state waiting for the funeral obsequies to be performed. If this be so, and the war that has been made upon me in consequence of advocating the Constitution and the Union is to result in my overthrow and in my destruction; and that flag, that glorious flag, the emblem of the Union, which was borne by Washington through a seven-years' struggle, shall be struck from the Capitol and trailed in the dust — when this Union is interred, I want no more honorable winding-sheet than that brave old flag, and no more glorious grave than to be interred in the tomb of the Union. [Applause in the galleries.] For it I have stood; for it I will continue to stand; I care not whence the blows come; and some will find, before this contest is over, that while there are blows to be given, there will be blows to receive; and that, while others can thrust, there are some who can parry. God preserve my country from the desolation that is threatening her, from treason and traitors!

> "Is there not some chosen curse,
> Some hidden thunder in the stores of heaven,
> Red with uncommon wrath, to blast the man
> Who owes his greatness to his country's ruin?"

[Applause in the galleries.]

In conclusion, Mr. President, I make an appeal to the conservative men of all parties. You see the posture of public affairs; you see the condition of the country; you see along the line of battle the various points of conflict; you see the struggle which the Union men have to maintain in many of the States. You ought to know and feel what is necessary to sustain those who, in their hearts, desire the preservation of this Union of States. Will you sit with stoic indifference, and see those who are willing to stand by the Constitution and uphold the pillars of the Government driven away by the raging surges that are now sweeping over some portions of the country? As conservative men, as patriots, as men who desire the preservation of this great, this good, this unparalleled Government, I ask you to save the country; or let the propositions be submitted to the people, that the heart of the nation may respond to them. I have an abiding confidence in the intelligence, the patriotism, and the integrity of the great mass of the people; and I feel in my own heart that, if this subject could be got before them, they would settle the question, and the Union of these States would be preserved. [Applause in the galleries.]

REPLY TO SENATOR LANE OF OREGON.

DELIVERED IN THE SENATE OF THE UNITED STATES, MARCH 2, 1861.

The Senate having under consideration the Report of the Peace Conference, and Mr. Lane of Oregon having concluded his speech, —

Mr. JOHNSON said: — Mr. President: it is painful to me to be compelled to occupy any of the time of the Senate upon the subject that has just been discussed by the Senator from Oregon. Had it not been for the extraordinary speech he has made, and the singular course he has taken, I should refrain from saying one word at this late hour of the day and of the session. But, sir, it must be apparent, not only to the Senate, but to the whole country, that, either by accident or by design, there has been an arrangement that any one who appeared in this Senate to vindicate the Union of these States should be attacked. Why is it that no one in the Senate or out of it, who is in favor of the Union of these States, has made an attack upon me? Why has it been left to those who have taken ground both openly and secretly in violation of the Constitution, for the disruption of the Government? Why has there been a concerted attack upon me from the beginning of this discussion to the present moment, not even confined within the ordinary courtesies of debate and of senatorial decorum? It is a question which lifts itself above personalities. I care not from what direction the Senator comes who indulges in personalities towards me; in that, I feel that I am above him, and that he is my inferior. [Applause in the galleries.]

The PRESIDING OFFICER[1] rapped with his mallet, and then said: The Chair will announce that if that disturbance is repeated in the galleries, they must be cleared. That is the order of the Senate for the purpose of conducting properly the deliberations of the Senate.

Mr. DOOLITTLE. I hope the Chair will enforce the order, and not threaten to do so. When applause is given on the expression of Union sentiments, in which I fully concur, I desire that the order shall be enforced, and there can then be no exception taken if we enforce the rules when applause may be given for any other sentiments uttered on this floor.

Mr. JOHNSON. Mr. President, I was alluding to the use of personalities. They are not arguments; they are the resort of men whose minds are low and coarse. It is very easy to talk about "cowards"; to draw autobiographical sketches; to recount the remarkable, the wonderful events and circumstances and exploits that we have performed. I have pre-

[1] Mr. Polk in the chair.

sented facts and authorities; and upon them I have argued; from them I have drawn conclusions; and why have they not been met? Why have they not been answered? Why abandon the great issues before the country, and go into personalities? In this discussion I shall act upon the principle laid down in Cowper's "Conversation," where he says, —

> "A moral, sensible, and well-bred man
> Will not affront me; and no other can."

But there are men who talk about cowardice, cowards, courage, and all that kind of thing; and in this connection, I will say, once for all, not boastingly, with no anger in my bosom, that these two eyes never looked upon any being in the shape of mortal man that this heart of mine feared.

Sir, have we reached a point of time at which we dare not speak of treason? Our forefathers talked about it; they spoke of it in the Constitution of the country; they have defined what treason is. Is it an offence, is it a crime, is it an insult to recite the Constitution that was made by Washington and his compatriots? What does the Constitution define treason to be?

> "Treason against the United States shall consist only in levying war against them, or in adhering to their enemies, giving them aid and comfort."

There it is defined clearly that treason shall consist only in levying war against the United States, and adhering to and giving aid and comfort to their enemies. Who is it that has been engaged in conspiracies? Who is it that has been engaged in making war upon the United States? Who is it that has fired upon our flag? Who is it that has given instructions to take your arsenals, to take your forts, to take your dock-yards, to seize your custom-houses, and rob your treasuries? Who is it that has been engaged in secret conclaves, and issuing orders for the seizure of public property in violation of the Constitution they were sworn to support? In the language of the Constitution of the United States, are not those who have been engaged in this nefarious work guilty of treason? I will now present a fair issue, and hope it will be fairly met. Show me the man who has been engaged in these conspiracies; show me who has been sitting in these nightly and secret conclaves, plotting the overthrow of the Government; show me who has fired upon our flag, has given instructions to take our forts and our custom-houses, our arsenals and our dock-yards, and I will show you a traitor! [Applause in the galleries.]

The PRESIDING OFFICER:[1] — The Sergeant-at-Arms will clear the galleries on the right of the Chair immediately.

Mr. JOHNSON. That is a fair proposition ——

The PRESIDING OFFICER. The Senator from Tennessee will pause until the order of the Chair is executed.

[1] Mr. Polk in the chair.

[Here a long debate ensued upon questions of order and the propriety of clearing the galleries.]

Mr. JOHNSON then continued: — I hope the execution of the order will be suspended, and I will go security for the gallery that they will not applaud any more. I should have been nearly through my remarks by this time but for this interruption.

The PRESIDING OFFICER here announced that the order for clearing the galleries would be suspended.

Mr. JOHNSON continued: — Mr. President, when I was interrupted by a motion to clear the galleries, I was making a general allusion to treason as defined in the Constitution of the United States, and to those who were traitors and guilty of treason within the scope and meaning of the law and the Constitution. My proposition was, that if they would show me who were guilty of the offences I have enumerated, I would show them who were the traitors. That being done, were I the President of the United States, I would do as Thomas Jefferson did in 1806 with Aaron Burr, who was charged with treason: I would have them arrested and tried for treason, and, if convicted, by the Eternal God they should suffer the penalty of the law at the hands of the executioner. Sir, treason must be punished. Its enormity and the extent and depth of the offence must be made known. The time is not distant, if this Government is preserved, its Constitution obeyed, and its laws executed in every department, when something of this kind must be done.

The Senator from Oregon, in his remarks, said that a mind that it required six weeks to stuff could not know much of anything. He intimated that I had been "stuffed." I made my speech on the 19th of December. The gentleman replied. I made another speech on the 5th and 6th of February. And now, after a lapse of about four weeks, and at the close of the session, when it is believed there will be no opportunity to respond on account of the great press of business which must necessarily be acted on, he makes a reply. How long has *he* been "stuffing"? *By whom* and how often has he been "stuffed"? [Laughter.] He has been stuffed twice; and if the stuffing operation was as severe and as laborious as the delivery has been, he has had a troublesome time of it; for his travail has been great, the delivery remarkable and excruciatingly painful. [Laughter.]

Again: he speaks of "triumphant ignorance and exulting stupidity." Repartee and satire are not limited to one. I have no disposition, however, to indulge in coarse flings; and, in fact, I think it is unsenatorial. Whatever may be the character of my mind, I have never obtrusively made it the subject of consideration. I may, nevertheless, have exhibited now and then the "exulting stupidity and triumphant ignorance" of which the Senator has spoken. Great and magnanimous minds pity ignorance. The Senator from Oregon, rich in intellectual culture, with a mind comprehensive enough to retain the wisdom of ages, and an eloquence to charm a listening Senate, deplores mine; but he should also be considerate enough to regard my humility. Unpretending in my ignorance, I am content to gaze at his lofty flights and glorious daring without aspiring to accompany him to regions for which my wings have not been plumed nor my eyes fitted. Gorgeously bright are those fair fields in which he revels. To me, alas! his heaven appears but as a murky region, dull, opaque, leaden. My pretension has been simply to do my duty to my State and to my country.

The Senator has thought proper to refer to the action of my State; and I may be permitted to remark, that we in the South understand some things as well as they are understood in the North; and when we find one who calls himself a Northern man, who boasts of his position there, making great professions of friendship, greater attachment to our institutions and our interests than we do ourselves, in some minds it may have a tendency to excite suspicion. The Senator from Oregon is *more* Southern than the South itself. He has taken under his wing of protection the peculiar guardianship of the Southern States, and his every utterance is upon "the equality of the States, their rights in the Union, or their independence out of it." I think Dr. Johnson advised that when a man comes to your house, and voluntarily makes great professions of his purity, his uprightness of purpose, his exalted character, of being far above suspicion and imputation, if you have any silver-ware hide it. When Northern Senators and Northern gentlemen make *greater* professions of devotion to our institutions than we do ourselves, our suspicions are somewhat excited.

The Senator has alluded to the action of my State; he has commented upon my devotion to the people; he has been reviewing my political history; he has even commented upon the nature and character of my mind; and he has failed to discover anything extraordinary in it. As to the character of my mind, as I before remarked, that is a subject which I have never obtruded upon any one. I have never made any pretensions to anything extraordinary, as regards intellect or extensive information; but, were the reverse of this all true, and had I the wisdom of Solomon, and a mind as strong, as clear, and as penetrating as the rays of the noonday sun when there is not a speck or a dot to obscure his disk, I should then even despair of breaking through the triple case of bigotry, superciliousness, and self-conceit, that surrounds the mind of the Senator from Oregon. Mind, did I say? I recall that term; I will not dignify it with the appellation of mind. No, it is the most miserable and the poorest caricature of a mind, that cannot even tell when it is upside up or upside down.

The Senator has reviewed my political history. He has not discovered that I ever introduced or projected any great measure except the "Homestead"; to that I had given great attention and labor. From what he has said on this occasion, I may infer that he was opposed to the Homestead policy. I believed it was a beneficent measure. It has been an object long near my heart to see every head of a family domiciliated. I thought it was important that every honest and industrious head of a family in this Republic should have a home and an abiding place for his wife and children. I think so still. I can well remember the period of time at which I could exult in the assurance that I had a home for my family; and I know how to sympathize with those who are not so blessed. Less gifted than the Senator from Oregon, I did not perceive that when, in the Senate, in the House of Representatives, and before the people, I advocated a measure that I thought had a tendency to alleviate and ameliorate the condition of the great mass of mankind, I was incurring the censure that is due to a crime. Lamentably devoid of his wisdom, if I had succeeded in accomplishing the great object I contemplated, the measure of my ambition would have been full. I have labored for it long; I labor still. In 1846 it was introduced into the House of Representatives with but few friends. In 1852 it received a two-thirds vote of that House. It came to the Senate of the United States, and during the last session of Congress forty-four Senators voted for it, and only eight against it. The Senator from Oregon himself, though he doubted and wavered, recorded *his* vote for it; but he is opposed to it now. I think it was one of the best acts of his life; and if it had succeeded I think it would have been better for the country.

But he intimates that I have been voting and acting with Senators who are not so intensely Southern as *he* pretends to be. Sir, look at the Senator's course this morning. *Who* has tried to defeat the measures that are so well calculated to restore peace? Who is trying to cast out the olive-branch that has been brought into the Senate? Why does he not stand with his noble colleague when this measure of peace is presented to the country?

But he refers to what has been the action of my State. Well, sir, we all know that the issue was directly made; and what has been the result? Tennessee has spoken in language not to be misunderstood. She has spoken in thunder-tones that she is against violations of the Constitution and the treasonable schemes which would result in breaking up the Government. The Senator assumes a special guardianship over Tennessee. He had better try to take care of Oregon, and leave my colleague and myself, and the Representatives from Tennessee, to attend to Tennessee affairs. Where does he stand? His colleague is in favor of measures to restore peace and sustain the country, and he is against them; and did it occur to him that others might ask how he stood with the people of Oregon? Tennessee stands redeemed, regenerated, and disenthralled by the exercise of the elective franchise, that glorious Franklin-rod which conducts the thunder of tyranny from the heads of the people. If the people of our sister States had enjoyed the same privilege of going to the ballot-box, and passing their judgment upon the ordinances of secession, I believe more of them would now be standing side by side with Tennessee, sustaining the laws and the Constitution. But the people have been overslaughed, a system of usurpation has been adopted, and a reign of terror instituted.

The Senator is exceedingly solicitous about Tennessee. I am inclined to think — I do not intend to be censorious or personal, but entirely senatorial — that at twelve o'clock on Monday next, or a few minutes before, when the hand of the dial is moving round to mark that important point of time when his term of office shall expire, instead of thinking about the action of my State, he may soliloquize in the language of Cardinal Wolsey, and exclaim, —

> "Nay, then, farewell!
> I have touched the highest point of all my greatness;
> And, from that full meridian of my glory,
> I haste now to my setting: I shall fall
> Like a bright exhalation in the evening,
> And no man see me more."

If the Senator has received the news from Tennessee, if the information has broken through that triple case of bigotry, superciliousness, and self-conceit which ensconce his caricature of a mind, with all his allusions to courage, and blood, and cowardice, he might feel like Macbeth, who, so long deceived by the juggling fiends, when told by Macduff that he was not of woman born, but from his mother's womb untimely ripped, in agony exclaimed, —

> "Accursed be that tongue that tells me so,
> For it hath cowed my better part of man:
> And be these juggling fiends no more believed,
> That palter with us in a double sense;
> That keep the word of promise to our ear,
> And break it to our hope."

Yes, Mr. President, I have alluded to treason and traitors, and shall not shrink from the responsibility of having done so, come what will; and while I, her humble representative, was speaking, Tennessee sent an echo back, in tones of thunder, which has carried terror and dismay through the whole camp of conspirators.

The Senator has alluded to my political course. What had that to do with the pending question? I did not attack the Senator from Oregon; he has attacked me. I had not even made an allusion to him in my speech, except in general terms; but he inquires into my consistency. How consistent has *he* been? We know how he stands upon popular or squatter sovereignty. On that subject he spoke at Concord, New Hampshire, where he maintained that the inhabitants of the Territories were the best judges; that they were the very people to settle all these questions. I will read what the Senator said on that occasion: —

"There is nothing in the law, gentlemen, but what every enlightened American heart should approve. *The idea incorporated in the Kansas-Nebraska bill is the true American principle; for the bill does not establish or prohibit slavery; but leaves the people of these Territories perfectly free to regulate their own local affairs in their own way.* Is there any man who can object to that idea? Is there any American citizen who can oppose that principle?

"Gentlemen, I desire to say to you that the principle incorporated into the Kansas-Nebraska bill is the very principle in defence of which your forefathers entered into the service of their country in the Revolutionary War; for the American colonies, two years previous to the Declaration of Independence, asserted this same principle we now find incorporated in the Kansas-Nebraska bill.

"Upon examination, you will find that the Declaration of Rights, made October 14, 1774, asserts *that the people of the several colonies 'are entitled to a free and exclusive power of legislation in their several provincial legislatures in all cases of internal polity.'* This was refused by the Crown, but reasserted by our forefathers. Upon this issue the battles of the Revolution were fought; by the blood of our fathers this principle of self-government was established. This right, refused by the King, was secured, consecrated, and established by the best blood that ever flowed in the veins of man. Would you now refuse to the people of the Territories the rights your noble sires demanded of the Crown, and won by their blood — thus placing yourselves in opposition to the right of self-government in the Territories, thereby occupying the very position towards the Territories that George III. did to the colonies?

"The simple question involved here is, 'are the people capable of regulating their internal affairs, or must Congress regulate those affairs for them?' It is strictly the doctrine of congressional non-intervention. Now, if that idea is the correct one — if it is true that the American people are capable of self-government — then the principles of the Kansas-Nebraska bill are right, and opposition to that bill is wrong; consequently, dangerous to the best interests of the country.

"The question of slavery is a most perplexing one, and ought not to be agitated. We should leave it with the State where it constitutionally exists, and the people of the Territories, to prohibit or establish, as to them may seem right and proper.

"All that the Democracy asks in relation to this matter is, that the people of the Territory should be left perfectly free to settle the question of slavery for themselves, without the interference of New Hampshire, Massachusetts, or any other State."

During the last Congress, however, the Senator made a speech, in which he repeated, I cannot tell how many times, "the equality of the States, the rights of the States in the Union, and their rights out of the Union;" and he thus shifted his course and repudiated his former position on squatter sovereignty. That speech was made on the 24th of May last. From it I will read the following extract: —

"I only desire to say, in relation to the series of resolutions, a portion of which I have already voted in favor of, that I shall vote in favor of the rest; for the whole of them together meet with my hearty approbation. They assert the truth; they assert the great principle that the constitutional rights of the States are equal; that the States have equal rights in this country under the Constitution; and, as I understand it, they must be maintained in that equality. These resolutions only assert that principle; and I say that it is a misfortune to the country, in my opinion, that the principles laid down in these resolutions had not been asserted sooner. They ought to have been asserted by the Democratic party, in plain English, ten years ago. If they had been, you would have had no trouble in this country to-day; the Democratic party would have been united and strong, and the equality and constitutional rights of the States would have been maintained in the Territory, and in all other things; squatter sovereignty would not have been heard of, and to-day we would be united."

If the conflict between his speech made in Concord in 1856 and his speech made here on the 24th day of May last can be reconciled, according to any rules of construction, it is fair to reconcile the conflict. If the discrepancy is so great between his speech made then and his speech on the 24th of May last as not to be reconciled, of course the discrepancy is against him; but I am willing to let one speech go as a set-off to the other, which will make honors easy, so far as speech-making is concerned.

Then how does the matter stand? The speech made at Concord, extracts from which I have read, is on the one side, and that made in the Senate on the 24th of May last, to which I have referred, is on the other side. Now we will come to the sticking place. We will now make a test from which there is no escape. You have seen the equivocation to-day. You have seen the cuttle-fish attempt to becloud the water and elude the grasp of its pursuer. I intend to stick his inconsistencies to him as close and as tight as what I have heard sometimes called "Jew David's Adhesive Plaster." Now to the record, and we will see how the Senator's vote stands as compared with his speeches. By referring to the record, it will be found that Mr. Clingman offered the following as an amendment to the fourth resolution of the series introduced by Mr. Davis: —

"*Resolved*, That the existing condition of the Territories of the United States does not require the intervention of Congress for the protection of property in slaves."

What was the vote on the amendment proposed to that resolution by Mr. Brown, to strike out the word "not"? I want the Senator's attention, for I am going to cite the record from which there is no appeal. How would it read to strike out the word "not"?

"That the existing condition of the Territories of the United States does require the intervention of Congress for the protection of property in slaves."

Among those who voted against striking out the word "not," who declared that protection of slavery in the Territories by legislation of Congress was unnecessary, was the Senator from Oregon. When was that? On the 25th day of May last. The Senator, under the solemn sanction of his oath, declared that legislation was not necessary. *Now* where do we find him? Here is a proposition to amend the Constitution to protect the institution of slavery in the States, and here is the proposition brought forward by the Peace Conference, and we find the Senator standing against the one, and I believe he recorded his vote against the other.

But we will proceed further with the investigation. The Senator voted that it was not necessary to legislate by Congress for the protection of slave property. Mr. Brown then offered the amendment to the resolution submitted by Mr. Davis, to strike out all after the word "resolved," and to insert in lieu thereof, —

> "That experience having already shown that the Constitution and the common law, unaided by statutory enactment, do not afford adequate and sufficient protection to slave property — some of the Territories having failed, others having refused, to pass such enactments — it has become the duty of Congress to interpose, and pass such laws as will afford to slave property in the Territories that protection which is given to other kinds of property."

We have heard a great deal said here to-day of "other kinds," and every description of property. There is a naked, clear proposition. Mr. Brown says it is needed; that the court and the common law do not give ample protection; and then the Senator from Oregon is called upon; but what is his vote? We find, in the vote upon this amendment, that but three Senators voted for it; and the Senator from Oregon records his vote, and says "no," it shall not be established; and every Southern Senator present, save three, voted against it also. When was that? On the 25th day of May last. Here is an amendment, now, to protect and secure the States against any encroachment upon the institution within the States, and there the Senator from Oregon swore that no further legislation was necessary to protect it in the Territories. Then, all the amendments being voted down, the Senate came to the vote upon this resolution, —

> "That, if experience should at any time prove that the judicial and executive authority do not possess means to insure adequate protection to constitutional rights in a Territory, and if the territorial government should fail or refuse to provide the necessary remedies for that purpose, it will be the duty of Congress to supply such deficiency, within the limits of its constitutional powers."

Does not the resolution proceed upon the idea that it was not necessary then; but if hereafter the Territories should refuse, and the courts and the common law could not give ample protection, then it would be the duty of Congress to do this thing? What has transpired since the 25th day of May last? Is not the decision of the court with us? Is there not the Constitution carrying it there? Why was not this resolution, declaring protection necessary, passed during the last Congress? The presidential election was on hand.

I have been held up, and indirectly censured, because I have stood by the people; because I have advocated those measures that are sometimes called demagogical. I would to God that we had a few more men here who were for the people in fact, and who would legislate in conformity with their will and wishes. If we had, the difficulties and dangers that surround us now would be postponed and set aside; they would not be upon us. But in

May last we could not vote that it was necessary to pass a slave code for the Territories. Oh, no, the presidential election was on hand. We were very willing then to try to get Northern votes; to secure their influence in the passage of resolutions; and to crowd some men down, and let others up. It was all very well then; but since the people have determined that some one else should be President of the United States, all at once the grape has got to be very sour, and gentlemen do not have as good an opinion of the people as they had before; they have changed their views in regard to the people. They have not thought quite as well of some of the aspirants as they desired; and, as they could not get to be President and Vice-President of all these United States, rather than miss it altogether, they would be perfectly willing to be President and Vice-President of a part, and therefore they will divide — yes, they will divide. They are in favor of secession; of breaking up the Union; of having the rights of the States out of the Union; and as they signally failed in being President and Vice-President of all, as the people have decided against them, they have reached that precise point of time at which the Government ought to be dissevered and broken up. It looks a little that way.

I have no disposition, Mr. President, to press this controversy further. If the Senator from Oregon is satisfied with the reply he has made to my speech or speeches, I am more than satisfied. I am willing that his speeches and mine shall go to the country; and, as to the application and understanding of the authorities that are recited in each, I am willing to leave for the determination of an intelligent public. I shall make no issue with him on that subject. I feel to-day — and I say it in no spirit of egotism — that, in the reply I made to his speech, I vanquished every position he assumed; I nailed many of his statements to the counter as spurious coin; and I felt that I had the arguments, that I had the authority; and so feeling, I know when I have my adversary in my power; I know when I have an argument that cannot be explained away, and a fact that cannot be upturned. The Senator felt it. I know he felt it from his former manifestations, and from the manner in which he has poured forth the wrath so long nursed in his bosom. Yes, sir, in that contest, figuratively speaking, he was impaled and left writhing in bitter agony. He felt it. I saw he felt it, and now I have no disposition, in concluding my remarks, to mutilate the dead, or add one single pang to the tortures of the already politically damned. I am a humane man; I will not add another pang to the intolerable sufferings of the distinguished Senator from Oregon. [Laughter.] I sought no controversy with him; I have made no issue with him; it has been forced upon me. How many have attacked me; and is there a single man, North or South, who is in favor of this glorious Union, who has dared to make an assault upon me? Is there one? No, not one. But it is all from secession; it is all from that reign of terror which usurpation has inaugurated. The Senator has made the set-to; and it is for the Senate and the country to determine who has been crushed in the tilt. I am satisfied, if he is. I am willing, as I said before, that his speech and mine shall go to the country, and let an intelligent people read and understand, and see who is right and who is wrong on this great issue.

But, sir, I alluded to the fact that secession has been brought about by usurpation. During the last forty days six States of this Confederacy have been taken out of the Union; how? By the voice of the people? No; it is demagogism to talk of the people. By the voice of the freemen of the country? No. By whom has it been done? Have the people of South Carolina passed upon the ordinance adopted by their convention? No; but a system of usurpation was instituted, and a reign of terror inaugurated. How was it in Georgia? Have the people there passed upon the ordinance of secession? No. We know that there was a powerful party there, of passive, conservative men, who have been overslaughed, borne down; and tyranny and usurpation have triumphed. A convention passed an ordinance to take the State out of the Confederacy; and the very same convention appointed delegates to go to a congress to make a constitution, without consulting the people. So with

Louisiana; so with Mississippi; so with all the six States which have undertaken to form a new confederacy. Have the people been consulted? Not in a single instance. We are in the habit of saying that man is capable of self-government; that he has the right, the unquestioned right, to govern himself; but here a government has been assumed over him; it has been taken out of his hands, and at Montgomery a set of usurpers are enthroned, legislating, and making constitutions and adopting them, without consulting the freemen of the country. Do we not know it to be so? Have the people of Alabama, of Georgia, of any of those States, passed upon it? No; but a constitution is adopted by those men, with a provision that it may be changed by a vote of two thirds. Four votes in a convention of six can change the whole organic law of a people constituting six States. Is not this a *coup-d'état* equal to any of Napoleon? Is it not a usurpation of the people's rights?

In some of those States even the flag of our country has been changed. One State has a palmetto, another has a pelican, and another has the rattlesnake run up instead of the Stars and Stripes. On a former occasion I spoke of the origin of secession; and I traced its early history to the Garden of Eden, when the serpent's wile and the serpent's wickedness beguiled and betrayed our first mother. After that occurred, and they knew light and knowledge, when their Lord and Master appeared, they seceded, and hid themselves from his presence. The serpent's wile and the serpent's wickedness first started secession; and now secession brings about a return of the serpent. Yes, sir; the wily serpent, the rattlesnake, has been substituted as the emblem on the flag of one of the seceding States, and that old flag, the Stars and the Stripes, under which our fathers fought and bled and conquered, and achieved our rights and our liberties, is pulled down and trailed in the dust. Will the American people tolerate it? They will be indulgent; time, I think, will be given; but they will not submit to it.

A word more in conclusion. Give the border States that security which they desire, and the time will come when the other States will come back; when they will be brought back — how? Not by the coercion of the border States, but by the coercion of the people; and those leaders who have taken them out will fall beneath the indignation and the accumulating force of that public opinion which will ultimately crush them. The gentlemen who have taken those States out are not the men to bring them back.

I have already suggested that the idea may have entered into some minds, "if we cannot get to be President and Vice-President of the whole United States, we may divide the Government, set up a new establishment, have new offices, and monopolize them ourselves when we take our States out." Here we see a President made, a Vice-

President made, cabinet officers appointed, and yet the great mass of the people not consulted, nor their assent obtained in any manner whatever. The people of the country ought to be aroused to this condition of things; they ought to buckle on their armor; and, as Tennessee has done, (God bless her!) by the exercise of the elective franchise, by going to the ballot-box under a new set of leaders, repudiate and put down those men who have carried these States out and usurped a government over their heads. I trust in God that the old flag of the Union will never be struck. I hope it may long wave, and that we may long hear the national air sung: —

> "The Star-Spangled banner, O long may it wave
> O'er the land of the free and the home of the brave."

Long may we hear Hail Columbia, that good old national air; long may we hear, and never repudiate, the old tune of Yankee Doodle! Long may wave that gallant old flag which went through the Revolution, and which was borne by Tennessee and Kentucky at the battle of New Orleans. And in the language of another, while it was thus proudly and gallantly unfurled as the emblem of the Union, the Goddess of Liberty hovered around, when "the rockets' red glare" went forth through the heavens, indicating that the battle was raging, and the voice of the old chief could be heard rising above the din of the storm, urging his gallant men on to the stern encounter, and watched the issue as the conflict grew fierce, and the result was doubtful; but when, at length, victory perched upon your standard, it was then, from the plains of New Orleans, that the Goddess made her loftiest flight, and proclaimed victory in strains of exultation. Will Tennessee ever desert the grave of him who bore it in triumph, or desert the flag that he waved with success? No, never; she was in the Union before some of these States were in existence; and she intends to remain in, and insist upon — as she has the confident belief she shall get — all her constitutional rights and protection in the Union, and under the Constitution of the country. [Applause in the galleries.]

The PRESIDING OFFICER:[1] — It will become the unpleasant but imperative duty of the Chair to clear the galleries.

Mr. JOHNSON. I have done.

[The applause was renewed, and was louder and more general than before. Hisses were succeeded by applause, and cheers were given and reiterated, with "Three cheers more for JOHNSON of Tennessee!"]

[As Mr. JOHNSON sat down, the spectators in the densely crowded galleries rose in order to leave, when, after the lapse of a few seconds, a faint cheer, followed by the clapping of a single pair of hands, was raised in the southeast corner of the ladies' gallery. This was hesitatingly imitated by two or three

[1] Mr. Fitch in the chair.

persons further on in the south range of the same gallery, but, instantaneously gathering strength, it lighted up the enthusiasm of the packed galleries in the west and northwest quarters, and a tremendous outburst of applause, putting to silence the powerful blows from the hammer of the Presiding Officer, succeeded. Three cheers were given for the Union, and three for ANDREW JOHNSON of Tennessee; and as by this time the Senators on the floor gave the strongest token of indignation and outraged dignity, the retreating crowd uttered a shower of hisses. Altogether, the exhibition was the most vociferous and unrepressed that ever took place in the galleries of either house of Congress.]

SPEECH AT CINCINNATI, OHIO.

DELIVERED JUNE 19, 1861.

Fellow-Citizens: — In reply to the cordial welcome which has just been tendered to me, through your chosen organ, — in reply to what has been said by the gentlemen chosen by you to bid me welcome to Cincinnati, I have not language adequate to express my feelings of gratitude. I cannot find language to thank you for the tender of good-fellowship which has been made to me on the present occasion. I came here without any expectation that such a reception was in store for me. I had no expectation of being received and welcomed in the language, I may say, the eloquent and forcible language of your chosen organ. I am deserving of no such tender.

I might conclude what little I am going to say by merely responding to and indorsing every single sentence uttered on this occasion, in welcoming me to your midst. [Applause.]

For myself, I feel that while I am a citizen of a Southern State — a citizen of the South, and of the State of Tennessee, I feel, at the same time, that I am also a citizen of the United States. [Applause.]

Most cordially do I respond to what has been said in reference to the maintenance of the Constitution of the United States, in all its bearings, in all its principles therein contained. The Constitution of the United States lays down the basis upon which the Union of all the States of this confederacy can and may be maintained and preserved, if it be literally and faithfully carried out. [Applause.] So far as I am concerned, feeling that I am a citizen of the Union — that I am a citizen of the United States, I am willing to abide by that Constitution. I am willing to live under a government that is built upon and perpetuated upon the principles laid down by the Constitution, which was framed by Washington and his compeers, after coming from the heat and strife of bloody revolution. [Applause.]

I repeat, again, that I have not language adequate to express my gratitude and appreciation of the kindness which has been manifested in regard to my humble self. I cannot sufficiently thank you for the manifestation of your appreciation of the course I have pursued in regard to the crisis which is now upon this country. I have no words to utter, or rather I have words which will not give utterance to the feelings that I entertain on this occasion. [Applause.] I feel, to-day, a confidence in my own bosom that the cordiality, and the sympathy, and the response that comes here from the people of Ohio, is heartfelt and sincere. I feel that in reference to the great question now before the people, those whom I see before me are honest and sincere. [Applause.] I repeat again, and for the third time, that I have no language with which I can express my gratitude to you, and at the same time my devotion to the principles of the Constitution, and the flag and emblem of our glorious Union of States. [Applause.]

I know that there has been much said about the North, much said about the South. I am proud here, to-day, to hear the sentiments which have been uttered in reference to the North and the South, and the relations that exist between these two sections. [Applause.] I am glad to hear it said in such a place as this, that the pending difficulties — I might say, the existing war — which are now upon this country, do not grow out of any animosity to the local institution of any section. [Applause.] I am glad to be assured that it grows out of a determination to maintain the glorious principles upon which the Government itself rests, — the principles contained in the Constitution, — and, at the same time, to rebuke and to bring back, as far as may be practicable, within the pale of the Constitution, those individuals, or States even, who have taken it upon themselves to exercise a principle and doctrine at war with all government, with all association — political, moral, and religious. [Applause.] I mean the doctrine of secession, which is neither more nor less than a heresy —

a fundamental error — a political absurdity, coming in conflict with all organized government, with everything that tends to preserve law and order in the United States, or wherever else the odious and abominable doctrine may be attempted to be exercised. I look upon the doctrine of secession as coming in conflict with all organism, moral and social. I repeat, without regard to the peculiar institutions of the respective States composing this confederacy, without regard to any government that may be founded in the future, or exists in the present, this odious doctrine of secession should be crushed out, destroyed, and totally annihilated. No government can stand, no religious, or moral, or social organization can stand, where this doctrine is tolerated. [Applause.] It is disintegration — universal dissolvement — in making war upon everything that has a tendency to promote and ameliorate the condition of the mass of mankind. [Applause.] Therefore I repeat, that this odious and abominable doctrine — you must pardon me for using a strong expression — I do not say it in a profane sense — but this doctrine I conceive to be — *hell-born and hell-bound*, and one which will carry everything in its train, unless it is arrested and crushed out from our midst. [Great Applause.]

In response to what has been said to me here today, I confess, when I lay my hand upon my bosom, I feel gratified at hearing the sentiments that have been uttered — that we are all willing to stand up for the constitutional rights guaranteed to every State, every community, — that we are all determined to stand up for the prerogatives secured to us in the Constitution as citizens of States, composing one grand confederacy, whether we belong to the North or to the South, to the East or to the West. I say that I am gratified to hear such sentiments uttered here to-day. I regard them as the most conclusive evidence that there is no disposition on the part of any citizens of the loyal States to make war upon any peculiar institution of the South, [Applause,] whether it be slavery or anything else, — leaving that institution under the Constitution, to be controlled by time, circumstances, and the great laws which lie at the foundation of all things which political legislation can control. [Applause.]

While I am before you, my countrymen, I am in hopes it will not be considered out of place for me to make a single remark or two in reference to myself as connected with the present crisis. My position in the Congress of the United States during its last session is, I suppose, familiar to most, if not all, of you. You know the doctrine I laid down then, and I can safely say that the opinions I entertain now on the questions of the day are as they were then. I have not changed them. I have seen no reason to change them. I believe that a government without the power to enforce its laws made in conformity with the Constitution, is no government at all. [Applause.] We have arrived at that period in our national history at which it has become necessary for this Government to say to the civilized, as well as to the pagan world, whether it is in reality a government, or whether it is but a pretext for a government. If it has power to preserve its existence, and to maintain the principles of the Constitution and the laws, that time has now arrived. If it is a government, that authority should be asserted. I say, then, let the civilized world see that we have a government. Let us dispel the delusion under which we have been laboring since the inauguration of the Government in 1789, — let us show that it is not an ephemeral institution, that we have not merely imagined we had a government, and when the test came, that the government frittered away between our fingers and quickly faded in the distance. [Applause.] The time has come when the government reared by our fathers should assert itself, and give conclusive proof to the civilized world that it is a reality and a perpetuity. [Applause.] Let us show to other nations that this doctrine of secession is a heresy; that States coming into the confederacy, that individuals living in the confederacy, under the Constitution have no right nor authority, upon their own volition, to set the laws and the Constitution aside, and to bid defiance to the authority of the government under which they live. [Applause.]

I substantially cited the best authority that could

be produced upon this subject, and took this position during the last session of Congress. I stand here to-day before you and advocate the same principles for which I then contended. As early as 1833, (let me here say I am glad to find that the committee which have waited upon me on this occasion represent all the parties among which we have been divided,) — as early as 1833, I say, I formed my opinions in reference to this doctrine of secession in the nullification of the laws of the United States. I held these doctrines up to the year 1850, and I maintain them still. [Applause.] I entertained these opinions down to the latest sitting of Congress, and I have reiterated them. I entertain and express them here to-day. [Applause.] In this connection I may be permitted to remark, that, during our last struggle for the Presidency, all parties contended for the preservation of the Union. Without going further back, what was that struggle? Senator Douglas, of the State of Illinois, was a candidate. His friends presented him as the best Union man. I shall speak upon this subject in reference to my position. Mr. Breckinridge's friends presented him to the people as the Union candidate. I was one of Mr. Breckinridge's friends. The Bell men presented the claims of the Hon. John Bell of Tennessee for the Presidency upon the ground that he was the best Union candidate. The Republican party, so far as I understand them, have always been in favor of the Union. Then here was the contest between four candidates presented to the consideration of the people of the United States.

Now, where do we find ourselves? In times gone by you know we had our discussions and our quarrels. It was bank and anti-bank questions, tariff and anti-tariff, internal improvement and anti-internal improvement, or the distribution of the money derived from the sale of public land among the several States. Such measures as these were presented to the people, and the aim in the solution of all was how best to preserve the union of these States. One party favored the measures as calculated to promote the welfare of our common country; another opposed them to bring about the same result. Then what was the former contest? Bringing it down to the present time, there has been no disagreement between Republicans, Bell men, Douglas men, and Breckinridge men, as regards the preservation of the union of States. Now, however, these measures are all laid aside; all these party questions are left out of consideration, and the great question comes up as to the Constitution, as adopted by the old Articles of Confederation, and afterwards reaffirmed in the adoption of the Constitution of the United States. Now, when this great question arises, involving the preservation and existence of the United States, I am proud to meet this vast concourse of people, and hear them say they are willing to lay aside all party measures, all party considerations, and come up to join in one fraternal hug to sustain the bright Stars and broad Stripes of our glorious Union, — all willing to coöperate for the consummation of a sublime purpose, without regard to former party differences, — that we are all determined to stand fast by the union of these States. [Applause.]

So far as I am concerned, I am willing to say in this connection that I am proud to stand here among you as one of the humble upholders and supporters of the Stars and Stripes that have been borne by Washington through a seven years' revolution, — a bold and manly struggle for our independence, and separation from the mother-country. That is my flag — that flag was borne by Washington in triumph. Under it I want to live, and under no other. It is that flag that has been borne in triumph by the Revolutionary fathers over every battle-field, when our brave men, after toil and danger, laid down and slept on the cold ground, with no covering but the inclement sky, and arose in the morning and renewed their march over the frozen ground, as the blood trickled from their feet, — all to protect that banner and bear it aloft triumphantly. I have intimated that I should make some allusion to myself. I have indicated to you what were my opinions and my views from 1838 down to the moment I stand before you. With the facts in relation to the contest which took place recently in the State of Tennessee, you are all familiar. No longer ago than last February there was an extra session of the Legislature called. There was then a law passed authorizing a convention to be called. The people of that State voted it down by a majority of sixty-four thousand.

In a very short time afterwards another session of the Legislature was called. This Legislature went into secret session in a very short time. While the Southern Confederacy, or its agents, had access to it, and were put in possession of the doings and proceedings of this secret session, the great mass of my own State were not permitted even to put their ears to the keyhole, or to look through a crevice in the doors, to ascertain what was being done. A league with the Southern Confederacy has been formed, and the State has been handed over to the Southern Confederacy, with Jefferson Davis at its head. We, the people of Tennessee, have been handed over to this Confederacy, I say, like sheep in the shambles, bound hand and foot, to be disposed of as Jefferson Davis and his cohorts may think proper. This Ordinance was passed by the Convention with a proviso that it should be submitted to the people. The Governor was authorized to raise fifty-five thousand men. Money was appropriated to enable him to carry out this diabolical and nefarious scheme, depriving the people of their rights, disposing of them as stock in the market, — handing them over, body and soul, to the Southern Confederacy.

Now you may talk about slaves and slavery, but in most instances when a slave changes his master, even he has the privilege of choosing whom he desires for his next master; but in this instance the sovereign people of a free State have not been allowed the power or privilege of choosing the master they desired to serve. They have been given a master without their consent or advice. No trouble was taken to ascertain what their desires were, — they were at once handed over to this Southern Confederacy.

Mr. JOHNSON here referred to the provisions of the Tennessee Secession Ordinance, &c. Noticing the persecution of the Union men in Tennessee, he remarked: —

But while this contest has been going on, a portion of our fellow-citizens have been standing up for the Constitution and the Union, and because they have dared to stand upon the great embattlement of constitutional liberties, exercising the freedom and the liberty of speech, a portion of our people have declared that we are traitors; they have said that our fate was to be the fate of traitors; and that hemp was growing, and that the day of our execution was approaching, — that the time would come when those who dare stand by the Constitution and the principles therein embraced, would expiate their deeds upon the gallows. We have met all these things. We have met them in open day. We have met them face to face — toe to toe — at least in one portion of the State. We have told them that the Constitution of the United States defines treason, and that definition is, that treason against the United States shall consist only in levying war against the General Government of the United States. We have told them that the time would come when the principles of the Constitution and the law defining treason would be maintained. We have told them that the time would come when the judiciary of the Government would be sustained in such a manner that it could define what was treason under the Constitution and the law made in conformity with it, and that when defined, they would ascertain who were the traitors, and who it was that would stretch the hemp they had prepared for us. [Applause.]

I know that, in reference to myself and others, rewards have been offered, and it has been said that warrants have been issued for our arrest. Let me say to you here to-day, that I am no fugitive, especially no fugitive from justice. [Laughter.] If I were a fugitive, I would be a fugitive from tyranny — a fugitive from the reign of terror. But, thank God, the country in which I live, and that division of the State from which I hail, will record a vote of twenty-five thousand against the Secession Ordinance. The county in which I live gave a majority of two thousand and seven against this odious, diabolical, nefarious, hell-born and hell-bound doctrine.

SPEECH ON THE WAR FOR THE UNION.

DELIVERED IN THE SENATE OF THE UNITED STATES, JULY 27, 1861.

The Senate having under consideration the joint resolution to approve and confirm certain acts of the President of the United States for suppressing insurrection and rebellion, Mr. Johnson said: —

Mr. President: When I came from my home to the seat of Government, in compliance with the proclamation of the President of the United States calling us together in extra session, it was not my intention to engage in any of the discussions that might transpire in this body; but since the session began, in consequence of the course that things have taken, I feel unwilling to allow the Senate to adjourn without saying a few words in response to many things that have been submitted to the Senate since its session commenced. What little I shall say to-day will be without much method or order. I shall present the suggestions that occur to my mind, and shall endeavor to speak of the condition of the country as it is.

On returning here, we find ourselves, as we were when we adjourned last spring, in the midst of a civil war. That war is now progressing, without much hope or prospect of a speedy termination. It seems to me, Mr. President, that our Government has reached one of three periods through which all governments must pass. A nation, or a people, have first to pass through a fiery ordeal in obtaining their independence or separation from the government to which they were attached. We passed through such an one in the Revolution; we were seven years in effecting the separation, and in taking our position amongst the nations of the earth as a separate and distinct power. Then, after having succeeded in establishing its independence, and taken its position among the nations of the earth, a nation must show its ability to maintain that position, that separate and distinct independence against other powers, against foreign foes. In 1812, in the history of our Government, this ordeal commenced, and terminated in 1815.

There is still another trial through which a nation must pass. It has to contend against internal foes; against enemies at home; against those who have no confidence in its integrity, or in the institutions that may be established under its organic law. We are in the midst of this third ordeal, and the problem now being solved before the nations of the earth, and before the people of the United States, is, whether we can succeed in maintaining ourselves against the internal foes of the Government; whether we can succeed in putting down traitors and treason, and in establishing the great fact that we have a

Government with sufficient strength to maintain its existence against whatever combination may be presented in opposition to it.

This brings me to a proposition laid down by the Executive in his recent message to the Congress of the United States. In that message the President said, —

> "This is essentially a people's contest. On the side of the Union it is a struggle for maintaining in the world that form and substance of government whose leading object is to elevate the condition of men; to lift artificial weights from all shoulders; to clear the paths of laudable pursuit for all; to afford all an unfettered start, and a fair chance in the race of life. Yielding to partial and temporary departures, from necessity, this is the leading object of the Government for whose existence we contend."

I think the question is fairly and properly stated by the President, that it is a struggle whether the people shall rule; whether the people shall have a government based upon their intelligence, upon their integrity, upon their purity of character, sufficient to govern themselves. I think this is the true issue; and the time has now arrived when the energies of the nation must be put forth, when there must be union and concert among all who agree in man's capability of self-government, in order to demonstrate that great proposition, without regard to former party divisions or prejudices.

Since this discussion commenced, it has been urged in argument, by Senators on one side, that there was a disposition to change the nature and character of the Government; and that, if we proceeded as we were going, it would result in establishing a dictatorship. It has been said that the whole framework, nature, genius, and character of the Government would be entirely changed; and great apprehensions have been expressed that it would result in a consolidation of the Government or a dictatorship. We find, in the speech delivered by the distinguished Senator from Kentucky[1] the other day, the following paragraph, alluding to what will be the effect of the passage of this joint resolution approving the action of the President: —

"Here in Washington, in Kentucky, in Missouri, everywhere where the authority of the President extends, in his discretion he will feel himself warranted by the action of Congress upon this resolution to subordinate the civil to the military power; to imprison citizens without warrant of law; to suspend the writ of *habeas corpus*; to establish martial law; to make seizures and searches without warrant; to suppress the press; to do all those acts which rest in the will and in the authority of a military commander. In my judgment, sir, if we pass it, we are upon the eve of putting, so far as we can, in the hands of the President of the United States the power of a dictator."

Then, in reply to the Senator from Oregon,[2] he seems to have great apprehension of a radical change in our form of government. The Senator goes on to say, —

"The pregnant question, Mr. President, for us to decide is, whether the Constitution is to be respected in this struggle; whether we are to be called upon to follow the flag over the

[1] Mr. Breckinridge. [2] Mr. Baker.

ruins of the Constitution? Without questioning the motives of any, I believe that the whole tendency of the present proceedings is to establish a government without limitation of powers, and to change radically our frame and character of government."

Sir, I most fully concur with the Senator that there is a great effort being made to change the nature and character of our Government. I think that effort is being demonstrated and manifested most clearly every day; but we differ as to the parties who are making this great effort.

The Senator alludes in his speech to a conversation he had with some very intelligent gentleman who formerly represented our country abroad. It appears from that conversation that foreigners were accustomed to say to Americans, "I thought your Government existed by consent; now how is it to exist?" and the reply was, "We intend to change it; we intend to adapt it to our condition; these old colonial geographical divisions and States will ultimately be rubbed out, and we shall have a government strong and powerful enough." The Senator seemed to have great apprehensions based on those conversations. He read a paragraph from a paper, indicating that State lines were to be rubbed out. In addition to all this he goes on to state that the writ of *habeas corpus* has been violated, and he says that since the Government commenced there has not been a case equal to the one which has recently transpired in Maryland. I shall take up some of his points in their order, and speak of them as I think they deserve to be spoken of. The Senator says, —

> "The civil authorities of the country are paralyzed, and a practical martial law is being established all over the land. The like never happened in this country before, and would not be tolerated in any country in Europe which pretends to the elements of civilization and regulated liberty. George Washington carried the thirteen colonies through the war of the Revolution without martial law. The President of the United States cannot conduct the Government three months without resorting to it."

The Senator puts great stress on the point, and speaks of it in very emphatic language, that General Washington carried the country through the seven years of the Revolution without resorting to martial law during all that period of time. Now, how does the matter stand? When we come to examine the history of the country, it would seem that the Senator had not hunted up all the cases. We can find some, and one in particular, not very different from the case which has recently occurred, and to which he alluded. In 1777, the second year of the war of the Revolution, numbers of the Society of Friends in Philadelphia were arrested on suspicion of being disaffected to the cause of American freedom. A publication now before me says, —

> "The persons arrested, to the number of twenty," . . . . "were taken into custody, by military force, at their homes or usual places of business; many of them could not obtain any knowledge of the cause of their arrest, or of any one to

whom they were amenable, and they could only hope to avail themselves of the intervention of some civil authority.

"The Executive Council [of the State of Pennsylvania], being formed of residents of the city and county of Philadelphia, had a better knowledge of the Society of Friends and of their individual characters than the members of Congress assembled from the various parts of the country, and ought to have protected them. But instead of this, they caused these arrests of their fellow-citizens to be made with unrelenting severity, and from the 1st to the 4th day of September, 1777, the party was taken into confinement in the Mason's Lodge, in Philadelphia.

"On the minutes of Congress of 3d September, 1777, it appears that a letter was received by them from George Bryan, Vice-President of the Supreme Executive Council, dated 2d September, stating that arrests had been made of persons inimical to the American States, and desiring the advice of Congress particularly whether Augusta and Winchester, in Virginia, would not be proper places at which to secure prisoners." . . . .

"Congress must have been aware that it was becoming a case of very unjust suffering, for they passed their resolution of 6th September, 1777, as follows:—

"'That it be recommended to the Supreme Executive Council of the State of Pennsylvania to hear what the said remonstrants can allege to remove the suspicions of their being disaffected or dangerous to the United States.'

"But the Supreme Executive Council on the same day, referring to the above,

"'*Resolved*, That the President do write to Congress to let them know that the Council has not time to attend to that business in the present alarming crisis, and that they were, agreeably to the recommendation of Congress, at the moment the resolve was brought into Council, disposing of everything for the departure of the prisoners.'"

. . . .

"As the recommendation of Congress of the 6th of September, to give the prisoners a hearing, was refused by the Supreme Executive Council, the next minute made by Congress was as follows: —

"'In Congress, 8th September, 1777.

"'*Resolved*, That it would be improper for Congress to enter into a hearing of the remonstrants or other prisoners in the Mason's Lodge, they being inhabitants of Pennsylvania; and therefore, as the Council declines giving them a hearing for the reasons assigned in their letter to Congress, that it be recommended to said Council to order the immediate departure of such of the said prisoners as yet refuse to swear or affirm allegiance to the State of Pennsylvania, to Staunton, in Virginia.'

"The remonstrances made to Congress, and to the Supreme Executive Council, being unavailing, the parties arrested were ordered to depart for Virginia, on the 11th September, 1777, when, as their last resource, they applied, under the laws of Pennsylvania, to be brought before the judicial court by writs of *habeas corpus*.

"The departure of the prisoners was committed to the care of Colonel Jacob Morgan, of Bucks County, and they were guarded by six of the light-horse, commanded by Alexander Nesbitt and Samuel Caldwell, who were to obey the despatches from the Board of War, of which General Horatio Gates was president, directed to the lieutenants of the counties through which the prisoners were to pass.

"The writs of *habeas corpus*, on being presented to the Chief Justice, were marked by him, 'Allowed by Thomas McKean,' and they were served on the officers who had the prisoners in custody, when they had been taken on their journey as far as Reading, Pennsylvania, on the 14th day of September, but the officers refused to obey them.

"It appears by the Journal of the Supreme Executive Council of the 16th of September, that Alexander Nesbitt, one of the officers, had previously obtained information about the writs, and made a report of them; when the Pennsylvania Legislature, at the instance of the Supreme Executive Council, passed a law on the 16th of September, 1777, to suspend the *habeas corpus* act; and although it was an *ex post facto* law, as it related to their case, the Supreme Executive Council on that day ordered the same to be carried into effect."

Continuing the history of this case, we find that —

"The party consisted of twenty persons, of whom seventeen were members of the Society of Friends. They were ordered first to Staunton, then a frontier town in the western settlement of Virginia, but afterwards to be detained at Winchester, where they were kept in partial confinement nearly eight months, without provision being made for their support; for the only reference to this was by a resolution of the Supreme Executive Council of Pennsylvania, dated April 8, 1778, as follows: —

"'*Ordered*, That the whole expenses of arresting and confining the prisoners sent to Virginia, the expenses of their journey, and all other incidental charges, be paid by the said prisoners.'

"During the stay of the exiles at Winchester, nearly all of them suffered greatly from circumstances unavoidable in their situation — from anxiety, separation from their families left unprotected in Philadelphia, then a besieged city, liable at any time to be starved out or taken by assault; while from sickness and exposure during the winter season, in accommodations entirely unsuitable for them, two of their number departed this life in the month of March, 1778."

Thus, Mr. President, we find that the writ of *habeas corpus* was suspended by the authorities of Pennsylvania, during the Revolution, in the case of persons who were considered dangerous and inimical to the country. A writ was taken out and served upon the officers, and they refused to surrender the prisoners, or even to give them a hearing. If the Senator from Kentucky had desired an extreme case, and wished to make a display of his legal and historical information, it would have been very easy for him to have cited this case — much more aggravated, much more extravagant, much more striking, than the one in regard to which he was speaking. Let it be remembered, also, that this case, although it seems to be an extravagant and striking one, occurred during the war of the Revolution, under General Washington, before we had a President. We find that at that time the writ of *habeas corpus* was suspended, and twenty individuals were denied even the privilege of a hearing, because they were considered inimical and dangerous to the liberties of the country. In the midst of the Revolution, when the writ of *habeas corpus* was as well understood as it is now, when they were familiar with its operation in Great Britain, when they knew and understood all the rights and privileges it granted to the citizen, we find that the Legislature of Pennsylvania passed a law suspending the writ of *habeas corpus*, and went back and relieved the officers who refused to obey the writs, and indemnified them from the operation of any wrong they might have done. If the Senator wanted a strong and striking case, one that would bear comment, why did he not go back to this case, that occurred in the Revolution, during the very period referred to by him? But no; all these cases seem to have been forgotten, and the mind was fixed upon one of recent occurrence. There is a great similarity in them; but the one to which I have alluded is a much stronger case than that referred to by the Senator. It was in Philadelphia, where Congress was sitting; it was in Pennsylvania, where these persons, who were considered inimical to the freedom of the country, were found. Congress was appealed to, but Congress executed the order; and the Legislature of Pennsylvania afterwards passed a law indemnifying the persons who in execution of the order violated the right to the writ of *habeas corpus*. What is our case now? We are not struggling for the establishment of our nationality, but we are now struggling for the existence of the Government. Suppose the writ of *habeas corpus* has been suspended: the question arises whether it was not a justifiable suspension at the time; and ought we not now to indorse what we would ourselves have done if we had been here at the time the power was exercised?

The impression is sought to be made on the public mind that this is the first and only case where the power has been exercised. I have shown that there is one tenfold more striking, that occurred during our struggle for independence. Is this the first time that persons in the United States have been placed under martial law? In 1815, when New Orleans was about to be sacked, when a foreign foe was upon the soil of Louisiana, New Orleans was put under martial law, and Judge Hall was made a prisoner because he attempted to interpose. Is there a man here, or in the country, who condemns General Jackson for the exercise of the power of proclaiming martial law in 1815? Could that city have been saved without placing it under martial law, and making Judge Hall submit to it? I know that General Jackson submitted to be arrested, tried, and fined $1000; but what did Congress do in that case? It did just we are called on to do in this case. By the restoration of his fine — an act passed by an overwhelming majority in the two houses of Congress — the nation said "We approve what you did." Suppose, Mr. President, (and it may have been the case,) that the existence of the Government depended upon the protection and successful defence of New Orleans; and suppose, too, it was in violation of the strict letter of the Constitution for General Jackson to place New Orleans under martial law, but without placing it under martial law the Government would have been overthrown: is there any reasonable, any intelligent man in or out of Congress who would not indorse and approve the exercise of a power which was indispensable to the existence and maintenance of the Government? The Constitution was likely to be overthrown, the law was about to be violated, and the Government trampled under foot; and whenever it becomes necessary to prevent this, even by exercising a power that comes in conflict with the Constitution in time of peace, it surely ought to be exercised. If General Jackson had lost the city of New Orleans, and the Government had been overthrown through a refusal on his part to place Judge Hall and the city of New Orleans under martial law, he ought to have lost his head. But he acted as a soldier; he acted as a patriot; he acted as a statesman, — as one devoted to the institutions and the preservation and the existence of his Government; and the grateful homage of a nation was his reward.

Then, sir, the power which has been exercised in this instance is no new thing. In great emergencies, when the life of a nation is in peril, when its very existence is endangered, to question too nicely, to scan too critically, its acts in the very midst of that crisis, when the Government is liable to be overthrown, is to make war upon it, and to try to paralyze its energies. If those who seem to violate the laws of the United States in their efforts to preserve the Government are to be called to an account, wait until the country passes out of its peril; wait until the country is relieved from its difficulty; wait until the crisis passes by, and then come forward, dispassionately, and ascertain to what extent the law has been violated, if indeed it has been violated at all.

A great ado has been made in reference to the Executive proclamation calling out the militia of the States to the extent of seventy-five thousand men. That call was made under the authority of the act of 1795, and is perfectly in accordance with the law. It has been decided by the Supreme Court of the United States that that act is constitutional, and that the President alone is the judge of the question whether the exigency has arisen. This decision was made in the celebrated case of Martin *vs.* Mott. Let me read from the opinion of the court, delivered by Judge Story: —

"It has not been denied here that the act of 1795 is within the constitutional authority of Congress, or that Congress may not lawfully provide for cases of imminent danger of invasion, as well as for cases where an invasion has actually taken place. In our opinion, there is no ground for a doubt on this point, even if it had been relied on; for the power to provide for repelling invasion includes the power to provide against the attempt and danger of invasion, as the necessary and proper means to effectuate the object. One of the best means to repel invasion is to provide the requisite force for action before the invader himself has reached the soil.

"The power thus confided by Congress to the President is, doubtless, of a very high and delicate nature. A free people are naturally jealous of the exercise of military power; and the power to call the militia into actual service is certainly felt to be one of no ordinary magnitude. But it is not a power which can be executed without a correspondent responsibility. It is, in its terms, a limited power, confined to cases of actual invasion, or of imminent danger of invasion. If it be a limited power, the question arises, by whom is the exigency to be judged of and decided? Is the President the sole and exclusive judge whether the exigency has arisen, or is it to be considered as an open question, upon which every officer, to whom the orders of the President are addressed, may decide for himself, and equally open to be contested by every militia man who shall refuse to obey the orders of the President? We are all of opinion that the authority to decide whether the exigency has arisen belongs exclusively to the President, and that his decision is conclusive upon all other persons. We think that this construction necessarily results from the nature of the power itself and from the manifest object contemplated by the act of Congress. The power itself is to be exercised upon sudden emergencies, upon great occasions of state, and under circumstances which may be vital to the existence of the Union. A prompt and unhesitating obedience to orders is indispensable to the complete attainment of the object. The service is a military service, and the command of a military nature; and in such cases every delay and every obstacle to an efficient and immediate compliance necessarily tend to jeopard the public interests." — *Martin* vs. *Mott*, 12 Wheaton's *Reports*, p. 29.

We see, then, that the power is clear as to calling out the militia; and we have seen that we have precedents for the suspension of the writ of *habeas corpus*.

The next objection made is, that the President had no power to make additions to the Navy and Army. I say that in this he is justified by the great law of necessity. At the time, I believe it was necessary to the existence of the Government; and it being necessary, he had a right to exercise all those powers that, in his judgment, the crisis demanded for the maintenance of the existence of the Government itself. The real question — if you condemn the President for acting in the absence of law — is, Do you condemn the propriety of his course ; do you condemn the increase of the Army ; do you condemn the increase of the Navy ? If you oppose the measure simply upon the ground that the Executive called them forth anticipating law, I ask what will you do now ? The question presents itself at this time, Is it not necessary to increase the Army and the Navy ? If you condemn the exercise of the power by the Executive in the absence of law, what will you do now, as the law-making power, when it is manifest that the Army and Navy should be increased ? You make war upon the Executive for anticipating the action of Congress. Does not the Government need an increase of the Army and the Navy ? Where do gentlemen stand now ? Are they for it ? Do they sustain the Government ? Are they giving it a helping hand ? No ; they go back and find fault with the exercise of a power that they say was without law ; but now, when they have the power to make the law, and when the necessity is apparent, they stand back and refuse. Where does that place those who take that course ? It places them against the Government, and against placing the means in the hands of the Government to defend and perpetuate its existence. The object is apparent, Mr. President. We had enemies of the Government here last winter ; in my opinion, we have enemies of the Government here now.

I said that I agreed with the Senator from Kentucky that there was a design — a deliberate determination — to change the nature and character of our Government. Yes, sir, it has been the design for a long time. All the talk about slavery and compromise has been but a pretext. We had a long disquisition, and a very feeling one, from the Senator from Kentucky. He became pathetic on the hopelessness of compromises. Did not the Senator from California[1] the other day show unmistakably that it was not compromises they wanted? I will add, that compromise was the thing they most feared; and their great effort was to get out of Congress before any compromise could be made. From the first, their cry was for peaceable secession and reconstruction. They talked not of compromise; and, I repeat, their greatest dread and fear was, that something would be agreed upon; that their last and only pretext would be swept from under them, and that they would stand before the country naked and exposed. The Senator from California pointed out to you a number of these men who stood here and did not vote for certain propositions of compromise, and by their means those propositions were lost.

What was the action before the committee of thirteen? Why did not that committee agree? Some of the most ultra men from the North were members of that committee, and they proposed to amend the Constitution so as to provide that Con-

[1] Mr. Latham.

gress in the future never should interfere with the subject of slavery. The committee failed to agree, and some of its members at once telegraphed to their States that they must go out of the Union at once. But after all that transpired in the early part of the session, what was done? We know what the argument has been, in times gone by, again and again. It has been said that one great object of the North was, first to abolish slavery in the District of Columbia and the slave-trade between the States, as a kind of initiative measure; next, to exclude it from the Territories; and when the free States constituted three fourths of all the States, so as to have power to change the Constitution, they would amend the Constitution so as to give Congress power to legislate upon the subject of slavery in the States, and expel it from the States in which it is now. Has not that been the argument? Now, how does the matter stand? At the last session of Congress seven States withdrew; it may be said that eight withdrew; reducing the remaining slave States down to one fourth of the whole number of States. The charge has been made, that, whenever the free States constituted a majority in the Congress of the United States sufficient to amend the Constitution, they would so amend it as to legislate upon the institution of slavery within the States, and that the institution of slavery would be overthrown. This has been the argument; it has been repeated again and again, and hence the great struggle about the Territories. The argument was, that we must prevent the creation of free States; we did not want to be reduced to that point where, under the sixth article of the Constitution, three fourths could amend the Constitution so as to exclude slavery from the States. This has been the great point; this has been the rampart over which it has been urged that the free States wanted to pass. Now, how does the fact stand? Let us "render unto Cæsar the things that are Cæsar's." We reached, at the last session, just the point where we were in the power of the free States, and then what was done? Instead of an amendment to the Constitution of the United States conferring power upon Congress to legislate upon the subject of slavery, what was done? This joint resolution was passed by a two-thirds majority in each House: —

> "*Resolved by the Senate and House of Representatives of the United States of America in Congress assembled*, That the following article be proposed to the Legislatures of the several States, as an amendment to the Constitution of the United States, which, when ratified by three fourths of said Legislatures, shall be valid, to all intents and purposes, as part of the said Constitution, viz:
>
> "Art. 13. No amendment shall be made to the Constitution which will authorize or give to Congress the power to abolish or interfere, within any State, with the domestic institutions thereof, including that of persons held to service or labor by the laws of said State."

Is not that very conclusive? Here is an amendment to the Constitution of the United States to make the Constitution unamendable upon that subject, as it is upon some other subjects; that Congress, in the future, should have no power to legislate on the subject of slavery within the States. Talk about "compromise," and about the settlement of this question; how can you settle it more substantially? How can you get a guaranty that is more binding than such an amendment to the Constitution? This places the institution of slavery in the States entirely beyond the control of Congress. Why have not the Legislatures that talk about "reconstruction" and "compromise" and "guaranties," taken up this amendment to the Constitution and adopted it? Some States have adopted it. How many Southern States have done so? Take my own State, for instance. Instead of accepting guaranties protecting them in all future time against the legislation of Congress on the subject of slavery, they undertake to pass ordinances violating the Constitution of the country, and taking the State out of the Union and into the Southern Confederacy. It is evident to me from all these things, that with many the talk about compromise and the settlement of this question is mere pretext, especially with those who understand the question.

What more was done at the last session of Congress, when the North had the power? Let us tell the truth. Three territorial bills were brought forward and passed. You remember in 1847, when the agitation arose in reference to the Wilmot proviso. You remember in 1850 the contest about slavery prohibition in the Territories. You remember in 1854 the excitement in reference to the Kansas-Nebraska bill, and the power conferred on the Legislature by it. Now we have a Constitutional amendment, proposed at a time when the Republicans have the power; and at the same time they come forward with three territorial bills, and in neither of those bills can be found any prohibition, so far as slavery in the Territories is concerned. Colorado, Nevada, and Dakota are organized without any prohibition of slavery. But what do you find in these bills? Mark, Mr. President, that there is no slavery prohibition; mark too, the language of the sixth section, conferring power upon the Territorial Legislature, —

"SEC. 6. *And be it further enacted*, That the legislative power of the Territory shall extend to all rightful subjects of legislation consistent with the Constitution of the United States and the provisions of this act; but no law shall be passed interfering with the primary disposal of the soil; no tax shall be imposed upon the property of the United States; nor shall the lands or other property of non-residents be taxed higher than the lands or other property of residents; nor shall any law be passed impairing the rights of private property; nor shall any discrimination be made in taxing different kinds of property; but all property subject to taxation shall be in proportion to the value of the property taxed."

Can there be anything more clear and conclusive? First, there is no prohibition; next, the Legislature shall have no power to legislate so as to impair the rights of private property, and shall not tax one description of property higher than another. Now, Mr. President, I ask any reasonable, intelligent man throughout the Union, to take the amendment to the Constitution, take the three territorial bills, put them all together, and how much of the slavery question is left? Is there any of it left? Yet we hear talk about compromise; and it is said the Union must be broken up because you cannot get compromise. Does not this settle the whole question? I should like to know how much more secure we can be in regard to this question of slavery? These three territorial bills cover every square inch of territory we have got; and here is an amendment to the Constitution embracing the whole question, so far as the States and the public lands of the United States are concerned. I know there are some who are sincere in this talk about compromise; but there are others who are merely making it a pretext, who come here claiming something in the hope that it will be refused, and that then, upon that refusal, their States may be carried out of the Union.

I am as much for compromise as any one can be; and there is no one who would desire more than myself to see peace and prosperity restored to the land; but when we look at the condition of the country, we find that rebellion is rife, that treason has reared its head. A distinguished Senator from Georgia once said, "When traitors become numerous enough, treason becomes respectable." Traitors are getting to be so numerous now that I suppose treason has almost got to be respectable; but God being willing, whether traitors be many or few, as I have hitherto waged war against traitors and treason, and in behalf of the Government which was constructed by our fathers, I intend to continue it to the end. [Applause in the galleries.]

The PRESIDENT *pro tempore.* Order!

Mr. JOHNSON continued: — Mr. President, we are in the midst of a civil war; blood has been shed; life has been sacrificed. Who commenced it? Of that we will speak hereafter. I am speaking now of the talk about compromise. Traitors and rebels are standing with arms in their hands, and it is said that we must go forward and compromise with them. They are in the wrong; they are making war upon the Government; they are trying to upturn and destroy our free institutions. I say to them that the compromise I have to offer under the existing circumstances is, — "Ground your arms; obey the laws; acknowledge the supremacy of the Constitution; — when you do that, I will talk to you about compromises." All the compromise that I have to make is the compromise of the Constitution of the United States. It is one of the best compromises that can be made. We lived under it from 1789 down to the 20th of December, 1860, when South Carolina undertook to go out of the Union. We prospered; we advanced in wealth, in commerce, in agriculture, in trade, in manufactures, in all the arts and sciences, and in religion, more than any people upon the face of God's earth had ever done before in the same time. What better compromise do you want? You lived under it until you got to be a great and prosperous people. It was made by our fathers, and cemented by their blood. When you talk to me about compromise, I hold up to you the Constitution under which you derived all your greatness, and which was made by the fathers of your country. It will protect you in all your rights.

But it is said we had better divide the country, and make a treaty and restore peace. If, under the Constitution which was framed by Washington and Madison and the patriots of the Revolution, we cannot live as brothers, as we have in times gone by, I ask, can we live quietly under a treaty, separated, as enemies? Suppose you make a treaty of peace and a division, our geographical and physical position will remain just the same; and if the same causes of irritation, if the same causes of division continue to exist, and we cannot now live as brothers in fraternity under the Constitution made by our fathers, and as friends in the same Government, how can we live in peace as aliens and enemies under a treaty? It cannot be done; it is impracticable.

But, Mr. President, I concur fully with the distinguished Senator from Kentucky in the dislike expressed by him to a change in the form of our

Government. He seemed to be apprehensive of a dictatorship. He feared there might be a change in the nature and character of our institutions. I could, if I chose, refer to many proofs to establish the fact that there has been a design to change the nature of our Government. I could refer to Mr. Rhett; I could refer to Mr. Inglis; I could refer to various others to prove this. The "Montgomery Daily Advertiser," one of the organs of the so-called Southern Confederacy, says, —

"Has it been a precipitate revolution? It has not. With coolness and deliberation the subject has been thought of for forty years; for ten years it has been the all-absorbing theme in political circles. From Maine to Mexico all the different phases and forms of the question have been presented to the people, until nothing else was thought of, nothing else spoken of, and nothing else taught in many of the political schools."

This, in connection with other things, shows that this movement has been long contemplated, and that the idea has been to separate from and break up this Government, to change its nature and character; and now, after they have attempted the separation, if they can succeed, their intention is to subjugate and overthrow and make the other States submit to their form of government.

To carry out the idea of the Senator from Kentucky, I want to show that there is conclusive proof of a design to change our Government.

I quote from the "Georgia Chronicle": —

"Our own republican Government has failed midway in its trial, and with it have nearly vanished the hopes of those philanthropists who, believing in man's capacity for self-government, believed, therefore, in spite of so many failures, in the practicability of a republic."

"If this Government has gone down," asks the editor, "what shall be its substitute?" And he answers by saying that, as to the present generation, "it seems their only resort must be to a constitutional monarchy." Hence you see the Senator and myself begin to agree in the proposition that the nature and character of the Government are to be changed.

William Howard Russell, the celebrated correspondent of the "London Times," spent some time in South Carolina, and he writes: —

"From all quarters have come to my ears the echoes of the same voice; it may be feigned, but there is no discord in the note, and it sounds in wonderful strength and monotony all over the country. Shades of George III., of North, of Johnson, of all who contended against the great rebellion which tore these colonies from England, can you hear the chorus which rings through the State of Marion, Sumter, and Pinckney, and not clap your ghostly hands in triumph? That voice says, 'If we could only get one of the royal race of England to rule over us, we should be content!' Let there be no misconception on this point. That sentiment, varied in a hundred ways, has been repeated to me over and over again. There is a general admission that the means to such an end are wanting, and that the desire cannot be gratified. But the admiration for monarchical institutions on the English model, for privileged classes, and for a landed aristocracy and gentry, is undisguised and apparently genuine. With the pride of having achieved their independence, is mingled in the South Carolinian's heart a strange regret at the result and consequences, and many are they who 'would go back to-morrow if we could.' An intense affection for the British connection, a love of British habits and customs, a respect for British sentiment, law, authority, order, civilization, and literature, preeminently distinguish the inhabitants of this State," &c.

This idea was not confined to localities. It was extensively prevalent, though policy prompted its occasional repudiation. At a meeting of the people of Bibb County, Georgia, the proposal of a constitutional monarchy for the Southern States, "as recommended by some of the advocates of immediate disunion," was discussed but not concurred in." Here is evidence that the public mind had been sought to be influenced in that direction; but the people were not prepared for it. Mr. Toombs, of Georgia, during the delivery of a speech by Mr. A. H. Stephens, before the Legislature of that State, did not hesitate to express a preference for the form of the British Government over our own.[1]

Not long since — some time in the month of May — I read in the "Richmond Whig," published at the place where their government is now operating, — the centre from which they are directing their armies which are making war upon this Government, — an article in which it is stated that, rather than submit to the Administration now in power in the city of Washington, they would prefer passing under the constitutional reign of the ami-

[1] See *The Rebellion Record.*

able Queen of Great Britain. I agree, therefore, with the Senator from Kentucky, that there is a desire to change this Government. We see it emanating from every point in the South. Mr. Toombs was not willing to wait for the movement of the people. Mr. Stephens, in his speech to the Legislature of Georgia, preferred the calling of a convention; but Mr. Toombs was unwilling to wait. Mr. Stephens was unwilling to see any violent action in advance of the action of the people; but Mr. Toombs replied, — "I will not wait; I will take the sword in my own hand, disregarding the will of the people, even in the shape of a convention;" and history will record that he kept his word. He and others had become tired and dissatisfied with a government of the people; they have lost confidence in man's capacity for self-government; and, furthermore, they would be willing to form an alliance with Great Britain; or, if Great Britain were slow in forming the alliance, with France; and they know they can succeed there, on account of the hate and malignity which exist between the two nations. They would be willing to pass under the reign of the amiable and constitutional Queen of Great Britain! Sir, I love woman, and woman's reign in the right place; but when we talk about the amiable and accomplished Queen of Great Britain, I must say that all our women are ladies, all are queens, all are equal to Queen Victoria, and many of them greatly her superiors. They desire no such thing; nor do we. Hence we see whither this movement is tending. It is to a change of government; in that the Senator and myself most fully concur.

The Senator from Kentucky was wonderfully alarmed at the idea of a "dictator," and replied with as much point as possible to the Senator from Oregon, who made the suggestion. But, sir, what do we find in the "Richmond Examiner," published at the seat of government of the so-called Confederate States?

"In the late debates of the congress of this Confederacy, Mr. Wright of Georgia showed a true appreciation of the crisis when he advocated the grant of power to the president that would enable him to make immediate defence of Richmond, and to bring the whole force of the Confederacy to bear on the affairs of Virginia. It is here that the fate of the Confederacy is to be decided; and the time is too short to permit red tape to interfere with public safety. No power in executive hands can be too great, no discretion too absolute, at such moments as these. We need a dictator. Let lawyers talk when the world has time to hear them. Now let the sword do its work. Usurpations of power by the chief, for the preservation of the people from robbers and murderers, will be reckoned as genius and patriotism by all sensible men in the world now, and by every historian that will judge the deed hereafter."

The articles in their leading papers, the "Whig" and the "Examiner," and the speeches of their leading men, all show unmistakably that their great object is to change the character of the Government. Hence we come back to the proposition that it is a contest whether the people shall govern or not. I have here an article that appeared in the "Memphis Bulletin," of my own State, from which it appears that under this reign of secession, this reign of terror, that is destructive of all good, and the accomplishment of nothing that is right, they have got things beyond their control: —

"In times like these there must be one ruling power to which all others must yield. 'In a multitude of counsellors,' saith the Book of Books, 'there is safety;' but nowhere are we told, in history or revelation, that there is aught of safety in a multitude of rulers. Any 'rule of action,' sometimes called the 'law,' is better than a multitude of conflicting, irreconcilable statutes. Any one head is better than forty, each of which may conceive itself the nonpareil, *par excellence*, supreme '*caput*' of all civil and military affairs.

"Let Governor Harris be king, if need be, and Baugh a despot."

"Let Governor Harris be king, and Baugh a despot," says the "Bulletin." Who is Baugh? The Mayor of Memphis. The mob "reign of terror" gotten up under this doctrine of secession is so great that we find that they are appealing to the one-man power. They are even willing to make the mayor of the city a despot, and Isham G. Harris, a little petty Governor of Tennessee, a king. He is to be made king over the State that contains the bones of the immortal, the illustrious Jackson. Isham G. Harris a king! Or Jeff Davis a dictator, and Isham G. Harris one of his satraps. He a king over the free and patriotic people of Tennessee! Isham G. Harris to be my king. Yes, sir, my king! I know the man. I know his elements. I know the ingredients that constitute the compound called Isham G. Harris. King Harris to be my master, and the master of the people that I have the proud and conscious satisfaction of representing on this floor! Mr. President, he should not be my slave. [Applause in the galleries.]

The PRESIDENT *pro tempore.* Order! A repetition of the offence will compel the Chair to order the galleries to be cleared forthwith. The order of the Senate must and shall be preserved. No demonstrations of applause or of disapprobation will be allowed. The Chair hopes not to be compelled to resort to the extremity of clearing the galleries of the audience.

Mr. JOHNSON. I was proceeding with this line of argument to show that the Senator from Kentucky and myself agree in the general proposition that there was a fixed determination to change the character and nature of the Government; and so far I think I have succeeded very well. And now, when we are looking at the elements of which this Southern Confederacy is composed, it may be well enough to examine the principles of the elements out of which is to be made a government that they prefer to this. We have shown, so far as the slavery question is concerned, that the whole question is settled; and it is shown to the American people and to the world that the people of the Southern States have now got no right which they said they had lost before they went out of this Union; but, on the contrary, many of their rights have been diminished, and oppression and tyranny have been inaugurated in their stead. Let me ask you, sir, to-day, and let me ask the nation, what right has any State in this so-called confederacy lost under the Constitution of the United States? Let me ask each individual citizen in the United States, what right has he lost by the continuance of this Government based on the Constitution of the United States? Is there a man North or South, East or West, who can put his finger on one single privilege, or one single right, of which he has been deprived by the Constitution or Union of these States? Can he do it? Can he see it? Can he feel it? No, sir; there is no one right that he has lost. But how many rights and privileges, and how much protection have they lost by going out of the Union, and violating the Constitution of the United States!

Pursuing this line of argument in regard to the formation of their government, let us take South Carolina, for instance, and see what her notions of government are. She is the leading spirit, and will constitute one of the master elements in the formation of this proposed Confederate Government. Let us see what are her notions of government — a State that will contribute to the formation of the government that is to exist hereafter. In the constitution of South Carolina it is provided that —

> "No person shall be eligible to a seat in the House of Representatives, unless he is a free white man, of the age of twenty-one years, and hath been a citizen and resident of this State three years previous to his election. If a resident in the election district, he shall not be eligible to a seat in the House of Representatives, unless he be legally seized and possessed, in his own right, of a settled freehold estate of five hundred acres of land and ten negroes."

This is the notion that South Carolina has of the necessary qualifications of a member of the lower branch of the State Legislature. Now, I desire to ask the distinguished Senator from Kentucky — who seems to be so tenacious about compromises, about rights, and about the settlement of this question, and who can discover that the Constitution has been violated so often and so flagrantly by the Administration now in power, yet never can see that it has been violated anywhere else — if he desires to seek under this South Carolina government for his lost rights? I do not intend to be personal. I wish he were in his seat, for he knows that I have the greatest kindness for him. I am free to say, in connection with what I am about to observe, that I am a little selfish in this; because if I lived in South Carolina, with these disabilities or qualifications affixed upon a member, I would not be eligible to a seat in the lower branch of the Legislature.

That would be a poor place for me to go and get my rights; would it not? I doubt whether the Senator from Kentucky is eligible to-day to a seat in the lower branch of the Legislature of South Carolina. I should not be, and I believe I am just as good as any who do take seats there.

In looking further into the constitution of South Carolina, in order to ascertain what are her principles of government, what do we find? We find it provided that, in the apportionment of these representatives, the whole number of white inhabitants is to be divided by sixty-two, and every sixty-second part is to have one member. Then all the taxes are to be divided by sixty-two, and every sixty-second part of the taxes is to have one member also. Hence we see that slaves, constituting the basis of property, would get the largest amount of representation; and we see that property goes in an equal representation to all the numbers, while those numbers constitute a part of the property-holders. That is the basis of their representation.

Sir, the people whom I represent desire no such form of government. Notwithstanding they have been borne down; notwithstanding there has been an army of fifty-five thousand men created by the Legislature; notwithstanding $5,000,000 of money have been appropriated to be expended against the Union; and notwithstanding the arms manufactured by the Government, and distributed among the States for the protection of the people, have been denied to them by this little petty tyrant of a king, and are now turned upon the Government for its overthrow and destruction, those people, when left to themselves to carry out their own government and the honest dictates of their own consciences, will be found to be opposed to this revolution.

Mr. President, while the congress of the Confederate States was engaged in the formation of their constitution, I find a protest from South Carolina against a decision of that congress in relation to the slave-trade published in the "Charleston Mercury," of February 13. It is written by L. W. Spratt to "Hon. John Perkins, delegate from Louisiana." It begins in this way: —

> "From the abstract of the constitution for the provisional government, published in the papers this morning, it appears that the slave-trade, except with the slave States of North America, shall be prohibited. The congress, therefore, not content with the laws of the late United States against it, which, it is to be presumed, were readopted, have unalterably fixed the subject, by a provision of the constitution."

He goes on and protests. We all know that that constitution is made for the day, just for the time being, a mere tub thrown out to the whale, to amuse and entertain the public mind for a time. We know this to be so. But in making his argument, Mr. Spratt, a commissioner who went to Florida, a member of the convention that took the State of

South Carolina out of the Union, says, in this protest, —

" The South is now in the formation of a *slave* republic. This, perhaps, is not admitted generally. There are many contented to believe that the South, as a geographical section, is in mere assertion of its independence; that it is instinct with no especial truth — pregnant of no distinct social nature; that for some unaccountable reason the two sections have become opposed to each other; that for reasons equally insufficient there is disagreement between the people that direct them; and that from no overruling necessity, no impossibility of coexistence, but as mere matter of policy, it has been considered best for the South to strike out for herself, and establish an independence of her own. This, I fear, is an inadequate conception of the controversy."

This indicates the whole scheme.

" The contest is not between the North and South as geographical sections, for between such sections merely there can be no contest; nor between the people of the North and the people of the South, for our relations have been pleasant; and on neutral grounds there is still nothing to estrange us. We eat together, trade together, and practise yet, in intercourse, with great respect, the courtesies of common life. But the real contest is between the two forms of society which have become established, the one at the North, and the other at the South."

The protest continues: —

" With that perfect economy of resources, that just application of power, that concentration of forces, that security of order which results to slavery from the permanent direction of its best intelligence, there is no other form of human labor that can stand against it, and it will build itself a home, and erect for itself, at some point within the present limits of the

Southern States, a structure of imperial power and grandeur — a glorious confederacy of States that will stand aloft and serene for ages amid the anarchy of democracies that will reel around it." . . . . .

"But it may be that to this end another revolution may be necessary. It is to be apprehended that this contest between democracy and slavery is not yet over. It is certain that both forms of society exist within the limits of the Southern States; both are distinctly developed within the limits of Virginia; and there, whether we perceive the fact or not, the war already rages. In that State there are about five hundred thousand slaves to about one million of whites; and as at least as many slaves as masters are necessary to the constitution of slave society, about five hundred thousand of the white population are in legitimate relation to the slaves, and the rest are in excess."

Hence we see the propriety of Mr. Mason's letter, in which he declared that all those who would not vote for secession must leave the State, and thereby you get clear of the excess of white population over slaves. They must emigrate.

"Like an excess of alkali or acid in chemical experiments, they are unfixed in the social compound. Without legitimate connection with the slave, they are in competition with him."

The protest continues:—

"And even in this State [South Carolina] the ultimate result is not determined. The slave condition here would seem to be established. There is here an excess of one hundred and twenty thousand slaves; and here is fairly exhibited the normal nature of the institution. The officers of the State are slave-owners, and the representatives of slave-owners. In their public acts they exhibit the consciousness of a superior position. Without unusual individual ability, they exhibit the elevation of tone and composure of public sentiment proper to a master class. There is no appeal to the mass, for there is no mass to appeal to; there are no demagogues, for there is no populace to breed them; judges are not forced upon the stump; governors are not to be dragged before the people; and when there is cause to act upon the fortunes of our social institution, there is perhaps an unusual readiness to meet it."

Again: —

"It is probable that more abundant pauper labor may pour in, and it is to be feared that even in this State, the purest in its slave condition, democracy may gain a foothold, and that here also the contest for existence may be waged between them.

"It thus appears that the contest is not ended with a dissolution of the Union, and that the agents of that contest still exist within the limits of the Southern States. The causes that have contributed to the defeat of slavery still occur; our slaves are still drawn off by higher prices to the West. There is still foreign pauper labor ready to supply their place. Maryland, Virginia, Kentucky, Missouri, possibly Tennessee and North Carolina, may lose their slaves, as New York, Pennsylvania, and New Jersey have done. In that condition they must recommence the contest. There is no avoiding that necessity. The systems cannot mix; and thus it is that slavery, like the Thracian horse returning from the field of victory, still bears a master on his back; and, having achieved one revolution to escape democracy at the North, it must still achieve another to escape it at the South. That it will ultimately triumph none can doubt. It will become redeemed and vindicated, and the only question now to be determined is, shall there be another revolution to that end?" . . . . .

"If, in short, you shall own slavery as the source of your

authority, and act for it, and erect, as you are commissioned to erect, not only a Southern, but a slave republic, the work will be accomplished." . . . . .

"But if you shall not; if you shall commence by ignoring slavery, or shall be content to edge it on by indirection; if you shall exhibit care but for the republic, respect but a democracy; if you shall stipulate for the toleration of slavery, as an existing evil, by admitting assumptions to its prejudice, and restrictions to its power and progress, you reinaugurate the blunder of 1789; you will combine States, whether true or not, to slavery; you will have no tests of faith; some will find it to their interests to abandon it; slave labor will be fettered; hireling labor will be free; your confederacy is again divided into antagonistic societies; the irrepressible conflict is again commenced; and as slavery can sustain the structure of a stable government, and will sustain such structure, and as it will sustain no structure but its own, another revolution comes; but whether in the order and propriety of this, is gravely to be doubted."

In another part of this protest I find this paragraph: —

"If the clause be carried into the permanent government, our whole movement is defeated. It will abolitionize the border slave States — it will brand our institution. Slavery cannot share a government with democracy — it cannot bear a brand upon it; thence another revolution. It may be painful, but we must make it. The constitution cannot be changed without. The border States, discharged of slavery, will oppose it. They are to be included by the concession; they will be sufficient to defeat it. It is doubtful if another movement will be as peaceful."[1]

In this connection, let me read the following paragraph from De Bow's "Review": —

[1] See *The Rebellion Record.*

"*All government begins with usurpation, and is continued by force.* Nature puts the ruling elements uppermost, and the masses below and subject to those elements. Less than this is not government. The right to govern resides in a very small minority, the duty to obey is inherent in the great mass of mankind."

We find by an examination of all these articles, that the whole idea is to establish a republic based upon slavery exclusively, in which the great mass of the people are not to participate. We find an argument made here against the admission of non-slaveholding States into their Confederacy. If they refuse to admit a non-slaveholding State into the Confederacy, for the very same reason they will exclude an individual who is not a slaveholder, in a slaveholding State, from participating in the exercise of the powers of the Government. Take the whole argument through, and that is the plain meaning of it. Mr. Spratt says, that sooner or later it will be done; and if the present revolution will not accomplish it, it must be brought about even if another revolution has to take place. We see, therefore, that it is most clearly contemplated to change the character and nature of the Government so far as they are concerned. They have lost confidence in the integrity, in the capability, in the virtue and intelligence of the great mass of the people to govern. Sir, in the section of the country where I live, notwithstanding we reside in a slave State, we believe that freemen are capable of self-government. We care not in what shape their property exists; whether it is in the shape of slaves or otherwise. We hold that it is upon the intelligent free white people of the country that all Governments should rest, and by them all Governments should be controlled.

I think, therefore, sir, that the President and the Senator from Kentucky have stated the question aright. This is a struggle between two forms of government. It is a struggle for the existence of the Government we have. The issue is now fairly made up. All who favor free government must stand with the Constitution, and in favor of the Union of the States as it is. That Union being once restored, the Constitution again becoming supreme and paramount, when peace, law, and order shall be restored, when the Government shall be restored to its pristine position, then, if necessary, we can come forward under proper and favorable circumstances to amend, change, alter, and modify the Constitution, as pointed out by the fifth article of the instrument, and thereby perpetuate the Government. This can be done, and this should be done.

We have heard a great deal said in reference to the violation of the Constitution. The Senator from Kentucky seems exceedingly sensitive about violations of the Constitution. Sir, it seems to me, admitting that his apprehensions are well founded, that a violation of the Constitution for the preservation of the Government, is more tolerable than one for its destruction. In all these complaints, in all these arraignments of the present Government for violation of law and disregard of the Constitution, have you heard, as was forcibly and eloquently said by the Senator from Illinois,[1] before me, one word uttered against violations of the Constitution and the trampling under foot of law by the States, or the party, now making war upon the Government of the United States? Not one word, sir.

The Senator enumerates what he calls violations of the Constitution, — the suspension of the writ of *habeas corpus*, the proclaiming of martial law, the increase of the Army and Navy, and the existing war; and then he asks, "Why all this?" The answer must be apparent to all.

But first, let me supply a chronological table of events on the other side.

1860. December 27. Fort Moultrie and Castle Pinckney, at Charleston, seized.

December 27. The revenue-cutter *William Aiken* surrendered by her commander, and taken possession of by South Carolina.

December 30. The United States arsenal at Charleston seized.

1861. January 2. Fort Macon and the United States arsenal at Fayetteville seized by North Carolina.

January 3. Forts Pulaski and Jackson, and the United States arsenal at Savannah, seized by Georgia troops.

January 4. Fort Morgan and the United States arsenal at Mobile seized by Alabama.

1 Mr. Browning.

January 8. Forts Johnson and Caswell, at Smithville, seized by North Carolina; restored by order of Governor Ellis.

January 9. The *Star of the West*, bearing reinforcements for Major Anderson, fired at in Charleston harbor.

January 12. Fort McRae, at Pensacola, seized by Florida.

January 10. The steamer *Marion* seized by South Carolina; restored on the 11th.

January 11. The United States arsenal at Baton Rouge, and Forts Pike, St. Philip, and Jackson, seized by Louisiana.

January 12. Fort Barrancas and the navy-yard at Pensacola seized by Florida.

These forts cost $5,947,000, are pierced for one thousand and ninety-nine guns, and are adapted for a war garrison of five thousand four hundred and thirty men.

We find, as was shown here the other day, and as has been shown on former occasions, that the State of South Carolina seceded, or attempted to secede from this Confederacy of States without cause. In seceding, her first step was a violation of the Constitution. She seceded on the 20th of last December, making the first innovation and violation of the law and the Constitution of the country. On the 27th day of December what did she do? She seized Fort Moultrie and Castle Pinckney, and caused your little band of sixty or seventy men under the command of Major Anderson to retire to a little pen in the ocean — Fort Sumter. She commenced erecting batteries, arraying cannon, preparing for war; in effect, proclaiming herself at once our enemy. Seceding from the Union, taking Fort Moultrie and Castle Pinckney, driving your men in fact into Fort Sumter, I say were practical acts of war. You need not talk to me about technicalities, and the distinction that you have got no war until Congress declares it. Congress could legalize it, or could make war, it is true; but that was practical war. Who began it? Then, sir, if South Carolina secedes, withdraws from the Union, becomes our common enemy, is it not the duty, the constitutional duty of the Government and of the President of the United States to make war, or to resist the attacks and assaults made by an enemy? Is she not as much our enemy as Great Britain was in the Revolutionary struggle? Is she not to-day as much our enemy as Great Britain was during the war of 1812?

In this connection I desire to read some remarks made by the Senator from Missouri[1] in his speech the other day, in regard to this general idea of who made the war. He said, speaking of the war, —

"This has all been brought about since the adjournment of the last Congress — since the 4th of March; indeed, since the 15th of April. Congress has declared no war. The Constitution of the United States says 'that Congress shall be authorized to declare war;' and yet, sir, though Congress

[1] Mr. Polk.

has declared no war, we are in the midst of a war monstrous in its character, and hugely monstrous in its proportions. That war has been brought on by the President of the United States since the 4th of March, of his own motion, and of his own wrong; and under what circumstances? Before the close of the last Congress, as early as the month of January, secession was an accomplished fact. Before the close of the last Congress, as many States had seceded from the Union, or had claimed to secede, as had on the 15th of April; and yet the last Congress made no declaration of war; the last Congress passed no legislation calculated to carry on a war; the last Congress refused to pass bills having this direction, or having any purpose of coercion. Now, sir, how has this war been brought on? I have said that, in my judgment, it has been brought on by the President of the United States; and a portion of the procedure which has resulted in it is named in the preamble of this joint resolution, which it is proposed that we shall approve and legalize."

The Senator from Kentucky[1] spoke in similar language. Alluding to the refusal of Kentucky to respond to the first call of the President for seventy-five thousand men, he said, —

"She believed that the calling forth of such an immense armament was for the purpose of making a war of subjugation on the Southern States, and upon that ground she refused to furnish the regiments called for. The Senator seems to be a little offended at the neutrality of Kentucky. Sir, Kentucky has assumed a position of neutrality, and I only hope that she may be able to maintain it. She has assumed that position because there is no impulse of her patriotic heart that desires her to imbrue her hands in a brother's blood, whether he be from the North or the South. Kentucky looks upon this war as unholy, unrighteous, and unjust. Kentucky

[1] Mr. Powell.

believes that this war, if carried out, can result in nothing else than a final disruption of this Confederacy. She hopes, she wishes, she prays, that this Union may be maintained. She believes that cannot be done by force of arms; that it must be done by compromise and conciliation, if it can be done at all; and hence, being devoted truly to the Union, she desires to stay this war, and desires measures of peace to be presented for the adjustment of our difficulties."

I desire in this connection to place before the Senate the remarks of both the Senators from Kentucky and the Senator from Missouri, and to answer them at the same time. The Senator from Missouri says the war was brought on since the 4th of March by the President of the United States of his own motion. The Senator from Kentucky pronounces it an unjust, an unrighteous, and an unholy war. Sir, I think it is an unjust, an unrighteous, and an unholy war.

But, sir, I commenced enumerating the facts with the view of showing who commenced the war. How do they stand? I have just stated that South Carolina seceded — withdrew from the Confederacy; and in the very act of withdrawing, she makes practical war upon the Government, and becomes its enemy. The *Star of the West*, on the 7th of January, laden simply with provisions to supply those starving men in Fort Sumter, attempted to enter the harbor, and was fired upon, and had to tack about, and leave the men in the forts to perish or do the best they could. We also find, that on the 11th of April General Beauregard had an interview with Major Anderson, and made a proposition to him to surrender. Major Anderson stated, in substance, that he could do no such thing; that he could not strike the colors of his country, and refused to surrender; but he said, at the same time, that by the 15th of the month his provisions would give out, and if not reinforced and supplied, starvation must take place. It seems that at this time, Mr. Pryor, from Virginia, was in Charleston. The convention of Virginia was sitting, and it was important that the cannon's roar should be heard in the land. Virginia was to be taken out of the Union, although a majority of the delegates in the convention were elected against secession, and in favor of the Union. We find that after being in possession of the fact that by the 15th of the month the garrison would be starved out and compelled to surrender, on the morning of the 12th they commenced the bombardment, fired upon your fort and upon your men. They knew that in three days the troops in Fort Sumter would be compelled to surrender; but they wanted war. It was indispensable to produce an excitement in order to hurry Virginia out of the Union, and they commenced the war. The firing was kept up until such time as the fort was involved in smoke and flames, and Major Anderson and his men were compelled to lie on the floor with their wet handkerchiefs to their faces to save them from suffocation and death. Even in the midst of all this, they refused to cease their firing, but kept it up until he was compelled to surrender.

Who then commenced the war? Who struck the first blow? Who violated the Constitution in the first place? Who trampled the law under foot, and violated the law morally and legally? Was it not South Carolina, in seceding? And yet you talk about the President having brought on the war by his own motion, when these facts are incontrovertible. No one dare attempt to assail them. But after Fort Sumter was attacked and surrendered, what do we find stated in Montgomery when the news reached there? Here is the telegraphic announcement of the reception of the news there: —

"MONTGOMERY, Friday, *April* 12, 1861.

"An immense crowd serenaded President Davis and Secretary Walker, at the Exchange Hotel, to-night."

Mr. Davis refused to address the audience, but his Secretary of War did. The Secretary of War, Mr. Walker, said, —

"No man could tell where the war this day commenced would end, but he would prophesy that the flag which now flaunts the breeze here would float over the dome of the Old Capitol at Washington, before the 1st of May. Let them try Southern chivalry and test the extent of Southern resources, and it might float eventually over Faneuil Hall itself."

What is the announcement? We have attacked Fort Sumter, and it has surrendered, and no one can tell where this war will end. By the first of

May our flag will wave in triumph from the dome of the Old Capitol at Washington, and ere long perhaps from Faneuil Hall in Boston. Then, was this war commenced by the President on his own motion? You say the President of the United States did wrong in ordering out seventy-five thousand men, and in increasing the Army and Navy under the exigency. Do we not know, in connection with these facts, that so soon as Fort Sumter surrendered they took up the line of march for Washington? Do not some of us who were here know that we did not even go to bed very confidently and securely, for fear the city would be taken before the rising sun? Has it not been published in the Southern newspapers that Ben McCulloch was in readiness, with five thousand picked men, in the State of Virginia, to make a descent and attack the city, and take it?

What more do we find? We find that the Congress of this same pseudo-republic, this same Southern Confederacy that has sprung up in the South, as early as the 6th of March passed a law preparing for this invasion — preparing for this war which they commenced. Here it is: —

"That in order to provide speedily forces to repel invasion, maintain the rightful possession of the Confederate States of America in every portion of territory belonging to each State, and to secure the public tranquillity and independence against threatened assault, the President be, and he is hereby, authorized to employ the militia, military, and naval forces of the Confederate States of America, and ask for and accept the services of any number of volunteers, not exceeding one hundred thousand."

When your forts were surrendered, and when the President of the so-called Southern Confederacy was authorized to call out the entire militia, naval, and military force, and then to receive into the service of the Confederate States one hundred thousand men, the President calls for seventy-five thousand men to defend the capital and the public property. Are we for the Government, or are we against it? That is the question. Taking all the facts into consideration, do we not see that an invasion was intended? It was even announced by Mr. Iverson upon this floor that ere long their Congress would be sitting here and this Government would be overthrown. When the facts are all put together we see the scheme, and it is nothing more nor less than executing a programme deliberately made out; and yet Senators hesitate, falter, and complain, and say the President has suspended the writ of *habeas corpus*, increased the Army and Navy, and they ask, where was the necessity for all this? With your forts taken, your men fired upon, your ships attacked at sea, and one hundred thousand men called into the field by this so-called Southern Confederacy, with the additional authority to call out the entire military and naval force of those States, Senators talk about the enormous call of the President for seventy-five thousand men, and the increase he has made of the Army and Navy. Mr. President, it all goes to show, in my opinion, that the sympathies of Senators are with the one government and against the other. Admitting that there was a little stretch of power; admitting that the margin was pretty wide when the power was exercised, the query now comes, when you have got the power, when you are sitting here in a legislative attitude, are you willing to sustain the Government and give it the means to sustain itself? It is not worth while to talk about what has been done before. The question on any measure should be, is it necessary now? If it is, it should not be withheld from the Government.

Senators talk about violating the Constitution and the laws. A great deal has been said about searches and seizures, and the right of protection of persons and of papers. I reckon it is equally as important to protect a Government from seizure as it is an individual. I reckon the morality and the law of the case would be just as strong in seizing upon that which belonged to the Federal Government as it would upon that belonging to an individual. What belongs to us in the aggregate is protected and maintained by the same law, moral and legal, as that which applies to an individual. These rebellious States, after commencing this war, after violating the Constitution, seized our forts, our arsenals, our dock-yards, our custom-houses, our public buildings, our ships, and last, though not least, plundered the independent treasury at New Orleans of $1,000,000. And yet Senators talk about violations of the law and the Constitution. They say the Constitution is disregarded, and the Government is about to be overthrown. Does not this talk about violations of the Constitution and law come with a beautiful grace from that side of the House? I repeat again, sir, are not violations of the Constitution necessary for its protection and vindication more tolerable, than violations of that sacred instrument aimed at the overthrow and destruction of the Government. We have seen instances, and other instances might occur, where it might be indispensably necessary for the Government to exercise a power and to assume a position that was not clearly legal and constitutional, in order to resist the entire overthrow and upturning of the Government and all our institutions.

But the President issued his proclamation. When did he issue it, and for what? He issued his proclamation calling out seventy-five thousand men after the Congress of the so-called Southern Confederacy had passed a law to call out the entire militia, and to receive into their service one hundred thousand men. The President issued his proclamation after they had taken Fort Moultrie and Castle Pinckney; after they had fired upon and reduced Fort Sumter. Fort Sumter was taken on the 12th, and on the 15th he issued his proclamation. Taking all these circumstances together, it showed that they intended to advance, and that their object was to extend their power, to subjugate the other States, and to overthrow the Constitution and the laws and the Government.

Senators talk about violations of the Constitution. Have you heard any intimation of complaint from those Senators about this Southern Confederacy — this band of traitors to their country and their country's institutions? I repeat, substantially, the language of the Senator from Illinois,[1] "Have you heard any complaint or alarm about violations of constitutional law on that side? Oh, no! But we must stand still; the Government must not move while they are moving with a hundred thousand men; while they have the power to call forth the entire militia and the army and the navy. While they are reducing our forts, and robbing us of our property, we must stand still; the Constitution and the laws must not be violated; and an arraignment is made to weaken and paralyze the Government in its greatest peril and trial."

On the 15th of April the proclamation was issued calling out seventy-five thousand men, after the Confederate States had authorized one hundred thousand men to be received by their President, — this man Davis, who stood up here and made a retiring speech, —a man educated and nurtured by the Government;

[1] Mr. Browning.

who sucked its pap; who received all his military instruction at the hands of this Government; a man who got all his distinction, civil and military, in the service of this Government, beneath the Stars and Stripes, and then, without cause, — without being deprived of a single right or privilege, — the sword he unsheathed in vindication of that flag in a foreign land, given to him by the hand of his cherishing mother, he stands this day prepared to plunge into her bosom! Such men as these have their apologists here in Congress, to excuse and extenuate their acts, either directly or indirectly. You never hear from them of law or Constitution being violated down there. Oh, no; that is not mentioned.

On the 15th the President issued his proclamation calling seventy-five thousand men into the service of the United States, and on the 17th this same Jefferson Davis, President of the Southern Confederacy, in retaliation for the proclamation issued by the President of the United States, and in violation of the constitution of this pseudo-confederacy, issued his proclamation proposing to issue letters of marque and reprisal. In other words, he proposed to open an office and say, we will give out licenses to rob the citizens of the United States of all their property, wherever it can be picked up upon the high seas. This he proposed to do not only in violation of the constitution of the Confederate States, but in violation of the law of nations; for no people — I care not by what name you call it — has a right to issue letters of marque and reprisal until its independence is first acknowledged as a separate and distinct power. Has that been done? I think, therefore, Senators can find some little violation of constitution and law down there among themselves. Sir, they have violated the law and the Constitution every step they progressed in going there, and now they violate it in trying to come this way. There was a general license offered, a premium to every freebooter, to every man who wanted to plunder and play the pirate on the high seas, to come and take a commission, and plunder in the name of the Southern Confederacy; to take, at that time, the property of Tennessee or the property of Kentucky, — your beef, your pork, your flour, and every other product making its way to a foreign market. Mr. Davis authorized letters of marque and reprisal to pick them up and appropriate them. After that, their Congress saw that he had gone ahead of their constitution and the law of nations, and they passed a law modifying the issuance of letters of marque and reprisal, that they should prey upon the property of the citizens of the United States, excepting certain States, — excepting Kentucky and Tennessee, — holding that out as a bait, as an inducement to get them in.

I do not think, therefore, when we approach the subject fairly and squarely, that there was any very great wrong in the President of the United States, on the 19th, issuing his proclamation blockading their ports, saying you shall not have the opportunity, so far as I can prevent it, of plundering and appropriating other people's property on the high seas. I think he did precisely what was right. He would have been derelict to his duty, and to the high behest of the American people, if he had sat here and failed to exert every power within his reach and scope to protect the property of citizens of the United States on the high seas.

Senators seem to think it is no violation of the Constitution to make war on your Government; and when its enemies are stationed in sight of the capital, there is no alarm, no dread, no scare, no fright. Some of us would not feel so very comfortable if they were to get this city. I believe there are others who would not be very much disturbed. I do not think I could sleep right sound if they were in possession of this city; not that I believe I am more timid than most men, but I do not believe there would be much quarter for me; and, by way of self-protection, and enjoying what few rights I have remaining, I expect it would be better, if they were in possession of this city, for me to be located in some other point, not too inconvenient or too remote. I believe there are others who would feel very comfortable here.

Then, Mr. President, in tracing this subject along, I cannot see what great wrong has been committed by the Government in taking the course it has taken. I repeat again, this Government is now passing through its third ordeal; and the time has arrived when it should put forth its entire power, and say to rebels and traitors wherever they are, that the supremacy of the Constitution, and laws made in pursuance thereof, shall be sustained; that those citizens who have been borne down and tyrannized over, and who have had laws of treason passed against them in their own States, and who have been threatened with confiscation of property, shall be protected. I say it is the paramount duty of this Government to assert its power and maintain its integrity. I say it is the duty of this Government to protect those States, or the loyal citizens of those States, in the enjoyment of a republican form of government; for we have seen one continued system of usurpation carried on, from one end of the Southern States to the other; disregarding the popular will, setting at defiance the judgment of the people, disregarding their rights, paying no attention to their State constitutions in any way whatever. We are bound, under the Constitution, to protect those States and their citizens. We are bound to guarantee to them a republican form of government; it is our duty to do it. If we have no Government, let the delusion be dispelled; let the dream pass away; and let the people of the United States, and the nations of the earth, know at once that we have no Government. If we have a Government, based on the intelligence and virtue of the American people, let that great fact be now established, and once established, this Government will be on a more enduring and permanent basis than it ever was before. I still have confidence in the integrity, the virtue, the intelligence, and the patriotism of the great mass of the people; and so believing, I intend to stand by the Government of my fathers to the last extremity.

In the last presidential contest I am free to say that I took some part. I advocated the pretensions and claims of one of the distinguished sons of Kentucky, as a Democrat. I am a Democrat to-day; I expect to die one. My Democracy rests upon the great principle I have stated; and in the support of measures, I have always tried to be guided by a conscientious conviction of right; and I have laid down for myself as a rule of action, in all doubtful questions, to pursue principle; and in the pursuit of a great principle I can never reach a wrong conclusion. I intend, in this case, to pursue principle. I am a Democrat, believing the principles of this Government are Democratic. It is based upon the Democratic theory. I believe Democracy can stand, notwithstanding all the taunts and jeers that are thrown at it throughout the Southern Confederacy. The principles which I call Democracy — I care not by whom they are sustained, whether by Republicans, by Whigs, or not — are the great principles that lie at the foundation of this Government, and they will be maintained. We have seen that so far the experiment has succeeded well; and now we should make an effort, in this last ordeal through which we are passing, to crush out the fatal doctrine of secession and those who are upholding it in the shape of rebels and traitors.

I advocated the professions of a distinguished son of Kentucky at the late election, for the reason that I believed he was a better Union man than any other candidate in the field. Others advocated the claims of Mr. Bell, believing him to be a better Union man; others those of Mr. Douglas. In the South we know that there was no Republican ticket. I was a Union man then; I was a Union man in 1833; I am a Union man now. And what has transpired since the election in November last that has produced sufficient cause to break up this Government? The Senator from California enumerated the facts up to the 25th day of May, 1860, when there was a vote taken in this body declaring that further legislation was not necessary for the protection of slave property in the Territories. Now, from the 6th of November up to the 20th of December, tell me what transpired of sufficient cause to break up this Government? Was there any innovation, was there any additional step taken in reference to the rights of the States or the institution of slavery? If the candidate whose claims I advocated had been elected President, — I speak of him as a candidate, of course not meaning to be personal, — I do not believe this Government would have been broken up. If Stephen A. Douglas had been elected, I do not believe this Government would have been broken up. Why? Because those who advocated the pretensions of Mr. Lincoln would have done as all parties have done heretofore: they would have yielded to the high behest of the American people.

Then, is the mere defeat of one man, and the election of another, according to the forms of law and the Constitution, sufficient cause to break up this Government? No; it is not sufficient cause. Do we not know, too, that if all the seceding Senators had stood here as faithful sentinels, representing the interests of their States, they had it in their power to check any advance that might be made by the incoming Administration? I showed these facts, and enumerated them at the last session. They were shown here the other day. On the 4th of March, when President Lincoln was inaugurated, we had a majority of six upon this floor in opposition to his Administration. Where, then, is there even a pretext for breaking up the Government upon the idea that he would have encroached upon our rights? Does not the nation know that Mr. Lincoln could not have made his Cabinet without the consent of the majority of the Senate? Do we not know that he could not even have sent a minister abroad without the majority of the Senate confirming the nomination? Do we not know that if any minister whom he sent abroad should make a treaty inimical to the institutions of the South, that treaty could not have been ratified without a majority of two thirds of the Senate.

With all these facts staring them in the face, where is the pretence for breaking up this Government? Is it not clear that there has been a fixed purpose, a settled design to break up the Government, and change the nature and character and whole genius of the Government itself? Does it not prove conclusively, as there was no cause, that they simply selected it as an occasion that was favorable to excite the prejudices of the South, and thereby enable them to break up this Government and establish a Southern confederacy?

Then when we get at it, what is the real cause? If Mr. Breckinridge, or Mr. Davis, or some other favorite of those who are now engaged in breaking up the Government, had been elected President of the United States, it would have been a very nice thing; they would have respected the judgment of the people, and no doubt their confidence in the capacity of the people for self-government would have been increased; but it so happened that the people thought proper to elect somebody else, according to law and the Constitution. Then, as all parties had done heretofore, it was the duty of the whole people to acquiesce; if he made a good President, to sustain him; if he became a bad one, to condemn him; if he violated the law and the Constitution, to impeach him. We had our remedy under the Constitution and in the Union.

What is the real cause? Disappointed ambition; an unhallowed ambition. Certain men could not wait any longer, and they seized this occasion to do what they had been wanting to do for a long time — to break up the Government. If they could not rule a large country, they thought they might rule a small one. Hence one of the prime movers in the Senate ceased to be a Senator, and passed out to be President of the Southern Confederacy. Another, who was bold enough on this floor to proclaim himself a rebel, retired as a Senator, and became Secretary of State. All perfectly disinterested, no ambition about it! Another, Mr. Benjamin of Louisiana, — one who understands something about the idea of dividing garments; who belongs to the tribe that parted the garments of our Saviour, and upon his vesture cast lots, — went out of this body and was made Attorney-General, to show his patriotism and disinterestedness — nothing else! Mr. Slidell, disinterested altogether, is to go as minister to France. I might enumerate many such instances. This is all patriotism, pure disinterestedness! Do we not see where it all begins? In disappointed, impatient, unhallowed ambition. There has been no cause for breaking up this Government; there have been no rights denied, no privileges trampled upon under the Constitution and Union, that might not have been remedied more effectually in the Union than outside of it. What rights are to be attained outside of the Union? The seceders have violated the Constitution, trampled it under foot; and what is their condition now? Upon the abstract idea that they had a right to secede, they have gone out; and what is the consequence? Oppression, taxation, blood, and civil war. They have gone out of the Union; and, I repeat again, they have got taxes, usurpations, blood, and civil war.

I said just now that I had advocated the election to the Presidency of the distinguished Senator from Kentucky, on the ground that he was a good Union man. I wish we could now hear his eloquent voice in favor of the old Government of our fathers, and in vindication of the Stars and Stripes, that have been borne in triumph everywhere. I hold in my hand a document which was our text-book in the campaign. It is headed "Breckinridge and Lane Campaign Document No. 16. Who are the disunionists? Breckinridge and Lane the true Union candidates." It contains an extract which I will read from the Senator's address on the removal of the Senate from the old to the new Chamber. I would to God he was as good a Union man to-day as I think he was then: —

"Such is our country; ay, and more — far more than my mind could conceive or my tongue could utter. Is there an American who regrets the past? Is there one who will deride his country's laws, pervert her Constitution, or alienate her people? If there be such a man, let his memory descend to posterity laden with the execrations of all mankind." . . . . . "Let us devoutly trust that another Senate, in another age, shall bear to a new and larger Chamber this Constitution, vigorous and inviolate, and that the last generation of posterity shall witness the deliberations of the Representatives of American States, still united, prosperous, and free."

Now this was the text — an extract from a speech of the Senator, after the nomination was made: —

"When that convention selected me as one of its candidates, looking at my humble antecedents and the place of my habitation, it gave to the country, so far as I was concerned, a personal and geographical guaranty that its interest was in the Union."

In addition to that, in Tennessee we headed our electoral ticket as if to give unmistakable evidence of our devotion to the Union, and the reason why we sustained him, "National Democratic Ticket. 'Instead of dissolving the Union, we intend to lengthen it and to strengthen it.' — *Breckinridge*." Where are his eloquent tones now? They are heard arraigning the Administration for what he conceives to be premature action, in advance of the law, or a slight departure from the Constitution. Which is the most tolerable, premature action, action in advance of law, a slight departure from the Constitution, (putting it on his own ground,) or an entire overthrow of the Government? Are there no advances, are there no inroads, being made to-day upon the Constitution and the existence of the Government itself? Let us look at the question plainly and fairly. Here is an invading army almost within cannon-shot of the capital, headed by Jeff Davis and Beauregard. Suppose they advance on the city to-night; subjugate it; depose the existing authorities; expel the present Government: what kind of government have you then? Is there any Constitution in it? Is there any law in it? The Senator can stand here almost in sight of the enemy, see the citadel of freedom, the Constitution, trampled upon, and there is no apprehension; but he can look with an eagle eye, and, with an analytic process almost unsurpassed, discriminate against and attack those who are trying to manage your Government for its safety and preservation. He has no word of condemnation for the invading army that threatens to overthrow the capital, that threatens to trample the Constitution and the law under foot. I repeat, suppose Davis, at the head of his advancing columns, should depose your Government and expel your authority: what kind of government will you have? Will there be any Constitution left? How eloquent my friend was upon constitutions. He told us the Constitution was the measure of power, and that we should understand and feel constitutional restraints; and yet when your Government is perhaps within a few hours of being overthrown, and the law and Constitution trampled under foot, there are no apprehensions on his part; no words of rebuke for those who are endeavoring to accomplish such results.

The Old Dominion has got the brunt of the war upon her hands. I sympathize with her most deeply, and especially with the loyal portion of her citizens, who have been browbeaten and domineered over. Now the war is transferred to Virginia, and her plains are made to run with blood; and when this is secured, what do we hear in the far South? Howell Cobb, another of these disinterested patriots, said not long since, in a speech in Georgia: —

> "The people of the Gulf States need have no apprehensions; they might go on with their planting and their other business as usual; the war would not come to their section; its theatre would be along the border of the Ohio River and in Virginia."

Virginia ought to congratulate herself upon that position, for she has got the war. Now they want to advance. Their plans and designs are to get across into Maryland, and carry on a war of subjugation. There is wonderful alarm among certain gentlemen here at the term "subjugate." They are alarmed at the idea of making citizens who have violated the law simply conform to it by enforcing their obedience. If a majority of the citizens in a State have violated the Constitution, have trampled it under foot, and violated the law, is it subjugation to assert the supremacy of the Constitution and the law? Is it any more than a simple enforcement of the law? It would be one of the best subjugations that could take place if some of them were subjugated, and brought back to the constitutional position that they occupied before. I would to God that Tennessee stood to-day where she did three months ago.

Mr. President, it is provided in the Constitution of the United States that "no State shall, without the consent of Congress, lay any duty of tonnage, keep troops or ships of war in time of peace, enter into any agreement or compact with another State, or with a foreign Power, or engage in war unless actually invaded, or in such imminent danger as will not admit of delay." The State authorities of Tennessee, before her people had even voted upon an ordinance to separate her from the Union, formed a league by which they transferred fifty-five thousand men, the whole army, over to the Confederate States for the purpose of prosecuting their war. Is it not strange that such a palpable violation of the Constitution should not be referred to and condemned by any one? Here is a member of the Union, without even having the vote taken upon an ordinance of separation or secession, forming a league, by its commissioners or ministers, and handing over fifty-five thousand men to make war upon the Government of the United States, though they were themselves then within the Union. No one seems to find fault with that. The fact is, that, in the whole progress of secession, the Constitution and the law have been violated at every step from its incipiency to the present point. How have the people of my State been treated? I know that this may not interest the Senate to any very great extent; but I must briefly refer to it. The people of a portion of that State, having devotion and attachment to the Constitution and the Government as framed by the sires of the Revolution, still adhering to it, gave a majority of more than twenty thousand votes in favor of the Union at the election. After that, this portion of the State, East Tennessee, called a convention, and the convention published an address, in which they sum up some of the grievances which we have been bearing in that portion of the country. They say: —

"The 'Memphis Appeal,' a prominent disunion paper, published a false account of our proceedings, under the head 'The Traitors in Council,' and styled us, who represented every county but two in East Tennessee, '*the little* batch of disaffected traitors who hover around the noxious atmosphere of Andrew Johnson's home.' Our meeting was telegraphed to the 'New Orleans Delta,' and it was falsely said that we had passed a resolution recommending submission if seventy thousand votes were not cast against secession. The despatch added that 'the Southern-Rights men are determined to hold possession of the State, though they should be in a minority.'"

They had fifty-five thousand men and $5,000,000 to sustain them, the State authorities with them, and made the declaration that they intended to hold the State though they should be in a minority. This shows the advance of tyranny and usurpation. By way of showing to the Senate some of the wrongs borne and submitted to by that people, who are loyal to the Government — who have been deprived of the arms furnished by the Government for their protection — withheld by this little man Harris, the Governor of the State, — I will read a few paragraphs from the address: —

"It has passed laws declaring it treason to say or do anything in favor of the Government of the United States, or against the Confederate States; and such a law is now before, and we apprehend will soon be passed by, the Legislature of Tennessee.

"It has involved the Southern States in a war whose success is hopeless, and which must ultimately lead to the ruin of the people.

"Its bigoted, overbearing, and intolerant spirit has already subjected the people of East Tennessee to many petty grievances; our people have been insulted; our flags have been fired upon and torn down; our houses have been rudely entered; our families subjected to insult; our peaceable meetings interrupted; our women and children shot at by a merciless soldiery; our towns pillaged; our citizens robbed, and some of them assassinated and murdered.

"No effort has been spared to deter the Union men of East Tennessee from the expression of their free thoughts. The penalties of treason have been threatened against them, and murder and assassination have been openly encouraged by leading secession journals. As secession has been thus overbearing and intolerant while in the minority in East Tennessee, nothing better can be expected of the pretended majority than wild, unconstitutional, and oppressive legislation; an utter contempt and disregard of law; a determination to force every Union man in the State to swear to the support of a constitution he abhors; to yield his money and property to aid a cause he detests; and to become the object of scorn and derision, as well as the victim of intolerable and relentless oppression."

These are some of the wrongs that we are enduring in that section of Tennessee; not nearly all of them, but a few which I have presented that the country may know what we are submitting to. Since I left my home, having only one way to leave the State through two or three passes coming out through Cumberland Gap, I have been advised that they had even sent their armies to blockade these passes in the mountains, as they say, to prevent Johnson from returning with arms and munitions to place in the hands of the people to vindicate their rights, repel invasion, and put down domestic insurrection and rebellion. Yes, sir, there they stand in arms, environing a population of three hundred and twenty-five thousand loyal, brave, patriotic, and unsubdued people; but yet powerless, and not in a condition to vindicate their rights. Hence I come to the Government, and I do not ask it as a suppliant, but I demand it as a constitutional right, that you give us protection, give us arms and munitions; and if they cannot be got there in any other way, to take them there with an invading army, and deliver the people from the oppression to which they are now subjected. We claim to be the State. The other divisions may have seceded and gone off; and if this Government will stand by and permit those portions of the State to go off, and not enforce the laws and protect the loyal citizens there, we cannot help it; but we still claim to be the State, and if two thirds have fallen off, or have been sunk by an earthquake, it does not change our relation to this Government. If the Government will let them go, and not give us protection, the fault is not ours; but if you will give us protection we intend to stand as a State, as a part of this Confederacy, holding to the Stars and Stripes, the flag of our country. We demand it according to law; we demand it upon the guaranties of the Constitution. You are bound to guarantee to us a republican form of government, and we ask it as a constitutional right. We do not ask you to interfere as a party, as your feelings or prejudices may be one way or another in reference to the parties of the country; but we ask you to interfere as a Government, according to the Constitution. Of course we want your sympathy, and your regard, and your respect; but we ask your interference on constitutional grounds.

The amendments to the Constitution which constitute the Bill of Rights declare that "a well regulated militia being necessary to the security of a free State, the right of the people to keep and bear arms shall not be infringed." Our people are denied this right, secured to them in their own constitution and the Constitution of the United States; yet we hear no complaints here of violations of the Constitution in this respect. We ask the Government to interpose to secure us this constitutional right. We want the passes in our mountains opened, we want deliverance and protection for a downtrodden and oppressed people who are struggling for their independence without arms. If we had had ten thousand stand of arms and ammunition when the contest commenced, we should have asked no further assistance. We have not got them. We are a rural people; we have villages and small towns — no large cities.

Our population is homogenous, industrious, frugal, brave, independent; but now harmless and powerless, and oppressed by usurpers. You may be too late in coming to our relief; or you may not come at all, though I do not doubt that you will come; they may trample us under foot; they may convert our plains into graveyards, and the caves of our mountains into sepulchres; but they will never take us out of this Union, or make us a land of slaves — no, never! We intend to stand as firm as adamant, and as unyielding as our own majestic mountains that surround us. Yes, we will be as fixed and as immovable as are they upon their bases. We will stand as long as we can; and if we are overpowered, and liberty shall be driven from the land, we intend, before she departs, to take the flag of our country, with a stalwart arm, a patriotic heart, and an honest tread, and place it upon the summit of the loftiest and most majestic mountain. We intend to plant it there, and leave it, to indicate to the inquirer who may come in after-times, the spot where the Goddess of Liberty lingered and wept for the last time, before she took her flight from a people once prosperous, free, and happy.

We ask the Government to come to our aid. We love the Constitution as made by our fathers. We have confidence in the integrity and capacity of the people to govern themselves. We have lived entertaining these opinions: we intend to die entertaining them. The battle has commenced. The President has placed it upon the true ground. It is an issue on the one hand for the people's Government, and its overthrow on the other. We have commenced the battle of Freedom. It is Freedom's cause. We are resisting usurpation and oppression. We will triumph; we must triumph. Right is with us. A great and fundamental principle of right, that lies at the foundation of all things, is with us. We may meet with impediments, and may meet with disasters, and here and there a defeat; but ultimately Freedom's cause must triumph, for —

> "Freedom's battle once begun,
> Bequeathed from bleeding sire to son,
> Though baffled oft, is ever won."

Yes, we must triumph. Though sometimes I cannot see my way clear, in matters of this kind as in matters of religion, when my facts give out, when my reason fails me, I draw largely upon my faith. My faith is strong, based on the eternal principles of right, that a thing so monstrously wrong as is this rebellion, cannot triumph. Can we submit to it? Can bleeding Justice submit to it? Is the Senate, are the American people, prepared to give up the graves of Washington and Jackson, to be encircled and governed and controlled by a combination of traitors and rebels? I say let the battle go on — it is Freedom's cause — until the Stars and Stripes (God bless them!) shall again be unfurled upon every cross-road, and from every house-top, throughout the Confederacy, North and South. Let the Union be reinstated; let the law be enforced; let the Constitution be supreme.

If the Congress of the United States were to give up the tombs of Washington and Jackson, we should have rising up in our midst another Peter the Hermit, in a much more righteous cause, — for ours is true, while his was a delusion, — who would appeal to the American people and point to the tombs of Washington and Jackson, in the possession of those who are worse than the infidel and the Turk who held the Holy Sepulchre. I believe the American people would start of their own accord, when appealed to, to redeem the graves of Washington and Jackson and Jefferson, and all the other patriots who are lying within the limits of the Southern Confederacy. I do not believe they would stop the march, until again the flag of this Union would be placed over the graves of those distinguished men. There will be an uprising. Do not talk about Republicans now; do not talk about Democrats now; do not talk about Whigs or Americans now; talk about your country and the Constitution and the Union. Save that; preserve the integrity of the Government; once more place it erect among the nations of the earth; and then if we want to divide about questions that may arise in our midst, we have a Government to divide in.

I know it has been said that the object of this war is to make war on Southern institutions. I have been in free States and I have been in slave States, and I thank God that, so far as I have been, there has been one universal disclaimer of any such purpose. It is a war upon no section; it is a war upon no peculiar institution; but it is a war for the integrity of the Government, for the Constitution, and the supremacy of the laws. That is what the nation understands by it.

The people whom I represent appeal to the Government and to the nation to give us the constitutional protection that we need. I am proud to say that I have met with every manifestation of that kind in the Senate, with only a few dissenting voices. I am proud to say, too, that I believe old Kentucky (God bless her!) will ultimately rise and shake off the stupor which has been resting upon her; and instead of denying us the privilege of passing through her borders, and taking arms and munitions of war to enable a downtrodden people to defend themselves, will not only give us that privilege, but will join us and help us in the work. The people of Kentucky love the Union; they love the Constitution; they have no fault to find with it; but in that State they have a duplicate to the Governor of ours. When we look all round, we see how the Governors of the different States have been involved in this conspiracy, — the most stupendous and gigantic conspiracy that was ever formed, and as corrupt and as foul as that attempted by Catiline in the days of Rome. We know it to be so. Have we not known men to sit at their desks in this Chamber, using the

Government's stationery to write treasonable letters; and while receiving their pay, sworn to support the Constitution and sustain the law, engaging in midnight conclaves to devise ways and means by which the Government and the Constitution should be overthrown? The charge was made and published in the papers. Many things we know that we cannot fully prove; but we know from the regular steps that were taken in this work of breaking up the Government, or trying to break it up, that there was system, concert of action. It is a scheme more corrupt than the assassination planned and conducted by Catiline in reference to the Roman Senate. The time has arrived when we should show to the nations of the earth that we are a nation capable of preserving our existence, and give them evidence that we will do it.

I have already detained the Senate much longer than I intended when I rose, and I shall conclude in a few words more. Although the Government has met with a little reverse within a short distance of this city, no one should be discouraged and no heart should be dismayed. It ought only to prove the necessity of bringing forth and exerting still more vigorously the power of the Government in maintenance of the Constitution and the laws. Let the energies of the Government be redoubled, and let it go on with this war, — not a war upon sections, not a war upon peculiar institutions anywhere; but let the Constitution and the Union be inscribed on its banners, and the supremacy and enforcement of the laws be its watchword. Then it can, it will, go on triumphantly. We must succeed. This Government must not, cannot fail. Though your flag may have trailed in the dust; though a retrogade movement may have been made; though the banner of our country may have been sullied, let it still be borne onward; and if, for the prosecution of this war in behalf of the Government and the Constitution, it is necessary to cleanse and purify that banner, I say let it be baptized in fire from the sun and bathed in a nation's blood! The nation must be redeemed; it must be triumphant. The Constitution — which is based upon principles immutable, and upon which rests the rights of man and the hopes and expectations of those who love freedom throughout the civilized world — must be maintained.

SPEECH ON THE PROPOSED EXPULSION OF MR. BRIGHT.

DELIVERED IN THE SENATE OF THE UNITED STATES, JAN. 31, 1862.

THE Senate having under consideration the following resolution, submitted by MR. WILKINSON on the 16th of December, 1861, and which had been reported upon adversely by the Committee on the Judiciary: —

Whereas, Hon. JESSE D. BRIGHT heretofore, on the 1st day of March, 1861, wrote a letter, of which the following is a copy, —

MY DEAR SIR: Allow me to introduce to your acquaintance my friend Thomas B. Lincoln, of Texas. He visits your capital mainly to dispose of what he regards a great improvement in fire-arms. I recommend him to your favorable consideration as a gentleman of the first respectability, and reliable in every respect.

Very truly yours, JESSE D. BRIGHT.

To His Excellency JEFFERSON DAVIS,

President of the Confederation of States.

And whereas we believe the said letter is evidence of disloyalty to the United States, and is calculated to give aid and comfort to the public enemies: Therefore,

Be it resolved, That the said JESSE D. BRIGHT is expelled from his seat in the Senate of the United States.

Mr. JOHNSON said: — Mr. President, when this resolution for the expulsion of the Senator from Indiana was first presented to the consideration of the Senate, it was not my intention to say a single word upon it. Presuming that action would be had upon it at a very early day, I intended to content myself with casting a silent vote. But the question has assumed such a shape that, occupying the position I do, I cannot consent to record my vote without giving some of the reasons that influence my action.

I am no enemy of the Senator from Indiana. I have no personally unkind feelings towards him. I never had any, and have none now. So far as my action on this case is concerned, it will be controlled absolutely and exclusively by public considerations, and with no reference to partisan or personal feeling. I know that since the discussion commenced, an intimation has been thrown out, which I was pained to hear, that there was a disposition on the part of some to hound down the Senator from Indiana. Sir, I know that I have no disposition to "hound" any man. I would to God that I could think it otherwise than necessary for me to say a single word upon this question, or even to cast a vote upon it. So far as I know, there has never been any unkind feeling between the Senator and myself from the time we made our advent into public life down to this moment. Although party and party associations and party considerations influence all of us more or less, — and I do not pretend to be free from the influence of party more than others, — I know, if I know myself, that no such considerations influence me now. Not many years ago there was a contest before the Senate as to his admission as a Senator from the State of Indiana; we all remember the struggle that took place. I will not say that the other side of the House were influenced by party considerations when the vote upon that question of admission took place; but if my memory serves me correctly, there was upon one side of the Chamber a nearly strict party vote that he was not entitled to his seat, while on the other side his right was sustained entirely by a party vote. I was one of those who voted for the Senator's admission to a seat upon this floor under the circumstances. I voted to let him into the Senate, and I am constrained to say that, before his term has expired, I am compelled to vote to expel him from it. In saying this, I repeat that if I know myself, and I think I do as well as ordinary men know themselves, I cast this vote upon public considerations entirely, and not from party or personal feeling.

Mr. President, I hold that under the Constitution of the United States we clearly have the power to expel a member, and that, too, without our assuming the character of a judicial body. It is not necessary to have articles of impeachment preferred by the other House; it is not necessary to organize ourselves into a court for the purpose of trial; but the principle is broad and clear, inherent in the very organization of the body itself, that we have the power and the right to expel any member from the Senate whenever we deem that the public interests are unsafe in his hands, and that he is unfit to be a member of the body. We all know, and the country understands, that provision of the Constitution which confers this power upon the Senate. Judge Story, in commenting upon the case of John Smith, in connection with the provision of the Constitution to which I have referred, used the following language: —

> "The precise ground of the failure of the motion does not appear; but it may be gathered, from the arguments of his counsel, that it did not turn upon any doubt that the power of the Senate extended to cases of misdemeanor not done in the presence or view of the body; but most probably it was decided upon some doubt as to the facts. It may be thought difficult to draw a clear line of distinction between the right to inflict the punishment of expulsion and any other punishment upon a member, founded on the time, place, or nature of the offence. The power to expel a member is not in the British House of Commons confined to offences committed by the party as a member, or during the session of Parliament; but it extends to all cases where the offence is such as, in the judgment of the House, unfits him for parliamentary duties.[1]

The rule in the House of Commons was undoubtedly in the view of the framers of our Constitution; and the question is, has the member unfitted himself, has he disqualified himself, in view of the extraordinary condition of the country, from discharging the duties of a Senator? Looking at

[1] *Story's Commentaries on the Constitution.*

his connection with the Executive; looking at the condition, and, probably, the destinies of the country, we are to decide — without prejudice, without passion, without excitement — can the nation and does the nation have confidence in committing its destinies to the Senator from Indiana, and others who are situated like him?

If we were disposed to bring to our aid, and were willing to rely upon, the public judgment, what should we find? When you pass through the country, the common inquiry is, "Why has not Senator Bright, and why have not others like him, been expelled from the Senate?" I have had the question asked me again and again. I do not intend, though, to predicate my action as a Senator upon what may be simply rumor and popular clamor or popular indignation; but still it is not often the case that, when there is a public judgment formed in reference to any great question before the country, that public judgment is not well founded, though it is true there are sometimes exceptions.

Having shown our power in the premises to be clear, according to the general authority granted by the Constitution and the broad principle stated by Judge Story in its elucidation, I next turn my attention to the case itself. The Senator from Indiana is charged with having written a letter on the first of March last to the chief of the rebellion, and this is the basis of this proceeding against him.

What was the condition of the country at the time that letter was written? Did war then exist or not? for really that is the great point in the case. On that point, allow me to read an extract from the charge of Judge David A. Smalley to the grand jury of the United States District Court for the Southern District of New York, published in the "National Intelligencer" of January 21, 1861: —

"It is well known that war, civil war, exists in portions of the Union; that persons owing allegiance to the United States have confederated together, and with arms, by force and intimidation, have prevented the execution of the constitutional acts of Congress, have forcibly seized upon and hold a custom-house and post-office, forts, arsenals, vessels, and other property belonging to the United States, and have actually fired upon vessels bearing the United States flag and carrying United States troops. This is a usurpation of the authority of the Federal Government; it is high treason by levying war. Either one of those acts will constitute high treason. There can be no doubt of it."

The judge here defines high treason, and he goes on to say, —

"What amounts to adhering to and giving aid and comfort to our enemies, it is somewhat difficult in all cases to define; but certain it is that furnishing them with arms," —

It really seems that, by some kind of intuition, the judge had in his mind the precise case now under our consideration, and had anticipated it last January, —

— "certain it is that furnishing them with arms or munitions of war, vessels or other means of transportation, or any materials which will aid the traitors in carrying out their traitorous purposes, with a knowledge that they are intended for such purposes, or inciting and encouraging others to engage in or aid the traitors in any way, does come within the provisions of the act."

In this view, even if we were sitting as a court, bound by the rules and technicalities of judicial proceedings, should we not be bound to hold that this case comes within this legal definition?

"And it is immaterial," adds Judge Smalley, "whether such acts are induced by sympathy with the rebellion, hostility to the Government, or a design for gain."

In view of these authorities, let us look at the letter. It was written on the 1st of March, 1861. The opinion of Judge Smalley was published in the "Intelligencer" of the 21st of January, 1861, and must, of course, have been delivered before that time. It would be doing the Senator's intelligence great injustice to presume that he was not as well informed on the subject as the judge was who was charging the grand jury in reference to an act of Congress passed at an early day in the history of the Government. It would be doing him great injustice to suppose that he was not familiar with the statute. It would be doing him great injustice to suppose that he had not observed the fact that the attention of the country was being called by the courts to the treason that was rampant throughout the land. The letter complained of is as follows: —

WASHINGTON, *March* 1, 1861.

MY DEAR SIR: Allow me to introduce to your acquaintance my friend Thomas B. Lincoln, of Texas. He visits your capital mainly to dispose of what he regards a great improvement in fire-arms. I recommend him to your favorable consideration as a gentleman of the first respectability, and reliable in every respect.

Very truly yours, JESSE D. BRIGHT.

To His Excellency JEFFERSON DAVIS,
President of the Confederation of States.

According to the charge of Judge Smalley, which I have already read, the flag of the United States had been fired upon before the 21st of January, 1861, and war then did in fact exist. When the rebels were taking our forts; when they were taking possession of our post-offices; when they were seizing our custom-houses; when they were taking possession of our mints and the depositories of the public money, can it be possible that the Senator from Indiana did not know that war existed, and that rebellion was going on? It is a fact that the ordinance of the convention of Texas seceding from the Union and attaching herself to the Southern Confederacy, was dated back as far as the 1st of February, 1861. Then, at the time the letter was written, Thomas B. Lincoln was a citizen of a rebel State; a traitor and a rebel himself. He comes to the Senator asking him to do what? To write a letter by which he could be facilitated in his scheme of selling an improved fire-arm, an implement of war and of death. Can there be any mistake about it? He asks for a letter recommending an improved fire-arm to the President of the rebel States, who was then in actual war; the man who asked for this being himself from a State that was in open rebellion, and he himself a traitor.

Now, sir, if we were a court, how would the case be presented? I know the Constitution says that "no person shall be convicted of treason unless on the testimony of two witnesses to the same overt act, or on confession in open court." Here is an overt act; it is shown clearly and plainly. We have the Senator's confession in open Senate that he did write the letter. Shall we with this discretion, in view of the protection of this body and the safety of the Government, decide the case upon special pleas or hunt up technicalities by which the Senator can escape, as you would quash an indictment in a criminal court?

The case of John Smith has already been stated to the Senate. A true bill had been found against him for his connection with Burr's treason, but upon a technicality, the proof not being made out according to the Constitution, and Burr having been tried first and acquitted, the bill against Smith was quashed, as he was only an accomplice. He was, therefore, turned out of court; the proceedings against him were quashed upon a technicality; but John Smith was a Senator, and he came here to this body. He came again to take his seat in the

Senate of the United States, and what did the Senate do? They took up his case; they investigated it. Mr. Adams made a report, able, full, complete. I may say he came well-nigh exhausting the whole subject. The committee reported a resolution for his expulsion, and how did the vote stand? It is true that Mr. Smith was not expelled for the want of some little formality in this body, the vote standing 19 to 10. It only lacked one vote to put him out by a two-thirds majority, according to the requirements of the Constitution. What was the judgment of the nation? It was that John Smith was an accomplice of Burr, and the Senate condemned him and almost expelled him, not narrowing itself down to those rules and technicalities that are resorted to in courts and by which criminals escape. To show the grounds upon which the action in that case was based, I beg leave to read some extracts from Mr. John Quincy Adams's report in that case: —

"In examining the question whether these forms of judicial proceedings or the rules of judicial evidence ought to be applied to the exercise of that censorial authority which the Senate of the United States possesses over the conduct of its members, let us assume as the test of their application either the dictates of unfettered reason, the letter and spirit of the Constitution, or precedents domestic or foreign, and your committee believe that the result will be the same: that the power of expelling a member must in its nature be discretionary, and in its exercise always more summary than the tardy process of judical proceedings.

"The power of expelling a member for misconduct results,

on the principles of common sense, from the interests of the nation that the high trust of legislation should be invested in pure hands. When the trust is elective, it is not to be presumed that the constituent body will commit the deposit to the keeping of worthless characters. But when a man, whom his fellow-citizens have honored with their confidence on the pledge of a spotless reputation, has degraded himself by the commission of infamous crimes, which become suddenly and unexpectedly revealed to the world, defective, indeed, would be that institution which should be impotent to discard from its bosom the contagion of such a member; which should have no remedy of amputation to apply until the poison had reached the heart."

. . . .

"But when a member of a legislative body lies under the imputation of aggravated offences, and the determination upon his case can operate only to remove him from a station of extensive powers and important trusts, this disproportion between the interest of the public and the interest of the individual disappears; if any disproportion exists, it is of an opposite kind. It is not better that ten traitors should be members of this Senate, than that one innocent man should suffer expulsion. In either case, no doubt, the evil would be great; but in the former, it would strike at the vitals of the nation; in the latter it might, though deeply to be lamented, only be the calamity of an individual."

. . . .

"Yet in the midst of all this anxious providence of legislative virtue, it has not authorized the constituent body to recall in any case its representative. It has not subjected him to removal by impeachment; and when the darling of the people's choice has become their deadliest foe, can it enter the imagination of a reasonable man, that the sanctuary of their legislation must remain polluted with his presence, until a court of common law, with its pace of snail, can ascertain whether his crime was committed on the right or on the left bank of a river; whether a puncture of difference can be found between the words of the charge and the words of the proof; whether the witnesses of his guilt should or should not be heard by his jury; and whether he was punishable, because present at an over act, or intangible to public justice because he only contrived and prepared it? Is it conceivable that a traitor to that country which has loaded him with favors, guilty to the common understanding of all mankind, should be suffered to return unquestioned to that post of honor and confidence where, in the zenith of his good fame, he had been placed by the esteem of his countrymen, and in defiance of their wishes, in mockery of their fears, surrounded by the public indignation, but inaccessible to its bolt, pursue the purposes of treason in the heart of the national councils? Must the assembled rulers of the land listen with calmness and indifference, session after session, to the voice of notorious infamy, until the sluggard step of municipal justice can overtake his enormities? Must they tamely see the lives and fortunes of millions, the safety of present and future ages, depending upon his vote, recorded with theirs, merely because the abused benignity of general maxims may have remitted to him the forfeiture of his life?"

"Such, in very supposable cases, would be the unavoidable consequences of a principle which should offer the crutches of judicial tribunals as an apology for crippling the congressional power of expulsion. Far different, in the opinion of your committee, is the spirit of our Constitution. They believed that the very purpose for which this power was given was to preserve the Legislature from the first approaches of infection; that it was made discretionary, because it could not exist under the procrastination of general rules. That its process must be summary, because it would be rendered nugatory by delay."

Mr. President, suppose Aaron Burr had been a Senator, and after his acquittal he had come back here to take his seat in the Senate, what would have been done? According to the doctrine avowed in this debate, that we must sit as a court and subject the individual to all the rules and technicalities of criminal proceedings, could he have been expelled? And yet is there a Senator here who would have voted to allow Aaron Burr to take a seat in the Senate after his acquittal by a court and jury? No; there is not a Senator here who would have done it. Aaron Burr was tried in court, and he was found not guilty; he was turned loose; but was the public judgment of this nation less satisfied of his guilt than if he had not been acquitted? What is the nation's judgment, settled and fixed? That Aaron Burr was guilty of treason, notwithstanding he was acquitted by a court and jury.

It is said by some Senators that the Senator from Indiana wrote this letter simply as a letter of friendship. Sir, just think of it! A Senator of the United States was called upon to write a letter for a rebel, for a man from a rebel State, after the courts of the country had pronounced that civil war existed; after the judicial tribunals had defined what aiding and adhering to the enemies of the country was! Under such circumstances, what would have been the course of loyalty and of patriotism? Suppose a man who had been your friend, sir, who had rendered you many acts of kindness, had come to you for such a letter. You would have asked where he was going with it. You would have said: "There is a Southern Confederacy; there is a rebellion; my friend, you cannot ask me to write a letter to anybody there; they are at war with the United States; they are at war with my Government; I cannot write you a letter giving you aid and assistance in selling your improved fire-arm there." Why? "Because that fire-arm may be used against my own country and against my own fellow-citizens." Would not that have been the language of a man who was willing to recognize his obligations of duty to his country?

What was the object of writing the letter? It certainly was to aid, to facilitate the selling of his fire-arms, to inspire the rebel chief with confidence in the individual. It was saying substantially, "I know this man; I write to you because I know you have confidence in me; I send him to you because I know you need fire-arms; you need improved fire-arms; you need the most deadly and destructive weapons of warfare to overcome this great and this glorious country; I recommend him to you, and I recommend his fire-arms; he is a man in whom entire confidence may be placed." That, sir, is the letter. I have already shown the circumstances under which it was written. If such a letter had been written in the purest innocence of intention, with no treasonable design, with no desire to injure his own Government, yet, in view of all the circumstances, in view of the facts which had transpired, a Senator who would be so unthoughtful, and so negligent, and so regardless of his country's interests as to write such a letter, is not entitled to a seat on this floor. [Applause in the galleries.]

The PRESIDING OFFICER.[1] Order! order!

Mr. JOHNSON. Then, Mr. President, what has been the bearing and the conduct of the Senator from Indiana since? I desire it to be understood that I refer to him in no unkindness, for God knows I bear him none; but my duty I will perform. "Duties are mine, consequences are God's." What has been the Senator's bearing generally? Have you heard of his being in the field? Have you heard of his voice and his influence being raised for his bleeding and distracted country? Has his influence been brought to bear officially, socially, politically, or in any way for the suppression of the rebellion? If so, I am unaware of it. Where is the evidence of devotion to his country in his speeches and in his votes? Where the evidence of the disposition on his part to overthrow and put down the rebellion? I have been told, Mr. President, by honorable gentlemen, as an evidence of the Senator's devotion to his country and his great opposition to this Southern movement, that they heard him, and perhaps with tears in his eyes, remonstrate with the leaders of the rebellion that they should not leave him here in the Senate, or that they should not persist in their course after the relations that had existed between them and him,

1 Mr. Sherman.

and the other Democrats of the country; that he thought they were treating him badly. This was the kind of remonstrance he made. Be it so. I am willing to give the Senator credit for all he is entitled to, and I would to God I could credit him with more.

But do Senators remember that when this battle was being fought in the Senate I stood here on this side, solitary and alone, on the 19th day of December, 1860, and proclaimed that the Government was at an end if you denied it the power to enforce its laws? I declared then that a government which had not the power to coerce obedience on the part of those who violated the law was no government at all, and had failed to carry out the objects of its creation, and was, *ipso facto*, dissolved. When I stood on this floor and fought the battle for the supremacy of the Constitution and the enforcement of the laws, has the Senate forgotten that a bevy of conspirators gathered in from the other House, and that those who were here crowded around, with frowns and scowls, and expressions of indignation and contempt toward me, because I dared to raise my feeble voice in vindication of the Constitution and the enforcement of the laws of the Union? Have you forgotten the taunts, the jeers, the derisive remarks, the contemptuous expressions that were indulged in? If you have, I have not. If the Senator felt such great reluctance at the departure from the Senate of the chiefs of the rebellion, I should have been glad to receive one encouraging smile from him when I was fighting the battles of the country. I did not receive one encouraging expression; I received not a single sustaining look. It would have been peculiarly encouraging to me, under the circumstances, to be greeted and encouraged by one of the Senator's talents and long standing in public life; but he was cold as an iceberg, and I stood solitary and alone amidst the gang of conspirators that had gathered around me. So much for the Senator's remonstrances and expressions of regret for the retirement of those gentlemen.

The bearing of the Senator since he wrote this letter has not been unobserved. I have not compared notes; I have not hunted up the record in reference to it; but I have a perfect recollection of it. Did we not see, during the last session of Congress, the line being drawn between those who were devoted to the Union and those who were not? Cannot we sometimes see a great deal more than is expressed? Does it require us to have a man's sentiments written down in burning and blazing characters, before we are able to judge what they are? Has it not been observable all through this history where the true Union heart has stood? What was the Senator's bearing at the last session of Congress? Do we not know that in the main he stood here opposed substantially to every measure which was necessary to sustain the Government in its trial and peril? He may perhaps have voted for some measures that were collateral, remote, indirect in their bearing; but do we not know that his vote and his influence were cast against the measures which were absolutely necessary to sustain the Government in its hour of peril?

Some gentlemen have said, and well said, that we should not judge by party. I say so, too. I voted to let the Senator from Indiana into the body, and as a Democrat my bias and prejudice would rather be in his favor. I am a Democrat now; I have been one all my life; I expect to live and die one; and the corner-stone of my Democracy rests upon the enduring basis of the Union. Democrats may come and go, but they shall never divert me from the polar star by which I have ever been guided from early life, — the great principle of Democracy upon which this Government rests, and which cannot be carried out without the preservation of the Union of these States. The pretence hitherto employed by many who are now in the traitors' camp has been, "We are for the Union; we are not for dissolution; but we are opposed to coercion." How long, Senators, have you heard that syren song? Where are now most of those who sang those syren tones to us? Look back to the last session, and inquire where now are the men who then were singing that song in our ears? Where is Trusten Polk, who then stood here so gently craving for peace? He is in the rebel camp.

Where is John C. Breckinridge? — a man for whose promotion to the Presidency I did what I could, physically, mentally, and pecuniarily; but when he satisfied me that he was for breaking up this Government, and would ere long be a traitor to his country, I dropped him as I would the Senator from Indiana. He was here at the last session of Congress; and everybody could see then that he was on the road to the traitors' camp. Instead of sustaining the Government, he, too, was crying out for peace; but he was bitter against "Lincoln's government." Sir, when I talk about preserving this great Government, I do not have its executive officer in my mind. The executive head of the Government comes in and goes out of office every four years. He is the mere creature of the people. I talk about the Government without regard to the particular executive officers who have charge of it. If they do well, we can continue them; if they do wrong, we can turn them out. Mr. Lincoln having come in according to the forms of law and the Constitution, I, loving my Government and the Union, felt it to be my duty to stand by the Government, and to stand by the Administration in all those measures that I believed to be necessary and proper for the preservation and perpetuation of the Union.

Mr. Polk has gone; Mr. Breckinridge has gone; my namesake, the late Senator from Missouri, has gone. Did you not see the line of separation at the last session? Although Senators make speeches, in which they give utterance to disclaimers, we can see their bearing. It is visible now; and the obligations of truth and duty to my country require me to speak of it. I believe there are treasonable tendencies here now; and how long it will be before they will lead to the traitors' camp, I shall not undertake to say. The great point with these gentlemen is, that they are opposed to coercion and to the enforcement of the laws. Without regard to the general bearing of the Senator from Indiana upon that point, let me quote the conclusion of his letter of the 7th of September, 1861, to J. Fitch. I will read only the concluding portion of the letter, as it does him no injustice to omit the remainder: —

"And hence I have opposed, and so long as my present convictions last shall continue to oppose, the entire coercive policy of the Government. I hope this may be satisfactory to my friends. For my enemies I care not."

Does not this correspond with the Senator's general bearing? Has he given his aid or countenance or influence, in any manner, towards the efforts of the Government to sustain itself? What has been his course? We know that great stress has been laid upon the word "coercion," and it has been played upon effectually for the purpose of prejudicing the Southern mind, in connection with the other term, "subjugation of the States," which has been used so often. We may as well be honest and fair, and admit the truth of the great proposition, that a government cannot exist — in other words, it is no government — if it is without the power to enforce its laws and coerce obedience to them. That is all there is of it; and the very instant you take that power from this Government, it is at an end; it is a mere rope of sand that will fall to pieces of its own weight. It is idle, utopian, chimerical, to talk about a Government existing without the power to enforce its laws. How is the Government to enforce its laws? The Constitution says that Congress shall have power "to provide for calling forth the militia to execute the laws of the Union, suppress insurrections, and repel invasions." Let me ask the Senator from Indiana, with all his astuteness, how is rebellion to be put down, how is it to be resisted, unless there is some power in the Government to enforce its laws?

If there be a citizen who violates your post-office laws, who counterfeits the coin of the United States, or who commits any other offence against the laws of the United States, you subject him to trial and punishment. Is not that coercion? Is not that enforcing the laws? How is rebellion to be put down without coercion, without enforcing the laws? Can it be done? The Constitution provides that, —

"The United States shall guarantee to every State in this Union a republican form of government, and shall protect each of them from invasion; and on application of the Legislature, or of the Executive, (when the Legislature cannot be convened,) against domestic violence."

How is this Government to put down domestic violence in a State without coercion? How is the nation to be protected against insurrection without coercing the citizens to obedience? Can it be done? When the Senator says he is against the entire coercive policy of the Government, he is against the vital principle of all government. I look upon this as the most revolutionary and destructive doctrine that ever was preached. If this Government cannot call forth the militia, if it cannot repel invasion, if it cannot put down domestic violence, if it cannot suppress rebellion, I ask if the great objects of the Government are not at an end?

Look at my own State, by way of illustration. There is open rebellion there; there is domestic violence; there is insurrection. An attempt has been made to transfer that State to another power. Let me ask the Senator from Indiana if the Constitution does not require you to guarantee us a republican form of government in that State? Is not that your sworn duty? We ask you to put down this unholy rebellion. What answer would he give us? We ask you to protect us against insurrection and domestic violence. What is his reply? "I am against your whole coercive policy; I am against the enforcement of the laws." I say that if that principle be acted on, your Government is at an end; it fails utterly to carry out the object of its creation. Such a principle leads to the destruction of the Government, for it must inevitably result in anarchy and confusion. "I am opposed to the entire coercive policy of the Government," says the Senator from Indiana. That cuckoo note has been reiterated to satiety; it is understood; men know the nature and character of their Government, and they also know that to cry out against "coercion" and "subjugation" is mere *ad captandum*, idle, and unmeaning slang-whanging.

Sir, I may be a little sensitive on this subject upon the one hand, while I know I want to do ample justice upon the other. I took an oath to support the Constitution of the United States. There is rebellion in the land; there is insurrection against the authority of this Government. Is the Senator from Indiana so unobservant or so obtuse that he does not know now that there has been a deliberate design for years to change the nature and character and genius of this Government? Do we not know that these schemers have been deliberately at work, and that there is a party in the South, with some associates in the North, and even in the West, that have become tired of free government, in which they have lost confidence? They raise an outcry against "coercion," that they may paralyze the Government, cripple the exercise of the great powers with which it was invested, and finally to change its form and subject us to a Southern despotism. Do we not know it to be so? Why disguise this great truth? Do we not know that they have been anxious for a change of Government for years? Since this rebellion commenced it has manifested itself in many quarters. How long is it since the organ of the government at Richmond, the "Richmond Whig," declared that rather than live under the Government of the United States, they preferred to take the constitutional Queen of Great Britain as their protector; that they would make an alliance with Great Britain for the purpose of preventing the enforcement of the laws of the United States? Do we not know this? Why then play "hide and go seek"? Why say, "Oh, yes, I am for the Union," while every act, influence, conversation, vote, is against it? What confidence can we have in one who takes such a course?

The people of my State, down-trodden and oppressed by the iron heel of Southern despotism, appeal to you for protection. They ask you to protect them against domestic violence. They want you to help them to put down this unholy and damnable rebellion. They call upon this Government for the execution of its constitutional duty to guarantee to them a republican form of government, and to protect them against the tyranny and despotism which is stalking abroad. What is the cold reply? "I am against the entire coercive policy; I am not for enforcing the laws." Upon such a doctrine Government crumbles to pieces, and anarchy and despotism reign throughout the land.

Indiana, God bless her, is as true to the Union as the needle is to the pole. She has sent out her "columns"; she has sent her thousands into the field, for what? To sustain the Constitution and to enforce the laws; and as they march with strong arms and brave hearts to relieve a suffering people, who have committed no offence save devotion to this glorious Union; as they march to the rescue of the Constitution and to extend its benefits again to a people who love it dearly, and who have been ruthlessly torn from under its protecting ægis, what does their Senator say to them? "I am against the entire policy of coercion." Do you ever hear a Senator who thus talks make any objection to the exercise of unconstitutional and tyrannical power by the so-called Southern Confederacy, or say a word against its practice of coercion? In all the speeches that have been delivered on that point, has one sentence against usurpation, against despotism, against the exercise of doubtful and unconstitutional powers by that Confederacy, been uttered? Oh, no! Have you heard any objection to their practising not only coercion but usurpation? Have they not usurped government? Have they not oppressed, and are they not now tyrannizing over the people? The people of my State are coerced, borne down, trodden beneath the iron heel of power. We appeal to you for protection. You stand by and see us coerced; you stand by and see tyranny triumphing, and no sympathy, no kindness, no helping hand can be extended to us. Your Government is paralyzed; your Government is powerless; that which you have called a government is a dream, an idle thing. You thought you had a government, but you have none. My people are appealing to you for protection under the Constitution. They are arrested by hundreds and by thousands; they are dragged away from their homes and incarcerated in dungeons. They ask you for protection. Why do you not give it? Some of them are lying chained in their lonely prison-house. The only response to their murmur is the rattling and clanking of the chains that bind their limbs. The only response to their appeals is the grating of the hinges of their dungeon. When we ask for help under the Constitution, we are told that the Government has no power to enforce the laws. Our people are oppressed and down-trodden, and you give them no remedy. They were taught to love and respect the Constitution of the United States. What is their condition to-day? They are hunted and pursued like the beasts of the forest by the secession and disunion hordes who are enforcing their doctrine of coercion. They are shot or hung for no crime save a desire to stand by the Constitution of the United States. Helpless children and innocent females are murdered in cold blood. Our men are hung and their bodies left upon the gibbet. They are shot and left lying in the gorges of the mountains, not even thrown into the caves there to lie, but are left exposed to pass through all the loathsome stages of decomposition, or to be devoured by the birds of prey. We appeal for protection, and are told by the Senator from Indiana and others, "We cannot enforce the laws; we are against the entire coercive policy." Do you not hear their groans? Do you not hear their cries? Do you not hear the shrieks of oppressed and down-trodden women and children? Sir, their tones ring out so loud and clear, that even listening angels look from heaven in pity.

I will not pursue this idea further, for I perceive that I am consuming more time than I intended to occupy. I think it it clear, without going further into the discussion, that the Senator from Indiana has sympathized with the rebellion. The conclusion is fixed upon my mind that the Senator from Indiana has disqualified himself, has incapacitated himself to discharge the duties in this body of a loyal Senator. I think it is clear that, even if we were a court, we should be bound to convict him; but I do not narrow the case down to the close rules that would govern a court of justice.

But, sir, in the course of the discussion one palliating fact was submitted by the distinguished Senator from New Jersey,[1] and he knows that I do not refer to him in any spirit of unkindness. There was more of legal learning and special pleading in his suggestion than solidity or sound argument. He

[1] Mr. Ten Eyck.

suggested that there was no proof that this letter had ever been delivered to Jefferson Davis, and that therefore the Senator from Indiana ought not to be convicted. Well, sir, on the other hand, there is no proof that it was not delivered. It is true, the letter was found in Mr. Lincoln's possession; but who knows that Davis did not read the letter, and hand it back to Lincoln? It may have been that, being from his early friend, a man whom he respected, Lincoln desired to keep the letter and show it to somebody else. We have as much right to infer that the letter was delivered as that it was not; but be that as it may, does it lessen the culpability of the Senator from Indiana? He committed the act, and so far as he was concerned it was executed. It would be no palliation of his offence if the man did not deliver the letter to Davis. The intent and the act were just as complete as if it had been delivered.

During the war of the Revolution, in 1780, Major André, a British spy, held a conference with Benedict Arnold. Arnold prepared his letters, six in number, and they were handed over to Major André, who put them between the soles of his feet and his stockings, and he started on his way to join Sir Henry Clinton. Before he reached his destination, however, John Paulding and his two associates arrested Major André. They pulled off his boots and his stockings, and they got the papers; they kept them, and Major André was tried and hung as a spy. Arnold's papers were not delivered to Sir Henry Clinton; but is there anybody here who doubts that Arnold was a traitor? Has public opinion ever changed upon that subject? He was not convicted in a court, nor were the treasonable despatches which were to expose the condition of West Point, and make the British attack upon it easy and successful, ever delivered to Sir Henry Clinton, and yet André was hung as a spy. Because Sir Henry Clinton did not receive the treasonable documents, was the guilt of Benedict Arnold any the less? I do not intend to argue this question in a legal way; I simply mention this circumstance by way of illustration of the point which has been urged in the present case, and leave it for the public judgment to determine.

Sir, it has been said by the distinguished Senator from Delaware[1] that the questions in controversy might all have been settled by compromise. He dealt rather extensively in the party aspect of the case, and seemingly desired to throw the *onus* of the present condition of affairs entirely on one side. He told us that if so and so had been done these questions could have been settled, and that now there would have been no war. He referred particularly to the resolution offered during the last Congress by the Senator from New Hampshire,[2] and upon the vote on that he based his argument. I do not mean to be egotistical, but if he will give

[1] Mr. Saulsbury. [2] Mr. Clark.

me his attention I intend to take the staple out of that speech, and show how much of it is left on that point.

The speech of the Senator from Delaware was a very fine one. I have not the power, as he has, to con over and get by rote, and memorize handsomely rounded periods, and make a great display of rhetoric. It is my misfortune that I am not so skilled. I have to seize on fugitive thoughts as they pass through my mind, make the best application of them I can, and express them in my own crude way. I am not one of those who prepare rounding, sounding, bounding rhetorical flourishes, read them over twenty times before I come into the Senate Chamber, make a great display, and have it said, "Oh, that is a fine speech!" I have heard many such fine speeches; but when I have had time to follow them up, I have found that it never took long to analyze them, and reduce them to their original elements; and that when they were reduced, there was not very much of them. [Laughter.]

The Senator told us that the adoption of the Clark amendment to the Crittenden resolutions defeated the settlement of the questions of controversy; and that, but for that vote, all could have been peace and prosperity now. We were told that the Clark amendment defeated the Crittenden Compromise, and prevented a settlement of the controversy. On this point I will read a portion of the speech of my worthy and talented friend from California,[1] and when I speak of him thus, I do it in no unmeaning sense. I intend that he, not I, shall answer the Senator from Delaware. I know that sometimes, when gentlemen are fixing up their pretty rhetorical flourishes, they do not take time to see all the sharp corners they may encounter. If they can make a readable sentence, and float on in a smooth, easy stream, all goes well, and they are satisfied. As I have said, the Senator from Delaware told us that the Clark amendment was the turning-point in the whole matter; that from it had flowed rebellion, revolution, war, the shooting and imprisonment of people in different States, — perhaps he meant to include my own. This was the Pandora's box that has been opened, out of which all the evils that now afflict the land have flown. Thank God, I still have hope that all will yet be saved. My worthy friend from California,[1] during the last session of Congress, made one of the best speeches he ever made. I bought five thousand copies of it for distribution, but I had no constituents to send them to; [laughter;] and they have been lying in your document-room ever since, with the exception of a few, which I thought would do good in some quarters. In the course of that speech, upon this very point, he made use of these remarks: —

"Mr. President, being last winter a careful eye-witness of all that occurred, I soon became satisfied that it was a deliber-

[1] Mr. Latham.

ate, wilful design, on the part of some representatives of Southern States, to seize upon the election of Mr. Lincoln merely as an excuse to precipitate this revolution upon the country. One evidence, to my mind, is the fact that South Carolina never sent her Senators here."

Then they certainly were not influenced by the Clark amendment.

"An additional evidence is, that when gentlemen on this floor, by their votes, could have controlled legislation, they refused to cast them for fear that the very propositions submitted to this body might have an influence in changing the opinions of their constituencies. Why, sir, when the resolutions submitted by the Senator from New Hampshire [Mr. Clark] were offered as an amendment to the Crittenden propositions, for the manifest purpose of embarrassing the latter, and the vote taken on the 16th of January, 1861, I ask, what did we see? There were fifty-five Senators at that time upon this floor in person. The 'Globe' of the second session, Thirty-Sixth Congress, part 1, page 409, shows that upon the call of the yeas and nays immediately preceding the vote on the substituting of Mr. Clark's amendment, there were fifty-five votes cast. I will read the vote from the 'Globe':

"'Yeas — Messrs. Anthony, Baker, Bingham, Cameron, Chandler, Clark, Collamer, Dixon, Doolittle, Durkee, Fessenden, Foot, Foster, Grimes, Hale, Harlan, King, Seward, Simmons, Sumner, Ten Eyck, Trumbull, Wade, Wilkinson, and Wilson — 25.

"'Nays — Messrs. Bayard, Benjamin, Bigler, Bragg, Bright, Clingman, Crittenden, Douglas, Fitch, Green, Gwin, Hemphill, Hunter, Iverson, Johnson of Arkansas, Johnson of Tennessee, Kennedy, Lane, Latham, Mason, Nicholson, Pearce, Polk, Powell, Pugh, Rice, Saulsbury, Sebastian, Slidell, and Wigfall — 30.'

"The vote being taken immediately after, on the Clark proposition, was as follows: —

"'Yeas — Messrs. Anthony, Baker, Bingham, Cameron, Chandler, Clark, Collamer, Dixon, Doolittle, Durkee, Fessenden, Foot, Foster, Grimes, Hale, Harlan, King, Seward, Simmons, Sumner, Ten Eyck, Trumbull, Wade, Wilkinson, and Wilson — 25.

"'Nays — Messrs. Bayard, Bigler, Bragg, Bright, Clingman, Crittenden, Fitch, Green, Gwin, Hunter, Johnson of Tennessee, Kennedy, Lane, Latham, Mason, Nicholson, Pearce, Polk, Powell, Pugh, Rice, Saulsbury, and Sebastian — 23.'

"Six Senators retained their seats and refused to vote, thus themselves allowing the Clark proposition to supplant the Crittenden resolution by a vote of twenty-five to twenty-three. Mr. Benjamin of Louisiana, Mr. Hemphill and Mr. Wigfall of Texas, Mr. Iverson of Georgia, Mr. Johnson of Arkansas, and Mr. Slidell of Louisiana, were in their seats, but refused to cast their votes."

I sat right behind Mr. Benjamin, and I am not sure that my worthy friend was not close by, when he refused to vote, and I said to him, "Mr. Benjamin, why do you not vote? Why not save this proposition, and see if we cannot bring the country to it?" He gave me rather an abrupt answer, and said he would control his own action without consulting me or anybody else. Said I, "Vote, and show yourself an honest man." As soon as the vote was taken, he and others telegraphed South, "We cannot get any compromise." Here were six Southern men refusing to vote, when the amendment would have been rejected by four majority if they had voted. Who, then, has brought these evils on the country? Was it Mr. Clark? He was acting out his own policy; but with the help we had from the other side of the Chamber, if all those on this side had been true to the Constitution and faithful to their constituents, and had acted with fidelity to the country, the amendment of the Senator from New Hampshire could have been voted down, the defeat of which, the Senator from Delaware says, would have saved the country. Whose fault was it? Who is responsible for it? Who did it? Southern traitors, as was said in the speech of the Senator from California. They did it. They wanted no compromise. They accomplished their object by withholding their votes; and hence the country has been involved in the present difficulty. Let me read another extract from this speech of the Senator from California: —

"I recollect full well the joy that pervaded the faces of some of those gentlemen at the result, and the sorrow manifested by the venerable Senator from Kentucky, [Mr. Crittenden.] The record shows that Mr. Pugh, from Ohio, despairing of any compromise between the extremes of ultra Republicanism and disunionists, working manifestly for the same end, moved, immediately after the vote was announced, to lay the whole subject on the table. If you will turn to page 443, in the same volume, you will find, when, at a late period, Mr. Cameron, from Pennsylvania, moved to reconsider the vote, appeals having been made to sustain those who were struggling to preserve the peace of the country, that the vote *was* reconsidered; and when, at last, the Crittenden propositions were submitted on the 2d day of March, these Southern States having nearly all seceded, they were then lost by but one vote. Here is the vote: —

"'Yeas — Messrs. Bayard, Bigler, Bright, Crittenden, Douglas, Gwin, Hunter, Johnson of Tennessee, Kennedy, Lane, Latham, Mason, Nicholson, Polk, Pugh, Rice, Sebastian, Thomson, and Wigfall — 19.

"'Nays — Messrs. Anthony, Bingham, Chandler, Clark, Dixon, Doolittle, Durkee, Fessenden, Foot, Foster, Grimes, Harlan, King, Morrill, Sumner, Ten Eyck, Trumbull, Wade, Wilkinson, and Wilson — 20.'

"If these seceding Southern Senators had remained, there would have passed, by a large vote, (as it did without them,) an amendment, by a two-thirds vote, forbidding Congress ever interfering with slavery in the States. The Crittenden proposition would have been indorsed by a majority vote, the subject finally going before the people, who have never yet, after consideration, refused justice, for any length of time, to any portion of the country.

"I believe more, Mr. President, that these gentlemen were acting in pursuance of a settled and fixed plan to break up and destroy this Government."

When we had it in our power to vote down the amendment of the Senator from New Hampshire, and adopt the Crittenden resolutions, certain Southern Senators prevented it; and yet, even at a late day of the session, after they had seceded, the Crittenden proposition was only lost by one vote. If rebellion and bloodshed and murder have followed, to whose skirts does the responsibility attach? I summed up all these facts myself in a speech during the last session; but I have preferred to read from the speech of the Senator from California, he being better authority, and having presented the facts better than I could.

What else was done at the very same session?

The House of Representatives passed, and sent to this body, a proposition to amend the Constitution of the United States, so as to prohibit Congress from ever hereafter interfering with the institution of slavery in the States, making that restriction a part of the organic law of the land. That constitutional amendment came here after the Senators from seven States had seceded; and yet it was passed by a two-thirds vote in the Senate. Have you ever heard of any one of the States which had then seceded, or which has since seceded, taking up that amendment to the Constitution, and saying they would ratify it, and make it a part of that instrument? No. Does not the whole history of this rebellion tell you that it was revolution that the leaders wanted, that they started for, that they intended to have? The facts to which I have referred show how the Crittenden proposition might have been carried; and when the Senators from the slave States were reduced to one fourth of the members of this body, the two Houses passed a proposition to amend the Constitution, so as to guarantee to the States perfect security in regard to the institution of slavery in all future time, and prohibiting Congress from legislating on the subject.

But what more was done? After Southern Senators had treacherously abandoned the Constitution and deserted their posts here, Congress passed bills for the organization of three new Territories,

Dakota, Nevada, and Colorado; and in the sixth section of each of those bills, after conferring, affirmatively, power on the Territorial Legislature, it went on to exclude certain powers by using a negative form of expression; and it provided, among other things, that the Legislature should have no power to legislate so as to impair the right to private property; that it should lay no tax discriminating against one description of property in favor of another; leaving the power on all these questions not in the Territorial Legislature, but in the people when they should come to form a State constitution.

Now, I ask, taking the amendment to the Constitution, and taking the three territorial bills, embracing every square inch of territory in the possession of the United States, how much of the slavery question was left? What better compromise could have been made? Still we are told that matters might have been compromised, and that if we had agreed to compromise, bloody rebellion would not now be abroad in the land. Sir, Southern Senators are responsible for it. They stood here with power to accomplish the result, and yet treacherously, and, I may say, tauntingly, they left this Chamber, and announced that they had dissolved their connection with the Government. Then, when we were left in the hands of those whom we had been taught to believe would encroach upon our rights, they gave us, in the constitutional amendment and in the three territorial bills, all that had ever been asked; and yet gentlemen talk about compromise. Why was not this taken and accepted?

No; it was not compromise that the leaders wanted; they wanted power; they wanted to destroy this Government, so that they might have place and emolument for themselves. They had lost confidence in the intelligence and virtue and integrity of the people, and their capacity to govern themselves; and they intended to separate and form a government, the chief corner-stone of which should be slavery, disfranchising the great mass of the people, of which we have seen constant evidence, and merging the powers of government in the hands of the few. I know what I say. I know their feelings and their sentiments. I served in the Senate here with them. I know they were a close corporation, that had no more confidence in or respect for the people than has the Dey of Algiers. I fought that close corporation here. I knew that they were no friends of the people. I knew that Slidell and Mason and Benjamin and Iverson and Toombs were the enemies of free government, and I know so now. I commenced the war upon them before a State seceded; and I intend to keep on fighting this great battle before the country for the perpetuity of free government. They seek to overthrow it, and to establish a despotism in its place. That is the great battle which is upon our hands. The great interests of civil liberty and free government call upon every patriot and every lover of popular rights to come forward and discharge his duty.

We see this great struggle; we see that the exercise of the vital principle of government itself is denied by those who desire our institutions to be overthrown and despotism established on their ruins. If we have not the physical and moral courage to exclude from our midst men whom we believe to be unsafe depositaries of public power and public trust, — men whose associates were rolling off honeyed accents against coercion, and are now in the traitors' camp, — if we have not the courage to force these men from our midst, because we have known them, and have been personal friends with them for years, we are not entitled to sit here as Senators ourselves. Can you expect your brave men, your officers and soldiers who are now in "the tented field," subject to all the hardships and privations pertaining to a civil war like this, to have courage, and to march on with patriotism to crush treason on every battle-field, when you have not the courage to expel it from your midst? Set those brave men an example; say to them by your acts and voice that you evidence your intention to put down traitors in the field by ejecting them from your midst, without regard to former associations.

I do not say these things in unkindness. I say them in obedience to duty, a high constitutional duty that I owe to my country; yes, sir, that I owe to my wife and children. By your failure to exercise the powers of this Government, by your failure to enforce the laws of the Union, I am separated from those most dear to me. Pardon me, sir, for this personal allusion. My wife and children have been turned into the street, and my house has been turned into a barrack, and for what? Because I stand by the Constitution and the institutions of the country that I have been taught to love, respect, and venerate. This is my offence. Where are my sons-in-law? One to-day is lying in prison; another is forced to fly to the mountains to evade the pursuit of the hell-born and hell-bound conspiracy of disunion and secession; and when their cries come up here to you for protection, we are told, "No; I am against the entire coercive policy of the Government."

The speech of the Senator from California the other day had the effect in some degree, and seemed to be intended to give the question a party tinge. If I know myself, — although, as I avowed before, I am a Democrat, and expect to live and die one, — I know no party in this great struggle for the existence of my country. The argument presented by the Senator from California was, that we need not be in such hot pursuit of Mr. Bright, or those Senators who entertain his sentiments, who are still here, because we had been a little dilatory in expelling other traitorous Senators heretofore, and he referred us to the resolution of the Senator from Maine,[1] which was introduced at the special session in March last, declaring that certain Senators having withdrawn, and their seats having thereby become vacant, the Secretary should omit their names from the roll of the Senate. I know there seemed to be a kind of timidity, a kind of fear, to make use of the word "expel" at that time; but the fact that we declared the seats vacant, and stopped there, did not preclude us from afterwards passing a vote of censure. The resolution, which was adopted in March, merely stated the fact that Senators had withdrawn, and left their seats vacant. At the next session a resolution was introduced to expel the other Senators from the seceded States who did not attend in the Senate; and my friend[2] moved to strike out of that very resolution the word "expelled," and insert "vacated"; so that I do not think he ought to be much offended at it. I simply allude to it to show how easy it is for us to forget the surrounding circumstances that influenced our action at the time it took place. We know that a year ago there was a deep and abiding hope that the rebellion would not progress as it has done; that it would cease; and that there might be circumstances which, at one time, would to some extent justify us in allowing a wide margin which, at another period of time would be wholly unjustifiable.

[1] Mr. Fessenden. [2] Mr. Latham.

All this, however, amounts to nothing. We have a case now before us that requires our action, and we should act upon it conscientiously in view of the facts which are presented. Because we neglected to expel traitors before, and omitted to have them arrested, and permitted them to go away freely, and afterwards declared their seats vacant because they had gone, we are not now prevented from expelling a Senator who is not worthy to be in the Senate. I do not say that other traitors may not be punished yet. I trust in God the time will come, and that before long, when these traitors can be overtaken, and we may mete out to them condign punishment, such as their offence deserves. I know who was for arresting them. I know who declared their conduct to be treason. Here in their midst I told them it was treason, and they might make the best of it they could.

Sir, to sum up the argument, I think there is but little in the point presented by the Senator from New Jersey, of there being no proof of the reception of the letter; and I think I have extracted the staple commodity entirely out of the speech of the Senator from Delaware; and so far as the force of the argument, based upon the Senate having at one session expelled certain members, while at the previous session it only vacated their seats, is concerned, I think the Senator from California answers that himself. As to the polished and ingenious statement of the case made by the Senator from New

York,[1] I think I have answered that by putting the case upon a different basis from the one presented by him, which seems to control his action.

Mr. President, I have alluded to the talk about compromise. If I know myself, there is no one who desires the preservation of this Government more than I do; and I think I have given as much evidence as mortal man could give of my devotion to the Union. My property has been sacrificed; my wife and children have been turned out-of-doors; my sons have been imprisoned; my son-in-law has had to run to the mountains; I have sacrificed a large amount of bonds in trying to give some evidence of my devotion to the Government under which I was raised. I have attempted to show you that, on the part of the leaders of this rebellion, there was no desire to compromise: compromise was not what they wanted; and now the great issue before the country is the perpetuation or the destruction of free government. I have shown how the resolution of the venerable Senator from Kentucky [2] was defeated, and that Southern men are responsible for that defeat, — six sitting in their places and refusing to vote. His proposition was only lost by two votes; and in the end, when the seceders had gone, by only one. Well do I remember, as was described by the Senator from California, the sadness, the gloom, the anguish that played over his venerable face when the result was announced; and I went

[1] Mr. Harris.

[2] Mr. Crittenden.

across the Chamber, and told him that here were men refusing to vote, and that to me was administered a rebuke by one of them for speaking to him on the subject.

Now, the Senator from Delaware tells us that if that compromise had been made, all these consequences would have been avoided. It is a mere pretence; it is false. Their object was to overturn the Government. If they could not get the control of this Government, they were willing to divide the country and govern a part of it. Talk not of compromise now. What, sir, compromise with traitors with arms in their hands! Talk about "our Southern brethren" when they present their swords at your throat and their bayonets at your bosoms! Is this a time to talk about compromise? Let me say, and I regret that I have to say it, that there is but one way to compromise this matter, and that is to crush the leaders of this rebellion and put down treason. You have got to subdue them; you have got to conquer them; and nothing but the sacrifice of life and blood will do it. The issue is made. The leaders of rebellion have decreed eternal separation between you and them. Those leaders must be conquered, and a new set of men brought forward who are to vitalize and develop the Union feeling in the South. You must show your courage here as Senators, and impart it to those who are in the field. If you were now to compromise, they would believe that they could whip you one to five, and you could not live in peace six months, or even three months. Settle the question now; settle it well; settle it finally; crush out the rebellion and punish the traitors. I want to see peace, and I believe that is the shortest way to get it. Blood must be shed, life must be sacrificed, and you may as well begin at first as last. I only regret that the Government has been so tardy in its operations. I wish the issue had been met sooner. I believe that if we had seen as much in the beginning as we see to-day, this rebellion would have been wound up and peace restored to the land by this time.

But let us go on; let us encourage the Army and the Navy; let us vote the men and the means necessary to vitalize and to bring into requisition the enforcing and coercive power of the Government; let us crush out the rebellion, and anxiously look forward to the day — God grant it may come soon — when that baleful comet of fire and of blood that now hovers over this distracted people may be chased away by the benignant star of peace. Let us look forward to the time when we can take the flag, the glorious flag of our country, and nail it below the cross, and there let it wave as it waved in the olden time, and let us gather around it, and inscribe as our motto, "Liberty and Union, now and forever, one and inseparable." Let us gather around it, and while it hangs floating beneath the cross, let us exclaim, "Christ first, our country next." Oh, how gladly rejoiced I should be to see the dove returning to the ark with the olive-leaf, indicating that land was found, and that the mighty waters had abated. I trust the time will soon come when we can do as they did in the olden times, when the stars sang together in the morning, and all creation proclaimed the glory of God. Then let us do our duty in the Senate and in the councils of the nation, and thereby stimulate our brave officers and soldiers to do theirs in the field.

Mr. President, I have occupied the attention of the Senate much longer than I intended. In view of the whole case, without personal unkind feeling towards the Senator from Indiana, I am of opinion that duty to myself, duty to my family, duty to the Constitution, duty to the country, obedience to the public judgment, all require me to cast my vote to expel Mr. Bright from the Senate, and when the occasion arrives I shall so record my vote.

APPEAL TO THE PEOPLE OF TENNESSEE.

FELLOW-CITIZENS: Tennessee assumed the form of a body politic, as one of the United States of America, in the year seventeen hundred and ninety-six, at once entitled to all the privileges of the Federal Constitution, and bound by all its obligations. For nearly sixty-five years she continued in the enjoyment of all her rights, and in the performance of all her duties, one of the most loyal and devoted of the sisterhood of States. She had been honored by the elevation of two of her citizens to the highest place in the gift of the American people, and a third had been nominated for the same high office, who received a liberal though ineffective support. Her population had rapidly and largely increased, and their moral and material interests correspondingly advanced. Never was a people more prosperous, contented, and happy than the people of Tennessee under the Government of the United States, and none less burdened for the support of the authority by which they were protected. They felt their Government only in the conscious enjoyment of the benefits it conferred and the blessings it bestowed.

Such was our enviable condition until within the

year just past, when, under what baneful influences it is not my purpose now to inquire, the authority of the Government was set at defiance, and the Constitution and laws contemned, by a rebellious, armed force. Men who, in addition to the ordinary privileges and duties of the citizen, had enjoyed largely the bounty and official patronage of the Government, and had, by repeated oaths, obligated themselves to its support, with sudden ingratitude for the bounty and disregard of their solemn obligation, engaged, deliberately and ostentatiously, in the accomplishment of its overthrow. Many, accustomed to defer to their opinions and to accept their guidance, and others, carried away by excitement or overawed by seditious clamor, arrayed themselves under their banners, thus organizing a treasonable power, which, for the time being, stifled and suppressed the authority of the Federal Government.

In this condition of affairs it devolved upon the President, bound by his official oath to preserve, protect, and defend the Constitution, and charged by the law with the duty of suppressing insurrection and domestic violence, to resist and repel this rebellious force by the military arm of the Government, and thus to reëstablish the Federal authority. Congress, assembling at an early day, found him engaged in the active discharge of this momentous and responsible trust. That body came promptly to his aid, and while supplying him with treasure and arms to an extent that would previously have been considered fabulous, they, at the same time, with almost absolute unanimity, declared "that this war is not waged on their part in any spirit of oppression, nor for any purpose of conquest or subjugation, nor purpose of overthrowing or interfering with the rights or the established institutions of these States; but to defend and maintain the supremacy of the Constitution and to preserve the Union, with all the dignity, equality, and rights of the several States unimpaired; and that as soon as these objects are accomplished, the war ought to cease." In this spirit, and by such coöperation, has the President conducted this mighty conquest, until, as Commander-in-Chief of the Army, he has caused the national flag again to float undisputed over the capitol of our State. Meanwhile the State government has disappeared. The Executive has abdicated; the Legislature has dissolved; the Judiciary is in abeyance. The great ship of state, freighted with its precious cargo of human interests and human hopes, its sails all set, and its glorious old flag unfurled, has been suddenly abandoned by its officers and mutinous crew, and left to float at the mercy of the winds, and to be plundered by every rover upon the deep. Indeed the work of plunder has already commenced. The archives have been desecrated; the public property stolen and destroyed; the vaults of the State Bank violated, and its treasures robbed, including the funds carefully gathered and consecrated for all time to the instruction of our children.

In such a lamentable crisis the Government of the United States could not be unmindful of its high constitutional obligation to guarantee to every State in this Union a republican form of government, an obligation which every State has a direct and immediate interest in having observed towards every other State; and from which, by no action on the part of the people in any State, can the Federal Government be absolved. A republican form of government, in consonance with the Constitution of the United States, is one of the fundamental conditions of our political existence, by which every part of the country is alike bound, and from which no part can escape. This obligation the national Government is now attempting to discharge. I have been appointed, in the absence of the regular and established State authorities, as Military Governor for the time being, to preserve the public property of the State, to give the protection of law actively enforced to her citizens, and, as speedily as may be, to restore her government to the same condition as before the existing rebellion.

In this grateful but arduous undertaking, I shall avail myself of all the aid that may be afforded by my fellow-citizens. And for this purpose I respectfully but earnestly invite all the people of Tennessee, desirous or willing to see a restoration of her ancient government, without distinction of party affiliations or past political opinions or action, to unite with me, by counsel and coöperative agency, to accomplish this great end. I find most, if not all of the offices, both State and Federal, vacated, either by actual abandonment, or by the action of the incumbents in attempting to subordinate their functions to a power in hostility to the fundamental law of the State, and subversive of her national allegiance. These offices must be filled temporarily, until the State shall be restored so far to its accustomed quiet, that the people can peaceably assemble at the ballot-box and select agents of their own choice. Otherwise anarchy would prevail, and no man's life or property would be safe from the desperate and unprincipled.

I shall therefore, as early as practicable, designate for various positions under the State and county governments, from among my fellow-citizens, persons of probity and intelligence, and bearing true allegiance to the Constitution and Government of the United States, who will execute the functions of their respective offices until their places can be filled by the action of the people. Their authority, when their appointment shall have been made, will be accordingly respected and observed.

To the people themselves the protection of the Government is extended. All their rights will be duly respected, and their wrongs redressed when made known. Those who through the dark and weary night of the rebellion have maintained their allegiance to the Federal Government will be honored. The erring and misguided will be welcomed on their return. And while it may become necessary, in vindicating the violated majesty of the law, and in reasserting its imperial sway, to punish intelligent and conscious treason in high places, no merely retaliatory or vindictive policy will be adopted. To those especially who, in a private, unofficial capacity, have assumed an attitude of hostility to the Government, a full and complete amnesty for all past acts and declarations is offered, upon the one condition of their again yielding themselves peaceful citizens to the just supremacy of the laws. This I advise them to do for their own good, and for the peace and welfare of our beloved State, endeared to me by the associations of long and active years, and by the enjoyment of her highest honors.

And appealing to my fellow-citizens of Tennessee, I point you to my long public life as a pledge for the sincerity of my motives, and an earnest for the performance of my present and future duties.

INAUGURAL ADDRESS.

DELIVERED IN THE SENATE OF THE UNITED STATES, MARCH 4, 1865.

SENATORS: I am here to-day as the chosen Vice-President of the United States; and as such, by constitutional provision, I am made the presiding officer of this body. I therefore present myself here in obedience to the high behests of the American people, to discharge a constitutional duty, and not presumptuously to thrust myself in a position so exalted. May I at this moment — it may not be irrelevant to the occasion — advert to the workings of our institutions under the Constitution which our fathers framed and Washington approved, as exhibited by the position in which I stand before the American Senate, in the sight of the American people? Deem me not vain or arrogant; yet I should be less than man if under such circumstances I were not proud of being an American citizen, for to-day one who claims no high descent, one who comes from the ranks of the people, stands, by the choice of a free constituency, in the second place of this Government. There may be those to whom such things are not pleasing; but those who have labored for the consummation of a free Government will appreciate and cherish institutions which exclude none, however obscure his origin, from places of trust and distinction. The people, in short, are the source of all power. You, Senators, you who constitute the bench of the Supreme Court of the United States, are but the creatures of the American people; your exaltation is from them; the power of this Government consists in its nearness and approximation to the great mass of the people. You, Mr. Secretary Seward, Mr. Secretary Stanton, the Secretary of the Navy, and the others who are your associates, — you know that you have my respect and my confidence, — derive not your greatness and your power alone from President Lincoln. Humble as I am, plebeian as I may be deemed, permit me in the presence of this brilliant assemblage to enunciate the truth that courts and cabinets, the President and his advisers, derive their power and their greatness from the people. A President could not exist here forty-eight hours if he were as far removed from the people as the autocrat of Russia is separated from his subjects. Here the popular heart sustains President and cabinet officers; the popular will gives them all their strength. Such an assertion of the great principles of this Government may be considered out of place, and I will not consume the time of these intelligent and enlightened people much longer; but I could not be insensible to these great truths when I, a plebeian, elected by the people the Vice-President of the United States, am here to enter upon the discharge of my duties. For those duties I claim not the aptitude of my respected predecessor. Although I have occupied a seat in both the House of Representatives and the Senate, I am not learned in parliamentary law, and I shall be dependent on the courtesy of those Senators who have become familiar with the rules which are requisite for the good order of the body and the dispatch of its business. I have only studied how I may best advance the interests of my State and of my country, and not the technical rules of order; and if I err I shall appeal to this dignified body of representatives of States for kindness and indulgence.

Before I conclude this brief inaugural address in the presence of this audience, — and I, though a plebeian boy, am authorized by the principles of the Government under which I live to feel proudly conscious that I am a man, and grave dignitaries are but men, — before the Supreme Court, the representatives of foreign governments, Senators, and the people, I desire to proclaim that Tennessee, whose representative I have been, is free. She has bent the tyrant's rod, she has broken the yoke of slavery, and to-day she stands redeemed. She waited not for the exercise of power by Congress; it was her own act, and she is now as loyal, Mr. Attorney-General, as is the State from which you came. It is the doctrine of the Federal Constitution that no State can go out of this Union; and moreover Congress cannot reject a State from this Union. Thank God, Tennessee has never been out of the Union! It is true the operations of her government were for a time interrupted; there was an interregnum; but she is still in the Union, and I am her representative. This day she elects her Governor and her Legislature, which will be convened on the first Monday of April, and again her Senators and Representatives will soon mingle with those of her sister States; and who shall gainsay it? for the Constitution requires that to every State shall be guaranteed a republican form of government.

I now am prepared to take the oath of office, and renew my allegiance to the Constitution of the United States.

APPENDIX.

IN THE SENATE OF THE UNITED STATES, THIRTY-SIXTH CONGRESS, SECOND SESSION, DECEMBER 13, 1860.

Mr. JOHNSON of Tennessee asked, and by unanimous consent obtained, leave to bring in the following joint resolution; which was read and passed to a second reading, and ordered to be printed.

JOINT RESOLUTION PROPOSING AMENDMENTS TO THE CONSTITUTION OF THE UNITED STATES.

Whereas the fifth article of the Constitution of the United States provides for amendments thereto, in the manner following, viz: "1. Congress, whenever two thirds of both Houses shall deem it necessary, shall propose amendments to this Constitution, or on the application of the legislatures of two thirds of the several States shall call a convention for proposing amendments, which, in either case, shall be valid to all intents and purposes, as part of this Constitution, when ratified by the legislatures of three fourths of the several States, or by conventions in three fourths thereof, as the one or the other mode of ratification may be proposed by Congress; provided that no amendment which may be made prior to the year one thousand eight hundred and eight, shall in any manner affect the first and fourth clauses in the ninth section of the first article; and that no State, without its consent, shall be deprived of its equal suffrage in the Senate": Therefore,

Be it resolved by the Senate and House of Representatives of the United States of America in Congress assembled, two thirds of both Houses concurring, That the following amendments to the Constitution of the United States be proposed to the legislatures of the several States, which when ratified by the legislatures of three fourths of the States, shall be valid to all intents and purposes as part of the Constitution:—

That hereafter the President and Vice-President of the United States shall be chosen by the people of the respective States, in the manner following:—Each State shall be divided, by the legislature thereof, in districts equal in number to the whole number of Senators and Representatives to which such State may be entitled in the Congress of the United States; the said districts to be composed of contiguous territory, and to contain, as nearly as may be, an equal number of persons entitled to be represented under the Constitution, and to be laid off, for the first time, immediately after the ratification of this amendment, and afterwards, at the session of the legislature next ensuing the apportionment of representatives by the Congress of the United States: that, on the first Thursday in August, in the year eighteen hundred and sixty-four, and on the same day every fourth year thereafter, the citizens of each State who possess the qualifications requisite for electors of the most numerous branch of the State legislatures, shall meet within their respective districts, and vote for a President and Vice-President of the United States; and the person receiving the greatest number of votes for President, and the one receiving the greatest number of votes for Vice-President in each district, shall be holden to have received one vote; which fact shall be immediately certified by the Governor of the State, to each of the Senators in Congress from such State, and to the President of the Senate and the Speaker of the House of Representatives. The Congress of the United States shall be in session on the second Monday in October, in the year eighteen hundred and sixty-four, and on the same day on every fourth year thereafter; and the President of the Senate, in the presence of the Senate and House of Representatives, shall open all the certificates, and the votes shall then be counted. The person having the greatest number of votes for President, shall be President, if such number be equal to a majority of the whole number of votes given; but if no person have such majority, then a second election shall be held on the first Thursday in the month of December then next ensuing, between the persons having the two highest numbers for the office of President; which second election shall be conducted, the result certified, and the votes counted, in the same manner as in the first; and the person having the greatest number of votes for President, shall be President. But, if two or more persons shall have received the greatest, and an equal number of votes, at the second election, then the person who shall have received the greatest number of votes in the greatest number of States, shall be President. The person having the greatest number of votes for Vice-President, at the first election, shall be Vice-President, if such number be equal to a majority of the whole number of votes given; and if no person have such majority, then a second election shall take place between the persons having the two highest numbers, on the same day that the second election is held for President; and the person having the highest number of the votes for Vice-President, shall be Vice-President. But if there should happen to be an equality of votes between the persons so voted for at the second election, then the person having the greatest number of votes in the greatest number of States, shall be Vice-President. But when a second election shall be necessary in the case of Vice-President, and not necessary in the case of President, then the Senate shall choose a Vice-President from the persons having the two highest numbers in the first election, as is now prescribed in the Constitution: *Provided*, That the President to be elected in the year eighteen hundred and sixty-four, shall be chosen from one of the slaveholding States, and the Vice-President from one of the non-slaveholding States; and, in the year eighteen hundred and sixty-eight, the President shall be chosen from one of the non-slaveholding States, and the Vice-President from one of the slaveholding States, and so alternating the President and Vice-President every four years between the slaveholding and the non-slaveholding States, during the continuance of the Government.

SEC. 2. *And be it further resolved*, That article one, section three, be amended by striking out the word "legislature," and inserting in lieu thereof the following words, viz: "persons qualified to vote for members of the most numerous branch of the legislature," so as to make the third section of said article, when ratified by three fourths of the States, read as follows, to wit: —

The Senate of the United States shall be composed of two Senators from each State, chosen by the persons qualified to vote for the members of the most numerous branch of the legislature thereof, for six years, and each Senator shall have one vote.

Sec. 3. *And be it further resolved*, That article three, section one, be amended by striking out the words "good behavior," and inserting the following words, viz: "the term of twelve years." And further, that said article and section be amended by adding the following thereto, viz: "and it shall be the duty of the President of the United States, within twelve months after the ratification of this amendment by three fourths of all the States, as provided by the Constitution of the United States, to divide the whole number of judges, as near as may be practicable, into three classes. The seats of the judges of the first class shall be vacated at the expiration of the fourth year from such classification; of the second class, at the expiration of the eighth year; and of the third class, at the expiration of the twelfth year, so that one third may be chosen every fourth year thereafter."

The article as amended will read as follows: —

Article 3. — Section 1. The judicial power of the United States shall be vested in one Supreme Court, and in such inferior courts as the Congress, from time to time, may ordain and establish. The judges, both of the Supreme and inferior courts, shall hold their offices during the term of twelve years, and shall, at stated times, receive for their services a compensation, which shall not be diminished during their continuance in office. And it shall be the duty of the President of the United States, within twelve months after the ratification of this amendment by three fourths of all the States, as provided by the Constitution of the United States, to divide the whole number of judges, as near as may be practicable, into three classes. The seats of the judges of the first class shall be vacated at the expiration of the fourth year from such classification; of the second class, at the expiration of the eighth year; and of the third class, at the expiration of the twelfth year, so that one third may be chosen every fourth year thereafter: *Provided, however,* That all vacancies occurring under the provisions of this section shall be filled by persons, one half of whom shall be chosen from the slaveholding States, and the other half with persons chosen from the non-slaveholding States; so that the Supreme Court will be equally divided between the slaveholding and the non-slaveholding States.

RECEPTION OF THE ILLINOIS DELEGATION.

On the 18th of April, 1865, a delegation of citizens of Illinois paid their respects to President Johnson, at his rooms in the Treasury Building.

Governor Oglesby presented the delegation, and made the subjoined address: —

Mr. President: I take much pleasure in presenting to you this delegation of the citizens of Illinois, representing almost every portion of the State. We are drawn together by the mournful events of the past few days, to give some feeble expression to the feelings we, in common with the whole nation, realize as pressing us to the earth, by appropriate and respectful ceremonies. We thought it not inappropriate before we should separate, even in this sad hour, to seek this interview with your Excellency, that, while the bleeding heart is pouring out its mournful anguish over the death of our beloved late President, the idol of our State and the pride of the whole country, we may earnestly express to you, the living head of this nation, our deliberate, full, and abiding confidence in you as the one who, in these dark hours, must bear upon yourself the mighty responsibility of maintaining, defending, and directing its affairs. In the midst of this sadness, through the oppressive gloom that surrounds us, we look to you and to a bright future for our country. The assassination of the President of the United States deeply depresses and seriously aggravates the entire nation; but under our blessed Constitution it does not delay, nor for any great length of time retard, its progress; does not for an instant disorganize or threaten its destruction. The record of your whole past life, familiar to all, the splendor of your recent gigantic efforts to stay the hand of treason and assassination, and restore the flag to the uttermost bounds of the Republic, assure that noble State which we represent, and, we believe, the people of the United States, that we may safely trust our destinies in your hands; and to this end we come, in the name of the State of Illinois, and, we confidently believe, fully and faithfully expressing the wishes of our people, to present and pledge to you the cordial, earnest, and unremitting purpose of our State to give your administration the strong support we have heretofore given to the administration of our lamented late President, the policy of whom we have heretofore, do now, and shall continue to endorse.

THE PRESIDENT'S REPLY.

President Johnson replied as follows: —

GENTLEMEN: I have listened with profound emotion to the kind words you have addressed to me. The visit of this large delegation to speak to me through you, sir, these words of encouragement, I had not anticipated. In the midst of the saddening circumstances which surround us, and the immense responsibility thrown upon me, an expression of the confidence of individuals, and still more of an influential body like that before me, representing a great commonwealth, cheers and strengthens my heavily burdened mind. I am at a loss for words to respond. In an hour like this, of deepest sorrow, were it possible to embody in words the feelings of my bosom, I could not command my lips to utter them. Perhaps the best reply I could make, and the one most readily appropriate to your kind assurances of confidence, would be to receive them in silence. [Sensation.] The throbbings of my heart since the sad catastrophe which has appalled us cannot be reduced to words; and, oppressed as I am with the new and great responsibility which has devolved upon me, and saddened with grief, I can with difficulty respond to you at all. But I cannot permit such expression of the confidence reposed in me by the people to pass without acknowledgment. To an individual like myself, who has never claimed much, but who has, it is true, received from a generous people many marks of trust and honor for a long time, an occasion like this and a manifestation of public feeling so well-timed are peculiarly acceptable. Sprung from the people myself, every pulsation of the popular heart finds an immediate answer in my own. By many men in public life such occasions are often considered merely formal. To me they are real. Your words of countenance and encouragement sank deep in my heart, and were I even a coward I could not but gather from them strength to carry out my convictions of right. Thus feeling, I shall enter upon the discharge of my great duty firmly, steadfastly, [applause,] if not with the signal ability exhibited by my predecessor, which is still fresh in our sorrowing minds. Need I repeat that no heart feels more sensibly than mine this great affliction? In what I say on this occasion I shall indulge in no petty spirit of anger, no feeling of revenge. But we have beheld a notable event in the history of mankind. In the midst of the American people, where every citizen is taught to obey law and observe the rules of Christian conduct, our Chief Magistrate, the beloved of all hearts, has been assassinated; and when we trace this crime to its cause, when we remember the source whence the assassin drew his inspiration, and then look at the result, we stand yet more astounded at this most barbarous, most diabolical assassination. Such a crime as the murder of a great and good man, honored and revered, the beloved and the hope of the people, springs not alone from a solitary individual of ever so desperate wickedness. We can trace its cause through successive steps, without my enumerating them here, back to that source which is the spring of all our woes. No one can say that if the perpetrator of this fiendish deed be arrested he should not undergo the extremest penalty the law knows for crime; none will say that mercy should interpose. But is he alone guilty? Here, gentlemen, you perhaps expect me to present some indication of my future policy. One thing I will say. Every era teaches its lesson. The times we live in are not without instruction. The American people must be taught — if they do not already feel — that treason is a crime and must be punished; [applause;] that the Government will not always bear with its enemies; that it is strong, not only to protect, but to punish. [Applause.] When we turn to the criminal code and examine the catalogue of crimes, we there find arson laid down as a crime with its appropriate penalty; we find there theft and robbery and murder given as crimes; and there, too, we find the last and highest of crimes, — treason. [Applause.] With other and inferior offences our people are familiar. But in our peaceful history treason has been almost unknown. The people must understand that it is the blackest of crimes, and will be surely punished. [Applause.] I make this allusion, not to excite the already exasperated feelings of the public, but to point out the principles of public justice which should guide our action at this particular juncture, and which accord with sound public morals. Let it be engraven on every heart that treason is a crime, and traitors shall suffer its penalty. [Applause.] While we are appalled, overwhelmed at the fall of one man in our midst by the hand of a traitor, shall we allow men — I care not by what weapons — to attempt the life of a State with impunity? While we strain our minds to comprehend the enormity of this assassination, shall we allow the nation to be assassinated? [Applause.] I speak in no spirit of unkindness. I leave the events of the future to be disposed of as they arise, regarding myself as the humble instrument of the American people. In this, as in all things, justice and judgment shall be determined by them. I do not harbor bitter or revengeful feelings toward any. In general terms I would say that public morals and public opinion should be established upon the sure and inflexible principles of justice. [Applause.] When the question of exercising mercy comes before me it will be considered calmly, judicially, — remembering that I am the Executive of the nation. I know men love to have their names spoken of in connection with acts of mercy; and how easy it is to yield to this impulse. But we must not forget that what may be mercy to the individual is cruelty to the State. [Applause.] In the exercise of mercy there should be no doubt left that this high prerogative is not used to relieve a few at the expense of the many. Be assured that I shall never forget that I am not to consult my own feelings alone, but to give an account to the whole people. [Applause.] In regard to my future course I will now make no professions, no pledges. I have been connected somewhat actively with public affairs, and to the history of my past public acts, which is familiar to you, I refer for those principles which have governed me heretofore, and will guide me hereafter. In general I will say I have long labored for the amelioration and elevation of the great mass of mankind. My opinions as to the nature of popular government have long been cherished; and constituted as I am, it is now too late in life for me to change them. I believe that government was made for man, not man for government. [Applause.] This struggle of the people against the most gigantic rebellion the world ever saw has demonstrated that the attachment of the people to their Government is the strongest national defence human wisdom can devise. [Applause.] So long as each man feels that the interests of the Government are his interests, so long as the public heart turns in the right direction, and the people understand and appreciate the theory of our Government and love liberty, our Constitution will be transmitted unimpaired. If the time ever comes when the people shall fail, the Government will fail, and we shall cease to be one of the nations of the earth. After having preserved our form of free government, and shown its power to maintain its existence through the vicissitudes of nearly a century, it may be that it was necessary for us to pass through this last ordeal of intestine strife to prove that this Government will not perish from internal weakness, but will stand to defend itself against all foes and punish treason. [Applause.] In the dealings of an inscrutable Providence and by the operation of the Constitution, I have been thrown unexpectedly into this position. My past life, especially my course during the present unholy Rebellion, is before you. I have no principles to retract; I defy any one to point to any of my public acts at variance with the fixed principles which have guided me through life. I have no professions to offer. Professions and promises would be worth nothing at this time. No one can foresee the circumstances that will hereafter arise. Had any man, gifted with prescience four years ago, uttered and written down in advance the events of this period, they would have seemed more marvellous than anything in the "Arabian Nights." I shall not attempt to anticipate the future. As events occur, and it becomes necessary for me to act, I shall dispose of each as it arises, deferring any declaration or message until it can be written, paragraph by paragraph, in the light of events as they transpire.

The members of the delegation were then severally introduced to the President by Governor Oglesby.

RECEPTION OF THE BRITISH AMBASSADOR.

On the 20th of April, 1865, Sir Frederick A. Bruce, Envoy Extraordinary and Minister Plenipotentiary of her Britannic Majesty to the United States Government, presenting his credentials to the President, spoke as follows: —

Mr. President: It is with deep and sincere concern that I have to accompany my first official act with expressions of condolence. On Saturday last the ceremony that takes place here to-day was to have been performed, but the gracious intentions of the late lamented President were frustrated by the events which have plunged this country in consternation and affliction, and which will call forth in Great Britain feelings of horror as well as of profound sympathy. It becomes, therefore, my duty, sir, to present the letter from my sovereign, of which I am the bearer, to you, as President of the United States, and it is with pleasure that I convey the assurances of regard and good-will which her Majesty entertains toward you, sir, as President of the United States. I am further directed to express her Majesty's friendly disposition towards the great Nation of which you are Chief

Magistrate, and her hearty good wishes for its peace, prosperity, and welfare. Her Majesty has nothing more at heart than to conciliate those relations of amity and good understanding which have so long and so happily existed between the two kindred nations of the United States and Great Britain, and it is in this spirit that I am directed to perform the duties of the important and honorable post confided to me. Permit me, sir, to say, that it shall be the object of my earnest endeavors to carry out my instructions faithfully in this respect, and to express the hope, sir, that you will favorably consider my attempts to merit your approbation, and to give effect to the friendly intentions of the Queen and of her Majesty's Government. I have the honor to place in your hands the letter of credence confided to me by her Majesty.

THE PRESIDENT'S REPLY.

To which President Johnson replied: —

SIR FREDERICK A. BRUCE: The very cordial and friendly sentiments which you have expressed on the part of her Britannic Majesty give me great pleasure. Great Britain and the United States, by the extended and various forms of commerce between them, the contiguity of portions of their possessions, and the similarity of their language and laws, are drawn into constant and intimate intercourse. At the same time they are, from the same causes, exposed to frequent occasions of misunderstanding, only to be averted by mutual forbearance. So eagerly are the people of the two countries engaged, throughout almost the whole world, in the pursuit of similar commercial enterprises, accompanied by natural rivalries and jealousies, that, at first sight, it would almost seem that the two Governments must be enemies, or at best cold and calculating friends. So devoted are the two nations throughout all their domain, and even in their most remote territory and colonial possessions, to the principles of civil rights and constitutional liberty, that, on the other hand, the superficial observer might erroneously count upon a continued concert of action and sympathy, amounting to an alliance between them. Each is charged with the development of the progress of the human race, and each in its sphere is subject to difficulties and trials not participated in by the other. The interests of civilization and of humanity require that the two should be friends. I have always known and accounted as a fact honorable to both countries, that the Queen of England is a sincere and honest well-wisher to the United States. I have been equally frank and explicit in the opinion that the friendship of the United States toward Great Britain is enjoined by all considerations of interest and of sentiment affecting the character of both. You will, therefore, be accepted as a Minister friendly and well-disposed to the maintenance of peace and the honor of both countries. You will find myself and all my associates acting in accordance with the same enlightened policy and consistent sentiments, and so I am sure that it will not occur in your case that either yourself or this Government will ever have cause to regret that such an important relationship existed at such a crisis.

RECEPTION OF THE DIPLOMATIC CORPS.

SOON after the reception of the British Minister, the members of the Diplomatic Corps were presented to President Johnson, when Baron von Gerolt addressed the President as follows: —

MR. PRESIDENT: The representatives of foreign nations have assembled here to express to your Excellency their feelings at the deplorable event of which they have been witnesses; to say how sincerely they share the national mourning for the cruel fate of the late President, Abraham Lincoln, and how deeply they sympathize with the Government and people of the United States in their great affliction. With equal sincerity we tender to you, Mr. President, our best wishes for the welfare and prosperity of the United States, and for your personal health and happiness. May we be allowed, also, Mr. President, to give utterance on this occasion to our sincerest hopes for an early reëstablishment of peace in this great country, and for the maintenance of the friendly relations between the Government of the United States and the governments which we represent.

REPLY OF THE PRESIDENT.

To which the President replied: —

GENTLEMEN OF THE DIPLOMATIC BODY: I heartily thank you, on behalf of the Government and people of the United States, for the sympathy which you have so feelingly expressed upon the mournful event to which you refer. The good wishes also which you kindly offer for the welfare and prosperity of the United States, and for my personal health and happiness, are gratefully received. Your hopes for the early restoration of peace in this country are cordially reciprocated by me, and you may be assured that I shall leave nothing undone towards preserving those relations of friendship which now fortunately exist between the United States and all foreign powers.

ADDRESS TO LOYAL SOUTHERNERS.

During the same month a deputation of loyal men from various Southern States waited on the President. In reply to a brief address, he said: —

It is hardly necessary for me on this occasion to say that my sympathies and impulses, in connection with this nefarious Rebellion, beat in unison with yours. Those who have passed through this bitter ordeal, and who participated in it to a great extent, are more competent, as I think, to judge and determine the true policy which should be pursued. [Applause.] I have but little to say on this question in response to what has been said. It enunciates and expresses my own feelings to the fullest extent, and in much better language than I can at the present moment summon to my aid. The most that I can say is that, entering upon the duties that have devolved upon me under circumstances that are perilous and responsible, and being thrown into the position I now occupy unexpectedly, in consequence of the sad event, the heinous assassination which has taken place, — in view of all that is before me and the circumstances that surround me, — I cannot but feel that your encouragement and kindness are peculiarly acceptable and appropriate. I do not think you, who have been familiar with my course, — you who are from the South, — deem it necessary for me to make any professions as to the future on this occasion, nor to express what my course will be upon questions that may arise. If my past life is no indication of what my future will be, my professions were both worthless and empty; and in returning you my sincere thanks for this encouragement and sympathy, I can only reiterate what I have said before, and, in part, what has just been read. As far as clemency and mercy are concerned, and the proper exercise of the pardoning power, I think I understand the nature and character of the latter. In the exercise of clemency and mercy, that pardoning power should be exercised with caution. I do not give utterance to my opinions on this point in any spirit of revenge or unkind feelings. Mercy and clemency have been pretty large ingredients in my composition, having been the Executive of a State, and thereby placed in a position in which it was necessary to exercise clemency and mercy. I have been charged with going too far, being too lenient, and have become satisfied that mercy without justice is a crime, and that when mercy and clemency are exercised by the Executive, it should always be done in view of justice, and in that manner alone is properly exercised that great prerogative. The time has come, as you who have had to drink this bitter cup are fully aware, when the American people should be made to understand the true nature of crime. Of crime generally our people have a high understanding, as well as of the necessity for its punishment; but in the catalogue of crimes there is one, and that the highest known to the laws and the Constitution, of which, since the days of Jefferson and Aaron Burr, they have become oblivious. That is — treason. Indeed, one who has become distinguished in treason and in this Rebellion said, that "when traitors become numerous enough treason becomes respectable, and to become a traitor was to constitute a portion of the aristocracy of the country." God protect the people against such an aristocracy. Yes, the time has come when the people should be taught to understand the length and breadth, the depth and height of treason. An individual occupying the highest position among us was lifted to that position by the free offering of the American people, — the highest position on the habitable globe. This man we have seen, revered, and loved, — one who, if he erred at all, erred ever on the side of clemency and mercy, — that man we have seen Treason strike, through a fitting instrument, and we have beheld him fall like a bright star falling from its sphere. Now, there is none but would say, if the question came up, what should be done with the individual who assassinated the Chief Magistrate of the nation, — He is but a man — one man, after all. But if asked what should be done with the assassin, what should be the penalty, the forfeit exacted? I know what response dwells in every bosom. It is, that he should pay the forfeit with his life. And hence we see there are times when mercy and clemency, without justice, become a crime. The one should temper the other, and bring about that proper means. And if we should say this when the case was the simple murder of one man by his fellow-man, what should we say when asked what should be done with him, or them, or those, who have raised impious hands to take away the life of a nation composed of thirty millions of people?

What would be the reply to that question? But while in mercy we remember justice, in the language that has been uttered, I say, justice toward the leaders, the conscious leaders; but I also say amnesty, conciliation, clemency, and mercy to the thousands of our countrymen whom you and I know have been deceived or driven into this infernal Rebellion. And so I return to where I started from, and again repeat that it is time our people were taught to know that treason is a crime, not a mere political difference, not a mere contest between two parties, in which one succeeded and the other has simply failed. They must know it is treason; for if they had succeeded, the life of the nation would have been reft from it, — the Union would have been destroyed. Surely the Constitution sufficiently defines treason. It consists in levying war against the United States, and in giving their enemies aid and comfort. With this definition it requires the exercise of no great acumen to ascertain who are traitors. It requires no great perception to tell who have levied war against the United States; nor does it require any great stretch of reasoning to ascertain who has given aid to the enemies of the United States; and when the Government of the United States does ascertain who are the conscious and intelligent traitors, the penalty and the forfeit should be paid. [Applause.] I know how to appreciate the condition of being driven from one's home. I can sympathize with him whose all has been taken from him, — with him who has been denied the place that gave his children birth. But let us, withal, in the restoration of true government, proceed temperately and dispassionately, and hope and pray that the time will come, as I believe, when all can return and remain at our homes, and treason and traitors be driven from our land, — [applause,] — when again law and order shall reign, and the banner of our country be unfurled over every inch of territory within the area of the United States. [Applause.] In conclusion, let me thank you most profoundly for this encouragement and manifestation of your regard and respect, and assure you that I can give no greater assurance regarding the settlement of this question, than that I intend to discharge my duty, and in that way which shall, in the earliest possible hour, bring back peace to our distracted country. And I hope the time is not far distant when our people can all return to their homes and firesides, and resume their various avocations.

SPEECH TO THE INDIANA DELEGATION.

At the close of the month of April, 1865, the President spoke as follows, in response to an address from a delegation from the State of Indiana: —

As my honorable friend [Governor Morton] knows, I long since took the ground that this Government was sent upon a great mission among the nations of the earth; that it had a great work to perform, and that in starting it, it was started in perpetuity. Look back for one single moment to the Articles of Confederation, and then come down to 1787, when the Constitution was formed, — what do you find? That we, "the People of the United States, in order to form a more perfect government," etc. Provision is made for the admission of new States, to be added to the old ones embraced within the Union. Now, turn to the Constitution; we find that amendments may be made by a recommendation of two thirds of the members of Congress, if ratified by three fourths of the States. Provision is made for the admission of new States; no provision is made for the secession of old ones. The instrument was made to be good in perpetuity, and you can take hold of it, not to break up the Government, but to go on perfecting it more and more as it runs down the stream of time. We find the Government composed of integral parts. An individual is an integer, and a State itself is an integer, and the various States form the Union, which is itself an integer, they all making up the Government of the United States. Now we come to the point of my argument, so far as concerns the perpetuity of the Government. We have seen that the Government is composed of parts, each essential to the whole, and the whole essential to each part. Now, if an individual [part of a State] declare war against the whole, in violation of the Constitution, he, as a citizen, has violated the law, and is responsible for the act as an individual. There may be more than one individual; it may go on until they become parts of States. Sometimes the rebellion may go on increasing in number till the State machinery is overturned, and the country becomes like a man that is paralyzed on one side. But we find in the Constitution a great panacea provided. It provides that the United States (that is the great integer) shall guarantee to each State (the integers composing the whole) in this Union a republican form of government. Yes, if rebellion has been rampant, and set aside the machinery of a State for a time, there stands the great law to remove the paralysis, and revitalize it and put it on its feet again. When we come to understand our system of government, though it be complex, we see how beautifully one part moves in harmony with another; then we see our Government is to be a perpetuity, there being no provision for pulling it down, the Union being its vitalizing power, imparting life to the whole of the States that move around it like planets around the sun, receiving thence light, and heat, and motion. Upon this idea of destroying States, my position has been heretofore well known, and I see no cause to change it now, and I am glad to hear its reiteration on the present occasion. Some are satisfied with the idea that States are to be lost in territorial and other divisions; are to lose their character as States. But their life-breath has only been suspended, and it is a high constitutional obligation we have to secure each of these States in the possession and enjoyment of a republican form of government. A State may be in the Government with a peculiar institution, and by the operation of rebellion lose that feature; but it was a State when it went into rebellion, and when it comes out without the institution, it is still a State. I hold it a solemn obligation in any one of these States where the rebel armies have been beaten back or expelled, I care not how small the ship of state, I hold it, I say, a high duty to protect and to secure to them a republican form of government. This is no new opinion. It is expressed in conformity with my understanding of the genius and theory of our Government. Then, in adjusting and putting the Government upon its legs again, I think the progress of this work must pass into the hands of its friends. If a State is to be nursed until it again gets strength, it must be nursed by its friends, not smothered by its enemies. Now, permit me to remark, that while I have opposed dissolution and disintegration on the one hand, on the other I am equally opposed to consolidation, or the centralization of power in the hands of a few.

INDEX.

41 *